W9-BGF-863

STUDY GUIDE

Financial Management Theory and Practice

Tenth Edition

Eugene F. Brigham
University of Florida

Michael C. Ehrhardt
University of Tennessee

STUDY GUIDE

Financial Management Theory and Practice

Tenth Edition

Eugene F. Brigham
University of Florida

Michael C. Ehrhardt
University of Tennessee

SOUTH-WESTERN
—————*—————™
THOMSON LEARNING

Australia · Canada · Mexico · Singapore · Spain · United Kingdom · United States

SOUTH-WESTERN

™

THOMSON LEARNING

Study Guide to accompany Financial Management Theory and Practice, Tenth Edition

Eugene F. Brigham, Michael C. Ehrhardt

COPYRIGHT © 2002
by South-Western, a division of
Thomson Learning. Thomson
Learning™ is a trademark used
herein under license.

Printed in the United States of
America
    3 4 5 04 03 02

ISBN: 0-03-032931-0

For more information
contact South-Western,
5191 Natorp Boulevard,
Mason, Ohio, 45040.
Or you can visit our Internet
site at:
http://www.swcollege.com

The text of this publication, or any
part thereof, may be reproduced
for use in classes for which
(Financial Management Theory
and Practice, Tenth Edition) by
(Eugene F. Brigham, Michael C.
Ehrhardt) is the adopted textbook.
It may not be reproduced in any
manner whatsoever for any other
purpose without written permission
from the publisher.
For permission to use material
from this text or product, contact
us by
Tel (800) 730-2214
Fax (800) 730-2215
http://www.thomsonrights.com

STUDY GUIDE

TABLE OF CONTENTS

PREFACE

This *Study Guide* is designed primarily to help you develop a working knowledge of the concepts and principles of financial management. Additionally, it will familiarize you with the types of true/false and multiple-choice test questions that are being used with increasing frequency in introductory finance courses.

The *Study Guide* follows the outline of *Financial Management: Theory and Practice.* You should read carefully the next section, "How to Use This *Study Guide*," to familiarize yourself with its specific contents and to gain some insights into how it can be used most effectively.

We would like to thank Dana Aberwald Clark, Tim Smith, Susan Purcell Whitman, and Tina Goforth for their considerable assistance in the preparation of this edition and Bob LeClair for his helpful ideas in prior editions which we carried over to this one.

We have tried to make the *Study Guide* as clear and error-free as possible. However, some mistakes may have crept in, and there are almost certainly some sections that could be clarified. Any suggestions for improving the *Study Guide* would be greatly appreciated and should be addressed to Mike Ehrhardt at the address given below. Since instructors almost never read study guides, we address this call for help to students!

Eugene F. Brigham

Michael C. Ehrhardt
Ehrhardt@utk.edu

College of Business Administration
PO Box 117167
University of Florida
Gainesville, FL 32611-7167

Finance Department, SMC 424
University of Tennessee
Knoxville, TN 37996-0540

February 2001

SUGGESTIONS FOR STUDENTS USING STUDY GUIDE

Different people will tend to use the *Study Guide* in somewhat different ways. This is natural because both introductory finance courses and individual students' needs vary widely. However, the tips contained in this section should help all students use the *Study Guide* more effectively, regardless of these differences.

Each chapter contains (1) an overview, (2) an outline, (3) definitional self-test questions, (4) conceptual self-test questions, (5) self-test problems, and (6) answers and solutions to the self-test questions and problems. You should begin your study by reading the overview; it will give you an idea of what is contained in the chapter and how this material fits into the overall scheme of things in financial management.

Next, read over the outline to get a better fix on the specific topics covered in the chapter. It is important to realize that the outline does not list every facet of every topic covered in the textbook the *Study Guide* is intended to highlight and summarize the textbook, not to supplant it. Also, note that Chapter Extension material is clearly marked as such within the outline. Thus, if your instructor does not assign a particular Chapter Extension, you may not want to study that portion of the outline.

The definitional self-test questions are intended to test your knowledge of, and also to reinforce your ability to work with, the terms and concepts introduced in the chapter. If you do not understand the definitions thoroughly, review the outline prior to going on to the conceptual questions and problems.

The conceptual self-test questions focus on the same kinds of ideas that the textbook end-of-chapter questions address, but in the *Study Guide*, the questions are set out in a true/false or multiple-choice format. Thus, for many students these questions can be used to practice for the types of tests that are being used with increasing frequency. However, regardless of the types of tests you must take, working through the conceptual questions will help drive home the key concepts of financial management.

The numeric problems are also written in a multiple-choice format. Generally, the problems are arranged in order of increasing difficulty. Also, note that some of the *Study Guide* problems are convoluted in the sense that information normally available to financial managers is withheld and information normally unknown is given. Such problems are designed to test your knowledge of a subject, and you must work "backwards" to solve them. Furthermore, such problems are included in the *Study Guide* in part because they provide a good test of how well you understand the material and in part because you may well be seeing similar problems on your exams.

Finally, each *Study Guide* chapter provides the answers and solutions to the self-test questions and problems. The rationale behind a question's correct answer is explained where necessary, but the problem solutions are always complete. Note that the problems in the early chapters generally provide both "table-based" and "financial calculator" solutions. In later chapters, only calculator solutions are shown. You should not be concerned if your answer differs from ours by a small amount which is caused by rounding errors.

Of course, each student must decide how to incorporate the *Study Guide* in his or her overall study program. Many students begin an assignment by reading the *Study Guide* overview and outline to get the "big picture," then read the chapter in the textbook. Naturally, the *Study Guide* overview and outline is also used extensively to review for exams. Most students work the textbook questions and problems, using the latter as a self-test and review tool. However, if you are stumped by a text problem, try the *Study Guide* problems first because their detailed solutions can get you over stumbling blocks.

CHAPTER 1
AN OVERVIEW OF FINANCIAL MANAGEMENT

OVERVIEW

This chapter provides an overview of financial management and should give you a better understanding of the following: (1) what career opportunities exist within the three interrelated areas of finance, (2) how businesses are organized, (3) what the goals of a firm are and how financial managers can contribute to the attainment of these goals, (4) what forces will affect financial management in the future, (5) the role of ethics and social responsibility, and (6) what agency relationships are and the primary agency relationships that exist within the financial management context.

OUTLINE

Finance consists of three interrelated areas: money and capital markets, investments, and financial management. Career opportunities within each field are varied and numerous, but financial managers must have a knowledge of all three areas.

■   Many finance majors go to work for financial institutions, including banks, insurance companies, mutual funds, and investment banking firms. The bank officer trainee is the most common initial job in this area.

■   Finance graduates who go into investments generally work for a brokerage house in sales or as a security analyst; for a bank, a mutual fund, or an insurance company in the management of investment portfolios; or for a financial consulting firm, advising individual investors or pension funds on how to invest their funds.

■   Financial management, the broadest of the three areas, and the one with the greatest number of job opportunities, is important to all types of businesses. The types of jobs one encounters in this area range from making decisions regarding plant expansions to choosing what types of securities to issue when financing an expansion.

The three main forms of business organization are the sole proprietorship, the partnership, and the corporation. About 80 percent of businesses operate as sole proprietorships, but

when based on dollar value of sales, 80 percent of all business is conducted by corporations. Although the three basic types of organization dominate the business scene, several hybrid forms are gaining popularity.

- A *sole proprietorship* is an unincorporated business owned by one individual.
  - Its advantages are: (a) it is easily and inexpensively formed, (b) it is subject to few government regulations, and (c) it avoids corporate income taxes. (However, all business earnings are taxed as personal income to the owner.)
  - Its disadvantages are: (a) it is limited in its ability to raise large sums of capital, (b) the proprietor has unlimited personal liability for business debts, and (c) it has a life limited to the life of the individual who created it.

- A *partnership* exists whenever two or more persons associate to conduct a noncorporate business.
  - Its major advantage is its low cost and ease of formation.
  - Its disadvantages are: (a) unlimited liability, (b) limited life, (c) difficulty of transferring ownership, and (d) difficulty of raising large amounts of capital.

- A *corporation* is a legal entity created by a state, and it is separate and distinct from its owners and managers.
  - Its advantages are: (a) unlimited life, (b) ownership which is easily transferred through the exchange of stock, and (c) limited liability. Because of these three factors, it is much easier for corporations to raise money in the capital markets.
  - Its disadvantages are: (a) corporate earnings may be subject to double taxation and (b) setting up a corporation and filing required state and federal reports are more complex and time consuming than for a sole proprietorship or partnership.
  - A charter must be filed with the state where the firm is incorporated, and bylaws which govern the management of the company must be prepared.

- Among the hybrid forms gaining popularity are the limited partnership, the limited liability partnership, and the professional corporation.
  - In a *limited partnership*, the limited partners are liable only for the amount of their investment in the partnership, while the general partners have unlimited liability. Limited partnerships are common in real estate, oil, and equipment leasing ventures.
  - The *limited liability partnership*, sometimes called a *limited liability company*, is a relatively new type of partnership that is now permitted in many states. In this type of partnership all partners enjoy limited liability with regards to the business's liabilities.
  - A *professional corporation* is common among professionals such as doctors, lawyers, and accountants. This form of organization provides most of the benefits of incorporation but does not relieve the participants of professional (malpractice) liability.

■ If certain requirements are met, particularly with regards to size and number of stockholders, one (or more) individuals can establish a corporation but elect to be taxed as if the business were a proprietorship or partnership. Such firms, which differ not in organizational form but only in how their owners are taxed, are called *S corporations*.

■ The value of any business, other than a very small one, will probably be maximized if it is organized as a corporation.

Maximizing the price of the firm's common stock is the most important goal of most corporations.

■ The same actions that maximize stock prices usually benefit society. Reasons include:
   ❏ To a large extent, the owners of stock are society.
   ❏ Consumers benefit because stock price maximization requires efficient, low-cost businesses that produce high-quality goods and services at the lowest possible cost.
   ❏ Employees benefit because companies that successfully increase stock prices also grow and add more employees, thus benefiting society.

■ Managers can enhance their firms' values (and stock prices) by increasing the size of the expected cash flows, by speeding up their receipt, and by reducing their riskiness.
   ❏ Three factors primarily determine cash flows: (1) unit sales, (2) after-tax operating margins, and (3) capital requirements.

■ Although managerial actions affect the value of a firm's stock, external factors also influence stock prices. Included among them are legal constraints, the general level of economic activity, tax laws, interest rates, and conditions in the stock market.

■ While a growing number of analysts rely on cash flow projections to assess performance, at least as much attention is still paid to accounting measures, especially EPS.
   ❏ Traditional accounting performance measures are appealing because (1) they are easy to use and understand; (2) they are calculated on the basis of standardized accounting principles; and (3) net income is supposed to reflect the firm's potential for producing cash flows over time.
   ❏ There are important distinctions between earnings and cash flow, and a firm's stock price is affected by both its performance this year and its expected performance in the future.
   ❏ Even though cash flows ultimately determine stockholder value, financial managers cannot ignore EPS, because earnings announcements send messages to investors.

Two increasingly important trends for financial management in recent years are (1) the focus on shareholder value maximization, (2) the globalization of business, and (3) the increased use of information technology.

- Four factors have led to increased globalization of businesses.
    - Transportation and communications improvements have lowered shipping costs, lowered trade barriers, and made international trade more feasible.
    - Increased political clout of consumers has also helped lower trade barriers.
    - Due to increased technology, higher development costs for new products have resulted, necessitating increased unit sales.
    - Competitive pressures have forced companies to shift manufacturing operations to lower-cost countries.

- Continued advances in computer technology and communications are revolutionizing the way financial decisions are made. Thus, the new generation of financial managers will need stronger computer and quantitative skills than were required in the past.

Business ethics can be thought of as a company's attitude and conduct toward its employees, customers, community, and stockholders.

- Most firms today have in place strong codes of ethical behavior; however, it is imperative that top management be openly committed to ethical behavior and that they communicate this commitment through their own personal actions as well as company policies.

- *Social responsibility* is the concept that businesses should be actively concerned with the welfare of society at large. It raises the question of whether businesses should operate strictly in their stockholders' best interests or also be responsible for the welfare of their employees, customers, and the communities in which they operate.
    - Any voluntary, socially responsible acts that raise costs will be difficult, if not impossible, in industries that are subject to keen competition.
    - Even highly profitable firms are generally constrained in exercising social responsibility by capital market forces because investors will normally prefer a firm that concentrates on profits over one excessively devoted to social action.
    - Socially responsible actions that increase costs may have to be put on a mandatory, rather than a voluntary, basis to ensure that the burden falls uniformly on all businesses.
    - Industry and government must cooperate in establishing the rules of corporate behavior, and the costs as well as the benefits of such actions must be estimated accurately and then taken into account.

An agency relationship arises whenever one or more individuals (the principals) hires another individual or organization (the agent) to perform some service, delegating decision making authority to that agent. Within the financial management context, the primary

agency relationships are those (1) between stockholders and managers and (2) between stockholders (through managers) and creditors (debtholders).

■ A potential *agency problem* arises whenever a manager of a firm owns less than 100 percent of the firm's common stock.
   ❑ Since the firm's earnings do not go solely to the manager, he or she may not concentrate exclusively on maximizing shareholder wealth.

■ A potential *moral hazard problem,* wherein agents take unobserved actions in their own behalf, arises, because it is virtually impossible for shareholders to monitor all managerial actions.

■ In general, to reduce both agency conflicts and the moral hazard problem, stockholders must incur *agency costs*, which include all costs borne by shareholders to encourage managers to maximize the firm's stock price rather than act in their own self-interests.
   ❑ There are three major categories of agency costs: (1) expenditures to monitor managerial actions; (2) expenditures to structure the organization in a way that will limit undesirable managerial behavior; and (3) opportunity costs which are incurred when shareholder imposed restrictions limit the ability of managers to take timely actions that would enhance shareholder wealth.

■ Specific mechanisms are used to motivate managers to act in shareholders' best interests. These include: (1) managerial compensation, (2) direct intervention by shareholders, (3) the threat of firing, and (4) the threat of takeovers.
   ❑ A *performance share* is stock that is awarded to executives on the basis of the company's performance.
   ❑ *Executive stock options* are granted to an executive as part of his or her compensation package and allow them to purchase stock at some future time at a given price.
   ❑ A relatively new measure of managerial performance, *economic value added (EVA)*, is being used by more and more firms to tie executive compensation to stockholder wealth maximization.
   ❑ A *hostile takeover* is the acquisition of a company over the opposition of its management. Hostile takeovers are most likely to occur when a firm's stock is undervalued relative to its potential because of poor management.

■ Another agency problem involves conflicts between stockholders (through managers) and creditors (debtholders).
   ❑ Conflicts arise if (a) management, acting for its stockholders, takes on projects that have greater risk than was anticipated by creditors or (b) the firm increases debt to a level higher than was anticipated. Both of these actions decrease the value of the debt outstanding.

❑   To best serve their shareholders in the long run, managers must play fairly with creditors. Managers, as agents of both shareholders and creditors, must act in a manner that is fairly balanced between the interest of the two classes of security holders. Similarly, management actions which would expropriate wealth from any of the firm's other *stakeholders* will ultimately be to the detriment of its shareholders. In our society, stock price maximization requires fair treatment for all parties whose economic positions are affected by managerial decisions.

SELFTEST QUESTIONS

Definitional

1.   Finance consists of three interrelated areas: (1) _____ _____ _____ _____, which deals with many of the topics covered in macroeconomics; (2) _____, which focuses on the decisions of individuals and financial institutions as they choose securities for their investment portfolios; and (3) _____ _____ or "business finance."

2.   Two increasingly important trends affecting financial management in recent years are the _____ of business, and the increased use of _____ _____.

3.   Sole proprietorships are easily formed, but often have difficulty raising _____, they subject proprietors to unlimited _____, and they have a limited _____.

4.   Partnership profits are taxed as _____ income in proportion to each partner's proportionate ownership.

5.   A partnership is dissolved upon the withdrawal or _____ of any one of the partners. In addition, the difficulty in _____ ownership is a major disadvantage of the partnership form of business organization.

6.   A(n) _____ is a legal entity created by a state, and it is separate from its owners and managers.

7.   The concept of _____ _____ means that a firm's stockholders are not personally liable for the debts of the business.

8.   Modern financial theory operates on the assumption that the goal of management is the _____ of shareholder _____. This goal is accomplished if the firm's _____ _____ is maximized.

9. Socially responsible activities that increase a firm's costs will be most difficult in those industries where _____ is most intense.

10. Firms with above average profit levels will find social actions _____ by capital market factors.

11. _____ _____ can be thought of as a company's attitude and conduct towards its employees, customers, community, and stockholders.

12. A(n) _____ relationship arises whenever one or more individuals (the principals) hire another individual or organization (the agent) to act on their behalf, delegating decision making authority to that agent.

13. Potential agency problems exist between a firm's shareholders and its _____ and also between shareholders (through managers) and _____.

14. Although the three basic types of organization dominate the business scene, several _____ forms are gaining popularity.

15. _____ _____ is the concept that businesses should be actively concerned with the welfare of society at large.

16. A(n) _____ _____ is stock which is awarded to executives on the basis of the company's performance.

17. _____ _____ _____ allow managers to purchase stock at some future time at a given price.

18. A(n) _____ _____ is the acquisition of a company over the opposition of its management.

19. A potential _____ _____ problem, wherein agents take unobserved actions in their own behalf, arises, because it is virtually impossible for shareholders to monitor all managerial actions.

20. A relatively new measure of managerial performance, _____ _____ _____, is being used by more and more firms to tie executive compensation to stockholder wealth maximization.

Conceptual

21. The primary objective of the firm is to maximize EPS.

    a. True   **b.** False

22. The types of actions that help a firm maximize stock price are generally not directly beneficial to society at large.

    a. True   **b.** False

23. There are factors that influence stock price over which managers have virtually no control.

    a. True   **b.** False

24. Which of the following factors tend to encourage management to pursue stock price maximization as a goal?

    a. Shareholders link management's compensation to company performance.
    b. Managers' reactions to the threat of firing and hostile takeovers.
    c. Managers do not have goals other than stock price maximization.
    d. Statements a and b are both correct.
    e. Statements a, b, and c are all correct.

25. The primary contribution of finance to total social welfare is its

    a. Function as a productive resource.
    b. Contribution to the efficient allocation and use of resources.
    c. Role as an exogenous variable.
    d. Positive impact on the externalities of "other variables."
    e. Contribution to environmental protection.

26. Which of the following represents a significant *disadvantage* to the corporate form of organization?

    a. Difficulty in transferring ownership.
    b. Exposure to taxation of corporate earnings and stockholder dividend income.
    c. Degree of liability to which corporate owners and managers are exposed.
    d. Level of difficulty corporations face in obtaining large amounts of capital in financial markets.
    e. All of the above are disadvantages to the corporate form of organization.

ANSWERS TO SELFTEST QUESTIONS

1. money and capital markets; investments; financial management
2. globalization; information technology
3. capital; liability; life
4. personal
5. death; transferring
6. corporation
7. limited liability
8. maximization; wealth; stock price
9. competition
10. constrained
11. Business ethics
12. agency
13. managers; creditors (or debtholders)
14. hybrid
15. Social responsibility
16. performance share
17. Executive stock options
18. hostile takeover
19. moral hazard
20. economic value added

21. b. An increase in earnings per share will not necessarily increase stock price. For example, if the increase in earnings per share is accompanied by an increase in the riskiness of the firm, stock price might fall. *The primary objective is the maximization of stock price.*

22. b. The actions that maximize stock price generally also benefit society by promoting efficient, low-cost operations; encouraging the development of new technology, products, and jobs; and requiring efficient and courteous service.

23. a. Managers have no control over factors such as (1) external constraints (for example, antitrust laws and environmental regulations), (2) the general level of economic activity, (3) taxes, (4) interest rates, and (5) conditions in the stock market, all of which affect the firm's stock price.

24. d. Specific mechanisms which tend to force managers to act in shareholders' best interests include (1) the proper structuring of managerial compensation, (2) direct intervention by shareholders, (3) the threat of firing, and (4) the threat of takeover.

25. b. Financial management plays a crucial role in the operation of successful firms because of finance's contribution to the efficient allocation and use of resources. Successful firms are absolutely necessary for a healthy, productive economy.

26. b. The double taxation of corporate earnings is a significant disadvantage of the corporate form of organization. The corporations' earnings are taxed, and then any earnings paid out as dividends are taxed again as income to stockholders.

CHAPTER 2
FINANCIAL STATEMENTS, CASH FLOW, AND TAXES

OVERVIEW

Financial management requires the consideration of the types of financial statements firms must provide to investors. Thus, this chapter begins with a discussion of the basic financial statements, how they are used, and what kinds of financial information users need.

The value of any asset depends on the usable, or after-tax, cash flows the asset is expected to produce, so the chapter explains the term net cash flow. Since the traditional financial statements are designed more for use by creditors than for corporate managers and stock analysts, the chapter discusses how to modify accounting data for managerial decisions. In addition, the concepts of Market Value Added (MVA) and Economic Value Added (EVA) are defined and explained. Finally, since it is the after-tax income that is important, the chapter provides an overview of the federal income tax system.

OUTLINE

Although the economic system has grown enormously since the early days of the barter system, the original reasons for accounting and financial statements still apply. Investors need them to make intelligent decisions, managers need them to see how effectively their enterprises are being run, and taxing authorities need them to assess taxes in a reasonable manner.

A firm's annual report to shareholders presents two important types of information. The first is a verbal statement of the company's recent operating results and its expectations for the coming year. The second is a set of quantitative financial statements that report what actually happened to the firm's financial position, earnings, and dividends over the past few years.

The balance sheet shows the firm's assets and the claims against those assets. Assets, found on the left-hand side of the balance sheet, are typically shown in the order of their liquidity. Claims, found on the right-hand side, are generally listed in the order in which they must be paid.

- ■ Only cash represents actual money.
  - ❑ Non-cash assets should produce cash flows eventually, but they do not represent cash in hand.
  - ❑ Note, though, that some types of marketable securities have a very short time until maturity, and can be converted very quickly into cash at prices close to their book values. These securities are called *cash equivalents*, and are included with cash.

- ■ Claims against the assets consist of liabilities and stockholders' equity:

  Assets – Liabilities – Preferred stock = Common stockholders' equity (Net worth).

- ■ The common equity section of the balance sheet is divided into two accounts: common stock and retained earnings. The common stock account arises from the issuance of stock to raise capital. Retained earnings are built up over time as the firm "saves" a part of its earnings rather than paying all earnings out as dividends.

- ■ Different methods, such as FIFO and LIFO, can be used to determine the value of inventory. These methods, in turn, affect the reported cost of goods sold, profits, and EPS.

- ■ Companies often use the most accelerated method permitted under the law to calculate depreciation for tax purposes but use straight-line depreciation, which results in a lower depreciation expense, for stockholder reporting.

- ■ The balance sheet may be thought of as a snapshot of the firm's financial position *at a point in time* (for example, end of year). The balance sheet changes every day as inventory is increased or decreased, as fixed assets are added or retired, as bank loans are increased or decreased, and so on.

The income statement summarizes the firm's revenues and expenses over a period of time (for example, the past year). Earnings per share (EPS) is called "the bottom line," denoting that of all the items on the income statement, EPS is the most important.

The statement of retained earnings reports changes in the equity accounts between balance sheet dates. The balance sheet account "retained earnings" represents a claim against assets, not assets per se. Retained earnings as reported on the balance sheet do not represent cash and are not "available" for the payment of dividends or anything else. Retained earnings represent funds that have already been reinvested in the firm's operating assets.

The statement of cash flows summarizes the changes in a company's cash position.

■ Net income, noncash adjustments to net income, changes in working capital, fixed assets, and security transactions are reflected in the statement of cash flows.

■ The statement of cash flows separates activities into three categories: operating activities, investing activities, and financing activities.

■ Financial managers generally use this statement, along with the cash budget, when forecasting their companies' cash positions.

■ Net cash flow is the sum of net income plus noncash adjustments.

■ The traditional financial statements are designed more for use by creditors and tax collectors than for managers and equity analysts. Certain modifications are used for corporate decision making and stock valuation.

■ To judge managerial performance one needs to compare managers' ability to generate operating income (EBIT) with the operating assets under their control.
   ❏ *Operating assets* consist of cash needed to sustain operations, accounts receivable, inventories, and fixed assets necessary to operate the business.
   ❏ *Nonoperating assets* include marketable securities (in excess or any cash equivalents needed to sustain operations), investments in subsidiaries, land held for future use, and the like.
   ❏ Operating assets can be further divided into working capital and plant and equipment.
   ❏ Those current assets used in operations are called *operating working capital*, and operating working capital less accounts payable and accruals is called *net operating working capital (NOWC)*. Short-term investments are normally excluded when calculating NOWC because they generally result from investment decisions made by the treasurer and are not used in the core operations.
   ❏ *Total operating capital* is the sum of net operating working capital and net fixed assets.

■ Net income does not always reflect the true performance of a company's operations or the effectiveness of its managers and employees.
   ❏ A better measure for comparing managers' performance is *net operating profit after taxes (NOPAT)*, which is the amount of profit a company would generate if it had no debt and held no financial assets.
   ❏ $NOPAT = EBIT(1 - T)$.
   ❏ The value of a company's operations depends on all the future expected free cash flows.

- ❑ *Free cash flow* is the cash flow actually available for distribution to investors after the company has made all the investments in fixed assets and working capital necessary to sustain ongoing operations.
- ❑ *Operating cash flow* is NOPAT plus any noncash adjustments as shown on the statement of cash flows.
- ❑ *Free cash flow* is calculated as operating cash flow less gross investment in operating capital. It also equals NOPAT less net investment in operating capital.

- ■ Free cash flow has five uses:
  - ❑ Pay net after-tax interest to debtholders.
  - ❑ Pay principal on debt.
  - ❑ Pay dividends to shareholders.
  - ❑ Repurchase stock from shareholders.
  - ❑ Buy marketable securities or other nonoperating assets.

- ■ The return on invested capital, ROIC, is the rate of return that the company is generating on its capital.
  - ❑ ROIC = NOPAT/Capital.

- ■ The weighted average cost of capital, WACC, is the rate of return that the company must generate to satisfy its investors.

- ■ Negative free cash flow is not always bad.
  - ❑ If ROIC is greater than WACC, then a negative free cash flow may be due to high growth. In this situation, as growth slows, the investment in new capital will also decrease, and free cash flow will become positive.

- ■ If free cash flow is negative because NOPAT is negative, this is a bad sign, because the company probably is experiencing operating problems.
  - ❑ Exceptions to this might be startup companies; companies that are incurring significant current expenses to launch a new product line; or high growth companies, which will have large investments in capital that cause low current free cash flow, but that will increase future free cash flow.

Neither traditional accounting data nor the modified data discussed above deal with stock prices. This is a serious omission, since the primary goal of management is to maximize the firm's stock price. In response to these limitations, analysts have come up with adjustments which provide alternative measures of performance. Two of these measures are Market Value Added (MVA) and Economic Value Added (EVA).

■ Shareholders' wealth is maximized by maximizing the difference between the market value of the firm's equity and the amount of equity capital that was supplied by shareholders. This difference is called the *Market Value Added (MVA)*.

> MVA = Market value of equity – Equity capital supplied by shareholders
> = (Shares outstanding)(Stock price) – Total common equity.

> Another expression for MVA that give the same value is:

> MVA = Total market value of the company – Total capital supplied by investors
> = [(Shares outstanding)(Stock price) + Value of debt]
> – [Total common equity + Debt].

■ Whereas MVA measures the effects of managerial actions since the very inception of a company, *Economic Value Added (EVA)* focuses on managerial effectiveness in a given year.

> EVA = NOPAT – After-tax dollar cost of capital used to support operations
> = EBIT $(1 - T)$ – (Operating Capital)(After-tax percentage cost).

> EVA can also be defined as:
> EVA = Capital (ROIC-WACC).

❑ EVA is an estimate of a business's true economic profit for the year.
❑ EVA differs sharply from accounting profit. EVA represents the residual income that remains after the cost of all capital, including equity capital, has been deducted, whereas accounting profit is determined without imposing a charge for equity capital.
❑ EVA provides a good measure of the extent to which the firm has added to shareholder value.
❑ EVA can be determined for divisions as well as for the company as a whole, so it provides a useful basis for determining managerial compensation at all levels.

■ There is a relationship between MVA and EVA, but it is not a direct one.
❑ If a company has a history of negative EVAs, then its MVA will probably be negative, and vice versa if it has a history of positive EVAs.
❑ A company with a history of negative EVAs could have a positive MVA, provided investors expect a turnaround in the future.

■ When EVAs or MVAs are used to evaluate managerial performance as part of an incentive compensation program, EVA is the measure that is typically used.

❑ MVA is used primarily to evaluate top corporate officers over periods of five to ten years, or longer.

Individuals pay taxes on wages and salaries, on investment income (dividends, interest, and profits from the sale of securities), and on the profits of proprietorships and partnerships.

■ U. S. income taxes are *progressive*; that is, the higher the income, the larger the percentage paid in taxes. Marginal tax rates begin at 15 percent and can go up to 39.6 percent.
   ❑ The *marginal tax rate* is the tax applicable to the last unit of income.
   ❑ The *average tax rate* is calculated as taxes paid divided by taxable income.
   ❑ *Taxable income* is gross income minus exemptions and allowable deductions as set forth in the Tax Code.
   ❑ *Bracket creep* is a situation that occurs when progressive tax rates combine with inflation to cause a greater portion of each taxpayer's real income to be paid as taxes.

■ Because dividends are paid from corporate income that has already been taxed (at rates going up as high as 39 percent), there is *double taxation* of corporate income. Interest on most state and local government securities, which are often called "*municipals*," is not subject to federal income taxes. This creates a strong incentive for individuals in high tax brackets to purchase such securities.

■ Gains and losses on the sale of *capital assets* such as stocks, bonds, and real estate have historically received special tax treatment.
   ❑ Capital gains tax rates have varied over time, but they have generally been lower than rates on ordinary income. The reason is simple. Congress wants the economy to grow, for growth we need investment in productive assets, and low capital gains tax rates encourage investments.
   ❑ *Short-term capital gains,* where the asset is sold within one year of the time it was purchased, are added to such ordinary income as wages, dividends, and interest and then are taxed at the same rate as ordinary income.
   ❑ If an asset has been held longer than 12 months, any profit is defined to be a *long-term capital gain*, and its rate is capped at 20 percent if the asset was acquired prior to 1/1/2001. If the asset was acquired on or after 1/1/2001 and held for more than 12 months, the capital gains rate is 18 percent.

Corporations pay taxes on profits.

■ Corporate tax rates are also progressive up to $18,333,333 of taxable income, but are constant thereafter at a rate of 35 percent. Marginal tax rates range from 15 to 39 percent.

■ Interest and dividend income received by a corporation are taxed.
   ❑ Interest is taxed as ordinary income at regular corporate tax rates.

- ❑ However, 70 percent of the dividends received by one corporation from another is excluded from taxable income. The remaining 30 percent is taxed at the ordinary rate. Thus, the effective tax rate on dividends received by a 35 percent marginal tax bracket corporation is 0.30(35%) = 10.5%.

- ■ The tax system favors debt financing over equity financing.
  - ❑ Interest paid is a tax-deductible business expense.
  - ❑ Dividends on common and preferred stock are not deductible. Thus, a 40 percent federal-plus-state tax bracket corporation must earn $1/(1.0 _ 0.40) = $1/0.60 = $1.67 before taxes to pay $1 of dividends, but only $1 of pretax income is required to pay $1 of interest.

- ■ Before 1987, long-term corporate capital gains were taxed at lower rates than ordinary income. However, at present, long-term corporate capital gains are taxed as ordinary income.

- ■ Ordinary corporate operating losses can be *carried back* to each of the preceding 2 years and *forward* for the next 20 years in the future to offset taxable income in those years. The purpose of permitting this loss treatment is to avoid penalizing corporations whose incomes fluctuate substantially from year to year.

- ■ The Internal Revenue Code imposes a penalty on corporations that improperly accumulate earnings if the purpose of the accumulation is to enable stockholders to avoid personal income tax on dividends.

- ■ If a corporation owns 80 percent or more of another corporation's stock, it can aggregate profits and losses and file a *consolidated* tax return. Thus, losses in one area can offset profits in another.

- ■ Small businesses which meet certain restrictions may be set up as *S corporations* which receive benefits of the corporate form——especially limited liability——yet are taxed as proprietorships or partnerships rather than as corporations. This treatment would be preferred by owners of small corporations in which all or most of the income earned each year is distributed as dividends because the income would be taxed only once at the individual level.

SELF-TEST QUESTIONS

Definitional

1. Of all its communications with shareholders, a firm's _____ report is generally the most important.

2. The income statement reports the results of operations during the past year, the most important item being _____ _____ _____.

3. The _____ _____ lists the firm's assets as well as claims against those assets.

4. Typically, assets are listed in order of their _____, while liabilities are listed in the order in which they must be paid.

5. Assets – Liabilities – Preferred stock = _____ worth, or _____ _____ equity.

6. The two accounts that normally make up the common equity section of the balance sheet are _____ _____ and _____ _____.

7. _____ _____ as reported on the balance sheet represent income earned by the firm in past years that has not been paid out as dividends.

8. The _____ ____ _____ _____ is designed to summarize the changes in a company's cash position.

9. The three major categories of the statement of cash flows are cash flows associated with _____ activities, _____-_____ _____ activities, and _____ activities.

10. The _____ _____ account arises from the issuance of stock to raise capital.

11. The _____ ____ _____ _____ reports changes in the equity accounts between balance sheet dates.

12. _____ _____ _____ is the sum of net income plus noncash adjustments.

13. The traditional financial statements are designed more for use by _____ and tax collectors than for _____ and equity analysts.

14. _____ _____ consist of cash, accounts receivable, inventories, and fixed assets necessary to operate the business.

15. _____ _____ include marketable securities, investments in subsidiaries, and land held for future use.

16. Those current assets used in operations are called _____ _____ _____.

17. Operating working capital less accounts payable and accruals is called _____ _____ _____ _____.

18. _____ _____ _____ is the sum of net operating working capital and net fixed assets.

19. A better measure for comparing managers' performance than net income is _____ _____ _____ _____ _____.

20. _____ _____ _____ is the cash flow actually available for distribution to investors after the company has made all the investments in fixed assets and working capital necessary to sustain ongoing operations.

21. _____ _____ _____ is calculated as net operating profit after taxes plus any noncash adjustments as shown on the statement of cash flows.

22. Shareholder wealth is maximized by maximizing the difference between the market value of the firm's equity and the amount of equity that was supplied by shareholders. This difference is called _____ _____ _____.

23. _____ _____ _____ focuses on managerial effectiveness in a given year and is an estimate of a business's true economic profit for the year.

24. A(n) _____ tax system is one in which tax rates are higher at higher levels of income.

25. A progressive tax structure, which when combined with inflation increases the government's share of GDP without any change in tax rates, is called _____ _____.

26. The marginal tax rate on the largest corporations, those with taxable incomes exceeding $18,333,333, is ____ percent, while that on the wealthiest individuals can go up as high as _____ percent.

27. Interest received on _____ bonds is generally not subject to federal income taxes. This feature makes them particularly attractive to investors in _____ tax brackets.

28. In order to qualify as a long-term capital gain or loss, an asset must be held for more than ____ months.

29. Gains or losses on assets held less than one year are referred to as _____-_____ transactions.

30. Interest income received by a corporation is taxed as _____ income. However, only ____ percent of dividends received from another corporation is subject to taxation.

31. Another important distinction exists between interest and dividends paid by a corporation. Interest payments are _____ _____, while dividend payments are not.

32. Ordinary corporate operating losses can first be carried back ____ years and then forward ____ years.

33. A firm that refuses to pay dividends in order to help stockholders avoid personal income taxes may be subject to a penalty for _____ _____ of earnings.

34. A corporation that owns 80 percent or more of another corporation's stock may choose to file _____ tax returns.

35. The Tax Code permits a corporation (that meets certain restrictions) to be taxed at the owners' personal tax rates and to avoid the impact of _____ taxation of dividends. This type of corporation is called a(n) ____ corporation.

Conceptual

36. The fact that 70 percent of intercorporate dividends received by a corporation is excluded from taxable income has encouraged debt financing over equity financing.

   a. True   **b.** False

37. An individual with substantial personal wealth and income is considering the possibility of opening a new business. The business will have a relatively high degree of risk, and losses may be incurred for the first several years. Which legal form of business organization would probably be best?

   a. Proprietorship   **d.** S corporation
   b. Corporation   **e.** Limited partnership

c. Partnership

38. Which of the following statements is most correct?

a. In order to avoid double taxation and to escape the frequently higher tax rate applied to capital gains, stockholders generally prefer to have corporations pay dividends rather than to retain their earnings and reinvest the money in the business. Thus, earnings should be retained only if the firm needs capital very badly and would have difficulty raising it from external sources.
b. Under our current tax laws, when investors pay taxes on their dividend income, they are being subjected to a form of double taxation.
c. The fact that a percentage of the interest received by one corporation, which is paid by another corporation, is excluded from taxable income has encouraged firms to use more debt financing relative to equity financing.
d. If the tax laws stated that $0.50 out of every $1.00 of interest paid by a corporation was allowed as a tax-deductible expense, this would probably encourage companies to use more debt financing than they presently do, other things held constant.
e. Statements b and d are both correct.

SELF-TEST PROBLEMS

(The following data apply to the next three Self-Test Problems.)

Ryngaert & Sons, Inc. has operating income (EBIT) of $2,250,000. The company's depreciation expense is $450,000, its interest expense is $120,000, and it faces a 40 percent tax rate.

1. What is the company's net income?

   a. $1,008,000   b. $1,278,000   c. $1,475,000   d. $1,728,000   e. $1,800,000

2. What is its net cash flow?

   a. $1,008,000   b. $1,278,000   c. $1,475,000   d. $1,728,000   e. $1,800,000
3. What is its operating cash flow?

   a. $1,008,000   b. $1,278,000   c. $1,475,000   d. $1,728,000   e. $1,800,000

4. Wayne Corporation had income from operations of $385,000, it received interest payments of $15,000, it paid interest of $20,000, it received dividends from another cor-

poration of $10,000, and it paid $40,000 in dividends to its common stockholders. What is Wayne's federal income tax?

   a. $122,760   **b.** $130,220   **c.** $141,700   **d.** 155,200   **e.** $163,500

5.   A firm purchases $10 million of corporate bonds that paid a 16 percent interest rate, or $1.6 million in interest. If the firm's marginal tax rate is 35 percent, what is the after-tax interest yield?

   a. 7.36%   **b.** 8.64%   **c.** 10.40%   **d.** 13.89%   **e.** 14.32%

6.   Refer to Self-Test Problem 5. The firm also invests in the common stock of another company having a 16 percent before-tax dividend yield. What is the after-tax dividend yield?

   a. 7.36%   **b.** 8.64%   **c.** 10.40%   **d.** 13.89%   **e.** 14.32%

7.   The Carter Company's taxable income and income tax payments are shown below for 1998 through 2001:

Year	Taxable Income	Tax Payment
1998	$10,000	$1,500
1999	5,000	750
2000	12,000	1,800
2001	8,000	1,200

Assume that Carter's tax rate for all 4 years was a flat 15 percent; that is, each dollar of taxable income was taxed at 15 percent. In 2002, Carter incurred a loss of $17,000. Using corporate loss carry-back, what is Carter's adjusted tax payment for 2001?

   a. $850   **b.** $750   **c.** $610   **d.** $550   **e.** $450

8.   A firm can undertake a new project that will generate a before-tax return of 20 percent or it can invest the same funds in the preferred stock of another company that yields 13 percent before taxes. If the only consideration is which alternative provides the highest relevant (after-tax) return and the applicable tax rate is 35 percent, should the firm invest in the project or the preferred stock?

   a. Preferred stock; its relevant return is 12 percent.
   b. Project; its relevant return is 1.36 percentage points higher.
   c. Preferred stock; its relevant return is 0.22 percentage points higher.
   d. Project; its after-tax return is 20 percent.
   e. Either alternative can be chosen; they have the same relevant return.

9. Cooley Corporation has $20,000 that it plans to invest in marketable securities. It is choosing between MCI bonds which yield 10 percent, state of Colorado municipal bonds which yield 7 percent, and MCI preferred stock with a dividend yield of 8 percent. Cooley's corporate tax rate is 25 percent, and 70 percent of its dividends received are tax exempt. What is the after-tax rate of return on the highest yielding security?

a. 7.4%   b. 7.0%   c. 7.5%   d. 6.5%   e. 6.0%

(The following data apply to the next two Self-Test Problems.)

GPD Corporation has operating income (EBIT) of $300,000, total assets of $1,500,000, and its capital structure consists of 40 percent debt and 60 percent equity. Total assets were equal to total operating capital. The firm's after-tax cost of capital is 10.5 percent and its tax rate is 40 percent. The firm has 50,000 shares of common stock currently out- standing and the current price of a share of stock is $27.00.

10. What is the firm's Market Value Added (MVA)?

a. $22,500   b. $87,575   c. $187,740   d. $450,000   e. $575,000

11. What is the firm's Economic Value Added (EVA)?

a. $22,500   b. $87,575   c. $187,740   d. $450,000   e. $575,000

(The following data apply to the next four Self-Test Problems.)

You have just obtained financial information for the past two years for the Smith Brothers Corporation.

Smith Brothers Corporation
Income Statements for Year Ending December 31
(Millions of Dollars)

	2001	2000
Sales	$360	$300
Oper. costs excluding deprec.	306	255
Depreciation	9	7
EBIT	$ 45	$ 38
Interest	7	6
EBT	$ 38	$ 32
Taxes (40%)	15	13
NI available to common stockholders	$ 23	$ 19
Common dividends	16	10

Smith Brothers Corporation
Balance Sheets as of December 31
(Millions of Dollars)

Assets	2001	2000
Cash & equivalents	$ 4	$ 3
ST investments	0	0
Accts. receivable	54	45
Inventories	54	60
Total CA	$112	$108
Net plant & equip.	90	75
Total assets	$202	$183
Liabilities and Equity		
Accts. payable	$ 32	$ 28
Notes payable	20	16
Accruals	22	18
Total CL	$ 74	$ 62
LT bonds	45	45
Total debt	$119	$107
Common stock (50,000,000 shares)	15	15
Retained earnings	68	61
Common equity	$ 83	$ 76
Total liabilities and equity	$202	$183

12. What is the net operating profit after taxes (NOPAT) in millions of dollars for 2001?

    a. $18   b. $27   c. $34   d. $40   e. $45

13. What is the net operating working capital in millions of dollars for 2001?

    a. $38   b. $54   c. $58   d. $87   e. $112

14. What is the total operating capital in millions of dollars for 2001?

    a. $90   b. $128   c. $144   d. $148   e. $177

15. What is the free cash flow in millions of dollars for 2001?

    a. $11   b. $16   c. $20   d. $25   e. $27

ANSWERS TO SELF-TEST QUESTIONS

1. annual
2. earnings per share
3. balance sheet
4. liquidity
5. Net; common stockholders'
6. common stock; retained earnings
7. Retained earnings
8. statement of cash flows
9. operating; long-term investing; financing
10. common stock
11. statement of retained earnings
12. Net cash flow
13. creditors; managers
14. Operating assets
15. Nonoperating assets
16. operating working capital
17. net operating working capital
18. Total operating capital
19. net operating profit after taxes
20. Free cash flow
21. Operating cash flow
22. Market Value Added (MVA)
23. Economic Value Added (EVA)
24. progressive
25. bracket creep
26. 35; 39.6
27. municipal; high
28. 18
29. short-term
30. ordinary; 30
31. tax deductible
32. 2; 20
33. improper accumulation
34. consolidated
35. double; S

36. b. Debt financing is encouraged by the fact that interest payments are tax deductible while dividend payments are not.

37. d. The S corporation limits the liability of the individual, but permits losses to be deducted against personal income.

38. b. Statement a is incorrect. To avoid double taxation, stockholders would prefer that corporations retain more of its earnings because long-term capital gains are taxed at a rate of 20 percent. Statement c is incorrect. Debt financing has been encouraged by the fact that interest on debt is tax deductible. Statement d is incorrect. Currently, interest on debt is fully tax deductible; allowing 50 percent of interest to be tax deductible would discourage debt financing.

SOLUTIONS TO SELF-TEST PROBLEMS

1. b.

EBIT	$2,250,000
Interest	120,000
EBT	$2,130,000
Taxes (40%)	852,000

Net Income $1,278,000

2.   d.   Net cash flow = Net income + Depreciation
$$= \$1,278,000 + \$450,000$$
$$= \$1,728,000.$$

3.   e.   Operating cash flow = NOPAT + Depreciation
$$= EBIT (1 - T) + Depreciation$$
$$= \$2,250,000(0.6) + \$450,000$$
$$= \$1,800,000.$$

4.   b.   The first step is to determine taxable income:

Income from operations	$385,000
Interest income (fully taxable)	15,000
Interest expense (fully deductible)	(20,000)
Dividend income (30% taxable)	3,000
Taxable income	$383,000

(Note that dividends are paid from after-tax income and do not affect taxable income.)

Based on the current corporate tax table, the tax calculation is as follows:

Tax = $113,900 + 0.34($383,000 – $335,000) = $113,900 + $16,320 = $130,220.

5.   c.   The after-tax yield (or dollar return) equals the before-tax yield (or dollar return) multiplied by one minus the effective tax rate, or AT = BT(1 – Effective T). Therefore,

AT = 16%(1 – 0.35) = 16%(0.65) = 10.40%.

6.   e.   Since the dividends are received by a corporation, only 30 percent are taxable, and the Effective T = Tax rate x 30%:

AT = BT(1 – Effective T)
$$= 16\%[1 - 0.35(0.30)]$$
$$= 16\%(1 - 0.105)$$
$$= 16\%(0.895)$$
$$= 14.32\%.$$

7. e.

Year	Taxable Income	Tax Payment	Adjusted Taxable Income	Adjusted Tax Payment
1998	$10,000	$1,500	$10,000	$1,500
1999	5,000	750	5,000	750
2000	12,000	1,800	0	0
2001	8,000	1,200	3,000	450

The carry-back can only go back 2 years. Thus, there were no adjustments made in 1998 and 1999. After a $12,000 adjustment in 2000, there was a $5,000 loss remaining to apply to 2001. The 2001 adjusted tax payment is $3,000(0.15) = $450. Thus, Carter received a total of $2,550 in tax refunds after the adjustment.

8. b. The project is fully taxable; thus its after-tax return is as follows:

$$AT = 20\%(1 - 0.35) = 20\%(0.65) = 13\%.$$

But only 30 percent of the preferred stock dividends are taxable; thus, its after-tax yield is $AT = 13\%[1 - 0.35(0.30)] = 13\%(1 - 0.105) = 13\%(0.895) = 11.64\%$. Therefore, the new project should be chosen since its after-tax return is 1.36 percentage points higher.

9. c. AT yield on Colorado bond = 7%.

AT yield on MCI bond = 10% – Taxes = 10% – 10%(0.25) = 7.5%.

Check: Invest $20,000 at 10% = $2,000 interest.
Pay 25% tax, so AT income = $2,000(1 – T) = $2,000(0.75) = $1,500.
AT rate of return = $1,500/$20,000 = 7.5%.

AT yield on MCI preferred stock = 8% – Taxes = 8% – 0.3(8%)(0.25)
= 8% – 0.6% = 7.4%.

Therefore, invest in MCI bonds.

10. d. Market Value Added = (Shares outstanding)(P_0) – Total common equity
= 50,000($27.00) – (0.6)($1,500,000)
= $1,350,000 – $900,000
= $450,000.

11.   a.   Economic Value Added $= \text{NOPAT} - $ AT dollar cost of capital used to support operations

$$= \text{EBIT}(1 - T) - (\text{Operating Capital})\left(\begin{array}{c}\text{After - tax} \\ \text{percentage cost}\end{array}\right)$$

$$= \$300,000(0.6) - (\$1,500,000)(0.105)$$
$$= \$180,000 - \$157,500$$
$$= \$22,500.$$

12.   b.   NOPAT $= \text{EBIT}(1 - \text{Tax rate})$
$$= \$45(0.6)$$
$$= \$27.$$

13.   c. NOWC_{01} $= \text{Operating current assets} - \text{operating current liabilities}$
$$= (\$4 + \$54 + \$54) - (\$32 + 22)$$
$$= \$112 - \$54 = \$58.$$

14.   d.   Operating capital$_{01}$ $= $ Net plant and equipment $+$ Net operating working capital
$$= \$90 + \$58$$
$$= \$148.$$

15.   b.   FCF $= \text{NOPAT} - \text{Net investment in operating capital}$
$$= \$27 - (\$148 - \$137)$$
$$= \$16.$$

CHAPTER 3
ANALYSIS OF FINANCIAL STATEMENTS

OVERVIEW

Financial analysis is designed to determine the relative strengths and weaknesses of a company. Investors need this information to estimate both future cash flows from the firm and the riskiness of those cash flows. Financial managers need the information provided by analysis both to evaluate the firm's past performance and to map future plans. Financial analysis concentrates on *financial statement analysis*, which highlights the key aspects of a firm's operations.

Financial statement analysis involves a study of the relationships between income statement and balance sheet accounts, how these relationships change over time (*trend analysis*), and how a particular firm compares with other firms in its industry (*benchmarking*). Although financial analysis has limitations, when used with care and judgment, it can provide some very useful insights into a company's operations.

OUTLINE

Financial statements are used to help predict the firm's future earnings and dividends. From an investor's standpoint, predicting the future is what financial statement analysis is all about. From management's standpoint, financial statement analysis is useful both to help anticipate future conditions and, more important, as a starting point for planning actions that will affect the future course of events. Financial ratios are designed to help one evaluate a firm's financial statements. Ratio analysis raises a red flag as to the questions managers and analysts should ask.

- Financial ratios are used by three main groups:
  - Managers, who employ ratios to help analyze, control, and thus improve their firm's operating performance.
  - Credit analysts, such as bank loan officers or bond rating analysts, who analyze ratios to help ascertain a company's ability to pay its debts.
  - Stock analysts and stockholders, who are interested in a company's efficiency, risk, and growth prospects to forecast earnings, dividends, and stock prices.

Liquidity ratios are used to measure a firm's ability to meet its current obligations as they come due.

- The *current ratio* measures the extent to which the claims of short-term creditors are covered by assets that are expected to be converted to cash fairly quickly. It is determined by dividing current assets by current liabilities. It is the most commonly used measure of short-term solvency.

- The *quick*, or *acid test, ratio* is calculated by deducting inventory from current assets and then dividing the remainder by current liabilities. Inventories are excluded because they are typically the least liquid of a firm's current assets, hence they are the assets on which losses are most likely to occur in the event of liquidation.

Asset management ratios measure how effectively a firm is managing its assets and whether or not the level of those assets is properly related to the level of operations as measured by sales.

- The *inventory turnover ratio* is defined as sales divided by inventories. It is often necessary to use average inventories rather than year-end inventories, especially if a firm's business is highly seasonal, or if there has been a strong upward or downward sales trend during the year.

- The *days sales outstanding (DSO),* also called the "average collection period" (ACP), is used to appraise accounts receivable, and it is calculated by dividing accounts receivable by average daily sales to find the number of days' sales tied up in receivables. Thus, the DSO represents the average length of time that the firm must wait after making a sale before receiving cash, which is the average collection period.
  - The DSO can also be evaluated by comparison with the terms on which the firm sells its goods.

- The *fixed assets turnover ratio* is the ratio of sales to net fixed assets. It measures how effectively the firm uses its plant and equipment.

- The *total assets turnover ratio* is calculated by dividing sales by total assets. It measures the utilization, or turnover, of all the firm's assets.

Debt management ratios measure the extent to which a firm is using debt financing, or financial leverage, and the degree of safety afforded to creditors.

- Financial leverage has three important implications: (1) By raising funds through debt, stockholders can maintain control of a firm while limiting their investment. (2) Creditors look to the equity, or owner-supplied funds, to provide a margin of safety, so if the stockholders have provided only a small proportion of the total financing, the firm's risks are borne mainly by its creditors. (3) If the firm earns more on investments financed with borrowed funds than it pays in interest, the return on the owners' capital is magnified, or "leveraged."

- ❑ Firms with relatively high debt ratios have higher expected returns when the economy is normal, but they are exposed to risk of loss when the economy goes into a recession.
- ❑ Firms with low debt ratios are less risky, but also forego the opportunity to leverage up their return on equity.
- ❑ Decisions about the use of debt require firms to balance higher expected returns against increased risk.

■ The text discusses two procedures analysts use to examine the firm's debt: (1) They check the balance sheet to determine the extent to which borrowed funds have been used to finance assets, and (2) they review the income statement to see the extent to which fixed charges are covered by operating profits.

■ The *debt ratio*, or ratio of total debt to total assets, measures the percentage of funds provided by creditors. Total debt includes both current liabilities and long-term debt. The lower the ratio, the greater the protection afforded creditors in the event of liquidation. Stockholders, on the other hand, may want more leverage because it magnifies expected earnings.

■ The *times-interest-earned (TIE) ratio* is determined by dividing earnings before interest and taxes (EBIT) by the interest charges. The TIE measures the extent to which operating income can decline before the firm is unable to meet its annual interest costs.

- ❑ Failure to meet this obligation can bring legal action by the firm's creditors, possibly resulting in bankruptcy.
- ❑ Note that EBIT, rather than net income, is used in the numerator. Because interest is paid with pre-tax dollars, the firm's ability to pay current interest is not affected by taxes.

■ The *EBITDA coverage ratio* is similar to the TIE ratio, but it is more inclusive because it recognizes that many firms lease assets and incur long-term obligations under lease contracts and sinking funds. It also recognizes that depreciation is a non-cash charge, and so can be used to cover interest and other payments.

Profitability ratios show the combined effects of liquidity, asset management, and debt on operating results.

■ The *profit margin on sales* is calculated by dividing net income by sales. It gives the profit per dollar of sales.

■   The *basic earning power (BEP) ratio* is calculated by dividing earnings before interest and taxes (EBIT) by total assets. It shows the raw earning power of the firm's assets, before the influence of taxes and leverage, and it is useful for comparing firms with different tax situations and different degrees of financial leverage.

■   The *return on total assets (ROA)* is the ratio of net income to total assets; it measures the return on all the firm's assets after interest and taxes.

■   The *return on common equity (ROE)* measures the rate of return on stockholders' investment. It is equal to net income divided by common equity.

Market value ratios relate the firm's stock price to its earnings and book value per share, and thus give management an indication of what investors think of the company's past performance and future prospects. If the liquidity, asset management, debt management, and profitability ratios are all good, then the market value ratios will be high, and the stock price will probably be as high as can be expected.

■   The *price/earnings (P/E) ratio*, or price per share divided by earnings per share, shows how much investors are willing to pay per dollar of reported profits. P/E ratios are higher for firms with strong growth prospects, other things held constant, but they are lower for riskier firms.

■   The *price/cash flow ratio*, or price per share divided by cash flow per share, shows how much investors are willing to pay per dollar of cash flow.

■   The *market/book (M/B) ratio*, defined as market price per share divided by book value per share, gives another indication of how investors regard the company. Higher M/B ratios are generally associated with firms with relatively high rates of return on common equity.

It is important to analyze trends in ratios as well as their absolute levels. Trend analysis can provide clues as to whether the firm's financial situation is likely to improve or to deteriorate.

■   In a *common size analysis*, all income statement items are divided by sales, and all balance sheet items are divided by total assets. Common size analysis facilitates comparisons of balance sheets and income statements over time and across companies.

■   In a *percentage change analysis*, growth rates are calculated for all income statement items and balance sheet accounts. This type of analysis pinpoints "problem" areas more quickly than looking at dollar amounts.

■ The conclusions reached in common size and percentage change analyses generally parallel those derived from ratio analysis. It is often useful to have all three analyses to drive home to management, in slightly different ways, the need to take corrective actions. Thus, a thorough financial statement analysis will include ratio, percentage change, and common size analyses, as well as a Du Pont analysis.

A modified Du Pont chart shows how return on equity is affected by assets turnover, profit margin, and leverage.

■ The profit margin times the total assets turnover is called the *Du Pont equation*. This equation gives the rate of return on assets (ROA):

$$\text{ROA} = \text{Profit margin} \times \text{Total assets turnover.}$$

■ The ROA times the *equity multiplier* (total assets divided by common equity) yields the return on equity (ROE). This equation is referred to as the *extended Du Pont equation:*

$$\text{ROE} = \text{Profit margin} \times \text{Total assets turnover} \times \text{Equity multiplier.}$$

■ If a company is financed only with common equity, the return on assets (ROA) and the return on equity (ROE) are the same because total assets will equal common equity. This equality holds only if the company uses no debt.

Ratio analysis involves comparisons because a company's ratios are compared with those of other firms in the same industry, that is, to industry average figures. Comparative ratios are available from a number of sources which include Dun & Bradstreet, Robert Morris Associates, and the U. S. Commerce Department. Benchmarking is the process of comparing the ratios of a particular company with those of a smaller group of "benchmark" companies, rather than with the entire industry.

■ Many companies also benchmark various parts of their overall operation against top companies, whether they are in the same industry or not.

■ Each of the data-supplying organizations uses a somewhat different set of ratios designed for its own purposes. So, when you select a comparative data source, you should be sure that your emphasis is similar to that of the agency whose ratios you plan to use.
  ❑ Be sure to verify the exact definitions of the ratios to ensure consistency with your own work.

There are some inherent problems and limitations to ratio analysis that necessitate care and judgment.

■ Ratios are often not useful for analyzing the operations of large firms which operate in many different industries because comparative ratios are not meaningful.

■ The use of industry averages may not provide a very challenging target for high-level performance.

■ Inflation affects depreciation charges, inventory costs, and therefore the value of both balance sheet items and net income. For this reason, the analysis of a firm over time, or a comparative analysis of firms of different ages, can be misleading.

■ Ratios may be distorted by seasonal factors, or manipulated by management to give the impression of a sound financial condition (*window dressing techniques*).

■ Different operating policies and accounting practices, such as the decision to lease rather than to buy equipment, can distort comparisons.

■ Many ratios can be interpreted in different ways, and whether a particular ratio is good or bad should be based upon a complete financial analysis rather than the level of a single ratio at a single point in time.

While it is important to understand and interpret financial statements, sound financial analysis involves more than just calculating and interpreting numbers. Good analysts recognize that certain qualitative factors must be considered when evaluating a company. Some of these factors are listed below.

■ Are the company's revenues tied to one key customer?

■ To what extent are the company's revenues tied to one key product?

■ To what extent does the company rely on a single supplier?

■ What percentage of the company's business is generated overseas?

■ Competition.

■ Future prospects.

■ Legal and regulatory environment.

SELF-TEST QUESTIONS

Definitional

1. The current ratio and acid test ratio are examples of _____ ratios. They measure a firm's ability to meet its _____-_____ obligations.

2. The days sales outstanding (DSO) ratio is found by dividing average sales per day into accounts _____. The DSO is the length of time that a firm must wait after making a sale before it receives _____.

3. Debt management ratios are used to evaluate a firm's use of financial _____.

4. The debt ratio, which is the ratio of _____ _____ to _____ _____, measures the percentage of funds supplied by creditors.

5. The _____-_____-_____ ratio is calculated by dividing earnings before interest and taxes by the amount of interest charges.

6. The combined effects of liquidity, asset management, and debt on operating results are measured by _____ ratios.

7. Dividing net income by sales gives the _____ _____ on sales.

8. The _____/_____ ratio measures how much investors are willing to pay for each dollar of a firm's reported profits.

9. Firms with higher rates of return on stockholders' equity tend to sell at relatively high ratios of _____ price to _____ value.

10. Individual ratios are of little value in analyzing a company's financial condition. More important are the _____ of a ratio over time and the comparison of the company's ratios to _____ average ratios.

11. A(n) ____ _____ chart shows how return on equity is affected by total assets turnover, profit margin, and leverage.

12. Return on assets is a function of two variables, the profit _____ and _____ _____ turnover.

13. Analyzing a particular ratio over time for an individual firm is known as _____ analysis.

14. The process of comparing a particular company with a smaller set of companies in the same industry is called _____.

15. Financial ratios are used by three main groups: (1) _____, who employ ratios to help analyze, control, and thus improve their firm's operating performance; (2) _____ _____, who analyze ratios to help ascertain a company's ability to pay its debts; and (3) _____ _____ and _____, who are interested in a company's efficiency, risk, and growth prospects to forecast earnings, dividends, and stock prices.

16. The _____ _____ _____ ratio measures how effectively the firm uses its plant and equipment.

17. The _____ _____ _____ ratio measures the utilization of all the firm's assets.

18. Two procedures analysts use to examine the firm's debt: (1) They check the _____ _____ to determine the extent to which borrowed funds have been used to finance assets, and, (2) they review the _____ _____ to see the extent to which fixed charges are covered by operating profits.

19. The _____ _____ _____ ratio is similar to the TIE ratio, but it is more inclusive because it recognizes that many firms lease assets and incur long-term obligations under lease contracts and sinking funds.

20. The _____ _____ _____ ratio is useful for comparing firms with different tax situations and different degrees of financial leverage.

21. If a company is financing only with common equity, the firm's return on assets and return on equity will be _____.

22. _____ _____ raises a red flag as to the questions managers and analysts should ask.

23. _____ _____ _____ facilitates comparisons of balance sheets and income statements over time and across companies.

24. In a(n) _____ _____ analysis, growth rates are calculated for all income statement items and balance sheet accounts.

Conceptual

25.   The equity multiplier can be expressed as 1 – (Debt/Assets).

    a. True   **b.** False

26.   A high quick ratio is *always* a good indication of a well-managed liquidity position.

    a. True   **b.** False

27.   International Appliances Inc. has a current ratio of 0.5. Which of the following actions would improve (increase) this ratio?

    a. Use cash to pay off current liabilities.
    b. Collect some of the current accounts receivable.
    c. Use cash to pay off some long-term debt.
    d. Purchase additional inventory on credit (accounts payable).
    e. Sell some of the existing inventory at cost.

28.   Refer to Self-Test Question 27. Assume that International Appliances has a current ratio of 1.2. Now, which of the following actions would improve (increase) this ratio?

    a. Use cash to pay off current liabilities.
    b. Collect some of the current accounts receivable.
    c. Use cash to pay off some long-term debt.
    d. Purchase additional inventory on credit (accounts payable).
    e. Use cash to pay for some fixed assets.

29.   Examining the ratios of a particular firm against the same measures for a small group of firms from the same industry, at a point in time, is an example of

    a. Trend analysis.
    b. Benchmarking.
    c. Du Pont analysis.
    d. Simple ratio analysis.
    e. Industry analysis.

30.   Which of the following statements is most correct?

    a. Having a high current ratio and a high quick ratio is always a good indication that a firm is managing its liquidity position well.
    b. A decline in the inventory turnover ratio suggests that the firm's liquidity position is improving.

c. If a firm's times-interest-earned ratio is relatively high, then this is one indication that the firm should be able to meet its debt obligations.

d. Since ROA measures the firm's effective utilization of assets (without considering how these assets are financed), two firms with the same EBIT must have the same ROA.

e. If, through specific managerial actions, a firm has been able to increase its ROA, then, because of the fixed mathematical relationship between ROA and ROE, it must also have increased its ROE.

31. Which of the following statements is most correct?

a. Suppose two firms with the same amount of assets pay the same interest rate on their debt and earn the same rate of return on their assets and that ROA is positive. However, one firm has a higher debt ratio. Under these conditions, the firm with the higher debt ratio will also have a higher rate of return on common equity.

b. One of the problems of ratio analysis is that the relationships are subject to manipulation. For example, we know that if we use some cash to pay off some of our current liabilities, the current ratio will always increase, especially if the current ratio is weak initially, for example, below 1.0.

c. Generally, firms with high profit margins have high asset turnover ratios and firms with low profit margins have low turnover ratios; this result is exactly as predicted by the extended Du Pont equation.

d. Firms A and B have identical earnings and identical dividend payout ratios. If Firm A's growth rate is higher than Firm B's, then Firm A's P/E ratio must be greater than Firm B's P/E ratio.

e. Each of the above statements is false.

SELF-TEST PROBLEMS

1. Info Technics Inc. has an equity multiplier of 2.75. The company's assets are financed with some combination of long-term debt and common equity. What is the company's debt ratio?

   a. 25.00%   b. 36.36%   c. 52.48%   d. 63.64%   e. 75.00%

2. Refer to Self-Test Problem 1. What is the company's common equity ratio?

   a. 25.00%   b. 36.36%   c. 52.48%   d. 63.64%   e. 75.00%

3. Cutler Enterprises has current assets equal to $4.5 million. The company's current ratio is 1.25, and its quick ratio is 0.75. What is the firm's level of current liabilities (in millions)?

    a. $0.8   **b.** $1.8   **c.** $2.4   **d.** $2.9   **e.** 3.6

4. Refer to Self-Test Problem 3. What is the firm's level of inventories (in millions)?

    a. $0.8   **b.** $1.8   **c.** $2.4   **d.** $2.9   **e.** $3.6

(The following financial statements apply to the next six Self-Test Problems.)

Roberts Manufacturing Balance Sheet
December 31, 2001
(Dollars in Thousands)

Cash	$ 200	Accounts payable	$ 205
Receivables	245	Notes payable	425
Inventory	625	Other current liabilities	115
Total current assets	$1,070	Total current liabilities	$ 745
Net fixed assets	1,200	Long-term debt	420
		Common equity	1,105
Total assets	$2,270	Total liabilities and equity	$2,270

Roberts Manufacturing Income Statement
for Year Ended December 31, 2001
(Dollars in Thousands)

Sales		$2,400
Cost of goods sold:		
Materials	$1,000	
Labor	600	
Heat, light, and power	89	
Indirect labor	65	
Depreciation	80	
		1,834
Gross profit		$ 566
Selling expenses		175
General and administrative expenses		216
Earnings before interest and taxes (EBIT)		$ 175
Less interest expense		35
Earnings before taxes (EBT)		$ 140
Less taxes (40%)		56
Net income (NI)		$ 84

5. Calculate the liquidity ratios, that is, the current ratio and the quick ratio.

    a. 1.20; 0.60   **b.** 1.20; 0.80   **c.** 1.44; 0.60   **d.** 1.44; 0.80   **e.** 1.60; 0.60

6. Calculate the asset management ratios, that is, the inventory turnover ratio, fixed assets turnover, total assets turnover, and days sales outstanding.

    a. 3.84; 2.00; 1.06; 36.75 days   **d.** 3.84; 2.00; 1.24; 34.10 days
    b. 3.84; 2.00; 1.06; 35.25 days   **e.** 3.84; 2.20; 1.48; 34.10 days
    c. 3.84; 2.00; 1.06; 34.10 days

7. Calculate the debt management ratios, that is, the debt and times-interest-earned ratios.

    a. 0.39; 3.16   **b.** 0.39; 5.00   **c.** 0.51; 3.16   **d.** 0.51; 5.00   **e.** 0.73; 3.16

8. Calculate the profitability ratios, that is, the profit margin on sales, return on total assets, return on common equity, and basic earning power of assets.

    a. 3.50%; 4.25%; 7.60%; 8.00%
    b. 3.50%; 3.70%; 7.60%; 7.71%
    c. 3.70%; 3.50%; 7.60%; 7.71%
    d. 3.70%, 3.50%; 8.00%; 8.00%
    e. 4.25%; 3.70%; 7.60%; 8.00%

9. Calculate the price/earnings ratio and the market/book value ratio. Roberts had an average of 10,000 shares outstanding during 2001, and the stock price on December 31, 2001, was $40.00.

    a. 4.21; 0.36   **b.** 3.20; 1.54   **c.** 3.20; 0.36   **d.** 4.76; 1.54   **e.** 4.76; 0.36

10. Use the extended Du Pont equation to determine Roberts' return on equity.

    a. 6.90%   **b.** 7.24%   **c.** 7.47%   **d.** 7.60%   **e.** 8.41%

11. Lewis Inc. has sales of $2 million per year, all of which are credit sales. Its days sales outstanding is 42 days. What is its average accounts receivable balance?

    a. $233,333   **b.** $266,667   **c.** $333,333   **d.** $350,000   **e.** $366,667

12. Southeast Jewelers Inc. sells only on credit. Its days sales outstanding is 60 days, and its average accounts receivable balance is $500,000. What are its sales for the year?

    a. $1,500,000   **b.** $3,000,000   **c.** $2,000,000   **d.** $2,750,000   **e.** $3,225,000

13. A firm has total interest charges of $20,000 per year, sales of $2 million, a tax rate of 40 percent, and a profit margin of 6 percent. What is the firm's times-interest-earned ratio?

   a. 10   **b.** 11   **c.** 12   **d.** 13   **e.** 14

14. Refer to Self-Test Problem 13. What is the firm's TIE, if its profit margin decreases to 3 percent and its interest charges double to $40,000 per year?

   a. 3.0   **b.** 2.5   **c.** 3.5   **d.** 4.2   **e.** 3.7

15. A fire has destroyed many of the financial records at Anderson Associates. You are assigned to piece together information to prepare a financial report. You have found that the firm's return on equity is 12 percent and its debt ratio is 0.40. What is its return on assets?

   a. 4.90%   **b.** 5.35%   **c.** 6.60%   **d.** 7.20%   **e.** 8.40%

16. Refer to Self-Test Problem 15. What is the firm's debt ratio if its ROE is 15 percent and its ROA is 10 percent?

   a. 67%   **b.** 50%   **c.** 25%   **d.** 33%   **e.** 45%

17. Rowe and Company has a debt ratio of 0.50, a total assets turnover of 0.25, and a profit margin of 10 percent. The president is unhappy with the current return on equity, and he thinks it could be doubled. This could be accomplished (1) by increasing the profit margin to 14 percent and (2) by increasing debt utilization. Total assets turnover will not change. What new debt ratio, along with the 14 percent profit margin, is required to double the return on equity?

   a. 0.55   **b.** 0.60   **c.** 0.65   **d.** 0.70   **e.** 0.75

18. Altman Corporation has $1,000,000 of debt outstanding, and it pays an interest rate of 12 percent annually. Altman's annual sales are $4 million, its federal-plus-state tax rate is 40 percent, and its net profit margin on sales is 10 percent. If the company does not maintain a TIE ratio of at least 5 times, its bank will refuse to renew the loan, and bankruptcy will result. What is Altman's TIE ratio?

   a. 9.33   **b.** 4.44   **c.** 2.50   **d.** 4.00   **e.** 6.56

19. Refer to Self-Test Problem 18. What is the maximum amount Altman's EBIT could decrease and its bank still renew its loan?

    a. $186,667   **b.** $45,432   **c.** $66,767   **d.** $47,898   **e.** $143,925

20. Pinkerton Packaging's ROE last year was 2.5 percent, but its management has developed a new operating plan designed to improve things. The new plan calls for a total debt ratio of 50 percent, which will result in interest charges of $240 per year. Management projects an EBIT of $800 on sales of $8,000, and it expects to have a total assets turnover ratio of 1.6. Under these conditions, the federal-plus-state tax rate will be 40 percent. If the changes are made, what return on equity will Pinkerton earn?

    a. 2.50%   **b.** 13.44%   **c.** 13.00%   **d.** 14.02%   **e.** 14.57%

(The following financial statements apply to the next three Self-Test Problems.)

Baker Corporation Balance Sheet
December 31, 2001

Cash and marketable securities $	50	Accounts payable	$ 250
Accounts receivable	200	Accruals	250
Inventory	250	Notes payable	500
Total current assets	$ 500	Total current liabilities	$1,000
Net fixed assets	1,500	Long-term debt	250
		Common stock	400
		Retained earnings	350
Total assets	$2,000	Total liabilities and equity	$2,000

21. What is Baker Corporation's current ratio?

    a. 0.35   **b.** 0.65   **c.** 0.50   **d.** 0.25   **e.** 0.75

22. If Baker uses $50 of cash to pay off $50 of its accounts payable, what is its new current ratio after this action?

    a. 0.47   **b.** 0.44   **c.** 0.54   **d.** 0.33   **e.** 0.62

23. If Baker uses its $50 cash balance to pay off $50 of its long-term debt, what will be its new current ratio?

    a. 0.35   **b.** 0.50   **c.** 0.55   **d.** 0.60   **e.** 0.45

(The following financial statements apply to the next Self-Test Problem.)

Whitney Inc. Balance Sheet
December 31, 2001

		Total current liabilities	$ 100
		Long-term debt	250
		Common stockholders' equity	400
Total assets	$750	Total liabilities and equity	$750

Whitney Inc. Income Statement
for Year Ended December 31, 2001

Sales		$1,000
Cost of goods sold (excluding depreciation)	$550	
Other operating expenses	100	
Depreciation	50	
Total operating costs		700
Earnings before interest and taxes (EBIT)		$ 300
Less interest expense		25
Earnings before taxes (EBT)		$ 275
Less taxes (40%)		110
Net income		$ 165

24. What are Whitney Inc.'s basic earning power and ROA ratios?

    a. 30%; 22%   **b.** 40%; 30%   **c.** 50%; 22%   **d.** 40%; 22%   **e.** 40%; 40%

(The following financial statements apply to the next Self-Test Problem.)

Cotner Enterprises Balance Sheet
December 31, 2001

		Total current liabilities	$ 300
		Long-term debt	500
		Common stockholders' equity	450
Total assets	$1,250	Total liabilities and equity	$1,250

Cotner Enterprises Income Statement
for Year Ended December 31, 2001

Sales		$1,700
Cost of goods sold (excluding depreciation)	$1,190	
Other operating expenses	135	
Depreciation	75	
Total operating costs		1,400
Earnings before interest and taxes (EBIT)		$ 300
Less interest expense		54
Earnings before taxes (EBT)		$ 246
Less taxes (35%)		86
Net income		$ 160

25. What are Cotner Enterprise's basic earning power and ROA ratios?

   a. 20%; 12.8%   d. 17.5%; 12.8%
   b. 24%; 12.8%   e. 24%; 10.5%
   c. 24%; 15.8%

26. Dauten Enterprises is just being formed. It will need $2 million of assets, and it expects to have an EBIT of $400,000. Dauten will own no securities, so all of its income will be operating income. If it chooses to, Dauten can finance up to 50 percent of its assets with debt which will have a 9 percent interest rate. Dauten has no other liabilities. Assuming a 40 percent federal-plus-state tax rate on all taxable income, what is the difference between the expected ROE if Dauten finances with 50 percent debt versus the expected ROE if it finances entirely with common stock?

   a. 7.2%   b. 6.6%   c. 6.0%   d. 5.8%   e. 9.0%

ANSWERS TO SELF-TEST QUESTIONS

1. liquidity; short-term (or current)
2. receivable; cash
3. leverage
4. total debt; total assets
5. times-interest-earned
6. profitability
7. profit margin
8. price/earnings
9. market; book
10. trend; industry
11. Du Pont
12. margin; total assets
13. trend

14. benchmarking

15. managers; credit analysts; stock analysts; shareholders

16. fixed assets turnover

17. total assets turnover

18. balance sheet; income statement

19. fixed charge coverage

20. basic earning power

21. equal

22. Ratio analysis

23. Common size analysis

24. percentage change

25. b. $1 - (\text{Debt/Assets}) = \text{Equity/Assets}$. The equity multiplier is equal to Assets/Equity.

26. b. Excess cash resulting from poor management could produce a high quick ratio. Similarly, if accounts receivables are not collected promptly, this could also lead to a high quick ratio.

27. d. This question is best analyzed using numbers. For example, assume current assets equal $50 and current liabilities equal $100; thus, the current ratio equals 0.5. For answer a, assume $5 in cash is used to pay off $5 in current liabilities. The new current ratio would be $45/$95 = 0.47. For answer d, assume a $10 purchase of inventory on credit (accounts payable). The new current ratio would be $60/$110 = 0.55, which is an increase over the old current ratio of 0.5. (Self-Test Problems 22 through 24 were set up to help visualize this question.)

28. a. Again, this question is best analyzed using numbers. For example, assume current assets equal $120 and current liabilities equal $100; thus, the current ratio equals 1.2. For answer a, assume $5 in cash is used to pay off $5 in current liabilities. The new current ratio would be $115/$95 = 1.21, which is an increase over the old current ratio of 1.2. For answer d, assume a $10 purchase of inventory on credit (accounts payable). The new current ratio would be $130/$110 = 1.18, which is a decrease over the old current ratio of 1.2.

29. b. The correct answer is benchmarking. A trend analysis compares the firm's ratios over time, while a Du Pont analysis shows how return on equity is affected by assets turnover, profit margin, and leverage.

30. c. Excess cash resulting from poor management could produce high current and quick ratios; thus statement a is false. A decline in the inventory turnover ratio suggests that either sales have decreased or inventory has increased, which suggests that the firm's liquidity position is *not* improving; thus statement b is false. ROA = Net income/Total assets, and EBIT does not equal net income. Two firms with the same EBIT could have different financing and different tax rates resulting in different net incomes. Also, two firms with the same EBIT do not necessarily have the same total assets; thus statement d is false. ROE = ROA × Assets/Equity. If ROA increases because total assets decrease, then the equity multiplier decreases, and depending on which effect is greater, ROE may or may not increase; thus statement e is false. Statement c is correct; the TIE ratio is used to measure whether the firm can meet its debt obligation, and a high TIE ratio would indicate this is so. (Self-Test Problems 25 and 26 were set up to help visualize statement d of this question.)

31. a. Ratio analysis is subject to manipulation; however, if the current ratio is less than 1.0 and we use cash to pay off some current liabilities, the current ratio will decrease, *not* increase; thus statement b is false. Statement c is just the reverse of what actually occurs. Firms with high profit margins have low turnover ratios and vice versa. Statement d is false; it does not necessarily follow that if a firm's growth rate is higher that its stock price will be higher. Statement a is correct. From the information given in statement a, one can determine that the two firms' net incomes are equal; thus, the firm with the higher debt ratio (lower equity ratio) will indeed have a higher ROE.

SOLUTIONS TO SELF-TEST PROBLEMS

1. d. $2.75 = A/E$
$E/A = 1/2.75$
$E/A = 36.36\%$.

$D/A = 1 - E/A$
$= 1 - 36.36\%$
$= 63.64\%$.

2. b. From #1 above, $E/A = 36.36\%$.

3.   e. CA = \$4.5 million; CA/CL = 1.25.

$$\$4.5/CL = 1.25$$
$$1.25\ CL = \$4.5$$
$$CL = \$3.6\ \text{million.}$$

4.   b. QR = 0.75; CA = \$4.5 million ; CL = \$3.6 million.

$$QR = \frac{CA - I}{CL}$$
$$0.75 = \frac{\$4.5 - I}{\$3.6}$$
$$\$2.7 = \$4.5 - I$$
$$I = \$1.8\ \text{million.}$$

5.   c. $\text{Current ratio} = \dfrac{\text{Current assets}}{\text{Current liabilities}} = \dfrac{\$1{,}070}{\$745} = 1.44.$

$$\text{Quick ratio} = \frac{\text{Current assets} - \text{Inventory}}{\text{Current liabilities}} = \frac{\$1{,}070 - \$625}{\$745} = 0.60.$$

6.   a. $\text{Inventory turnover} = \dfrac{\text{Sales}}{\text{Inventory}} = \dfrac{\$2{,}400}{\$625} = 3.84.$

$$\text{Fixed assets turnover} = \frac{\text{Sales}}{\text{Net fixed assets}} = \frac{\$2{,}400}{\$1{,}200} = 2.00.$$

$$\text{Total assets turnover} = \frac{\text{Sales}}{\text{Total assets}} = \frac{\$2{,}400}{\$2{,}270} = 1.06.$$

$$\text{DSO} = \frac{\text{Accounts receivable}}{\text{Sales}/360} = \frac{\$245}{\$2{,}400/360} = 36.75\ \text{days.}$$

7. d. Debt ratio = Total debt/Total assets = $1,165/$2,270 = 0.51.

TIE ratio = EBIT/Interest = $175/$35 = 5.00.

8. b. $\text{Profit margin} = \dfrac{\text{Net income}}{\text{Sales}} = \dfrac{\$84}{\$2,400} = 0.0350 = 3.50\%.$

$\text{ROA} = \dfrac{\text{Net income}}{\text{Total assets}} = \dfrac{\$84}{\$2,270} = 0.0370 = 3.70\%.$

$\text{ROE} = \dfrac{\text{Net income}}{\text{Common equity}} = \dfrac{\$84}{\$1,105} = 0.0760 = 7.60\%.$

$\text{BEP} = \dfrac{\text{EBIT}}{\text{Total assets}} = \dfrac{\$175}{\$2,270} = 0.0771 = 7.71\%.$

9. e. $\text{EPS} = \dfrac{\text{Net income}}{\text{Number of shares outstanding}} = \dfrac{\$84,000}{10,000} = \$8.40.$

$\text{P/E ratio} = \dfrac{\text{Price}}{\text{EPS}} = \dfrac{\$40.00}{\$8.40} = 4.76.$

$\text{Market/ Book value} = \dfrac{\text{Market price}}{\text{Book value}} = \dfrac{\$40(10,000)}{\$1,105,000} = 0.36.$

10. d. ROE = Profit margin × Total assets turnover × Equity multiplier

$\qquad = \dfrac{\$84}{\$2,400} \times \dfrac{\$2,400}{\$2,270} \times \dfrac{\$2,270}{\$1,105} = 0.035 \times 1.057 \times 2.054$

$\qquad = 0.0760 = 7.60\%.$

11. a. $\text{DSO} = \dfrac{\text{Accounts receivable}}{\text{Sales/ 360}}$

$42 \text{ days} = \dfrac{\text{AR}}{\$2,000,000 / 360}$

$\qquad \text{AR} = \$233,333.$

12. b.   DSO = Accounts receivable/(Sales/360)
       60 days = $500,000/(Sales/360)
   60(Sales/360) = $500,000
          Sales = $3,000,000.

13. b.   Net income = $2,000,000(0.06) = $120,000.

     Earnings before taxes = $120,000/(1 − 0.4) = $200,000.

     EBIT = $200,000 + $20,000 = $220,000.

     TIE = EBIT/Interest = $220,000/$20,000 = 11.

14. c.   Net income = $2,000,000(0.03) = $60,000.

     Earnings before taxes = $60,000/(1 − 0.4) = $100,000.

     EBIT = $100,000 + $40,000 = $140,000.

     TIE = EBIT/Interest = $140,000/$40,000 = 3.5.

15. d.   If Total debt/Total assets = 0.40, then Total equity/Total assets = 0.60, and the equity multiplier (Assets/Equity) = 1/0.60 = 1.667.

$$\frac{NI}{E} = \frac{NI}{A} \times \frac{A}{E}$$

ROE = ROA × EM
12% = ROA × 1.667
ROA = 7.20%.

16. d.   ROE = ROA × Equity multiplier
      15% = 10% × TA/Equity
       1.5 = TA/Equity
  Equity/TA = 0.67.

     Debt/TA = 1 − Equity/TA = 1 − 0.67 = 0.33 = 33%.

17.   c.   If Total debt/Total assets = 0.50, then Total equity/Total assets = 0.50 and the equity multiplier (Assets/Equity) = 1/0.50 = 2.0.

ROE = PM × Total assets turnover × EM.

Before: ROE = 10% × 0.25 × 2.00 = 5.00%.

After: 10.00% = 14% × 0.25 × EM; thus EM = 2.8571.

$$\text{Equity multiplier} = \frac{\text{Assets}}{\text{Equity}}$$

$$2.8571 = \frac{1}{\text{Equity}}$$

$$0.35 = \text{Equity}.$$

Debt = Assets − Equity = 100% − 35% = 65%.

18.   e.   TIE = EBIT/Interest, so find EBIT and Interest.

Interest = $1,000,000(0.12) = $120,000.

Net income = $4,000,000(0.10) = $400,000.

Pre-tax income = $400,000/(1 − T) = $400,000/0.6 = $666,667.

EBIT = $666,667 + $120,000 = $786,667.

TIE = $786,667/$120,000 = 6.56×.

19.   a.   TIE = EBIT/INT
         5 = EBIT/$120,000
EBIT = $600,000.

From Self-Test Problem 19, EBIT = $786,667, so EBIT could decrease by $786,667 − $600,000 = $186,667.

20.   b.   ROE = Profit margin × Total assets turnover × Equity multiplier
            = NI/Sales × Sales/TA × TA/Equity.

Now we need to determine the inputs for the equation from the data that were given. On the left we set up an income statement, and we put numbers in it on the right:

Sales (given)	$8,000
Cost	NA
EBIT (given)	$ 800
Interest (given)	240
EBT	$ 560
Taxes (40%)	224
Net income	$ 336

Now we can use some ratios to get some more data:

Total assets turnover = S/TA = 1.6 (given).

D/A = 50%, so E/A = 50%, and therefore TA/E = 1/(E/A) = 1/0.5 = 2.00.

Now we can complete the extended Du Pont equation to determine ROE:

ROE = $336/$8,000 × 1.6 × 2.0 = 13.44%.

21.   c.   Baker Corporation's current ratio equals Current assets/Current liabilities = $500/$1,000 = 0.50.

22.   a.   Baker Corporation's new current ratio equals ($500 − $50)/($1,000 − $50) = $450/$950 = 0.47.

23.   e.   Only the current asset balance is affected by this action. Baker's new current ratio = ($500 − $50)/$1,000 = $450/$1,000 = 0.45.

24.   d.   Whitney's BEP ratio equals EBIT/Total assets = $300/$750 = 40%.

Whitney's ROA equals Net income/Total assets = $165/$750 = 22%.

25.   b.   Cotner's BEP ratio equals EBIT/Total assets = $300/$1,250 = 24%.

Cotner's ROA equals Net income/Total assets = $160/$1,250 = 12.8%.

26. b. Known data: Total assets = $2,000,000; EBIT = $400,000; k_d = 9%, T = 40%.

D/A = 0.5 = 50%, so Equity = 0.5($2,000,000) = $1,000,000.

	D/A = 0%	D/A = 50%
EBIT	$400,000	$400,000
Interest	0	90,000*
Taxable income	$400,000	$310,000
Taxes (40%)	160,000	124,000
Net income (NI)	$240,000	$186,000

For D/A = 0%, ROE = NI/Equity = $240,000/$2,000,000 = 12%. For D/A = 50%, ROE = $186,000/$1,000,000 = 18.6%. Difference = 18.6% – 12.0% = 6.6%.

*If D/A = 50%, then half of the assets are financed by debt, so Debt = 0.5($2,000,000) = $1,000,000. At a 9 percent interest rate, INT = 0.09($1,000,000) = $90,000.

CHAPTER 4
FINANCIAL PLANNING AND
FORECASTING FINANCIAL STATEMENTS

OVERVIEW

Managers are vitally concerned with *future financial statements* and with the effects of alternative assumptions and policies on these *projected*, or *pro forma*, statements. The construction of pro forma statements begins with a *sales forecast*. On the basis of the sales forecast, the amount of assets necessary to support this sales level is determined. Although some liabilities will increase *spontaneously* with increased sales, if the sales growth rate is rapid, then external capital will be required to support the growth in sales.

Pro forma financial statements have three very important uses in the value creation process. Their first use is for estimating future free cash flows, which are necessary to implement the corporate valuation model. Second, pro forma state-ments can be used to plan for the financing that will be required to execute the operating plans. Last, pro forma statements provide a basis for setting targets used in the firm's compensation plan.

Proforma
3 important uses
- estimate future free cashflows
- used to plan for financing
- basis for setting targets

OUTLINE

Most companies have a mission statement, which is in many ways a condensed version of the firm's strategic plan.

■ Strategic plans usually begin with a statement of the overall *corporate purpose*.

■ The *corporate scope* defines a firm's lines of business and geographic area of operations.

■ The *corporate objectives* set forth specific goals for management to attain.
  ❑ These include both qualitative and quantitative objectives.
  ❑ Companies have multiple objectives.
  ❑ Companies revise their objectives as business conditions change.

- A firm needs to develop a strategy for achieving its goals. *Corporate strategies* are broad approaches rather than detailed plans.
  - Strategies should be both attainable and compatible with the firm's purpose, scope, and objectives.

Operating plans can be developed for any time horizon, but most companies use a five-year horizon.

- A five-year plan is most detailed for the first year, with each succeeding year's plan becoming less specific.

- The plan is intended to provide detailed implementation guidance, based on the corporate strategy, in order to meet the corporate objectives.
  - Large, multidivisional companies break down their operating plans by divisions.
  - Each division has its own goals, mission, and plan for meeting its objectives, and these plans are then consolidated to form the corporate plan.

The financial planning process is broken down into six steps.

- Set up a system of projected financial statements to analyze the effects of the operating plan on projected profits and various financial ratios.

- Determine the funds needed to support the five-year plan.

- Forecast funds availability over the next five years.

- Establish and maintain a system of controls governing the allocation and use of funds within the firm.

- Develop procedures for adjusting the basic plan if the economic forecasts upon which the plan was based do not materialize.

- Establish a performance-based management compensation system.

Well-run companies generally base their operating plans on a set of forecasted financial statements. A sales forecast for the next five years or so is developed, the assets required to meet the sales target are determined, and a decision is made concerning how to finance the required assets. These forecasts represent the "base case" and are a standard by which to judge alternate forecasts.

- The *sales forecast* generally begins with a review of sales for the past 5 to 10 years.
- If the sales forecast is off, the consequences can be serious. Thus, an accurate sales forecast is critical to the well being of the firm.

- ❏ If the market expands more than the firm has geared up for, the company will not be able to meet demand.
- ❏ If a firm's projections are overly optimistic, the firm could end up with too much plant, equipment, and inventory.

Any forecast of financial requirements involves (1) determining how much money the firm will need during a given period, (2) determining how much money the firm will generate internally during the same period, and (3) subtracting the funds generated from the funds required to determine the external financial requirements.

- ■ Two methods are used to estimate external requirements: the *percent of sales method,* which develops pro forma financial statements, and the *formula method.*

The most commonly used technique for forecasting future balance sheets and income statements is the percent of sales method.

- ■ The first step is to analyze the historical financial statements.

- ■ This method begins with a sales forecast, expressed as an annual growth rate in dollar sales revenues.
  - ❏ Population growth and inflation determine the *long-term sustainable growth rate* for most companies. Reasonable values for the sustainable growth rate are from 5 to 7 percent for most companies.
  - ❏ Companies often have a *competitive advantage period*, during which they can grow at rates higher than the long-term sustainable growth rate.

- ■ With the percent of sales forecasting method, many items on the income statement and balance sheet are assumed to increase proportionally with sales.
  - ❏ The remaining items on the forecasted statements—items that are not tied directly to sales—depend on the company's policies and managers' choices.

- ■ If the forecasted percentage of sales for each item is the same as in the last year of the actual statements, then all projected items will grow at the same rate as the growth rate in sales. This approach is called the *constant ratio method of forecasting.*
  - ❏ Managers should strive to have improving, not constant ratios.

The percent of sales method involves projecting the asset requirements for the coming period, then projecting the liabilities and equity that will be generated under normal operations, and subtracting the projected liabilities and capital from the required assets to estimate the additional funds needed (AFN).

■ The first step is to forecast next year's income statement.
   ❏ A sales forecast is needed.
   ❏ The percent of sales method assumes initially that all costs except depreciation are a specified percentage of sales.
   ❏ Depreciation can be assumed to be a fixed percentage of net plant and equipment.
   ❏ The primary objective of this step is to determine how much income the company will earn and retain for reinvestment during the forecasted year.
      ● The addition to retained earnings in the first-pass forecasted income statement will turn out to be too high because it understates next year's actual interest and dividends.

■ The second step is to forecast next year's balance sheet.
   ❏ If sales are to increase, then assets will have to increase.
   ❏ Cash, accounts receivable, and inventory are assumed to increase proportionally with sales. They are expressed as a percentage of sales.
   ❏ In the long term, there is a relatively close relationship between sales and fixed assets for all companies. Therefore, as a first approximation it is reasonable to assume that the long-term ratio of net plant and equipment to sales will be constant.
   ❏ Additional assets must be financed, so liabilities and equity must also increase.
      ● Some items on the liability side, such as accounts payable and accruals, can be expected to increase spontaneously with sales producing what are called *spontaneously generated funds*.
   ❏ Retained earnings will increase, but not proportionately with sales. The new retained earnings will be determined from the projected income statement.
   ❏ Other financing accounts, such as notes payable, long-term debt, preferred stock, and common stock, are not directly related to sales. Changes in these accounts result from managerial financing decisions; they do not increase spontaneously as sales increase.
   ❏ The difference between projected total assets and projected liabilities and capital is the amount of *additional funds needed (AFN)*. AFN are funds that a firm must raise externally through some combination of debt, preferred stock, and common stock.

■ The third step is the decision on how to finance the additional funds required. The financial staff will base the financial mix on several factors, including the firm's target capital structure, the effect of short-term borrowing on its current ratio, conditions in the debt and equity markets, and restrictions imposed by existing debt agreements.

■ One complexity that arises in financial forecasting relates to *financing feedbacks*: The external funds raised to pay for new assets create additional expenses which must be reflected in the income statement, and that lowers the initially forecasted addition to retained earnings.

- ❑ Financing feedbacks are handled by forecasting the additional interest expense and dividends that result from external financings.
- ❑ In each iteration of the forecasted financial statements, the additional financing becomes smaller and smaller and eventually the AFN is essentially zero. Spreadsheet software can do this iteration process so fast that it appears to occur instantaneously.

Although financial forecasting as described in this chapter can be done with a hand calculator, virtually all corporate forecasts are made using computerized forecasting models. Many models are based on spreadsheet programs, such as Microsoft Excel.

- ■ Spreadsheet models have two major advantages over pencil-and-paper calculations.
  - ❑ It is much faster to construct a spreadsheet model than to make a "by hand" forecast if the forecast period extends beyond two or three years.
  - ❑ A spreadsheet model can recompute the projected financial statements and ratios almost instantaneously when the input variables are changed, thus making it easy for managers to determine the effects of changes in variables such as sales.

- ■ Developing the forecasted financial statements is only the first part of a firm's total planning process.
  - ❑ The projected statements must be analyzed to whether they meet the firm's targets as set forth in the five-year financial plan.
  - ❑ If the statements do not meet targets, then elements of the operating plan must be analyzed to see if changes should be made.

- ■ Forecasting is an iterative process, both in the way the financial statements are generated and the way the financial plan is developed.

Most firms' forecasts of capital requirements are made by constructing pro forma financial statements as described above. However, when the ratios are expected to remain constant, then a simple forecasting formula is sometimes used.

- ■ The formula is as follows:

$$\begin{matrix} \text{Additional} \\ \text{funds} \\ \text{needed} \end{matrix} = \begin{matrix} \text{Required} \\ \text{increase} \\ \text{in assets} \end{matrix} - \begin{matrix} \text{Spontaneous} \\ \text{increase in} \\ \text{liabilities} \end{matrix} - \begin{matrix} \text{Increase in} \\ \text{retained} \\ \text{earnings} \end{matrix}$$

or

$$AFN = (A^*/S_0)\Delta\Delta S - (L^*/S_0)\Delta\Delta S - MS_1 (1 - d).$$

- ❑ $A*/S_0$ = percentage of required assets to sales, which shows the required dollar increase in assets per \$1 increase in sales.
- ❑ $L*/S_0$ = liabilities that increase spontaneously as a percentage of sales, or spontaneously generated financing per \$1 increase in sales.
- ❑ S_1 = total sales projected for next year (note that S_0 = last year's sales).
- ❑ ΔS = change in sales = $S_1 - S_0$.
- ❑ M = profit margin, or profit per \$1 of sales.
- ❑ d = the percentage of earnings paid out in common dividends (dividend payout ratio).

- ■ Inherent in the formula are the assumptions (1) that each asset item must increase in direct proportion to sales increases, (2) that accounts payable and accruals also grow at the same rate as sales, and (3) that the profit margin is constant.
  - ❑ Obviously, these assumptions do not always hold, so the formula does not always produce reliable results.
  - ❑ Therefore, the formula is used primarily to get a rough-and-ready forecast of financial requirements under "business as usual" conditions.

- ■ The faster a firm's growth rate in sales, the greater its need for additional financing.
  - ❑ Higher growth rates require managers to plan very carefully to decide if the additional financing needed is actually available to the firm. Otherwise, they should reconsider the feasibility of the expansion plans.
  - ❑ Dividend policy as reflected in the payout ratio also affects external capital requirements: the higher the payout ratio, the smaller the addition to retained earnings, and hence the greater the requirements for external capital. Dividend policy may be changed to satisfy internal financing requirements, but this may have a negative impact on stock price and may be met with resistance from investors.
  - ❑ The amount of assets required per dollar of sales, $A*/S_0$, is often called the *capital intensity ratio*. This factor has a major effect on capital requirements. If the capital intensity ratio is low, then sales can grow rapidly without much outside capital. However, if a firm is capital intensive, even a small growth in output will require a great deal of new outside capital.
  - ❑ Profit margin, M, also has an effect on capital requirements. The higher the profit margin, the lower the funds requirement, and the lower the profit margin, the higher the requirement. Thus, highly profitable firms can raise most of their capital internally.

The forecasting process is greatly complicated if the ratios of balance sheet items to sales are not constant at all levels of sales.

- ■ Where *economies of scale* occur in asset use, the ratio of that asset to sales will change as the size of the firm increases.

Can use % sales method *economies of scale, lumpy assets, excess capacity*

- In many industries, technological considerations dictate that fixed assets be added in large, discrete units, often referred to as *lumpy assets*. This automatically creates excess capacity immediately after a plant expansion.

- *Forecasting errors* can cause the actual asset/sales ratio for a given period to be quite different from the planned ratio. This situation can result in excess capacity.

If any of the above conditions apply (economies of scale, lumpy assets, or excess capacity), the A^*/S_0 ratio will not be a constant, and the percent of sales method should not be used. Rather, other techniques must be used to forecast asset levels to determine additional financing requirements. Two of these methods include simple linear regression and excess capacity adjustments.

- If one assumes that the relationship between a certain type of asset and sales is linear, then one can use *simple linear regression* techniques to estimate the requirements for that type of asset for any given sales increase. An estimated regression equation is determined which provides an estimated relationship between a given asset account and sales.

- If a firm's fixed assets are not operating at full capacity, then the calculation for the required level of fixed assets will need to be adjusted.
  - *Full capacity sales* is defined as actual sales divided by the percentage of capacity at which the fixed assets were operated to achieve these sales:

  $$\text{Full capacity sales} = \frac{\text{Actual sales}}{\substack{\text{Percentage of capacity at which} \\ \text{fixed assets were operated}}}.$$

  - The *target fixed assets-to-sales ratio* is equal to actual fixed assets divided by full capacity sales:

  $$\text{Target fixed assets-to-sales ratio} = \frac{\text{Actual fixed assets}}{\text{Full capacity sales}}.$$

  - The *required level of fixed assets* is equal to the target fixed assets-to-sales ratio times projected sales:

  $$\substack{\text{Required level} \\ \text{of fixed assets}} = (\text{Target fixed assets-to-sales ratio})(\text{Projected sales}).$$

❑ Theoretically, excess capacity could occur with other types of assets, but as a practical matter, excess capacity normally exists only with respect to fixed assets and inventories.

SELF-TEST QUESTIONS

Definitional

1. If various asset categories increase, _liabilities_ and/or _equity_ must also increase.

2. Typically, certain liabilities will rise _spontaneously_ with sales. These include accounts _payable_ and _accruals_.

3. _Bonds_, _preferred_ stock, _common_ stock, and _retained_ earnings are examples of accounts that do not increase proportionately with higher levels of sales.

4. As the dividend _payout ratio_ is increased, the amount of earnings available to finance new assets is _decreased_.

5. Retained earnings depend not only on next year's sales level and dividend payout ratio but also on the _profit margin_.

6. The amount of assets that are tied directly to sales, $A*/S_0$, is often called the _capital intensive ratio_.

7. A capital intensive industry will require large amounts of _external_ capital to finance increased growth.

8. The _percent of sales_ method involves projecting the asset requirements for the coming period, then projecting the liabilities and equity that will be generated under normal operations, and subtracting the projected liabilities and capital from the required assets to estimate the _additional funds needed_.

9. The assumption of constant percentage of sales ratios may not be accurate when assets must be added in discrete amounts, called _lumpy_ assets, or when _economies_ of scale are considered.

10. Two methods can be used to estimate external funding requirements: the _percent of sales_ and the _formula_ methods.

11. One complexity that arises in financial forecasting relates to _financing feedbacks_ which are the effects on the income statement and balance sheet of actions taken to finance asset increases.

12. Forecasting is a(n) _iterative_ process, both in the way financial statements are generated and the way the financial plan is developed.

13. The faster a firm's growth rate in sales, the _greater_ its need for additional financing.

14. If economies of scale, lumpy assets, or excess capacity exist, the capital intensity ratio will not be a constant, and the percent of sales method should not be used. Other techniques such as linear _regression_ and _excess capacity_ adjustment should be used.

15. _Full Capacity Sales_ is defined as actual sales divided by the percentage of capacity at which fixed assets were operated to achieve those sales.

16. The _____ _____ _____-to-_____ ratio is equal to actual fixed assets divided by full capacity sales.

17. The _required_ level of _fixed assets_ is equal to the target fixed assets-to-sales ratio times projected sales.

18. A(n) _mission statement_ is, in many ways, a condensed version of the firm's strategic plan.

19. Strategic plans usually begin with a statement of the overall _corporate purpose_.

20. The _corporate objectives_ set forth specific goals for management to attain.

21. The most commonly used technique for forecasting future balance sheets and income statements is the _percent of sales_ method.

22. Companies often have what is called a(n) _competitive advantage_ period, during which they can grow at rates higher than the long-term _sustainable_ growth rate.

Conceptual

23. An increase in a firm's inventory will call for additional financing unless the increase is offset by an equal or larger *decrease* in some other asset account.

 a. True   **b.** False

24. If the capital intensity ratio of a firm actually decreases as sales increase, use of the formula method will typically *overstate* the amount of additional funds required, other things held constant.

   a. True   **b.** False

25. If the dividend payout ratio is 100 percent, all ratios are held constant, and the firm is operating at full capacity, then any increase in sales will require additional financing.

   a. True   **b.** False

26. One of the first steps in the percent of sales method of forecasting is to identify those asset and liability accounts that increase spontaneously with retained earnings.

   a. True   **b.** False

27. Which of the following would <u>reduce</u> the additional funds required if all other things are held constant?

   a. An increase in the dividend payout ratio.
   b. A decrease in the profit margin.
   c. An increase in the capital intensity ratio.
   d. An increase in the expected sales growth rate.
   e. A decrease in the firm's tax rate.

28. Which of the following statements is most correct?

   a. Suppose economies of scale exist in a firm's use of assets. Under this condition, the firm should use the regression method of forecasting asset requirements rather than the percent of sales method.
   b. If a firm must acquire assets in lumpy units, it can avoid errors in forecasts of its need for funds by using the linear regression method of forecasting asset requirements because all the points will lie on the regression line.
   c. If economies of scale in the use of assets exist, then the AFN formula rather than the percent of sales method should be used to forecast additional funds requirements.
   d. Notes payable to banks are included in the AFN formula, along with a projection of retained earnings.
   e. One problem with the AFN formula is that it does not take account of the firm's dividend policy.

SELF-TEST PROBLEMS

1. United Products Inc. has the following balance sheet:

Current assets	$ 5,000	Accounts payable	$ 1,000
		Notes payable	1,000
Net fixed assets	5,000	Long-term debt	4,000
		Common equity	4,000
Total assets	$10,000	Total liabilities and equity	$10,000

Business has been slow; therefore, fixed assets are vastly underutilized. Management believes it can double sales next year with the introduction of a new product. No new fixed assets will be required, and management expects that there will be no earnings retained next year. What is next year's additional financing requirement?

a. $0   **b.** $4,000   **c.** $6,000   **d.** $13,000   **e.** $19,000

2. The 2001 balance sheet for American Pulp and Paper is shown below (in millions of dollars):

Cash	$ 3.0	Accounts payable	$ 2.0
Accounts receivable	3.0	Notes payable	1.5
Inventory	5.0		
Current assets	$11.0	Current liabilities	$ 3.5
Fixed assets	3.0	Long-term debt	3.0
		Common equity	7.5
Total assets	$14.0	Total liabilities and equity	$14.0

In 1998, sales were $60 million. In 2002, management believes that sales will increase by 20 percent to a total of $72 million. The profit margin is expected to be 5 percent, and the dividend payout ratio is targeted at 40 percent. No excess capacity exists. What is the additional financing requirement (in millions) for 2002 using the formula method?

a. $0.36   **b.** $0.24   **c.** $0   **d.** -$0.24   **e.** -$0.36

3. Refer to Self-Test Problem 2. How much can sales grow above the 2002 level of $60 million without requiring any additional funds?

a. 12.28%   **b.** 14.63%   **c.** 15.75%   **d.** 17.65%   **e.** 18.14%

4. Smith Machines Inc. has a net income this year of $500 on sales of $2,000 and is operating its fixed assets at full capacity. Management expects sales to increase by 25 percent next year and is forecasting a dividend payout ratio of 30 percent. The profit margin is not expected to change. If spontaneous liabilities are $500 this year and no excess funds are expected next year, what are Smith's total assets this year?

   a. $1,000   **b.** $1,500   **c.** $2,250   **d.** $3,000   **e.** $3,500

(The following data apply to the next three Self-Test Problems.)

Crossley Products Company's 2001 financial statements are shown below:

Crossley Products Company
Balance Sheet as of December 31, 2001
(Thousands of Dollars)

Cash	$ 600	Accounts payable	$ 2,400
Receivables	3,600	Notes payable	1,157
Inventory	4,200	Accruals	840
Total current assets	$ 8,400	Total current liabilities	$ 4,397
		Mortgage bonds	1,667
		Common stock	667
Net Fixed assets	7,200	Retained earnings	8,869
Total assets	$15,600	Total liabilities and equity	$15,600

Crossley Products Company
Income Statement for December 31, 2001
(Thousands of Dollars)

Sales	$12,000
Operating costs	10,261
Earnings	$ 1,739
Interest	339
Earnings before taxes	$ 1,400
Taxes (40%)	560
Net income	$ 840
Dividends (60%)	$ 504
Addition to retained earnings	$ 336

5. Assume that the company was operating at full capacity in 2001 with regard to all items except fixed assets; fixed assets in 1998 were utilized to only 75 percent of capacity. By what percentage could 2002 sales increase over 2001 sales without the need for an increase in fixed assets?

    a. 33%   **b.** 25%   **c.** 20%   **d.** 44%   **e.** 50%

6. Now suppose 2002 sales increase by 25 percent over 2001 sales. Assume that Crossley cannot sell any fixed assets. Use the percent of sales method to develop a pro forma balance sheet and income statement. Assume that any required financing is borrowed as notes payable, and ignore financing feedbacks. Use a pro forma income statement to determine the addition to retained earnings. How much additional external capital (in thousands) will be required?

    a. $825   **b.** $925   **c.** $750   **d.** $900   **e.** $850

7. Refer to Self-Test Problem 6. After the required financing is borrowed as notes payable, and ignoring any financing feedbacks, what is the firm's current and debt ratios?

    a. 1.73; 38.84%   **d.** 1.73; 43.64%
    b. 2.02; 38.84%   **e.** 2.02; 43.64%
    c. 1.73; 44.06%

    (The following data apply to the next two Self-Test Problems.)

    Taylor Technologies Inc.'s 2001 financial statements are shown below:

Taylor Technologies Inc.
Balance Sheet as of December 31, 2001

Cash	$ 90,000	Accounts payable	$ 180,000
Receivables	180,000	Notes payable	78,000
Inventory	360,000	Accruals	90,000
Total current assets	$ 630,000	Total current liabilities	$ 348,000
		Common stock	900,000
Net fixed assets	720,000	Retained earnings	102,000
Total assets	$1,350,000	Total liabilities and equity	$1,350,000

Taylor Technologies Inc.
Income Statement for December 31, 2001

Sales	$ 1,800,000
Operating costs	1,639,860
EBIT	$ 160,140
Interest	10,140
EBT	$ 150,000
Taxes (40%)	60,000
Net income	$ 90,000
Dividends (60%)	$ 54,000
Addition to retained earnings	$ 36,000

8. Suppose that in 2002, sales increase by 10 percent over 2001 sales. Construct the pro forma financial statements using the percent of sales method. Assume the firm operated at full capacity in 2001. How much additional capital will be required?

    a. $72,459   **b.** $70,211   **c.** $68,157   **d.** $66,445   **e.** $63,989

9. Refer to Self-Test Problem 8. Assume now that fixed assets are only being operated at 95 percent of capacity. Construct the proforma financial statements using the percent of sales method. How much additional capital will be required?

    a. $28,557   **b.** $32,400   **c.** $39,843   **d.** $45,400   **e.** $50,000

10. Your company's sales were $2,000 last year, and they are forecasted to rise by 50 percent during the coming year. Here is the latest balance sheet:

Cash	$ 100	Accounts payable	$ 200
Receivables	300	Notes payable	200
Inventory	800	Accruals	20
Total current assets	$ 1,200	Total current liabilities	$ 420
		Long-term debt	780
		Common stock	400
Net Fixed Assets	800	Retained earnings	400
Total assets	$2,000	Total liabilities and equity	$2,000

Fixed assets were used to only 80 percent of capacity last year, and year-end inventory holdings were $100 greater than were needed to support the $2,000 of sales. The other current assets (cash and receivables) were at their proper levels. All assets would be a constant percentage of sales if excess capacity did not exist; that is, all assets would increase at the same rate as sales if no excess capacity existed. The company's after-tax profit margin will be 3 percent, and its payout ratio will be 80 percent. If all additional funds needed (AFN) are raised as notes payable and financing feedbacks are ignored, what will the current ratio be at the end of the coming year?

   a. 2.47   **b.** 1.44   **c.** 1.21   **d.** 1.00   **e.** 1.63

11. The Bouchard Company's sales are forecasted to increase from $500 in 2001 to $1,000 in 2002. Here is the December 31, 2001, balance sheet:

Cash	$ 50	Accounts payable	$ 25
Receivables	100	Notes payable	75
Inventory	100	Accruals	25
Total current assets	$250	Total current liabilities	$125
		Long-term debt	200
		Common stock	50
Net fixed assets	250	Retained earnings	125
Total assets	$500	Total liabilities and equity	$500

Bouchard's fixed assets were used to only 50 percent of capacity during 2001, but its current assets were at their proper levels. All assets except fixed assets should be a constant percentage of sales, and fixed assets would also increase at the same rate if the current excess capacity did not exist. Bouchard's after-tax profit margin is forecasted to be 8 percent, and its payout ratio will be 40 percent. What is Bouchard's additional funds needed (AFN) for the coming year?

   a. $102   **b.** $152   **c.** $197   **d.** $167   **e.** $183

ANSWERS TO SELF-TEST QUESTIONS

1. liabilities; equity
2. spontaneously; payable; accruals
3. Bonds; preferred; common; retained
4. payout ratio; decreased
5. profit margin
6. capital intensity ratio
7. external
8. percent of sales; additional funds needed
9. lumpy; economies
10. percent of sales; formula
11. financing feedbacks

12. iterative
13. greater
14. regression; excess capacity
15. Full capacity sales
16. fixed assets; sales
17. required; fixed assets
18. mission statement
19. corporate purpose
20. corporate objectives
21. percent of sales
22. competitive advantage; sustainable

23. a. When an increase in one asset account is not offset by an equivalent decrease in another asset account, then financing is needed to reestablish equilibrium on the

balance sheet. Note, though, that this additional financing may come from a spontaneous increase in accounts payable or from retained earnings.

24. a. A decreasing capital intensity ratio, A^*/S_0, means that fewer assets are required, proportionately, as sales increase. Thus, the external funding requirement is overstated. Always keep in mind that the formula method assumes that the asset/sales ratio is constant regardless of the level of sales.

25. a. With a 100 percent payout ratio, there will be no retained earnings. When operating at full capacity, *all* assets are spontaneous, but *all* liabilities cannot be spontaneous since a firm must have common equity. Thus, the growth in assets cannot be matched by a growth in spontaneous liabilities, so additional financing will be required in order to keep the financial ratios (the debt ratio in particular) constant.

26. b. The first step is to identify those accounts which increase spontaneously with sales.

27. e. Answers a through d would increase the additional funds required, but a decrease in the tax rate would raise the profit margin and thus increase the amount of available retained earnings.

28. a. Statement a is correct; economies of scale cause the ratios to change over time, which violates the assumption of the percent of sales method. Statement b is false; the points will not all lie on the regression line. Statement c is false; the AFN formula requires a constant percentage of sales over time. Statement d is false; the AFN formula includes only spontaneous liabilities, and notes payable do not spontaneously increase with sales. Statement e is false; the AFN formula includes the dividend payout, so dividend policy is included.

SOLUTIONS TO SELF-TEST PROBLEMS

1. b. Look at next year's balance sheet:

Current assets	$10,000	Accounts payable	$ 2,000
Net fixed assets	5,000	Notes payable	1,000
		Current liabilities	$ 3,000
		Long-Term debt	$ 4,000
		Common equity	4,000
			$11,000
		AFN	4,000
Total assets	$15,000	Total liabilities and equity	$15,000

With no retained earnings next year, the common equity account remains at $4,000. Thus, the additional financing requirement is $15,000 – $11,000 = $4,000.

2. b. None of the items on the right side of the balance sheet rises spontaneously with sales except accounts payable. Therefore,

$$AFN = (A^*/S_0)(\Delta S) - (L^*/S_0)(\Delta S) - MS_1(1 - d)$$
$$= (\$14/\$60)(\$12) - (\$2/\$60)(\$12) - (0.05)(\$72)(0.6)$$
$$= \$2.8 - \$0.4 - \$2.16 = \$0.24 \text{ million.}$$

The firm will need $240,000 in additional funds to support the increase in sales.

3. d. Note that $g = $ Sales growth $= \Delta S/S_0$ and $S_1 = S_0(1 + g)$. Then,

$$
\begin{aligned}
AFN = \quad A^*g - L^*g - M[(S_0)(1 + g)](1 - d) &= 0 \\
\$14g - \$2g - 0.05[(\$60)(1 + g)](0.6) &= 0 \\
\$12g - [(\$3 + \$3g)(0.60)] &= 0 \\
\$12g - \$1.8 - \$1.8g &= 0 \\
\$10.20g &= \$1.80 \\
g &= 0.1765 = 17.65\%.
\end{aligned}
$$

4. c.
$$0 = (A^*/S_0)(\Delta S) - (L^*/S_0)(\Delta S) - MS_1(1 - d)$$
$$0 = (A^*/\$2,000)(\$500) - (\$500/\$2,000)(\$500) - (\$500/\$2,000)(\$2,500)(1 - 0.3)$$
$$0 = (\$500A^*/\$2,000) - \$125 - \$437.50$$
$$0 = (\$500A^*/\$2,000) - \$562.50$$
$$\$562.50 = 0.25A^*$$
$$A^* = \$2,250.$$

5. a. $$\text{Full capacity sales} = \frac{\text{Actual sales}}{\text{\% of capacity at which FA were operated}} = \frac{\$12,000}{0.75} = \$16,000.$$

$$\frac{\text{Percent increase}}{} = \frac{\text{New sales} - \text{Old sales}}{\text{Old sales}} = \frac{\$16,000 - \$12,000}{\$12,000} = 0.33 = 33\%.$$

Therefore, sales could expand by 33 percent before Crossley Products would need to add fixed assets.

6. e.

Crossley Products Company
Pro Forma Income Statement
December 31, 2002
(Thousands of Dollars)

	2001	Forecast Basis[a]	2002 Forecast
Sales	$12,000	1.25	$15,000
Operating costs	10,261	0.8551	12,826
EBIT	$ 1,739		$ 2,174
Interest	339		339
EBT	$ 1,400		$ 1,835
Taxes (40%)	560		734
Net income	$ 840		$ 1,101
Dividends (60%)	$ 504		$ 661
Addition to RE	$ 336		$ 440

Crossley Products Company
Pro Forma Balance Sheet
December 31, 2002
(Thousands of Dollars)

	2001	Forecast Basis[a]	2002 Forecast	AFN	2002 After AFN
Cash	$ 600	0.05	$ 750		$ 750
Receivables	3,600	0.30	4,500		4,500
Inventory	4,200	0.35	5,250		5,250
Total current assets	$ 8,400		$10,500		$10,500
Net fixed assets	7,200		7,200[b]		7,200
Total assets	$15,600		$17,700		$17,700
Accts. payable	$ 2,400	0.20	$ 3,000		$ 3,000
Notes payable	1,157		1,157	+850	2,007
Accruals	840	0.07	1,050		1,050
Total current liab.	$ 4,397		$ 5,207		$ 6,057
Mortgage bonds	1,667		1,667		1,667
Common stock	667		667		667
Retained earnings	8,869	440[c]	9,309		9,309
Total liabilities and equity	$15,600		$16,850		$17,700
			AFN =	$ 850	

Notes:

[a]Sales are increased by 25%. Operating costs, all assets except fixed assets, accruals, and accounts payable are divided by 2001 sales to determine the appropriate ratios to apply to 2002 sales to calculate 2002 account balances.

[b]From Self-Test Problem 5 we know that sales can increase by 33 percent before additions to fixed assets are needed.

[c]See income statement.

7.   d.   Current ratio $= CA/CL$

$$= \$10,500/\$6,057$$
$$= 1.73.$$

$$\text{Debt/Asset ratio} = \frac{(\$6,057 + \$1,667)}{\$17,700}$$
$$= 43.64\%.$$

8.   c.   The projected balance sheet indicates that the AFN = $68,157.

Taylor Technologies Inc.
Pro Forma Income Statement
December 31, 2002

	2001	Forecast Basis[a]	2002 Forecast
Sales	$1,800,000	1.10	$1,980,000
Operating costs	1,639,860	0.9110	1,803,846
EBIT	$ 160,140		$ 176,154
Interest	10,140		10,140
EBT	$ 150,000		$ 166,014
Taxes (40%)	60,000		66,406
Net income	$ 90,000		$ 99,608
Dividends (60%)	$ 54,000		$ 59,765
Addition to RE	$ 36,000		$ 39,843

Taylor Technologies Inc.
Pro Forma Balance Sheet
December 31, 2002

	2001	Forecast Basis[a]	2002 Forecast
Cash	$ 90,000	0.05	$ 99,000
Receivables	180,000	0.10	198,000
Inventory	360,000	0.20	396,000
Total current assets	$ 630,000		$ 693,000
Fixed assets	720,000	0.40	792,000
Total assets	$1,350,000		$1,485,000
Accts. payable	$ 180,000	0.10	$ 198,000
Notes payable	78,000		78,000
Accruals	90,000	0.05	99,000
Total current liabilities	$ 348,000		$ 375,000
Common stock	900,000		900,000
Ret. earnings	102,000	39,843[b]	141,843
Total liabilities and equity	$1,350,000		$1,416,843
		AFN =	$ 68,157

Notes:

[a]Sales are increased by 10%. Operating costs, all assets, accruals, and accounts payable are divided by 2001 sales to determine the appropriate ratios to apply to 2002 sales to calculate 2002 account balances.

[b]See income statement on previous page.

9. a.

Taylor Technologies Inc.
Pro Forma Income Statement
December 31, 2002

	2001	Forecast Basis[a]	2002 Forecast
Sales	$1,800,000	1.10	$1,980,000
Operating costs	1,639,860	0.9110	1,803,846
EBIT	$ 160,140		$ 176,154
Interest	10,140		10,140
EBT	$ 150,000		$ 166,014
Taxes (40%)	60,000		66,406
Net income	$ 90,000		$ 99,608
Dividends (60%)	$ 54,000		$ 59,765
Addition to RE	$ 36,000		$ 39,843

Taylor Technologies Inc.
Pro Forma Balance Sheet
December 31, 2002

	2001	Forecast Basis[a]	2002 Forecast
Cash	$ 90,000	0.05	$ 99,000
Receivables	180,000	0.10	198,000
Inventory	360,000	0.20	396,000
Total current assets	$ 630,000		$ 693,000
Fixed assets	720,000	32,400[b]	752,400
Total assets	$1,350,000		$1,445,400
Accts. payable	$ 180,000	0.10	$ 198,000
Notes payable	78,000		78,000
Accruals	90,000	0.05	99,000
Total current liabilities	$ 348,000		$ 375,000
Common stock	900,000		900,000
Ret. earnings	102,000	39,843[c]	141,843
Total liabilities and equity	$1,350,000		$1,416,843
		AFN =	$ 28,557

Notes:

[a]Sales are increased by 10%. Operating costs, all assets except fixed assets, accruals, and accounts payable are divided by 2001 sales to determine the appropriate ratios to apply to 2002 sales to calculate 2002 account balances.

$$^b\,\begin{array}{c}\text{Full}\\\text{capacity}\\\text{sales}\end{array} = \frac{\$1,800,000}{0.95} = \$1,894,737.$$

$$\text{Target fixed assets/ Sales ratio} = \frac{\$720,000}{\$1,894,737} = 38\%.$$

$$\begin{array}{l}\text{Required level}\\\text{of fixed assets}\end{array} = (0.38)(\$1,980,000)$$

$$= \$752,400.$$

Necessary FA increase = $752,400 - $720,000 = $32,400.

[c]See income statement.

10. e.

	Current Year	Forecast Basis[a]	1st Pass	AFN	2nd Pass
Cash	$ 100	0.05	$ 150		$ 150
Receivables	300	0.15	450		450
Inventory	800	+250[b]	1,050		1,050
Total curr. assets	$1,200		$1,650		$1,650
Net fixed assets	800	+160[c]	960		960
Total assets	$2,000		$2,610		$2,610
Accts. payable	$ 200	0.10	$ 300		$ 300
Notes payable	200		200	+ 482	682
Accruals	20	0.01	30		30
Total curr. liab.	$ 420		$ 530		$1,012
Long-term debt	780		780		780
Common stock	400		400		400
Ret. earnings	400	+ 18[d]	418		418
Total liab./equity	$2,000		$2,128		$2,610

AFN = $ 482

Notes:

[a]Cash, receivables, accounts payable, and accruals are divided by current year's sales to determine the appropriate ratios to apply to next year's sales to calculate next year's account balances.

[b]Target inventory/assets = ($800 − $100)/$2,000 = 35%.
Target inventory level = 0.35($3,000) = $1,050.
Since we already have $800 of inventories, we need:
Additional inventories = $1,050 − $800 = $250.

[c]Capacity sales = Sales/Capacity factor = $2,000/0.8 = $2,500.
Target FA/S ratio = FA/Capacity sales = $800/$2,500 = 32%.
Required FA = (Target ratio)(Forecasted sales) = 0.32($3,000) = $960.
Since we already have $800 of fixed assets, we need:
Additional fixed assets = $960 − $800 = $160.

[d]Additions to RE = $M(S_1)(1 − \text{Payout ratio}) = 0.03(\$3,000)(0.2) = \$18$.

The problem asks for the forecasted current ratio which is calculated as:
Forecasted current ratio = $1,650/$1,012 = 1.6304.

11. b.

	2001	Forecast Basis[a]	1st Pass 2002
Cash	$ 50	0.10	$100
Receivables	100	0.20	200
Inventory	100	0.20	200
Total current assets	$250		$500
Net fixed assets	250	+0[b]	250
Total assets	$500		$750
Accounts payable	$ 25	0.05	$ 50
Notes payable	75		75
Accruals	25	0.05	50
Total current liabilities	$125		$175
Long-term debt	200		200
Common stock	50		50
Retained earnings	125	+48[c]	173
Total claims	$500		$598

AFN = $152

Notes:

[a]Cash, receivables, inventory, accounts payable, an accruals are divided by 2001 sales to determine the appropriate ratios to apply to 2002 sales to calculate 2002 account balances.

[b]Capacity sales = Actual sales/Capacity factor = $500/0.5 = $1,000.
Target FA/S ratio = $250/$1,000 = 0.25.
Target FA = 0.25($1,000) = $250 = Required fixed assets.
Since Bouchard currently has $250 of FA, no new FA will be required.

[c]Addition to RE = $M(S_1)(1 - \text{Payout ratio}) = 0.08(\$1,000)(0.6) = \$48$.

CHAPTER 5
THE FINANCIAL ENVIRONMENT:
MARKETS, INSTITUTIONS, AND INTEREST RATES

OVERVIEW

It is critical that financial managers understand the environment and markets within which they operate. In this chapter, we examine the markets where capital is raised, securities are traded, and stock prices are established. We examine the institutions that operate in these markets and hence through which securities transactions are conducted. In the process, we shall see how money costs are determined, and we shall explore the principal factors that determine both the general level of interest rates in the economy and the interest rate on a particular debt security.

OUTLINE

Financial markets bring together people and organizations wanting to borrow money with those having surplus funds.

- There are many different financial markets in a developed economy, each dealing with a different type of instrument, serving a different set of customers, or operating in a different part of the country.

- The major types of financial markets include the following:
  - *Money markets* are the markets for short-term, highly liquid debt securities, those securities that mature in less than one year.
  - *Capital markets* are the markets for long-term debt and corporate stocks.
  - *Primary markets* are the markets in which corporations sell newly issued securities to raise capital.
  - *Secondary markets* are the markets in which existing, already outstanding securities are traded among investors.

- A healthy economy is dependent on efficient transfers of funds from people who are net savers to firms and individuals who need capital.

- Financial markets have experienced tremendous change during the 1980s and 1990s. Technological advances in computers and telecommunications, along with the globalization of banking and commerce, have led to deregulation, and this has increased competition throughout the world.

- Another important trend in recent years has been the increased use of derivatives.
  - A *derivative* is any security whose value is derived from the price of some other "underlying" asset.
  - The market for derivatives has grown faster than any other market in recent years, providing corporations with additional opportunities but also exposing them to new risks.
  - Derivatives can be used either to reduce risks or as speculative investments, which increase risk.
  - In theory, derivatives should allow companies to manage risk better, but it is not clear whether recent innovations have "increased or decreased the inherent stability of the financial system."

- Another major trend involves stock ownership patterns.
  - The number of individuals who have a stake in the stock market is increasing, but the number of individuals who own corporate shares is decreasing. Thus, more and more individuals are investing in the market, but they are doing so indirectly.
  - The direct ownership of stocks is being concentrated in institutions. If a fund holds a high percentage of a given corporation's shares, it would probably severely depress the stock's price if it tried to sell out. This has led to a phenomenon called *relationship investing*, where portfolio managers think of themselves as large, active, long-term investors in individual companies.

Transfers of capital between savers and borrowers take place in three different ways.

- *Direct transfers* of money and securities occur when a business sells its stocks or bonds directly to savers, without going through any type of financial institution.

- Transfers through an *investment banking house* occur when a brokerage firm, such as Merrill Lynch, serves as a middleman and facilitates the issuance of securities. These middlemen help corporations design securities that will be attractive to investors, buy these securities from the corporations, and then resell them to savers in the primary markets.

- Transfers through a *financial intermediary* occur when a bank or mutual fund obtains funds from savers, issues its own securities in exchange, and then uses these funds to purchase other securities.
  - Intermediaries literally create new forms of capital.

- ❑ Some major classes of intermediaries include commercial banks, savings and loan (S&L) associations, mutual savings banks, credit unions, life insurance companies, mutual funds, and pension funds.
- ❑ The result of the ongoing regulatory changes has been a blurring of the distinctions between the different types of financial institutions. As a result, in the United States the trend has been toward huge *financial service corporations*, which own any number of financial intermediaries with national and even global operations.

The stock market is one of the most important markets to financial managers because it is here that the price of each stock, and hence the value of all publicly-owned firms, is established. There are two basic types of stock markets.

- ■ The *organized security exchanges*, typified by the New York Stock Exchange (NYSE) and the American Stock Exchange (AMEX), are tangible, physical entities.

- ■ The *over-the-counter market* includes all facilities that are needed to conduct security transactions not conducted on the organized exchanges.
  - ❑ Brokers and dealers who participate in the over-the-counter market are members of a self-regulating body known as the *National Association of Securities Dealers (NASD)*, which licenses brokers and oversees trading practices.
  - ❑ In terms of numbers of issues, the majority of stocks are traded over the counter, and trading volume is greater on NASDAQ stocks than on the NYSE. However, because the stocks of most large companies are listed on the exchanges, more than half of the dollar volume of stock trading takes place on the exchanges.

Capital in a free economy is allocated through the price system. The interest rate is the price paid to borrow debt capital. The four most fundamental factors affecting the cost of money are (1) production opportunities, (2) time preferences for consumption, (3) risk, and (4) inflation.

- ■ The level of interest rates is determined by the supply of, and demand for, investment capital.
  - ❑ The demand for investment capital is determined by *production opportunities* available and the rates of return producers can expect to earn on invested capital.
  - ❑ The supply of investment capital depends on *consumers' time preferences* for current versus future consumption.

- ■ Two additional factors affecting the level of interest rates are *risk* and *inflation*. The higher the perceived risk, the higher the required rate of return, and the higher the expected rate of inflation, the higher the required return.

The quoted (or nominal) interest rate on a debt security, k, is composed of a real risk-free rate of interest, k*, plus several premiums that reflect inflation, the riskiness of the security, and the security's marketability (or liquidity):

$$k = k^* + IP + DRP + LP + MRP.$$
$$= k_{RF} + DRP + LP + MRP.$$

- ■ The *real risk-free rate of interest (k*)* is the interest rate that would exist on a riskless security if no inflation were expected, and it may be thought of as the rate of interest that would exist on short-term U. S. Treasury securities in an inflation-free world.
  - ❑ The real risk-free rate on long-term securities can be measured by the market yield on indexed U. S. Treasury bonds.

- ■ The *nominal, or quoted, risk-free rate of interest (k_{RF})* on a security such as a U.S Treasury bill is the real risk-free rate plus a premium for expected inflation: $k_{RF} = k^* + IP$.

- ■ The *inflation premium (IP)*, which is the average inflation rate *expected* over the life of the security, compensates investors for the expected loss of purchasing power.
  - ❑ Expectations for future inflation are closely, but not perfectly, correlated with rates experienced in the recent past.

- ■ The *default risk premium (DRP)* compensates investors for the risk that a borrower will default and hence not pay the interest or principal on a loan. DRP is zero for U. S. Treasury securities, but it rises as the riskiness of issuers increases.

- ■ A security which can be converted to cash quickly and at a "fair market value" is said to be *liquid*. A *liquidity premium (LP)* is also added to the real rate for securities that are not liquid.

- ■ Long-term securities are more price sensitive to interest rate changes than are short-term securities. Therefore, a *maturity risk premium (MRP)* is added to longer-term securities to compensate investors for interest rate risk. The MRP is higher the longer the years to maturity.
  - ❑ Although long-term bonds are heavily exposed to interest rate risk, short-term bills are heavily exposed to *reinvestment rate risk*. This is the risk that a decline in interest rates will lead to lower income when bonds mature and funds are reinvested.

In addition to inflation and liquidity, investors should consider other risk factors before investing overseas.

■　*Country risk* is the risk that arises from investing or doing business in a particular country.
 ❑ This risk depends on the country's economic, political, and social environment.
 ❑ Examples of country risk include the risk associated with changes in tax rates, regulations, currency conversion, and exchange rates. It also includes the risk that property will be expropriated without adequate compensation, as well as new host country stipulations about local production, sourcing or hiring practices, and damage or destruction of facilities due to internal strife.

■　Investors should keep in mind when investing overseas, more often than not, the security will be denominated in a currency other than the dollar. This means the value of the investment will depend on what happens to exchange rates, and this is known as *exchange rate risk*.
 ❑ Two factors can lead to exchange rate fluctuations.
 ❑ Changes in relative inflation will lead to changes in exchange rates. If expected inflation increases more within some foreign country than in the U. S., the value of the country's currency is likely to fall.
 ❑ An increase in country risk will also cause the country's currency to fall.

■　Inflation risk, country risk, and exchange rate risk are all interrelated.

The term structure of interest rates is the relationship between long- and short-term rates.

■　The plot of interest rates at different maturities is called a *yield curve*.

■　Yield curves have different shapes depending on expected inflation rates and perceptions about the relative riskiness of securities with different maturities.
 ❑ The "normal" yield curve is *upward sloping* because investors charge higher rates on longer-term bonds, even when inflation is expected to remain constant, because longer-term bonds have more interest rate risk than shorter-term bonds.
 ❑ An inverted, or *downward sloping*, yield curve signifies that investors expect inflation to decrease.

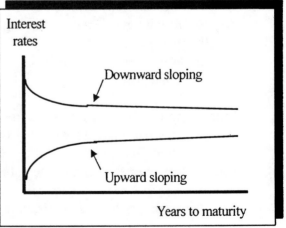

The shape of the yield curve depends on two key factors: (1) expectations about future inflation and (2) perceptions about the relative riskiness of securities with different maturities.

There are other factors that influence both the general level of interest rates and the shape of the yield curve. The four most important are (1) Federal Reserve policy; (2) the level of the federal budget deficit; (3) international factors, including the foreign trade balance and interest rates in other countries; and (4) the level of business activity.

■   Expansionary monetary policy (growth in monetary supply) by the Federal Reserve initially lowers the interest rate but inflationary pressures could cause a rise in the interest rate in the long term. Contractionary monetary policy has the opposite effect.

■   Federal budget deficits drive interest rates up due to increased demand for loanable funds, while surpluses drive rates down due to increased supply of loanable funds. The larger the federal deficit, other things held constant, the higher the level of interest rates. Whether long- or short-term rates are more affected depends on how the deficit is financed.

■   Foreign trade deficits (when imports are greater than exports) push interest rates up because deficits must be financed from abroad and rates must be high enough relative to world interest rates to draw foreign investors.

■   In relation to the business cycle, there is a general tendency for interest rates to decline during a recession.

The level of interest rates also has a significant effect on stock prices.

■   Interest rates have two effects on corporate profits.
    ❑   Because interest is a cost, the higher the interest rate, the lower a firm's profits, other things held constant.
    ❑   Interest rates affect the level of economic activity, and economic activity affects corporate profits.

■   Stocks and bonds compete in the marketplace for investors' capital. Therefore, a rise in interest rates will increase the rate of return on bonds, causing investors to transfer funds from the stock market to the bond market. The resultant selling of stocks lowers stock prices. The reverse occurs if interest rates decline.

Interest rate movements have a significant impact on business decisions.

■   Wrong decisions, such as using short-term debt to finance long-term projects just before interest rates rise, can be very costly.

■   It is extremely difficult, if not impossible, to predict future interest rate levels.

■ Sound financial policy calls for using a mix of long-term and short-term debt, and equity, to position the firm so that it can survive in almost any interest rate environment.

    ❑ The optimal financial policy depends in an important way on the nature of the firm's assets—the easier it is to sell off assets to generate cash, the more feasible it is to use large amounts of short-term debt. This makes it more feasible for a firm to finance its current assets than its fixed assets with short-term debt.

SELF-TEST QUESTIONS

Definitional

1. Markets for short-term debt securities are called _____ markets, while markets for long-term debt and equity are called _____ markets.

2. Firms raise capital by selling newly issued securities in the _____ markets, while existing, already outstanding securities are traded in the _____ markets.

3. An institution which issues its own securities in exchange for funds and then uses these funds to purchase other securities is called a financial _____.

4. A(n) _____ _____ firm facilitates the transfer of capital between savers and borrowers by acting as a middleman.

5. The two basic types of stock markets are the _____ _____ _____, such as the NYSE, and the _____-_____-_____ market.

6. The risk that a borrower will not pay the interest or principal on a loan is _____ risk.

7. ____ ____ _____ securities have zero default risk.

8. A(n) _____ premium is added to the real risk-free rate to protect investors against loss of purchasing power.

9. The nominal rate of interest is determined by adding a(n) _____ premium plus a(n) _____ risk premium plus a(n) _____ premium plus a(n) _____ risk premium to the real risk-free rate of return.

10. The relationship between long- and short-term rates is called the _____ _____ of interest rates, while the resulting plotted curve is the _____ curve.

11. The "normal" yield curve has a(n) _____ slope.

12. Because interest rates fluctuate, a sound financial policy calls for using a mix of _____-_____ and _____-_____ debt and _____.

13. _____ _____ bring together people and organizations wanting to borrow money with those having surplus funds.

14. _____ _____ of money and securities occur when a business sells its stock or bonds directly to savers, without going through any type of financial institution.

15. A(n) _____ is any security whose value is derived from the price of some other "underlying" asset.

16. The result of the ongoing regulatory changes has been a blurring of the distinctions between the different types of financial institutions. As a result, in the U. S. the trend has been toward huge _____ _____ corporations, which own any number of financial intermediaries with national and even global operations.

17. The _____ market is one of the most important markets to financial managers because it is here that the value of all publicly-owned firms is established.

18. The _____ _____ is the price paid to borrow debt capital.

19. A(n) _____ _____ premium is added to longer-term securities to compensate investors for interest rate risk.

20. _____ risk arises from investing or doing business in a particular country.

21. The value of an investment made overseas will depend on what happens to exchange rates, and this is known as _____ _____ risk.

22. _____ _____ is the phenomenon where portfolio managers think of themselves as large, active, long-term investors in individual companies because their fund holds a high percentage of a given corporation's shares.

23. The real risk-free rate on long-term securities can be measured by the market yield on _____ U. S. Treasury bonds.

24. A security which can be converted to cash quickly and at a "fair market value" is said to be _____.

25. A rise in interest rates will increase the rate of return on _____, causing investors to transfer funds from the _____ market to the _____ market.

Conceptual

26.   If management is sure that the economy is at the peak of a boom and is about to enter a recession, a firm which needs to borrow money should probably use short-term rather than long-term debt.

     a. True   **b.** False

27.   Long-term interest rates reflect expectations about future inflation. Inflation has varied greatly from year to year over the last 10 years, and, as a result, long-term rates have fluctuated more than short-term rates.

     a. True   **b.** False

28.   Suppose the Fed takes actions which lower expectations for inflation this year by 1 percentage point, but these same actions raise expectations for inflation in Years 2 and thereafter by 2 percentage points. Other things held constant, the yield curve becomes steeper.

     a. True   **b.** False

29.   Assume interest rates on 30-year government and corporate bonds were as follows: T-bond = 7.72%; AAA = 8.72%; A = 9.64%; BBB = 10.18%. The differences in rates among these issues are caused primarily by:

     a. Tax effects.   **d.** Inflation differences
     b. Default risk differences.   **e.** Both b and d.
     c. Maturity risk differences.

30.   Which of the following statements is most correct?

     a. The introduction of a new technology, such as computers, might be expected to improve labor productivity, making businesses more able and willing to pay a higher price for capital. This would put upward pressure on interest rates. However, the productivity improvements might give rise to lower inflationary expectations, which would put downward pressure on interest rates. Thus, the net effect of the new technology on interest rates might be uncertain.

     b. If future inflation were expected to remain constant at 6 percent for all future years, then for all bonds (government and corporate combined) we could measure the maturity risk premium as the difference between the yields on 30-year and 1-year bonds.

c. If investors expect the inflation rate to *decrease* over time, e.g., the expected inflation rate in Year t exceeds the expected rate in Year t + 1 for all values of t, then we can be *certain* that the yield curve for U. S. Treasury securities will be downward sloping.

d. Each of the above statements is correct.

e. Statements a and c are both correct.

31. Which of the following statements is most correct?

a. Suppose financial institutions, such as savings and loans, were required by law to make long-term, fixed-interest rate mortgages, but, at the same time, they were largely restricted, in terms of their capital sources, to taking deposits that could be withdrawn on demand. Under these conditions, these financial institutions should prefer a "normal" yield curve to an inverted curve.

b. You are considering establishing a new firm, the University Assistance Company (UAC). UAC would obtain funds in the short-term money market and write long-term mortgage loans to students so that they might buy condominiums rather than rent. A downward sloping yield curve, if it persisted over time, would be best for UAC.

c. The yield curve is upward sloping, or normal, if short-term rates are higher than long-term rates.

d. All of the above statements are correct.

e. Only statements a and b are correct.

32. Which of the following statements is most correct?

a. One of the major benefits of well-developed stock markets such as the New York Stock Exchange is that they increase liquidity, which makes it easier for firms to raise capital.

b. In the United States, we have a number of specialized financial institutions, but, according to the text, the trend is toward larger, more diversified institutions which offer broad arrays of financial services.

c. If the expected rate of inflation rose by 2 percentage points, from 5 to 7 percent, then the *real* risk-free rate (k^*) would also rise by 2 percentage points.

d. Statements a, b, and c are all true.

e. Only statements a and b are true.

SELF-TEST PROBLEMS

1. The real risk-free rate of interest is 2 percent. Inflation is expected to be 3 percent the next 2 years and 5 percent during the next 3 years after that. Assume that the maturity risk premium is zero. What is the yield on 3-year Treasury securities?

    a. 5.2%   **b.** 5.7%   **c.** 6.0%   **d.** 6.2%   **e.** 6.5%

2. Refer to Self-Test Problem 1. What is the yield on 5-year Treasury securities?

    a. 5.2%   **b.** 5.7%   **c.** 6.0%   **d.** 6.2%   **e.** 6.5%

3. A Treasury bond which matures in 20 years has a yield of 8 percent. A 20-year corporate bond has a yield of 11 percent. Assume that the liquidity premium on the corporate bond is 1.0 percent. What is the default risk premium on the corporate bond?

    a. 0.5%   **b.** 1.0%   **c.** 1.5%   **d.** 1.75%   **e.** 2.0%

4. You have determined the following data for a given bond: Real risk-free rate (k^*) = 3%; inflation premium = 8%; default risk premium = 2%; liquidity premium = 2%; and maturity risk premium = 1%. What is the nominal risk-free rate, k_{RF}?

    a. 10%   **b.** 11%   **c.** 12%   **d.** 13%   **e.** 14%

5. Refer to Self-Test Problem 4. What is the interest rate on long-term Treasury securities, or T-bonds, of the relevant maturity?

    a. 10%   **b.** 11%   **c.** 12%   **d.** 13%   **e.** 14%

6. Assume that a 3-year Treasury note has no maturity risk nor liquidity risk and that the real risk-free rate of interest falls to 2 percent. A 3-year T-note carries a yield to maturity of 12 percent. If the expected inflation rate is 12 percent for the coming year and 10 percent the year after, what is the implied expected inflation rate for the third year?

    a. 8%   **b.** 9%   **c.** 10%   **d.** 11%   **e.** 12%

7. Assume that the real risk-free rate is 2 percent, that the expected inflation rate during Year 2 is 3 percent, and that 2-year T-bonds yield 5.5 percent. If the maturity risk premium is zero, what is the inflation rate during Year 1?

    a. 3.0%   **b.** 5.0%   **c.** 3.5%   **d.** 4.0%   **e.** 2.5%

8. Refer to Self-Test Problem 7. Given the same information, what is the rate of return on 1-year T-bonds?

a. 5.5% **b.** 6.0% **c.** 5.0% **d.** 6.5% **e.** 4.5%

9. Assume that the real risk-free rate, k*, is 4 percent and that inflation is expected to be 7 percent in Year 1, 4 percent in Year 2, and 3 percent thereafter. Assume also that all Treasury bonds are highly liquid and free of default risk. If 2-year and 5-year Treasury bonds both yield 11 percent, what is the difference in the maturity risk premiums (MRPs) on the two bonds; that is, what is $MRP_5 - MRP_2$?

a. 0.5% **b.** 1.0% **c.** 2.25% **d.** 1.5% **e.** 1.25%

10. Due to the recession, the rate of inflation expected for the coming year is only 3.5 percent. However, the rate of inflation in Year 2 and thereafter is expected to be constant at some level above 3.5 percent. Assume that the real risk-free rate is k* = 2% for all maturities and that the expectations theory fully explains the yield curve, so there are no maturity premiums. If 3-year Treasury bonds yield 3 percentage points (0.03) more than 1-year Treasury bonds, what rate of inflation is expected after Year 1?

a. 4% **b.** 5% **c.** 7% **d.** 6% **e.** 8%

ANSWERS TO SELF-TEST QUESTIONS

1.	money; capital	**13.**	Financial markets
2.	primary; secondary	**14.**	Direct transfers
3.	intermediary	**15.**	derivative
4.	investment banking	**16.**	financial service
5.	organized security exchanges; over-the-counter (OTC)	**17.**	stock
		18.	interest rate
6.	default	**19.**	maturity risk
7.	U. S. Treasury	**20.**	Country
8.	inflation	**21.**	exchange rate
9.	inflation; default; liquidity; maturity	**22.**	Relationship investing
10.	term structure; yield	**23.**	indexed
11.	upward	**24.**	liquid
12.	short-term; long-term; equity	**25.**	bonds; stock; bond

26. a. The firm should borrow short-term until interest rates drop due to the recession, then go long-term. Predicting interest rates is extremely difficult, for managers can rarely be sure about what is going to happen to the economy.

27. b. Fluctuations in long-term rates are smaller because the long-term inflation premium is an average of inflation expectations over many years, and hence the IP on long-term bonds is quite stable relative to the IP on short-term bonds. Also, short-term rates fluctuate as a result of Federal Reserve policy (the Fed intervenes in the short-term rather than the long-term market).

28. a. The yield curve becomes steeper. Although interest rates in Year 1 decrease by 1 percent, interest rates in the following years increase by 2 percent, making the yield curve steeper.

29. b. $k = k^* + IP + DRP + LP + MRP$. Since each of these bonds has a 30-year maturity, the MRP and IP would all be equal. Thus, the differences in the interest rates among these issues are the default risk and liquidity premiums.

30. a. Statement b is false because $k = k^* + IP + DRP + LP + MRP$. $k^* + IP$ would be the same for the two bonds; however, the default risk premium and liquidity premium would not be the same for the two bonds. Thus, you could not simply subtract the two yields to determine the MRP. Statement c is false because the expectations theory is not the only theory proposed to explain the shape of the yield curve. The liquidity preference theory states that under normal conditions a positive maturity risk premium exists. So, we cannot be certain that the yield curve would be downward sloping.

31. a. Statement b is incorrect. If a downward-sloping yield curve existed, long-term interest rates would be lower than short-term rates. This would be very serious for UAC: UAC receives as income the interest it charges on its long-term mortgage loans, but it has to pay out interest for obtaining funds in the short-term money market. Therefore, UAC would be receiving low interest income, but it would be paying out even higher interest. Statement c is incorrect. An upward-sloping yield curve would indicate higher interest rates for long-term securities than for short-term securities.

32. e. Statement c is incorrect because the nominal rate ($k_{RF} = k^* + IP$) would increase (not the real risk-free rate, k^*) if inflation increased by 2 percentage points.

SOLUTIONS TO SELF-TEST PROBLEMS

1. b. $k^* = 2\%$; $I_1 = 3\%$; $I_2 = 3\%$; $I_3 = 5\%$; $I_4 = 5\%$; $I_5 = 5\%$; MRP = 0; $k_{T-3} = ?$
        Since these are Treasury securities, DRP = LP = 0.

    $k_{T-3} = k^* + IP_3$.
    $IP_3 = (3\% + 3\% + 5\%)/3 = 3.67\%$.
    $k_{T-3} = 2\% + 3.67\% = 5.67\% \approx 5.7\%$.

2. d. $k^* = 2\%$, $I_1 = 3\%$; $I_2 = 3\%$; $I_3 = 5\%$; $I_4 = 5\%$; $I_5 = 5\%$; MRP = 0; $k_{T-5} = ?$
        Since these are Treasury securities, DRP = LP = 0.

    $k_{T-5} = k^* + IP_5$.
    $IP_5 = (3\% + 3\% + 5\% + 5\% + 5\%)/5 = 4.2\%$.
    $k_{T-5} = 2\% + 4.2\% = 6.2\%$.

3. e. $k_{T-20} = 8\%$; $k_{C-20} = 11\%$; LP = 1.0%; DRP = ?

    $k = k^* + IP + DRP + LP + MRP$.
    $k_{T-20} = 8\% = k^* + IP + MRP$; DRP = LP = 0.
    $k_{C-20} = 11\% = k^* + IP + DRP + 1.0\% + MRP$.

    Because both bonds are 20-year bonds the inflation premium and maturity risk premium on both bonds are equal. The only differences between them are the liquidity and default risk premiums.

    $k_{C-20} = 11\% = k^* + IP + MRP + 1.0\% + DRP$. But we know from above that $k^* + IP + MRP = 8\%$; therefore,

    $k_{C-20} = 11\% = 8\% + 1.0\% + DRP$
    $\quad 2\% = DRP$.

4. b. $k_{RF} = k^* + IP = 3\% + 8\% = 11\%$.

5. c. There is virtually no risk of default on a U. S. Treasury security, and they trade in active markets, which provide liquidity, so

    $k = k^* + IP + DRP + LP + MRP$
    $\quad = 3\% + 8\% + 0\% + 0\% + 1\%$
    $\quad = 12\%$.

6. a. $k = k* + IP + DRP + LP + MRP$
$12\% = 2\% + IP + 0\% + 0\% + 0\%$
$IP = 10\%.$

Thus, the average expected inflation rate over the next three years (IP) is 10 percent. Given that the average expected inflation rate over the next three years is 10%, we can find the implied expected inflation rate for the third year by solving the equation that sets the two known and the one unknown expected inflation rates equal to 10%:

$$\frac{12\% + 10\% + I_3}{3} = 10\%$$

$$I_3 = 8\%.$$

7. d.

Year	k*	Inflation	Average Inflation	k_t
1	2%	?	$I_1/1 = ?$	?
2	2%	3	$(I_1 + 3\%)/2$	5.5%

$k_2 = 2\% + (I_1 + 3\%)/2 = 5.5\%.$ Solving for I_1, we find I_1 = Year 1 inflation = 4%.

8. b. $I_1 = IP = 4\%.$ $k_1 = k* + IP = 2\% + 4\% = 6\%.$

9. d. First, note that we will use the equation $k_t = 4\% + IP_t + MRP_t$. We have the data needed to find the IPs:

$IP_5 = (7\% + 4\% + 3\% + 3\% + 3\%)/5 = 20\%/5 = 4\%.$
$IP_2 = (7\% + 4\%)/2 = 5.5\%.$

Now we can substitute into the equation:

$k_2 = 4\% + 5.5\% + MRP_2 = 11\%.$
$k_5 = 4\% + 4\% + MRP_5 = 11\%.$

Now we can solve for the MRPs, and find the difference:

$MRP_5 = 11\% - 8\% = 3\%.$
$MRP_2 = 11\% - 9.5\% = 1.5\%.$
Difference = 3% - 1.5% = 1.5%.

10.   e. Basic relevant equations:

$k_t = k^* + IP_t + DRP_t + MRP_t + LP_t$. But $DRP_t = MRP_t = LP_t = 0$, so
$k_t = k^* + IP_t$.

$$IP_t = \frac{\text{Average}}{\text{inflation}} = \frac{I_1 + I_2 + \dots}{N}.$$

We know that $I_1 = IP_1 = 3.5\%$, and $k^* = 2\%$. Therefore,

$k_1 = 2\% + 3.5\% = 5.5\%$.
$k_3 = k_1 + 3\% = 5.5\% + 3\% = 8.5\%$.

But $k_3 = k^* + IP_3 = 2\% + IP_3 = 8.5\%$, so
$IP_3 = 8.5\% - 2\% = 6.5\%$.

We also know that $I_t = $ Constant after $t = 1$.
$IP_3 = (3.5\% + 2I)/3 = 6.5\%$; $2I = 16\%$, so $I = 8\%$.

We can set up this table:

Year	k^*	I_t	Avg. I = IP_t	$k = k^* + IP_t$
1	2%	3.5%	3.5%/1 = 3.5%	5.5%
2	2%	I	(3.5 % + I)/2 = IP_2	
3	2%	I	(3.5% + I + I)/3 = IP_3	8.5%, so $IP_3 =$ 8.5% − 2% = 6.5%

CHAPTER 6
RISK AND RETURN: THE BASICS

OVERVIEW

Risk is an important concept in financial analysis, especially in terms of how it affects security prices and rates of return. Investment risk is associated with the probability of low or negative future returns.

The riskiness of an asset can be considered in two ways: (1) on a *stand-alone basis,* where the asset's cash flows are analyzed all by themselves, or (2) in a *portfolio context,* where the cash flows from a number of assets are combined and then the consolidated cash flows are analyzed.

In a portfolio context, an asset's risk can be divided into two components: (1) a *diversifiable risk component,* which can be diversified away and hence is of little concern to diversified investors, and (2) a *market risk component,* which reflects the risk of a general stock market decline and which cannot be eliminated by diversification, hence does concern investors. Only market risk is *relevant*; diversifiable risk is irrelevant to most investors because it can be eliminated.

An attempt has been made to quantify market risk with a measure called *beta.* Beta is a measurement of how a particular firm's stock returns move relative to overall movements of stock market returns. The *Capital Asset Pricing Model (CAPM),* using the concept of beta and investors' aversion to risk, specifies the relationship between market risk and the required rate of return. This relationship can be visualized graphically with the Security Market Line (SML). The slope of the SML can change, or the line can shift upward or downward, in response to changes in risk or required rates of return.

OUTLINE

With most investments, an individual or business spends money today with the expectation of earning even more money in the future. The concept of return provides investors with a convenient way of expressing the financial performance of an investment.

■ One way of expressing an investment return is in *dollar terms*.

■ Dollar return = Amount received − Amount invested.

    ❑   Expressing returns in dollars is easy, but two problems arise.

    ❑   To make a meaningful judgment about the adequacy of the return, you need to know the scale (size) of the investment.

    ❑   You also need to know the timing of the return.

■   The solution to the scale and timing problems of dollar returns is to express investment results as *rates of return*, or *percentage returns*.

$$\text{Rate of return} = \frac{\text{Amount received} - \text{Amount invested}}{\text{Amount invested}}.$$

    ❑   The rate of return calculation "normalizes" the return by considering the return per unit of investment.

    ❑   Expressing rates of return on an annual basis solves the timing problem.

    ❑   Rate of return is the most common measure of investment performance.

Risk refers to the chance that some unfavorable event will occur. Investment risk is related to the probability of actually earning less than the expected return; thus, the greater the chance of low or negative returns, the riskier the investment.

■   An asset's risk can be analyzed in two ways: (1) on a *stand-alone basis,* where the asset is considered in isolation, and (2) on a *portfolio basis,* where the asset is held as one of a number of assets in a portfolio.

■   No investment will be undertaken unless the expected rate of return is high enough to compensate the investor for the perceived risk of the investment.

■   The *probability distribution* for an event is the listing of all the possible outcomes for the event, with mathematical probabilities assigned to each.

    ❑   An event's *probability* is defined as the chance that the event will occur.

■   The sum of the probabilities for a particular event must equal 1.0, or 100 percent.

■ *The expected rate of return* $(\hat{k})$ is the sum of the products of each possible outcome times its associated probability—it is a weighted average of the various possible outcomes, with the weights being their probabilities of occurrence:

$$\text{Expected rate of return} = \hat{k} = \sum_{i=1}^{n} P_i\, k_i \, .$$

❑ Where the number of possible outcomes is virtually unlimited, *continuous probability distributions* are used in determining the expected rate of return of the event.

❑ The tighter, or more peaked, the probability distribution, the more likely it is that the actual outcome will be close to the expected value, and, consequently, the less likely it is that the actual return will end up far below the expected return. Thus, the tighter the probability distribution, the lower the risk assigned to a stock.

■ One measure for determining the tightness of a distribution is the *standard deviation,* σ .

$$\text{Standard deviation} \ = \ \sigma \ = \ \sqrt{\sum_{i=1}^{n}(k_i - \hat{k})^2 P_i} \, .$$

❑ The standard deviation is a probability-weighted average deviation from the expected value, and it gives you an idea of how far above or below the expected value the actual value is likely to be.

■ Another useful measure of risk is the *coefficient of variation (CV)*, which is the standard deviation divided by the expected return. It shows the risk per unit of return, and it provides a more meaningful basis for comparison when the expected returns on two alternatives are not the same:

$$\text{Coefficient of variation (CV)} \ = \ \frac{\sigma}{\hat{k}} \, .$$

■ Most investors are *risk averse*. This means that for two alternatives with the same expected rate of return, investors will choose the one with the lower risk.

■ In a market dominated by risk-averse investors, riskier securities must have higher expected returns, as estimated by the marginal investor, than less risky securities, for if this situation does not hold, buying and selling in the market will force it to occur.

An asset held as part of a portfolio is less risky than the same asset held in isolation. This is important, because most financial assets are not held in isolation; rather, they are held as parts of portfolios. From the investor's standpoint, what is important is the return on his or her portfolio, and the portfolio's risk—not the fact that a particular stock goes up or down. Thus, the risk and return of an individual security should be analyzed in terms of how it affects the risk and return of the portfolio in which it is held.

■   The expected return on a portfolio,

$\hat{k}_p$, is the weighted average of the expected returns on the individual assets in the portfolio, with the weights being the fraction of the total portfolio invested in each asset:

$$\hat{k}_p = \sum_{i=1}^{n} w_i \hat{k}_i.$$

■   The riskiness of a portfolio, σ_P, is generally *not* a weighted average of the standard deviations of the individual assets in the portfolio; the portfolio's risk will be smaller than the weighted average of the assets' σ's. The riskiness of a portfolio depends not only on the standard deviations of the individual stocks, but also on the *correlation between the stocks*.

   ❑   The *correlation coefficient, r*, measures the tendency of two variables to move together. With stocks, these variables are the individual stock returns.

   ❑   Diversification does nothing to reduce risk if the portfolio consists of *perfectly positively correlated* stocks.

   ❑   As a rule, the riskiness of a portfolio will decline as the number of stocks in the portfolio increases.

   ❑   However, in the real world, where the correlations among the individual stocks are generally positive but less than +1.0, some, but not all, risk can be eliminated.

   ❑   In the real world, it is impossible to form completely riskless stock portfolios. Diversification can reduce risk, but cannot eliminate it.

■   While very large portfolios end up with a substantial amount of risk, it is not as much risk as if all the money were invested in only one stock. Almost half of the riskiness inherent in an average individual stock can be eliminated if the stock is held in a reasonably well-diversified portfolio, which is one containing 40 or more stocks.

   ❑   *Diversifiable risk* is that part of the risk of a stock which can be eliminated. It is caused by events that are unique to a particular firm.

   ❑   *Market risk* is that part of the risk which cannot be eliminated, and it stems from factors which systematically affect most firms, such as war, inflation, recessions, and high interest rates. It can be measured by the degree to which a given stock tends to move up or down with the market. Thus, market risk is the *relevant* risk, which reflects a security's contribution to the portfolio's risk.

❑ The *Capital Asset Pricing Model* is an important tool for analyzing the relationship between risk and rates of return. The model is based on the proposition that any stock's required rate of return is equal to the risk-free rate of return plus a risk premium, which reflects only the risk remaining after diversification. Its primary conclusion is: The relevant riskiness of an individual stock is its contribution to the riskiness of a well-diversified portfolio.

The tendency of a stock to move with the market is reflected in its beta coefficient, b, which is a measure of the stock's volatility relative to that of an average stock.

■ An *average-risk stock* is defined as one that tends to move up and down in step with the general market. By definition it has a beta of 1.0.

■ A stock that is twice as volatile as the market will have a beta of 2.0, while a stock that is half as volatile as the market will have a beta coefficient of 0.5.

■ Since a stock's beta measures its contribution to the riskiness of a portfolio, beta is the theoretically correct measure of the stock's riskiness.

■ The beta coefficient of a portfolio of securities is the weighted average of the individual securities' betas:

$$b_p = \sum_{i=1}^{n} w_i b_i.$$

■ Since a stock's beta coefficient determines how the stock affects the riskiness of a diversified portfolio, beta is the most relevant measure of any stock's risk.

The Capital Asset Pricing Model (CAPM) employs the concept of beta, which measures risk as the relationship between a particular stock's movements and the movements of the overall stock market. The CAPM uses a stock's beta, in conjunction with the average investor's degree of risk aversion, to calculate the return that investors require, k_s, on that particular stock.

■ The *Security Market Line (SML)* shows the relationship between risk as measured by beta and the required rate of return for individual securities. The SML equation can be used to find the required rate of return on Stock i:

$$SML: \ k_i = k_{RF} + (k_M - k_{RF})b_i.$$

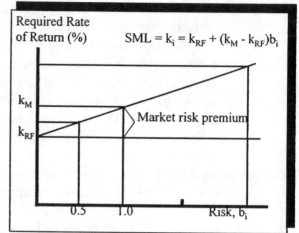

■ Here k_{RF} is the rate of interest on risk-free securities, b_i is the ith stock's beta, and k_M is the return on the market or, alternatively, on an average stock.

❑ The term $k_M - k_{RF}$ is the *market risk premium, RP_M*. This is a measure of the additional return over the risk-free rate needed to compensate investors for assuming an average amount of risk.

❑ In the CAPM, the market risk premium, $k_M - k_{RF}$, is multiplied by the stock's beta coefficient to determine the additional premium over the risk-free rate that is required to compensate investors for the risk inherent in a particular stock.

❑ This premium may be larger or smaller than the premium required on an average stock, depending on the riskiness of that stock in relation to the overall market as measured by the stock's beta.

❑ The risk premium calculated by $(k_M - k_{RF})b_i$ is added to the risk-free rate, k_{RF} (the rate on Treasury securities), to determine the total rate of return required by investors on a particular stock, k_s.

❑ The slope of the SML, $(k_M - k_{RF})$, shows the increase in the required rate of return for a one unit increase in risk. It reflects the degree of risk aversion in the economy.

■ The risk-free (also known as the nominal, or quoted) rate of interest consists of two elements: (1) a real inflation-free rate of return, k^*, and (2) an inflation premium, IP, equal to the anticipated rate of inflation.

❑ The real rate on long-term Treasury bonds has historically ranged from 2 to 4 percent, with a mean of about 3 percent.

❑ As the expected rate of inflation increases, a higher premium must be added to the real risk-free rate to compensate for the loss of purchasing power that results from inflation.

■ As risk aversion increases, so do the risk premium and, thus, the slope of the SML. The greater the average investor's aversion to risk, then (1) the steeper the slope of the line, (2) the greater the risk premium for all stocks, and (3) the higher the required rate of return on all stocks.

■ Many factors can affect a company's beta. When such changes occur, the required rate of return also changes.
- ❑ A firm can influence its market risk, hence its beta, through changes in the composition of its assets and also through its use of debt.
- ❑ A company's beta can also change as a result of external factors such as increased competition in its industry, the expiration of basic patents, and the like.

For a management whose primary goal is stock price maximization, the overriding consideration is the riskiness of the firm's stock, and the relevant risk of any physical asset must be measured in terms of its effect on the stock's risk as seen by investors.

A number of recent studies have raised concerns about the validity of the CAPM.

■ A recent study by Fama and French found no historical relationship between stocks' returns and their market betas.
- ❑ They found two variables which are consistently related to stock returns: (1) a firm's size and (2) its market/book ratio.
- ❑ After adjusting for other factors, they found that smaller firms have provided relatively high returns, and that returns are higher on stocks with low market/book ratios. By contrast, after controlling for firm size and market/book ratios, they found no relationship between a stock's beta and its return.

■ As an alternative to the traditional CAPM, researchers and practitioners have begun to look to more general multi-beta models that encompass the CAPM and address its shortcomings.
- ❑ In the multi-beta model, market risk is measured relative to a set of factors that determine the behavior of asset returns, whereas the CAPM gauges risk only relative to the market return.
- ❑ The risk factors in the multi-beta model are all nondiversifiable sources of risk.

Earnings volatility does not necessarily imply investment risk. You have to think about the causes of the volatility before reaching any conclusions as to whether earnings volatility indicates risk. However, stock price volatility does signify risk (except for stocks that are negatively correlated with the market, which are few and far between, if they exist at all).

SELF-TEST QUESTIONS

Definitional

1. Investment risk is associated with the _____ of low or negative returns; the greater the chance of loss, the riskier the investment.

2.   A listing of all possible _____, with a probability assigned to each, is known as a probability _____.

3.   Weighting each possible outcome of a distribution by its _____ of occurrence and summing the results give the expected _____ of the distribution.

4.   One measure of the tightness of a probability distribution is the _____ _____, a probability-weighted average deviation from the expected value.

5.   Investors who prefer outcomes with a high degree of certainty to those that are less certain are described as being _____ _____.

6.   Owning a portfolio of securities enables investors to benefit from _____.

7.   Diversification of a portfolio can result in lower _____ for the same level of return.

8.   Diversification of a portfolio is achieved by selecting securities that are not perfectly _____ correlated with each other.

9.   That part of a stock's risk that can be eliminated is known as _____ risk, while the portion that cannot be eliminated is called _____ risk.

10.   The _____ coefficient measures a stock's relative volatility as compared with a stock market index.

11.   A stock that is twice as volatile as the market would have a beta coefficient of _____, while a stock with a beta of 0.5 would be only _____ as volatile as the market.

12.   The beta coefficient of a portfolio is the _____ _____ of the betas of the individual stocks.

13.   The minimum expected return that will induce investors to buy a particular security is the _____ rate of return.

14.   The security used to measure the _____-_____ rate is the return available on U. S. Treasury securities.

15.   The risk premium for a particular stock may be calculated by multiplying the market risk premium times the stock's _____ _____.

16.   A stock's required rate of return is equal to the _____-_____ rate plus the stock's _____ _____.

17.   The risk-free rate on a short-term Treasury security is made up of two parts: the _____ _____-_____ rate plus a(n) _____ premium.

18.   Changes in investors' risk aversion alter the _____ of the Security Market Line.

19.   The concept of _____ provides investors with a convenient way of expressing the financial performance of an investment.

20.   An event's _____ is defined as the chance that the event will occur.

21.   Investment returns can be expressed in _____ terms or as _____ ____ _____, or percentage returns.

22.   The _____ ____ _____ shows the risk per unit of return, and it provides a more meaningful basis for comparison when the expected returns on two alternatives are not the same.

Conceptual

23.   The Y-axis intercept of the Security Market Line (SML) indicates the required rate of return on an individual stock with a beta of 1.0.

       a. True   **b.** False

24.   If a stock has a beta of zero, it will be riskless when held in isolation.

       a. True   **b.** False

25.   A group of 200 stocks each has a beta of 1.0. We can be certain that each of the stocks was positively correlated with the market.

       a. True   **b.** False

26.   Refer to Self-Test Question 25. If we combined these same 200 stocks into a portfolio, market risk would be reduced below the average market risk of the stocks in the portfolio.

       a. True   **b.** False

27.   Refer to Self-Test Question 26. The standard deviation of the portfolio of these 200 stocks would be lower than the standard deviations of the individual stocks.

       a. True   **b.** False

28.   Suppose k_{RF} = 7% and k_M = 12%. If investors became more risk averse, k_M would be likely to decrease.

    a. True   **b.** False

29.   Refer to Self-Test Question 28. The required rate of return for a stock with b = 0.5 would increase more than for a stock with b = 2.0.

    a. True   **b.** False

30.   Refer to Self-Test Questions 28 and 29. If the expected rate of inflation increased, the required rate of return on a b = 2.0 stock would rise by more than that of a b = 0.5 stock.

    a. True   **b.** False

31.   Which is the best measure of risk for an asset held in a well-diversified portfolio?

    a. Variance   **d.** Semi-variance
    b. Standard deviation   **e.** Expected value
    c. Beta

32.   In a portfolio of three different stocks, which of the following could *not* be true?

    a. The riskiness of the portfolio is less than the riskiness of each stock held in isolation.
    b. The riskiness of the portfolio is greater than the riskiness of one or two of the stocks.
    c. The beta of the portfolio is less than the beta of each of the individual stocks.
    d. The beta of the portfolio is greater than the beta of one or two of the individual stocks.
    e. The beta of the portfolio is equal to the beta of one of the individual stocks.

33.   If investors expected inflation to increase in the future, and they also became more risk averse, what could be said about the change in the Security Market Line (SML)?

    a. The SML would shift up and the slope would increase.
    b. The SML would shift up and the slope would decrease.
    c. The SML would shift down and the slope would increase.
    d. The SML would shift down and the slope would decrease.
    e. The SML would remain unchanged.

34.   Which of the following statements is most correct?

    a. The SML relates required returns to firms' market risk. The slope and intercept of this line *cannot* be controlled by the financial manager.

b. The slope of the SML is determined by the value of beta.

c. If you plotted the returns of a given stock against those of the market, and if you found that the slope of the regression line was negative, then the CAPM would indicate that the required rate of return on the stock should be less than the risk-free rate for a well-diversified investor, assuming that the observed relationship is expected to continue on into the future.

d. If investors become less risk averse, the slope of the Security Market Line will increase.

e. Statements a and c are both true.

35. Which of the following statements is most correct?

a. Normally, the Security Market Line has an upward slope. However, at one of those unusual times when the yield curve on bonds is downward sloping, the SML will also have a downward slope.

b. The market risk premium, as it is used in the CAPM theory, is equal to the required rate of return on an average stock minus the required rate of return on an average company's bonds.

c. If the marginal investor's aversion to risk decreases, then the slope of the yield curve would, other things held constant, tend to increase. If expectations for inflation also increased at the same time risk aversion was decreasing—say the expected inflation rate rose from 5 percent to 8 percent—the net effect could possibly result in a parallel upward shift in the SML.

d. According to the text, it is theoretically possible to combine two stocks, each of which would be quite risky if held as your only asset, and to form a 2-stock portfolio that is riskless. However, the stocks would have to have a correlation coefficient of expected future returns of -1.0, and it is hard to find such stocks in the real world.

e. Each of the above statements is false.

36. Which of the following statements is most correct?

a. The expected future rate of return, $\hat{k}$, is always *above* the past realized rate of return, $\overline{k}$, except for highly risk-averse investors.

b. The expected future rate of return, $\hat{k}$, is always *below* the past realized rate of return, $\overline{k}$, except for highly risk-averse investors.

c. The expected future rate of return, $\hat{k}$, is always *below* the required rate of return, k, except for highly risk-averse investors.

d. There is no logical reason to think that any relationship exists between the expected future rate of return, $\hat{k}$, on a security and the security's required rate of return, k.

e. Each of the above statements is false.

37. Which of the following statements is most correct?

   a. Someone who is highly averse to risk should invest in stocks with high betas (above +1.0), other things held constant.

   b. The returns on a stock might be highly uncertain in the sense that they could actually turn out to be much higher or much lower than the expected rate of return (that is, the stock has a high standard deviation of returns), yet the stock might still be regarded by most investors as being less risky than some other stock whose returns are less variable.

   c. The standard deviation is a better measure of risk when comparing securities than the coefficient of variation. This is true because the standard deviation "standardizes" risk by dividing each security's variance by its expected rate of return.

   d. Market risk can be reduced by holding a large portfolio of stocks, and if a portfolio consists of all traded stocks, market risk will be completely eliminated.

   e. The market risk in a portfolio declines as more stocks are added to the portfolio, and the risk decline is linear, that is, each additional stock reduces the portfolio's risk by the same amount.

SELF-TEST PROBLEMS

1. Stock A has the following probability distribution of expected returns:

Probability	Rate of Return
0.1	-15%
0.2	0
0.4	5
0.2	10
0.1	25

What is Stock A's expected rate of return and standard deviation?

   a. 8.0%; 9.5%   **d.** 5.0%; 6.5%
   b. 8.0%; 6.5%   **e.** 5.0%; 9.5%
   c. 5.0%; 3.5%

2. If $k_{RF} = 5\%$, $k_M = 11\%$, and $b = 1.3$ for Stock X, what is k_X, the required rate of return for Stock X?

   a. 18.7%   **b.** 16.7%   **c.** 14.8%   **d.** 12.8%   **e.** 11.9%

3. Refer to Self-Test Problem 2. What would k_X be if investors expected the inflation rate to increase by 2 percentage points?

    a. 18.7%   **b.** 16.7%   **c.** 14.8%   **d.** 12.8%   **e.** 11.9%

4. Refer to Self-Test Problem 2. What would k_X be if an increase in investors' risk aversion caused the market risk premium to increase by 3 percentage points? k_{RF} remains at 5 percent.

    a. 18.7%   **b.** 16.7%   **c.** 14.8%   **d.** 12.8%   **e.** 11.9%

5. Refer to Self-Test Problem 2. What would k_X be if investors expected the inflation rate to increase by 2 percentage points *and* their risk aversion increased by 3 percentage points?

    a. 18.7%   **b.** 16.7%   **c.** 14.8%   **d.** 12.8%   **e.** 11.9%

6. Jan Middleton owns a 3-stock portfolio with a total investment value equal to $300,000.

Stock	Investment	Beta
A	$100,000	0.5
B	100,000	1.0
C	100,000	1.5
Total	$300,000	

    What is the weighted average beta of Jan's 3-stock portfolio?

    a. 0.9   **b.** 1.3   **c.** 1.0   **d.** 0.4   **e.** 1.2

7. The Apple Investment Fund has a total investment of $450 million in five stocks.

Stock	Investment (Millions)	Beta
1	$130	0.4
2	110	1.5
3	70	3.0
4	90	2.0
5	50	1.0
Total	$450	

    What is the fund's overall, or weighted average, beta?

    a. 1.14   **b.** 1.22   **c.** 1.35   **d.** 1.46   **e.** 1.53

8. Refer to Self-Test Problem 7. If the risk-free rate is 12 percent and the market risk premium is 6 percent, what is the required rate of return on the Apple Fund?

    a. 20.76%   **b.** 19.92%   **c.** 18.81%   **d.** 17.62%   **e.** 15.77%

9. Stock A has a beta of 1.2, Stock B has a beta of 0.6, the expected rate of return on an average stock is 12 percent, and the risk-free rate of return is 7 percent. By how much does the required return on the riskier stock exceed the required return on the less risky stock?

    a. 4.00%   **b.** 3.25%   **c.** 3.00%   **d.** 2.50%   **e.** 3.75%

10. You are managing a portfolio of 10 stocks which are held in equal dollar amounts. The current beta of the portfolio is 1.8, and the beta of Stock A is 2.0. If Stock A is sold and the proceeds are used to purchase a replacement stock, what does the beta of the replacement stock have to be to lower the portfolio beta to 1.7?

    a. 1.4   **b.** 1.3   **c.** 1.2   **d.** 1.1   **e.** 1.0

11. Consider the following information for the Alachua Retirement Fund, with a total investment of $4 million.

Stock	Investment	Beta
A	$ 400,000	1.2
B	600,000	-0.4
C	1,000,000	1.5
D	2,000,000	0.8
Total	$4,000,000	

The market required rate of return is 12 percent, and the risk-free rate is 6 percent. What is its required rate of return?

    a. 9.98%   **b.** 10.45%   **c.** 11.01%   **d.** 11.50%   **e.** 12.56%

12. You are given the following distribution of returns:

Probability	Return
0.4	$30
0.5	25
0.1	-20

What is the coefficient of variation of the expected dollar returns?

    a. 206.2500   **b.** 0.6383   **c.** 14.3614   **d.** 0.7500   **e.** 1.2500

13. If the risk-free rate is 8 percent, the expected return on the market is 13 percent, and the expected return on Security J is 15 percent, then what is the beta of Security J?

    a. 1.40   **b.** 0.90   **c.** 1.20   **d.** 1.50   **e.** 0.75

ANSWERS TO SELF-TEST QUESTIONS

1.	probability	**12.**	weighted average
2.	outcomes; distribution	**13.**	required
3.	probability; return	**14.**	risk-free
4.	standard deviation	**15.**	beta coefficient
5.	risk averse	**16.**	risk-free; risk premium
6.	diversification	**17.**	real risk-free; inflation
7.	risk	**18.**	slope
8.	positively	**19.**	return
9.	diversifiable; market	**20.**	probability
10.	beta	**21.**	dollar; rates of return
11.	2.0; half	**22.**	coefficient of variation

23. b. The Y-axis intercept of the SML is k_{RF}, which is the required rate of return on a security with a beta of zero.

24. b. A zero beta stock could be made riskless if it were combined with enough other zero beta stocks, but it would still have company-specific risk and be risky when held in isolation.

25. a. By definition, if a stock has a beta of 1.0 it moves exactly with the market. In other words, if the market moves up by 7 percent, the stock will also move up by 7 percent, while if the market falls by 7 percent, the stock will fall by 7 percent.

26. b. Market risk is measured by the beta coefficient. The beta for the portfolio would be a weighted average of the betas of the stocks, so b_p would also be 1.0. Thus, the market risk for the portfolio would be the same as the market risk of the stocks in the portfolio.

27. a. Note that with a 200-stock portfolio, the actual returns would all be on or close to the regression line. However, when the portfolio (and the market) returns are quite high, some individual stocks would have higher returns than the portfolio, and some would have much lower returns. Thus, the range of returns, and the standard deviation, would be higher for the individual stocks.

28. b. RP_M, which is equal to $k_M - k_{RF}$, would rise, leading to an increase in k_M.

29. b. The required rate of return for a stock with $b = 0.5$ would increase less than the return on a stock with $b = 2.0$.

30. b. If the expected rate of inflation increased, the SML would shift parallel due to an increase in k_{RF}. Thus, the effect on the required rates of return for both the $b = 0.5$ and $b = 2.0$ stocks would be the same.

31. c. The best measure of risk is the beta coefficient, which is a measure of the extent to which the returns on a given stock move with the stock market.

32. c. The beta of the portfolio is a weighted average of the individual securities' betas, so it could not be less than the betas of all of the stocks. (See Self-Test Problem 6.)

33. a. The increase in inflation would cause the SML to shift up, and investors becoming more risk averse would cause the slope to increase. (This can be demonstrated by graphing the SML lines on the same graph in Self-Test Problems 2 through 5.)

34. e. Statement b is false because the slope of the SML is $k_M - k_{RF}$. Statement d is false because as investors become less risk averse the slope of the SML decreases. Statement a is correct because the financial manager has no control over k_M or k_{RF}. ($k_M - k_{RF}$ = slope and k_{RF} = intercept of the SML.) Statement c is correct because the slope of the regression line is beta and beta would be negative; thus, the required return would be less than the risk-free rate.

35. d. Statement a is false. The yield curve determines the value of k_{RF}; however, SML = $k_{RF} + (k_M - k_{RF})b$. The average return on the market will always be greater than the risk-free rate; thus, the SML will always be upward sloping. Statement b is false because RP_M is equal to $k_M - k_{RF}$. k_{RF} is equal to the risk-free rate, not the rate on an average company's bonds. Statement c is false. A decrease in an investor's aversion to risk would indicate a downward sloping yield curve. A decrease in risk aversion and an increase in inflation would cause the SML slope to decrease and to shift upward simultaneously.

36. e. All the statements are false. For equilibrium to exist, the expected return must equal the required return.

37. b. Statement b is correct because the stock with the higher standard deviation might not be highly correlated with most other stocks, hence have a relatively low beta, and thus not be very risky if held in a well-diversified portfolio. The other statements are simply false.

SOLUTIONS TO SELF-TEST PROBLEMS

1. e. $\hat{k}_A = 0.1(-15\%) + 0.2(0\%) + 0.4(5\%) + 0.2(10\%) + 0.1(25) = 5.0\%$.

    $$\begin{aligned} \text{Variance} = {} & 0.1(-0.15 - 0.05)^2 + 0.2(0.0 - 0.05)^2 + 0.4(0.05 - 0.05)^2 \\ & + 0.2(0.10 - 0.05)^2 + 0.1(0.25 - 0.05)^2 \\ = {} & 0.009. \end{aligned}$$

    Standard deviation = $\sqrt{0.009}$ = 0.0949 = 9.5%.

2. d. $k_X = k_{RF} + (k_M - k_{RF})b_X = 5\% + (11\% - 5\%)1.3 = 12.8\%$.

3. c. $k_X = k_{RF} + (k_M - k_{RF})b_X = 7\% + (13\% - 7\%)1.3 = 14.8\%$.

    A change in the inflation premium does *not* change the market risk premium $(k_M - k_{RF})$ since both k_M and k_{RF} are affected.

4. b. $k_X = k_{RF} + (k_M - k_{RF})b_X = 5\% + (14\% - 5\%)1.3 = 16.7\%$.

5. a. $k_X = k_{RF} + (k_M - k_{RF})b_X = 7\% + (16\% - 7\%)1.3 = 18.7\%$.

6. c. The calculation of the portfolio's beta is as follows:

    $b_p = (1/3)(0.5) + (1/3)(1.0) + (1/3)(1.5) = 1.0$.

7. d. $b_p = \sum_{i=1}^{5} w_i \, b_i$

    $= \dfrac{\$130}{\$450}(0.4) + \dfrac{\$110}{\$450}(1.5) + \dfrac{\$70}{\$450}(3.0) + \dfrac{\$90}{\$450}(2.0) + \dfrac{\$50}{\$450}(1.0) = 1.46$.

8. a. $k_p = k_{RF} + (k_M - k_{RF})b_p = 12\% + (6\%)1.46 = 20.76\%$.

9. c. We know $b_A = 1.20$, $b_B = 0.60$; $k_M = 12\%$, and $k_{RF} = 7\%$.

$k_i = k_{RF} + (k_M - k_{RF})b_i = 7\% + (12\% - 7\%)b_i$.

$k_A = 7\% + 5\%(1.20) = 13.0\%$.

$k_B = 7\% + 5\%(0.60) = 10.0\%$.

$k_A - k_B = 13\% - 10\% = 3\%$.

10. e. First find the beta of the remaining 9 stocks:

$1.8 = 0.9(b_R) + 0.1(b_A)$
$1.8 = 0.9(b_R) + 0.1(2.0)$
$1.8 = 0.9(b_R) + 0.2$
$1.6 = 0.9(b_R)$
$b_R = 1.78$.

Now find the beta of the new stock that produces $b_p = 1.7$.

$1.7 = 0.9(1.78) + 0.1(b_N)$
$1.7 = 1.6 + 0.1(b_N)$
$0.1 = 0.1(b_N)$
$b_N = 1.0$.

11. c. Determine the weight each stock represents in the portfolio:

Stock	Investment	w_i	Beta	w_i x Beta
A	400,000	0.10	1.2	0.1200
B	600,000	0.15	-0.4	-0.0600
C	1,000,000	0.25	1.5	0.3750
D	2,000,000	0.50	0.8	0.4000

$b_p = 0.8350$ = Portfolio beta

Write out the SML equation, and substitute known values including the portfolio beta. Solve for the required portfolio return.

$k_p = k_{RF} + (k_M - k_{RF})b_p = 6\% + (12\% - 6\%)0.8350$
$\quad = 6\% + 5.01\% = 11.01\%$.

12.   b.   Use the given probability distribution of returns to calculate the expected value, variance, standard deviation, and coefficient of variation.

P_i	k_i	$P_i k_i$	k_i	$\hat{k}$		$(k_i - \hat{k})$	$(k_i - \hat{k})^2$	$P(k_i - \hat{k})^2$
0.4	x $30	= $12.0	$30	- $22.5	=	$ 7.5	$ 56.25	$ 22.500
0.5	x 25	= 12.5	25	- 22.5	=	2.5	6.25	3.125
0.1	x -20	= -2.0	-20	- 22.5	=	-42.5	1,806.25	180.625
	$\hat{k}$	= $22.5					σ^2 = Variance =	$206.250

The standard deviation (σ) of $\hat{k}$ is $\sqrt{\$206.25} = \$14.3614$.

Use the standard deviation and the expected return to calculate the coefficient of variation: $\$14.3614/\$22.5 = 0.6383$.

13.   a.   Use the SML equation, substitute in the known values, and solve for beta.

$k_{RF} = 8\%$; $k_M = 13\%$; $k_J = 15\%$.

$$k_J = k_{RF} + (k_M - k_{RF})b_J$$
$$15\% = 8\% + (13\% - 8\%)b_J$$
$$7\% = (5\%)b_J$$
$$b_J = 1.4.$$

CHAPTER 7
RISK AND RETURN: PORTFOLIO THEORY AND ASSET PRICING MODELS

OVERVIEW

In Chapter 6 we presented the key elements of risk and return analysis. There we saw that much of the risk inherent in a stock can be eliminated by diversification, so rational investors should hold portfolios of stocks rather than just one stock. We also introduced the Capital Asset Pricing Model (CAPM), which links risk and required rates of return, using a stock's beta coefficient as the relevant measure of risk.

In this chapter, we extend the Chapter 6 material by presenting an in-depth treatment of portfolio concepts and the CAPM. We continue the discussion of risk and return by adding a risk-free asset to the set of investment opportunities. This leads all investors to hold the same well-diversified portfolio of risky assets, and then to account for differing degrees of risk aversion by combining the risky portfolio in different proportions with the risk-free asset. Additionally, we show how betas are actually calculated, and we discuss two alternative views of the risk/return relationship, the Arbitrage Pricing Theory (APT) and the Fama-French 3-Factor Model.

OUTLINE

The riskiness of a portfolio, because it is assumed to be a single asset held in isolation, is measured by the standard deviation of its return distribution. This equation is exactly the same as the one for the standard deviation of a single asset, except that here the asset is a portfolio of assets (for example, a mutual fund).

Portfolio standard deviation $= \sigma_p = \sqrt{\sum_{i=1}^{n} \left(k_{pi} - \hat{k}_p \right)^2 P_i}$.

Two key concepts in portfolio analysis are covariance and the correlation coefficient.

■ *Covariance* is a measure of the general movement relationship between two variables. It combines the variance or volatility of a stock's returns with the tendency of those returns to move up or down at the same time other stocks move up or down. The following equation defines the covariance (Cov) between Stocks A and B:

$$\text{Covariance} = \text{Cov (AB)} = \sum_{i=1}^{n} (k_{Ai} - \hat{k}_A)(k_{Bi} - \hat{k}_B)P_i.$$

❑ If the returns move together, the terms in parentheses will both be positive or both be negative, hence the product of the two terms will be positive, while if the returns move counter to one another, the products will tend to be negative.

❑ Cov(AB) will be large and positive if two assets have large standard deviations and tend to move together; it will be large and negative for two high σ assets which move counter to one another; and it will be small if the two assets' returns move randomly, rather than up or down with one another, or if either of the assets has a small standard deviation.

■ The *correlation coefficient* also measures the degree of comovement between two variables, but its values are limited to the range from -1.0 (perfect negative correlation) to +1.0 (perfect positive correlation).   The relationship between covariance and the correlation coefficient can be expressed as

$$\text{Correlation coefficient(AB)} \ = \ r_{AB} \ = \ \frac{\text{Cov(AB)}}{\sigma_A \sigma_B}.$$

❑ The correlation coefficient standardizes the covariance.

❑ The sign of the correlation coefficient is the same as the sign of the covariance, so a positive sign means that the variables move together, a negative sign indicates that they move in opposite directions, and if r is close to zero, they move independently of one another.

■ Under the assumption that the distributions of returns on the individual securities are normal, the following equation can be used to determine the riskiness of a two-asset portfolio:

$$\text{Portfolio SD} = \sigma_p = \sqrt{w_A^2 \sigma_A^2 + (1 - w_A)^2 \sigma_B^2 + 2w_A(1 - w_A)r_{AB}\sigma_A \sigma_B}.$$

❑ Here w_A is the fraction of the portfolio invested in Security A, so $(1 - w_A)$ is the fraction invested in Security B.

One important use of portfolio risk concepts is to select efficient portfolios. An efficient portfolio provides the highest expected return for any degree of risk, or the lowest degree of risk for any expected return.

■ While the riskiness of a multi-asset portfolio usually decreases as the number of stocks increase, the portfolio's risk depends on the degree of correlation among the stocks.

■ In general, the average correlation between two stocks is +0.5 to +0.7, and hence holding stocks in portfolios will reduce, but not eliminate, risk.

■ The *attainable*, or *feasible, set of portfolios* represents all portfolios that can be constructed from a given set of stocks.

The optimal portfolio is found by determining the efficient set of portfolios and then choosing from the efficient set the single portfolio that is best for the individual investor.

■ The efficient set of portfolios is also called the *efficient frontier*.
  ❑ Portfolios to the left of the efficient set are not possible because they lie outside the attainable set.
  ❑ Portfolios to the right of the boundary line (interior portfolios) are inefficient because some other portfolio would provide either a higher return with the same degree of risk or lower risk for the same rate of return.

■ An *indifference curve* (or risk/return trade-off function) reflects an individual investor's attitude towards risk. The optimal portfolio for each investor is found at the tangency point between the efficient set of portfolios and one of the investor's indifference curves. This tangency point marks the highest level of satisfaction the investor can attain.

The Capital Asset Pricing Model (CAPM) specifies the relationship between risk and required rates of return on assets when they are held in well-diversified portfolios.

■ As in all financial theories, a number of assumptions were made in the development of the CAPM. These assumptions are:
  ❑ All investors focus on a single holding period, and seek to maximize the expected utility of their terminal wealth.
  ❑ All investors can borrow or lend an unlimited amount at a given risk-free rate of interest.
  ❑ Investors have homogeneous expectations.
  ❑ All assets are perfectly divisible and perfectly liquid.
  ❑ There are no transactions costs.
  ❑ There are no taxes.
  ❑ All investors are price takers.
  ❑ The quantities of all assets are given and fixed.

■ Theoretical extensions in finance literature have relaxed some of the assumptions, and in general these extensions have led to conclusions that are reasonably consistent with the basic theory. However, even the extensions contain assumptions which are both strong and unrealistic, so the validity of the model can only be established through empirical tests.

The Capital Market Line (CML) specifies a linear relationship between expected return and risk for efficient portfolios.

■ The equation of the CML may be expressed as follows:

$$\hat{k}_p = k_{RF} + \left(\frac{\hat{k}_M - k_{RF}}{\sigma_M} \right) \sigma_p.$$

■ Here $\hat{k}_p$ is the expected (and in equilibrium, required) rate of return on an efficient portfolio, k_{RF} is the rate of interest on risk-free securities, $\hat{k}_M$ is the return on the market portfolio, σ_M is the standard deviation of the market portfolio, and σ_p is the standard deviation of the efficient portfolio in question.

■ In words, the expected rate of return on any efficient portfolio (that is, any portfolio on the CML) is equal to the riskless rate plus a risk premium, and the risk premium is equal to $(\hat{k}_M - k_{RF}) / \sigma_M$ multiplied by the portfolio's standard deviation, σ_p.

■ The slope of the CML reflects the aggregate attitude of investors toward risk.

■ An *efficient portfolio* is one that is well diversified, hence all of its unsystematic risk has been eliminated and its only remaining risk is market risk. Therefore, unlike individual stocks, the riskiness of an efficient portfolio is measured by its standard deviation, σ_p.

The relevant measure of risk for use in the Security Market Line (SML) equation is the stock's beta coefficient, which measures the volatility of a stock relative to that of a portfolio containing all stocks.

■ *Beta* is estimated by plotting historical returns on a particular stock versus returns on a market index. The slope of the regression line, or *characteristic line*, is the stock's beta coefficient. The statistical equation for beta is:

$$b_j = \frac{Cov(\overline{k}_j, \overline{k}_M)}{\sigma_M^2} = \frac{r_{jM}\sigma_j\sigma_M}{\sigma_M^2} = r_{jM}\left(\frac{\sigma_j}{\sigma_M} \right),$$

where,

b_j = the slope, or beta coefficient, for Stock j.

$\overline{k}_j$ = the historical (realized) rate of return on Stock j.

$\overline{k}_M$ = the historical (realized) rate of return on the market.

r_{jM} = the correlation between Stock j and the market.

σ_j = the standard deviation of Stock j.

σ_M = the standard deviation of the market.

- ❑ A stock's beta, hence its market risk, depends on its correlation with the stock market as a whole, r_{jM}, and its own variability, σ_j, relative to the variability of the market, σ_M.
- ❑ We assume that the historical relationship between Stock j and the market as a whole, as given by its characteristic line, will continue into the future.
- ❑ Besides general market movements, each firm also faces events that are unique to it and independent of the general economic climate. This component of total risk is the stock's *diversifiable*, or *company-specific, risk*, and rational investors will eliminate its effects by holding diversified portfolios of stocks.
- ❑ An individual stock tends to move with the market as economic conditions change. This component of total risk is the stock's *market*, or *non-diversifiable, risk*. Even well-diversified portfolios contain some market risk.
- ❑ Total risk (variance) equals market risk plus diversifiable risk.

$$\begin{array}{c} \text{Total} \\ \text{risk} \end{array} = \begin{array}{c} \text{Market} \\ \text{risk} \end{array} + \begin{array}{c} \text{Diversifiable} \\ \text{risk} \end{array}$$

$$\sigma_j^2 = b_j^2 \sigma_M^2 + \sigma_{e_j}^2 .$$

- ❑ If all the points plotted on the characteristic line, then all of the stock's total risk would be market risk. On the other hand, if the points are widely scattered about the regression line, much of the stock's total risk would be diversifiable.
- ❑ If the stock market never fluctuated, then stocks would have no market risk.
- ❑ Beta is the measure of relative market risk, but the stock's actual risk depends on both its beta (market risk), and on the volatility of the market.
- ❑ The diversifiable risk can and should be eliminated by diversification, so the *relevant risk* is market risk, not total risk.
- ❑ A stock's risk premium, $(k_M - k_{RF})b_j$, depends only on its market risk, not its total risk.

Since the CAPM depends on some unrealistic assumptions, it must be tested empirically to determine if it gives accurate estimates of k_i.

- ■ Betas are generally calculated for some past period, and the assumption is made that the relative volatility of a stock will remain constant in the future. However, conditions may change and alter a stock's future volatility, which is the item of real concern to investors.

■   The CAPM should use expected (future) data, yet only historical data are generally available.

■   Studies indicate that the CAPM is a better concept for structuring investment portfolios than it is for purposes of estimating the cost of capital for individual securities.

■   Studies of the CAPM based on the slope of the SML generally have shown a significant positive relationship between realized returns and systematic risk and that the relationship between risk and return appears to be linear.

■   According to the CAPM, high-beta stocks should provide higher returns than low-beta stocks. However, the Fama-French study revealed no relationship between historical betas and historical returns—low-beta stocks provided about the same returns as high-beta stocks.

The CAPM is extremely appealing at an intellectual level.

■   The CAPM framework is clearly a useful way to think about the riskiness of assets. Thus, as a conceptual model, the CAPM is of truly fundamental importance.

■   Estimates of k_i found through the use of the CAPM are subject to potentially large errors, because we do not know precisely how to measure any of the inputs required to implement the CAPM.

■   Because the CAPM is logical in the sense that it represents the way risk-averse people ought to behave, the model is a useful conceptual tool.

■   It is appropriate to think about many financial problems in a CAPM framework. However, it is equally important to recognize the limitations of the CAPM when using it in practice.

The CAPM assumes that required rates of return depend on only one risk factor, the stock's beta coefficient, but required returns may be a function of several risk factors. An approach called the Arbitrage Pricing Theory (APT) can include any number of risk factors.

$$\bar{k}_i = \hat{k}_i + \left(\bar{F}_1 - \hat{F}_1\right)b_{i1} + \cdots + \left(\bar{F}_j - \hat{F}_j\right)b_{ij} + e_i,$$

where,

        $\bar{k}_i$ = the realized rate of return on Stock i.

        $\hat{k}_i$ = the expected rate of return on Stock i.

$\overline{\mathbf{F}}_j$ = the realized value of economic Factor j.

$\hat{\mathbf{F}}_j$ = the expected value of Factor j.

$\mathbf{b}_{ij}$ = the sensitivity of Stock i to economic Factor j.

$\mathbf{e}_i$ = the effect of unique events on the realized return of Stock i.

■ This equation shows that the realized return on any stock is equal to the stock's expected return, increases or decreases which depend on unexpected changes in fundamental economic factors times the sensitivity of the stock to these changes, and a random term which reflects changes unique to the firm or industry.

■ Theoretically, one could construct a portfolio such that (1) the portfolio was riskless and (2) the net investment in it was zero. Such a zero investment portfolio must have a zero expected return, or else arbitrage operations would occur that would cause the prices of the underlying assets to change until the portfolio's expected return was zero.

■ The end result is APT:

$$k_i = k_{RF} + \left(k_1 - k_{RF}\right)b_{i1} + \cdots + \left(k_j - k_{RF}\right)b_{ij},$$

where kj is the required rate of return on a portfolio that is sensitive only to the jth economic factor ($b_j = 1.0$) and has zero sensitivity to all other factors.

■ The primary theoretical advantage of the APT is that it permits several economic factors to influence individual stock returns, whereas the CAPM assumes that the impact of all factors, except those unique to the firm, can be captured in a single measure, the volatility of the stock with respect to the market portfolio.
   ❑ The APT also requires fewer assumptions than the CAPM and hence is a more general theory.
   ❑ The APT does not assume that all investors hold the market portfolio, a CAPM requirement that clearly is not met in practice.

■ However, the APT does not identify the relevant factors, nor does it even tell us how many factors should appear in the model. The APT is in an early stage of development, and there are still many unanswered questions.

The Fama-French 3-Factor Model is a multi-factor model, like the APT, except it specifies three specific factors: (1) a market factor, like CAPM; (2) a size factor, based on the difference in returns between a portfolio with Small sized firms and a portfolio with Big sized firms (SMB); and (3) a factor base on the difference in returns between a portfolio with High ratios of Book value/Market value of equity (B/M ratios) and a portfolio with Low B/M ratios. The model is shown below:

$$\left(\bar{k}_i - \bar{k}_{RF} \right) = a_i + b_i \left(\bar{k}_M - \bar{k}_{RF} \right) + c_i \left(\bar{k}_{SMB} \right) + d_i \left(\bar{k}_{HML} \right) + e_i \ ,$$

where

$\bar{k}_i$ = historical (realized) rate of return on Stock i.

$\bar{k}_{RF}$ = historical (realized) rate of return on the risk free rate.

$\bar{k}_M$ = historical (realized) rate of return on the market.

$\bar{k}_{SMB}$ = historical (realized) rate of return on the small size portfolio minus the big size portfolio.

$\bar{k}_{HML}$ = historical (realized) rate of return on the high B/M portfolio minus the low B/M portfolio.

a_i = vertical axis intercept term for Stock i.

b_i, c_i and d_i = slope coefficients for Stock i.

e_i = random error, reflecting the difference between the actual return on Stock i in a given period and the return as predicted by the regression line.

■   Using the Fama-French 3-factor model, the expected return is:

$$k_i = k_{RF} + a_i + b_i \left(k_M - \bar{k}_{RF} \right) + c_i \left(k_{SMB} \right) + d_i \left(k_{HML} \right) \ ,$$

where k_{SMB} and k_{HML} are the expected returns on the Small Minus Big and High Minus Low portfolios.

SELF-TEST QUESTIONS

Definitional

1. _____ is a measure of the general movement relationship between two variables, while the _____ _____ also measures the degree of comovement between two stocks but its values are limited from -1.0 to +1.0.

2. A(n) _____ _____ is that portfolio which provides the highest expected return for any given degree of risk, or the lowest degree of risk for any expected return.

3. The _____, or _____, set of portfolios represents all portfolios that can be constructed from a given set of stocks.

4. The _____ _____ is found by determining the efficient set of portfolios and then choosing from the efficient set the single portfolio that is best for the individual investor.

5. The efficient set of portfolios is also called the _____ _____.

6. A(n) _____ _____ (or risk/return trade-off function) reflects an individual investor's attitude towards risk.

7. The _____ _____ _____ _____ specifies the relationship between risk and required rates of return on assets when they are held in well-diversified portfolios.

8. The _____ _____ _____ specifies a linear relationship between expected return and risk for efficient portfolios.

9. The relevant measure of risk for use in the Security Market Line (SML) equation is the stock's _____ _____, which measures the volatility of a stock relative to that of a portfolio containing all stocks.

10. Beta is estimated by plotting historical returns on a particular stock versus returns on a market index. The slope of the regression line, or _____ _____, is the stock's beta coefficient.

11. Besides general market movements, each firm also faces events that are unique to it and independent of the general economic climate. This component of total risk is the stock's _____, or _____-_____, risk, and rational investors will eliminate its effects by holding diversified portfolios of stocks.

12.   The relevant risk is _____ risk, not total risk.

13.   Studies indicate that the CAPM is a better concept for structuring _____ _____ than it is for purposes of estimating the cost of capital for individual _____.

14.   The _____ _____ _____ uses several risk factors for determining the required return on a stock.

15.   The most commonly used continuous distribution is the _____ _____, which is symmetric about the expected value and its tails extend out to plus and minus infinity.

16.   The _____ _____ standardizes the covariance.

17.   The sign of the correlation coefficient is the _____ as the sign of the covariance. A(n) _____ sign means that the variables move together, a(n) _____ sign indicates that they move in opposite directions, and if r is close to zero, they move _____ of one another.

18.   Portfolios to the _____ of the efficient set are not possible because they lie outside the attainable set, while portfolios to the _____ of the boundary line are inefficient because some other portfolio would provide either a higher return with the same degree of risk or lower risk for the same rate of return.

19.   The _____ of the CML reflects the aggregate attitude of investors toward risk.

20.   An individual stock tends to move with the market as economic conditions change. This component of total risk is the stock's _____, or _____-_____ risk.

21.   _____ risk equals market risk plus diversifiable risk.

22.   A stock's risk premium depends only on its _____ risk, not its total risk.

Conceptual

23.   The standard deviation of a portfolio is not the weighted average of the standard deviations of the individual stocks in the portfolio.

       a. True   **b.** False

24.   If the correlation coefficient between two stocks is +1.0, risk can be completely diversified away.

    a. True   **b.** False

25.   Total risk is relevant only for assets held in isolation.

    a. True   **b.** False

26.   The Arbitrage Pricing Theory identifies the relevant factors for determining the required return beforehand.

    a. True   **b.** False

27.   Which of the following statements is most correct?

    a. It is difficult to interpret the magnitude of the correlation coefficient, so a related statistic, the covariance, is often used to measure the degree of comovement between two variables.

    b. The sign of the correlation coefficient is the same as the sign of the covariance, so a positive sign means that the variables move together, a negative sign indicates that they move in opposite directions, and if the correlation coefficient is close to zero, they move independently of one another.

    c. Attainable portfolios are defined as those portfolios which provide the highest expected return for any degree of risk, or the lowest degree of risk for any expected return.

    d. The efficient set of portfolios is also called the efficient frontier.

    e. Statements b and d are both correct.

28.   Which of the following statements is most correct?

    a. The Capital Market Line (CML) specifies a curvilinear relationship between expected return and risk, whereas the Security Market Line (SML) specifies a linear relationship between expected return and risk.

    b. An efficient portfolio is one that is well diversified, so like individual stocks, all the riskiness of an efficient portfolio is measured by its standard deviation, σ_p.

    c. A stock's beta coefficient is the y-intercept of its characteristic line.

    d. Empirical tests of the stability of beta coefficients have indicated that the betas of individual stocks are stable, hence that past betas for individual securities are good estimators of their future risk, while betas of portfolios of ten or more randomly selected stocks are not stable, hence that past portfolio betas are not good estimators of future portfolio volatility.

e. All of the above statements are false.

SELF-TEST PROBLEMS

1. You are evaluating two potential investment opportunities: Stocks A and B. The expected rate of return on Stock A is 15.8% and its standard deviation is 2.8%. Stock B's expected rate of return is 20.5% with a standard deviation of 3.5%. What is the coefficient of variation (CV) for Stocks A and B, respectively?

   a. 0.12; 0.12   **b.** 0.18; 0.12   **c.** 0.18; 0.17   **d.** 0.25; 0.17   **e.** 0.25; 0.25

2. Refer to Self-Test Problem 1. Assume that Stocks A and B have a correlation coefficient of 0.65. What is the covariance between Stocks A and B?

   a. 3.89   **b.** 4.35   **c.** 5.12   **d.** 6.37   **e.** 7.19

3. Refer to Self-Test Problem 1. Assume that Stocks A and B have a covariance of -5.4. What is the correlation coefficient between Stocks A and B?

   a. -0.55   **b.** -0.70   **c.** -0.85   **d.** -0.92   **e.** -1.00

4. Given the information below, calculate the betas for Stocks A and B.

Year	Stock A	Stock B	Market
1	-5%	10%	-10%
2	10	20	10
3	25	30	30

   (Hint: Think rise over run.)

   a. 1.0; 0.5   **b.** 0.75; 0.5   **c.** 0.75; 1.0   **d.** 0.5; 0.5   **e.** 0.75; 0.25

   (The following data apply to the next two Self-Test Problems.)

   You are given the following information:

Year	Stock N	Market
1	-5%	10%
2	-8	15
3	7	-10

   The risk-free rate is equal to 7 percent, and the market required return is equal to 10 percent.

5.   What is Stock N's beta coefficient?

  a. 1.00   **b.** -0.50   **c.** 0.60   **d.** -0.75   **e.** -0.60

6.   What is Stock N's required rate of return?

  a. 6.40%   **b.** 5.20%   **c.** 8.80%   **d.** 5.90%   **e.** 7.00%

7.   Stock Y and the Market had the following rates of return during the last 4 years. What is Stock Y's beta? (Hint: You will need a financial calculator to calculate the beta coefficient.)

	Y	Market
1995	10.0%	10.0%
1996	16.0	13.5
1997	-7.5	-4.0
1998	0.0	5.5

  a. 1.25   **b.** 0.75   **c.** 1.00   **d.** 1.34   **e.** 1.57

8.   Stock Y, Stock Z, and the Market had the following rates of return during the last 4 years:

	Y	Z	Market
1995	10.0%	10.0%	10.0%
1996	16.0	11.5	13.5
1997	-7.5	1.0	-4.0
1998	0.0	6.0	5.5

The expected future return on the market is 15 percent, the real risk-free rate is 3.75 percent, and the expected inflation rate is a constant 5 percent. If the market risk premium rises by 3 percentage points, what will be the change in the required rate of return of the riskier stock?

  a. 4.01%   **b.** 3.67%   **c.** 4.88%   **d.** 3.23%   **e.** 4.66%

ANSWERS TO SELF-TEST QUESTIONS

1.	Covariance; correlation coefficient	5.	efficient frontier
2.	efficient portfolio	6.	indifference curve
3.	attainable; feasible	7.	Capital Asset Pricing Model
4.	optimal portfolio	8.	Capital Market Line

9.	beta coefficient	**17.**	same; positive; negative; independently
10.	characteristic line		
11.	diversifiable; company-specific	**18.**	left; right
12.	market	**19.**	slope
13.	investment portfolios; securities	**20.**	market; non-diversifiable
14.	Arbitrage Pricing Theory	**21.**	Total
15.	normal distribution	**22.**	market
16.	correlation coefficient		

23. a. The standard deviation of a portfolio depends on the correlations among the stocks as well as their individual standard deviations. The calculation for the portfolio standard deviation is:

$$\sigma_p = \sqrt{\sum_{i=1}^{n} \left(k_{pi} - \hat{k}_p \right)^2 P_i}\,.$$

24. b. A correlation coefficient of -1.0 is required to combine two stocks into a riskless portfolio.

25. a. When assets are combined into portfolios, then the relevant risk is an asset's market risk, which is the contribution of the asset to the riskiness of the portfolio.

26. b. The APT does not identify the relevant factors beforehand, nor does it even tell how many factors should appear in the model.

27. e. Statement a is false. It is difficult to interpret the magnitude of the covariance, so the correlation coefficient is used to measure comovement between two variables. Statement c is false; this statement is true only for efficient portfolios. Both statements b and d are true, so statement e is the correct choice.

28. e. Statement a is false. The CML specifies the relationship between risk and return for efficient portfolios, while the SML specifies the relationship between risk and return for individual securities. Statement b is false. The standard deviation of an individual stock should not be used to measure the stock's riskiness because some of its risk as reflected in the standard deviation can be eliminated by diversification. Statement c is false; beta is the slope of the characteristic line. Statement d is false; just the reverse is true. Betas of portfolios of 10 or more randomly selected stocks have been shown to be stable, while the betas of individual securities have been shown to be unstable. Consequently, statement e is the correct choice.

SOLUTIONS TO SELF-TEST PROBLEMS

1. c. Stock A: CV = 2.8%/15.8% = 0.18. Stock B: CV = 3.5%/20.5% = 0.17. Since the CV for Project A is higher, it has more risk per unit of expected return.

2. d. Cov(AB) = 0.65 (2.8) (3.5) = 6.37.

3. a. r_{AB} = -5.4/[(2.8)(3.5)] = -0.55.

4. b. Stock A: b_A = Rise/Run = [10 – (-5)]/[10 – (-10)] = 15/20 = 0.75.
        Stock B: b_B = Rise/Run = [20 – 10]/[10 – (-10)] = 10/20 = 0.50.

    This problem can also be worked using most financial calculators having statistical functions.

5. e. b_N = Rise/Run = [-8) – (-5)]/(15 – 10) = -3/5 = -0.60.

    Again, this problem can also be worked using most financial calculators having statistical functions.

6. b. k_N = 7% + (10% – 7%)(-0.60) = 7% + (-1.80%) = 5.20%.

7. d. Use the regression feature of the calculator. Enter data for the market and Stock Y, and then find $Beta_Y$ = 1.3374 rounded to 1.34.

8. a. We know k_M = 15%; k* = 3.75%; IP = 5%.
        Original RP_M = k_M – k_{RF} = 15% – (3.75% + 5%) = 6.25%.
        RP_M increases by 3% to 9.25%.
        Find the change in k = Δk for the riskier stock.
        First, find the betas for the two stocks. Enter data in the regression register, then find b_Y = 1.3374 and b_Z = 0.6161.

    Y is the riskier stock. Originally, its required return was k_Y = 8.75% + 6.25%(1.3374) = 17.11%. When RP_M increases by 3 percent, k_Y = 8.75% + (6.25% + 3%)(1.3374) = 21.12%. Difference = 21.12% – 17.11% = 4.01%.

CHAPTER 8
TIME VALUE OF MONEY

OVERVIEW

A dollar in the hand today is worth more than a dollar to be received in the future because, if you had it now, you could invest that dollar and earn interest. Of all the techniques used in finance, none is more important than the concept of *time value of money,* also called *discounted cash flow (DCF) analysis.* Future value and present value techniques can be applied to a single cash flow (lump sum), ordinary annuities, annuities due, and uneven cash flow streams. Future and present values can be calculated using interest factor tables, a regular calculator, a calculator with financial functions, or a spreadsheet program. When compounding occurs more frequently than once a year, the effective rate of interest is greater than the quoted rate.

OUTLINE

Time lines are used to help visualize what is happening in time value of money problems. Cash flows are placed directly below the tick marks, and interest rates are shown directly above the time line; unknown cash flows are indicated by a symbol for the particular item that is missing. Thus, to find the future value of $100 after 5 years at 5 percent interest, the following time line can be set up:

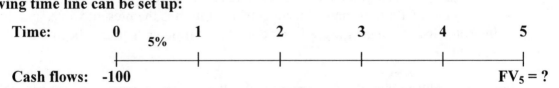

Finding the future value (FV), or compounding, is the process of going from today's values (or present values) to future amounts (or future values). It can be calculated as

$$FV_n = PV(1 + i)^n = PV(FVIF_{i,n}),$$

where PV = present value, or beginning amount; i = interest rate per year; and n = number of periods involved in the analysis. $FVIF_{i,n}$, the Future Value Interest Factor, is a short-hand way of writing the equation. This equation can be solved in one of three ways: numerically with a regular calculator, with a financial calculator, or with a spreadsheet program. For calculations, assume the following data that were presented in the time line

above: present value (PV) = $100, interest rate (i) = 5%, and number of years (n) = 5.

■   To solve numerically, use a regular calculator to find $1 + i = 1.05$ raised to the fifth power, which equals 1.2763. Multiply this figure by PV = $100 to get the final answer of $FV_s = 127.63.

■   With a financial calculator, the future value can be found by using the time value of money input keys, where N = number of periods, I = interest rate per period, PV = present value, PMT = payment, and FV = future value. By entering N = 5, I = 5, PV = -100, and PMT = 0, and then pressing the FV key, the answer 127.63 is displayed.

    ❑   Some financial calculators require that all cash flows be designated as either inflows or outflows, thus an outflow must be entered as a negative number (for example, PV = -100 instead of PV = 100).

    ❑   Some calculators require you to press a "Compute" key before pressing the FV key.

■   Spreadsheet programs are ideally suited for solving time value of money problems. The spreadsheet itself becomes a time line.

	A	B	C	D	E	F	G
1	Interest rate	.05					
2	Time	0	1	2	3	4	5
3	Cash flow	-100					
4	Future value		105.00	110.25	115.76	121.55	**127.63**

    ❑   Row 4 contains the spreadsheet formula for future value.

    ❑   The Excel formula in Cell G4 is written as **=-$B$3*(1+$B$1)^G2**. This gives us flexibility to change the interest rate in Cell B1 to see how the future value changes with changes in interest rates.

    ❑   An alternative Excel formula in Cell G4 could have been entered, **=FV(5%,5,0, -100,1)**. The first argument of this formula is the interest rate, the second the number of periods, the third the annual payments, the fourth is the present value, and the fifth indicates that payments are all made at the end rather than the beginning of each year.

■   Note that small rounding differences will often occur among the various solution methods.

■   In general, you should use the easiest approach.

■   A graph of the compounding process shows how any sum grows over time at various interest rates. The greater the interest rate, the faster the growth rate.

Finding present values is called discounting, and it is simply the reverse of compounding. In general, the present value of a cash flow due n years in the future is the amount which, if it were on hand today, would grow to equal the future amount. By solving for PV in the future value equation, the present value, or discounting, equation can be developed and written in several forms:

$$PV = \frac{FV_n}{(1+i)^n} = FV_n\left(\frac{1}{1+i}\right)^n = FV_n(PVIF_{i,n}).$$

- $PVIF_{i,n}$, the Present Value Interest Factor, is a short-hand way of writing the equation.
- To solve for the present value of $127.63 discounted back 5 years at a 5% opportunity cost rate, one can utilize any of the four solution methods:
  - Numerical solution: Divide $127.63 by 1.05 five times to get PV = $100.
  - Financial calculator solution: Enter N = 5, I = 5, PMT = 0, and FV = 127.63, and then press the PV key to get PV = -100.
  - Spreadsheet solution:

	A	B	C	D	E	F	G
1	Interest rate	.05					
2	Time	0	1	2	3	4	5
3	Cash flow		0	0	0	0	127.63
4	Present value	**100**					

Any of three formulas could be entered using Excel in Cell B4: (1) **=G3/(1+$B$1)^G2**, (2) **=NPV($B$1,C3:G3)**, or (3) **=PV(B1,G2,0,G3)**. The second formula finds the present value of each number in the range of cells from C3 to G3, discounted at 5 percent. The third formula find the present value of G3, when discounted for G2 periods at a rate of B1.

- A graph of the discounting process shows how the present value of any sum to be received in the future diminishes as the years to receipt increases. At relatively high interest rates, funds due in the future are worth very little today, and even at a relatively low discount rate, the present value of a sum due in the very distant future is quite small.

There are four variables in the time value of money compounding and discounting equations: PV, FV, i, and n. If three of the four variables are known, you can find the value of the fourth.

- If we are given PV, FV, and n, we can determine i by substituting the known values into either the present value or future value equations, and then solve for i. Thus, if you can buy a security at a price of $78.35 which will pay you $100 after 5 years, what is the interest rate earned on the investment?

- ❑ Numerical solution: Solve for i in the following equation using the exponential feature of a regular calculator: $\$100 = \$78.35(1 + i)^5$.
- ❑ Financial calculator solution: Enter N = 5, PV = -78.35, PMT = 0, and FV = 100, then press the I key, and I = 5 is displayed.
- ❑ Spreadsheet solution:

	A	B	C	D	E	F	G
1	Time	0	1	2	3	4	5
2	Cash flow	-78.35	0	0	0	0	100
3	Interest rate	5%					
4							

- ❑ The Excel formula in Cell B3 is entered as **=IRR(B2:G2)**. The formula calculates the internal rate of return, and its argument is the range of the cash flows. Alternatively, you could enter **=Rate(G1,0,B2,G2)**, which finds the rate given G1 periods, a present value of B2, and a future value of G2.

- ■ Likewise, if we are given PV, FV, and i, we can determine n by substituting the known values into either the present value or future value equations, and then solve for n. Thus, if you can buy a security with a 5 percent interest rate at a price of $78.35 today, how long will it take for your investment to return $100?
    - ❑ Numerical solution: Solve for n in the following equation using the natural logarithm feature of a regular calculator: $\$100 = \$78.35(1 + .05)^n$.
    - ❑ Financial calculator solution: Enter I = 5, PV = -78.35, PMT = 0, and FV = 100, then press the N key, and N = 5 is displayed.
    - ❑ Spreadsheet solution: Enter the formula **=NPER(.05,0,-78.35,100)**, which finds the number of periods, given a rate of 5%, a present value of –78.35, and a future value of 100.

An annuity is a series of equal payments made at fixed intervals for a specified number of periods. If the payments occur at the end of each period, as they typically do, the annuity is an ordinary (or deferred) annuity. If the payments occur at the beginning of each period, it is called an annuity due.

- ■ The future value of an annuity is the total amount one would have at the end of the annuity period if each payment were invested at a given interest rate and held to the end of the annuity period.
    - ❑ Defining FVA_n as the compound sum of an ordinary annuity of n years, and PMT as the periodic payment, we can write

$$FVA_n = PMT \sum_{t=1}^{n} (1+i)^{n-t} = PMT \left(\frac{(1+i)^n - 1}{i} \right) = PMT(FVIFA_{i,n}).$$

- $FVIFA_{i,n}$ is the future value interest factor for an ordinary annuity. This is a short-hand notation for the formula shown above.
- For example, the future value of a 3-year, 5 percent ordinary annuity of $100 per year would be $100(3.1525) = $315.25.
- The same calculation can be made using the financial function keys of a calculator. Enter N = 3, I = 5, PV = 0, and PMT = -100. Then press the FV key, and 315.25 is displayed.
- Most spreadsheets have a built-in function to find the future value of an annuity. In Excel the formula would be written as =FV(.05,3,-100).
- For an annuity due, each payment is compounded for one additional period, so the future value of the entire annuity is equal to the future value of an ordinary annuity compounded for one additional period. Thus:

$$FVA_n \text{ (Annuity due)} = PMT(FVIFA_{i,n})(1 + i).$$

- For example, the future value of a 3-year, 5 percent annuity due of $100 per year is $100(3.1525)(1.05) = $331.01.
- Most financial calculators have a switch, or key, marked "DUE" or "BEG" that permits you to switch from end-of-period payments (an ordinary annuity) to beginning-of-period payments (an annuity due). Switch your calculator to "BEG" mode, and calculate as you would for an ordinary annuity. Do not forget to switch your calculator back to "END" mode when you are finished.
- For an annuity due, the spreadsheet formula is written as =FV(.05,3,-100,0,1). The fourth term in the formula, 0, means that no extra payment is made at t = 0, and the last term, 1, tells the computer that this is an annuity due.

- The present value of an annuity is the single (lump sum) payment today that would be equivalent to the annuity payments spread over the annuity period. It is the amount today that would permit withdrawals of an equal amount (PMT) at the end (or beginning for an annuity due) of each period for n periods.
  - Defining PVA_n as the present value of an ordinary annuity of n years and PMT as the periodic payment, we can write

$$PVA_n = PMT \sum_{t=1}^{n} \left(\frac{1}{1+i} \right)^t = PMT \left(\frac{1 - \frac{1}{(1+i)^n}}{i} \right) = PMT(PVIFA_{i,n}).$$

- ❑ PVIFA$_{i,n}$ is the present value interest factor for an ordinary annuity. This is a short-hand notation for the formula shown above.
- ❑ For example, an annuity of $100 per year for 3 years at 5 percent would have a present value of $100(2.7232) = $272.32.
- ❑ Using a financial calculator, enter N = 3, I = 5, PMT = -100, and FV = 0, and then press the PV key, for an answer of $272.32.
- ❑ Spreadsheet solution:

	A	B	C	D	E
1	Interest rate	.05			
2	Time	0	1	2	3
3	Cash flow		100	100	100
4	Present value	$272.32			

- ❑ Two formulas can be used to solve this problem. Excel's NPV formula can be entered in Cell B4: **=NPV($B$1,C3:E3)**. The second formula that can be used is Excel's PV annuity function: **=PV(.05,3,-100)**.
- ❑ The present value for an annuity due is

$$PVA_n \text{ (Annuity due)} = PMT(PVIFA_{i,n})(1 + i).$$

- ❑ For example, the present value of a 3-year, 5 percent annuity due of $100 is $100(2.7232)(1.05) = $285.94.
- ❑ Using a financial calculator, switch to the "BEG" mode, and then enter N = 3, I = 5, PMT = -100, and FV = 0, and then press PV to get the answer, $285.94. Again, do not forget to switch your calculator back to "END" mode when you are finished.
- ❑ For an annuity due, the spreadsheet formula is written as **=PV(.05,3,-100,0,1)**. The fourth term in the formula, 0, means that you are not making any additional payments at t = 3, and the last term, 1, tells the computer that this is an annuity due.

An annuity that goes on indefinitely is called a perpetuity. The payments of a perpetuity constitute an infinite series.

- ■ The present value of a perpetuity is:

$$PV \text{ (Perpetuity)} = Payment/Interest \text{ rate} = PMT/i.$$

- ■ For example, if the interest rate were 12 percent, a perpetuity of $1,000 a year would have a present value of $1,000/0.12 = $8,333.33.

Many financial decisions require the analysis of uneven, or nonconstant, cash flows rather than a stream of fixed payments such as an annuity.

■ The present value of an uneven stream of income is the sum of the PVs of the individual cash flow components. Similarly, the future value of an uneven stream of income is the sum of the FVs of the individual cash flow components.

❑ With a financial calculator, enter each cash flow (beginning with the t = 0 cash flow) into the cash flow register, CF_j, enter the appropriate interest rate, and then press the NPV key to obtain the PV of the cash flow stream.

❑ Spreadsheets are especially useful for solving problems with uneven cash flows.

	A	B	C	D	E	F	G	H	I
1	Interest rate	.06							
2	Time	0	1	2	3	4	5	6	7
3	Cash flow		100	200	200	200	200	0	1,000
4	Present value	1,413.19							

❑ The Excel spreadsheet formula in Cell B4 is written as **=NPV(B1,C3:I3)**.

❑ Some calculators have a net future value (NFV) key which allows you to obtain the FV of an uneven cash flow stream.

■ If one knows the relevant cash flows, the effective interest rate can be calculated efficiently with either a financial calculator or a spreadsheet program. Using a financial calculator, enter each cash flow (beginning with the t = 0 cash flow) into the cash flow register, CF_j, and then press the IRR key to obtain the interest rate of an uneven cash flow stream.

Semiannual, quarterly, and other compounding periods more frequent than an annual basis are often used in financial transactions. Compounding on a nonannual basis requires an adjustment to both the compounding and discounting procedures discussed previously.

■ The *effective annual rate* (EAR or EFF%) is the rate that would have produced the final compounded value under annual compounding. The effective annual percentage rate is given by the following formula:

$$\text{Effective annual rate (EAR)} = \text{EFF\%} = (1 + i_{Nom}/m)^m - 1.0,$$

■ where i_{Nom} is the nominal, or quoted, interest rate and m is the number of compounding periods per year. The EAR is useful in comparing securities with different compounding periods.

■ For example, to find the effective annual rate if the nominal rate is 6 percent and semiannual compounding is used, we have:

$$\text{EAR} = (1 + 0.06/2)^2 - 1.0 = 6.09\%.$$

- For annual compounding use the formula to find the future value of a single payment (lump sum):

$$FV_n = PV(1 + i)^n.$$

- When compounding occurs more frequently than once a year, use this formula:

$$FV_n = PV(1 + i_{Nom}/m)^{mn}.$$

- Here m is the number of times per year compounding occurs, and n is the number of years.

- The amount to which $1,000 will grow after 5 years if quarterly compounding is applied to a nominal 8 percent interest rate is found as follows:

$$FV_n = \$1,000(1 + 0.08/4)^{(4)(5)} = \$1,000(1.02)^{20} = \$1,485.95.$$

  - Financial calculator solution: Enter N = 20, I = 2, PV = -1000, and PMT = 0, and then press the FV key to find FV = $1,485.95.
  - Spreadsheet solution: The spreadsheet developed to find the future value of a lump sum under quarterly compounding would look like the one for annual compounding, with two changes: The interest rate would be quartered, and the time line would show four times as many periods.

- The present value of a 5-year future investment equal to $1,485.95, with an 8 percent nominal interest rate, compounded quarterly, is found as follows:

$$\$1,485.95 = PV(1 + 0.08/4)^{(4)(5)}$$

$$PV = \frac{\$1,485.95}{(1.02)^{20}} = \$1,000.$$

  - Financial calculator solution: Enter N = 20, I = 2, PMT = 0, and FV = 1485.95, and then press the PV key to find PV = -$1,000.00.

  - Spreadsheet solution: The spreadsheet developed to find the present value of a lump sum under quarterly compounding would look like the one for annual compounding, with two changes: The interest rate would be quartered, and the time line would show four times as many periods.

The nominal rate is the rate that is quoted by borrowers and lenders. Nominal rates can only be compared with one another if the instruments being compared use the same number of compounding periods per year. Note also that the nominal rate is never shown on a time line, or used as an input in a financial calculator, unless compounding occurs only once a year. In general, nonannual compounding can be handled one of two ways.

■　　State everything on a periodic rather than on an annual basis. Thus, n = 6 periods rather than n = 3 years and i = 3% instead of i = 6% with semiannual compounding.

■　　Find the effective annual rate (EAR) with the equation below and then use the EAR as the rate over the given number of years.

$$EAR = \left(1 + \frac{i_{Nom}}{m}\right)^{m} - 1.0.$$

Fractional time periods are used when payments occur within periods, instead of at either the beginning or the end of periods. Solving these problems requires using the fraction of the time period for n, number of periods, and then solving either numerically, with a spreadsheet program, or with a financial calculator. (Some older calculators will produce incorrect answers because of their internal "solution" programs.)

An important application of compound interest involves amortized loans, which are paid off in equal installments over time.

■　　The amount of each payment, PMT, is found as follows: PV of the annuity = PMT(PVIFA$_{i,n}$), so PMT = PV of the annuity/PVIFA$_{i,n}$.

■　　With a financial calculator, enter N (number of years), I (interest rate), PV (amount borrowed), and FV = 0, and then press the PMT key to find the periodic payment.

■　　The spreadsheet is ideal for developing amortization tables. The set up is similar to Table 8-1 in the text, but you would want to include "input" cells for the interest rate, principal value, and the length of the loan.

■　　Each payment consists partly of interest and partly of the repayment of principal. This breakdown is often developed in a loan amortization schedule.
　　❑　The interest component is largest in the first period, and it declines over the life of the loan.
　　❑　The repayment of principal is smallest in the first period, and it increases thereafter.

SELF-TEST QUESTIONS

Definitional

1. The beginning value of an account or investment in a project is known as its _____ _____.

2. Using a savings account as an example, the difference between the account's present value and its future value at the end of the period is due to _____ earned during the period.

3. The equation $FV_n = PV(1 + i)^n$ determines the future value of a sum at the end of n periods. The factor $(1 + i)^n$ is known as the _____ _____ _____ _____.

4. The process of finding present values is often referred to as _____ and is the reverse of the _____ process.

5. The $PVIF_{i,n}$ for a 5-year, 5 percent investment is 0.7835. This value is the _____ of the $FVIF_{i,n}$ for 5 years at 5 percent.

6. For a given number of time periods, the $PVIF_{i,n}$ will decline as the _____ _____ increases.

7. A series of payments of a constant amount for a specified number of periods is a(n) _____. If the payments occur at the end of each period it is a(n) _____ annuity, while if the payments occur at the beginning of each period it is an annuity _____.

8. The present value of an uneven stream of future payments is the _____ of the PVs of the individual payments.

9. Since different types of investments use different compounding periods, it is important to distinguish between the quoted, or _____, rate and the _____ annual interest rate.

10. When compounding occurs more than once a year, divide the _____ _____ by the number of times compounding occurs and multiply the years by the number of _____ _____ per year.

11. _____ _____ are used to help visualize what is happening in time value of money problems.

12. An annuity that goes on indefinitely is called a(n) _____.

13. _____ loans are those which are paid off in equal installments over time.

14. The breakdown of each payment as partly interest and partly principal is developed in a(n) _____ _____ _____.

Conceptual

15. If a bank uses quarterly compounding for savings accounts, the nominal rate will be greater than the effective annual rate (EAR).

    a. True   **b.** False

16. If money has time value (that is, i > 0), the future value of some amount of money will always be more than the amount invested. The present value of some amount to be received in the future is always less than the amount to be received.

    a. True   **b.** False

17. You have determined the profitability of a planned project by finding the present value of all the cash flows from that project. Which of the following would cause the project to look less appealing, that is, have a lower present value?

    a. The discount rate decreases.
    b. The cash flows are extended over a longer period of time.
    c. The discount rate increases.
    d. Statements b and c are both correct.
    e. Statements a and b are both correct.

18. As the discount rate increases without limit, the present value of a future cash inflow

    a. Gets larger without limit.
    b. Stays unchanged.
    c. Approaches zero.
    d. Gets smaller without limit; that is, approaches minus infinity.
    e. Goes to e^{in}.

19.   Which of the following statements is most correct?

   a.   For all positive values of i and n, $FVIF_{i,n} \geq 1.0$ and $PVIFA_{i,n} \geq n$.
   b.   You may use the annuity formula to find the present value of an uneven series of payments.
   c.   If a bank uses quarterly compounding for savings accounts, the nominal rate will be greater than the effective annual rate.
   d.   The present value of a future sum decreases as either the nominal interest rate or the number of discounting periods per year increases.
   e.   All of the above statements are false.

20.   Which of the following statements is most correct?

   a.   Except in situations where compounding occurs annually, the periodic interest rate exceeds the nominal interest rate.
   b.   The effective annual rate always exceeds the nominal rate, no matter how few or many compounding periods occur each year.
   c.   If compounding occurs more frequently than once a year, and if payments are made at times other than at the end of compounding periods, it is impossible to determine present or future values, even with a financial calculator. The reason is that under these conditions, the basic assumptions of discounted cash flow analysis are not met.
   d.   Assume that compounding occurs quarterly, that the nominal interest rate is 8 percent, and that you need to find the present value of $1,000 due 6 months from today. You could get the correct answer by discounting the $1,000 at 2 percent for 2 periods.
   e.   Statements a, b, c, and d are all false.

SELF-TEST PROBLEMS

(Note: In working these problems, you may get an answer which differs from ours by a few cents due to differences in rounding. This should not concern you; just pick the closest answer.)

1.   Assume that you purchase a 6-year, 8 percent savings certificate for $1,000. If interest is compounded annually, what will be the value of the certificate when it matures?

   a. $630.17   b. $1,469.33   c. $1,677.10   d. $1,586.90   e. $1,766.33

2.   A savings certificate similar to the one in the previous problem is available with the exception that interest is compounded semiannually. What is the difference between the ending value of the savings certificate compounded semiannually and the one compounded annually?

    a. The semiannual is worth $14.10 more than the annual.
    b. The semiannual is worth $14.10 less than the annual.
    c. The semiannual is worth $21.54 more than the annual.
    d. The semiannual is worth $21.54 less than the annual.
    e. The semiannual is worth the same as the annual.

3. A friend promises to pay you $600 two years from now if you loan him $500 today. What annual interest rate is your friend offering?

    a. 7.5%   **b.** 8.5%   **c.** 9.5%   **d.** 10.5%   **e.** 11.5%

4. At an inflation rate of 9 percent, the purchasing power of $1 would be cut in half in just over 8 years (some calculators round to 9 years). How long, to the nearest year, would it take for the purchasing power of $1 to be cut in half if the inflation rate were only 4 percent?

    a. 12 years   **b.** 15 years   **c.** 18 years   **d.** 20 years   **e.** 23 years

5. You are offered an investment opportunity with the "guarantee" that your investment will double in 5 years. Assuming annual compounding, what annual rate of return would this investment provide?

    a. 40.00%   **b.** 100.00%   **c.** 14.87%   **d.** 20.00%   **e.** 18.74%

6. You decide to begin saving toward the purchase of a new car in 5 years. If you put $1,000 at the end of each of the next 5 years in a savings account paying 6 percent compounded annually, how much will you accumulate after 5 years?

    a. $6,691.13   **b.** $5,637.10   **c.** $1,338.23   **d.** $5,975.33   **e.** $5,732.00

7. Refer to Self-Test Problem 6. What would be the ending amount if the payments were made at the beginning of each year?

    a. $6,691.13   **b.** $5,637.10   **c.** 1,338.23   **d.** $5,975.33   **e.** $5,732.00

8. Refer to Self-Test Problem 6. What would be the ending amount if $500 payments were made at the end of each 6-month period for 5 years and the account paid 6 percent compounded semiannually?

    a. $6,691.13   **b.** $5,637.10   **c.** $1,338.23   **d.** $5,975.33   **e.** $5,732.00

9. Calculate the present value of $1,000 to be received at the end of 8 years. Assume an interest rate of 7 percent.

    a. $582.00   **b.** $1,718.19   **c.** $531.82   **d.** $5,971.30   **e.** $649.37

10. How much would you be willing to pay today for an investment that would return $800 each year at the end of each of the next 6 years? Assume a discount rate of 5 percent.

    a. $5,441.53   **b.** $4,800.00   **c.** $3,369.89   **d.** $4,060.56   **e.** $4,632.37

11. You have applied for a mortgage of $60,000 to finance the purchase of a new home. The bank will require you to make annual payments of $7,047.55 at the end of each of the next 20 years. Determine the interest rate in effect on this mortgage.

    a. 8.0%   **b.** 9.8%   **c.** 10.0%   **d.** 5.1%   **e.** 11.2%

12. If you would like to accumulate $7,500 over the next 5 years, how much must you deposit each six months, starting six months from now, given a 6 percent interest rate and semiannual compounding?

    a. $1,330.47   **b.** $879.23   **c.** $654.22   **d.** $569.00   **e.** $732.67

13. A company is offering bonds which pay $100 per year indefinitely. If you require a 12 percent return on these bonds—that is, the discount rate is 12 percent—what is the value of each bond?

    a. $1,000.00   **b.** $962.00   **c.** $904.67   **d.** $866.67   **e.** $833.33

14. What is the present value (t = 0) of the following cash flows if the discount rate is 12 percent?

```
0              1        2        3        4        5
    12%
|-------+--------+--------+--------+--------+--------+
0       2,000    2,000    2,000    3,000    -4,000
```

    a. $4,782.43   **b.** $4,440.50   **c.** $4,221.79   **d.** $4,041.23   **e.** $3,997.98

15. What is the effective annual percentage rate (EAR) of 12 percent compounded monthly?

    a. 12.00%   **b.** 12.55%   **c.** 12.68%   **d.** 12.75%   **e.** 13.00%

16.   Martha Mills, manager of Plaza Gold Emporium, wants to sell on credit, giving customers 4 months in which to pay. However, Martha will have to borrow from her bank to carry the accounts payable. The bank will charge a nominal 18 percent, but with monthly compounding. Martha wants to quote a nominal rate to her customers (all of whom are expected to pay on time at the end of 4 months) *which will exactly cover her financing costs*. What nominal annual rate should she quote to her credit customers? (Note: Interest factor tables cannot be used to solve this problem.)

   a. 15.44%   b. 19.56%   c. 17.11%   d. 18.41%   e. 16.88%

17.   Self-Test Problem 11 refers to a 20-year mortgage of $60,000. This is an amortized loan. How much principal will be repaid in the second year?

   a. $1,152.30   b. $1,725.70   c. $5,895.25   d. $7,047.55   e. $1,047.55

18.   You have $1,000 invested in an account which pays 16 percent compounded annually. A commission agent (called a "finder") can locate for you an equally safe deposit which will pay 16 percent, compounded quarterly, for 2 years. What is the maximum amount you should be willing to pay him now as a fee for locating the new account?

   a. $10.92   b. $13.78   c. $16.14   d. $16.81   e. $21.13

19.   The present value (t = 0) of the following cash flow stream is $11,958.20 when discounted at 12 percent annually. What is the value of the missing t = 2 cash flow?

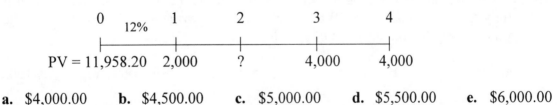

   a. $4,000.00   b. $4,500.00   c. $5,000.00   d. $5,500.00   e. $6,000.00

20.   Today is your birthday, and you decide to start saving for your college education. You will begin college on your 18th birthday and will need $4,000 per year at the *end* of each of the following 4 years. You will make a deposit 1 year from today in an account paying 12 percent annually and continue to make an identical deposit each year up to and including the year you begin college. If a deposit amount of $2,542.05 will allow you to reach your goal, what birthday are you celebrating today?

   a. 13   b. 14   c. 15   d. 16   e. 17

21. Assume that your aunt sold her house on December 31 and that she took a mortgage in the amount of $50,000 as part of the payment. The mortgage has a stated (or nominal) interest rate of 8 percent, but it calls for payments every 6 months, beginning on June 30, and the mortgage is to be amortized over 20 years. Now, one year later, your aunt must file Schedule B of her tax return with the IRS informing them of the interest that was included in the two payments made during the year. (This interest will be income to your aunt and a deduction to the buyer of the house.) What is the total amount of interest that was paid during the first year?

    a. $1,978.95   **b.** $526.17   **c.** $3,978.95   **d.** $2,000.00   **e.** $750.02

22. Assume that you inherited some money. A friend of yours is working as an unpaid intern at a local brokerage firm, and her boss is selling some securities which call for five payments, $75 at the end of each of the next 4 years, plus a payment of $1,075 at the end of Year 5. Your friend says she can get you some of these securities at a cost of $960 each. Your money is now invested in a bank that pays an 8 percent nominal (quoted) interest rate, but with quarterly compounding. You regard the securities as being just as safe, and as liquid, as your bank deposit, so your required effective annual rate of return on the securities is the same as that on your bank deposit. You must calculate the value of the securities to decide whether they are a good investment. What is their present value to you?

    a. $957.75   **b.** $888.66   **c.** $923.44   **d.** $1,015.25   **e.** $970.51

23. Your company is planning to borrow $500,000 on a 5-year, 7 percent, annual payment, fully amortized term loan. What fraction of the payment made at the end of the second year will represent repayment of principal?

    a. 76.29%   **b.** 42.82%   **c.** 50.28%   **d.** 49.72%   **e.** 60.27%

24. Your firm can borrow from its bank for one month. The loan will have to be "rolled over" at the end of the month, but you are sure the rollover will be allowed. The nominal interest rate is 14 percent, but interest will have to be paid at the end of each month, so the bank interest rate is 14 percent, monthly compounding. Alternatively, your firm can borrow from an insurance company at a nominal rate which would involve quarterly compounding. What nominal quarterly rate would be equivalent to the rate charged by the bank? (Note: Interest factor tables cannot be used to solve this problem.)

    a. 12.44%   **b.** 14.16%   **c.** 13.55%   **d.** 13.12%   **e.** 12.88%

25. Assume that you have $15,000 in a bank account that pays 5 percent annual interest. You plan to go back to school for a combination MBA/law degree 5 years from today. It will take you an additional 5 years to complete your graduate studies. You figure you will need a fixed income of $25,000 in today's dollars; that is, you will need $25,000 of today's dollars during your first year and each subsequent year. (*Thus, your real income will decline while you are in school.*) You will withdraw funds for your annual expenses at the beginning of each year. Inflation is expected to occur at the rate of 3 percent per year. How much must you save during each of the next 5 years in order to achieve your goal? The first increment of savings will be deposited one year from today.

a. $20,241.66
b. $19,224.55
c. $18,792.11

d. $19,559.42
e. $20,378.82

26. You plan to buy a new HDTV. The dealer offers to sell the set to you on credit. You will have 3 months in which to pay, but the dealer says you will be charged a 15 percent interest rate; that is, the nominal rate is 15 percent, quarterly compounding. As an alternative to buying on credit, you can borrow the funds from your bank, but the bank will make you pay interest each month. At what nominal bank interest rate should you be indifferent between the two types of credit?

a. 13.7643%   b. 14.2107%   c. 14.8163%   d. 15.5397%   e. 15.3984%

27. Assume that your father is now 40 years old, that he plans to retire in 20 years, and that he expects to live for 25 years after he retires, that is, until he is 85. He wants a fixed retirement income that has the same purchasing power at the time he retires as $75,000 has today (he realizes that the real value of his retirement income will decline year-by-year after he retires). His retirement income will begin the day he retires, 20 years from today, and he will then get 24 additional annual payments. Inflation is expected to be 4 percent per year from today forward; he currently has $200,000 saved up; and he expects to earn a return on his savings of 7 percent per year, annual compounding. To the nearest dollar, how much must he save during each of the next 20 years (with deposits being made at the end of each year) to meet his retirement goal?

a. $31,105.90
b. $35,709.25
c. $54,332.88

d. $41,987.33
e. $62,191.25

ANSWERS TO SELF-TEST QUESTIONS

1. present value
2. interest
3. future value interest factor
4. discounting; compounding
5. reciprocal
6. interest rate
7. annuity; ordinary; due

8. sum
9. nominal; effective
10. nominal rate; compounding periods
11. Time lines
12. perpetuity
13. Amortized
14. loan amortization schedule

15. b. The EAR is always greater than or equal to the nominal rate.

16. a. Both these statements are correct.

17. d. The slower the cash flows come in and the higher the interest rate, the lower the present value.

18. c. As the discount rate increases, the present value of a future sum decreases and eventually approaches zero.

19. d. As a future sum is discounted over more and more periods, the present value will get smaller and smaller. Likewise, as the discount rate increases, the present value of a future sum decreases and eventually approaches zero.

20. d. Statement a is false because the periodic interest rate is equal to the nominal rate divided by the number of compounding periods, so it will be equal to or smaller than the nominal rate. Statement b is false because the EAR will equal the nominal rate if there is one compounding period per year (annual compounding). Statement c is false because we can determine present or future values under the stated conditions. Statement d is correct; using a financial calculator, enter $N = 2$, $I = 2$, $PMT = 0$, and $FV = 1000$ to find $PV = -961.1688$.

SOLUTIONS TO SELF-TEST PROBLEMS

1. **d.**

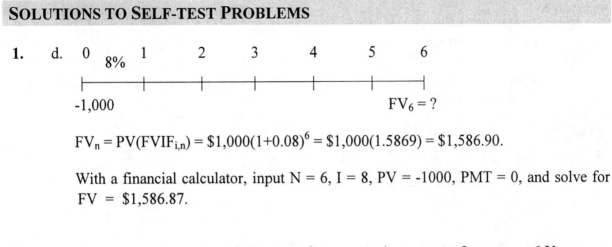

$$FV_n = PV(FVIF_{i,n}) = \$1,000(1+0.08)^6 = \$1,000(1.5869) = \$1,586.90.$$

With a financial calculator, input N = 6, I = 8, PV = -1000, PMT = 0, and solve for FV = $1,586.87.

2. **a.**

$$FVIF_{i,n} = (1+0.04)^{12} = 1.6010.$$ Thus, $FV_n = \$1,000(1.6010) = \$1,601.00.$ The difference, $1,601.00 - $1,586.90 = $14.10, is the additional interest.

With a financial calculator, input N = 12, I = 4, PV = -1000, and PMT = 0, and then solve for FV = $1,601.03. The difference, $1,601.03 - $1,586.87 = $14.16.

3. **c.**

$$\$600 = \$500(1+i)^2$$
$$\$600/\$500 = (1+i)^2$$
$$(1+i)^2 = 1.200$$
$$(1+i) = (1.200)^{1/2} = 1.0954$$
$$i = 0.0954 = 9.54\%.$$

With a financial calculator, input N = 2, PV = -500, PMT = 0, FV = 600, and solve for I = 9.54%.

4. c. 0   N = ?
      4%

1.00   0.50

With a financial calculator, input I = 4, PV = -1.00, PMT = 0, and FV = 0.50. Solve for N = 17.67 ≈ 18 years.

5. c. 0   1   2   3   4   5
      i = ?

-1   2

Assume any value for the present value and double it:

$FV_5 = PV(FVIF_{i,5})$
$\$2/\$1 = (1+i)^5$
$(1+i)^5 = 2$
$(1+i) = (2)^{1/5} = 1.1487$
$i = 0.1487 = 14.87\%.$

With a financial calculator, input N = 5, PV = -1, PMT = 0, FV = 2, and solve for I = 14.87%.

6. b. 0   1   2   3   4   5
      6%

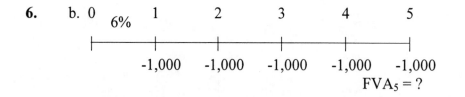

      -1,000   -1,000   -1,000   -1,000   -1,000
                                          FVA_5 = ?

$FVA_5 = PMT(FVIFA_{6\%,5}) = \$1,000([(1+i)^n-1]/i) = \$1,000(5.6371)=\$5,637.10.$
$FVA_5 = \$1,000([(1+0.06)^5-1]/0.06) = \$5,637.10.$

With a financial calculator, input N = 5, I = 6, PV = 0, PMT = -1000, and solve for FV = $5,637.09.

7. **d.**

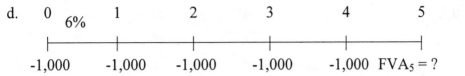

FVA_5(Annuity due) = $PMT(FVIFA_{6\%,5})(1 + i)$ = $1,000(5.6371)(1.06)$ = $5,975.33.$
See above for calculation of $FVIFA_{6\%,5}$.
FVA_5(Annuity due) = $1,000(5.6371)(1.06) = $5,975.33.$

With a financial calculator, switch to "BEG" mode, then input N = 5, I = 6, PV = 0, PMT = -1000, and solve for FV = $5,975.32$. Be sure to switch back to "END" mode.

8. **e.**

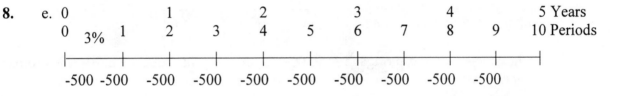

$FVA_{10} = ?$

$FVA_{10} = PMT(FVIFA_{3\%,10}) = $500([(1+i)^n-1]/i).$
$FVA_{10} = $500([(1+0.03)^{10}-1]/0.03) = $500(11.464) = $5,732.00.$

With a financial calculator, input N = 10, I = 3, PV = 0, PMT = -500, and solve for FV = $5,731.94$.

9. **a.**

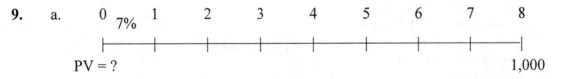

PV = ?

$PV = FV_8(PVIF_{7\%,8}) = $1,000(1/(1+0.07)^8) = $1,000(0.5820) = $582.00.$

With a financial calculator, input N = 8, I = 7, PMT = 0, FV = 1000, and solve for PV = $-$582.01.$

(Note: Annual compounding is assumed if not otherwise specified.)

10. d.

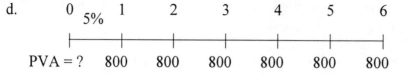

$$PVA_6 = PMT(PVIFA_{5\%,6}) = PMT\ [(1-[1/(1+i)^n])/i] = \$800\ [(1-[1/(1+0.05)^6])/0.05]$$
$$PVA_6 = \$800(5.0757) = \$4,060.56.$$

With a financial calculator, input N = 6, I = 5, PMT = 800, FV = 0, and solve for PV = - $4,060.55 .

11. c.

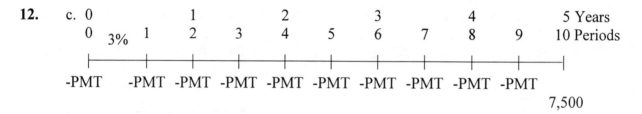

The amount of the mortgage ($60,000) is the present value of a 20-year ordinary annuity with payments of $7,047.55. Therefore,

With a financial calculator, input N = 20, PV = 60000, PMT = -7047.55, FV = 0, and solve for I = 10.00%.

12. c.

	0		1		2		3		4		5 Years
0	3%	1	2	3	4	5	6	7	8	9	10 Periods

-PMT   -PMT -PMT -PMT -PMT -PMT -PMT -PMT -PMT -PMT

7,500

$$FVA_{10} = PMT(FVIFA_{3\%,10})$$
$$FVIFA_{3\%,10} = [(1+i)^n-1]/i = [(1+0.03)^{10}-1]/0.03 = 11.464.$$
$$\$7,500 = PMT(11.464)$$
$$PMT = \$654.22.$$

With a financial calculator, input N = 10, I = 3, PV = 0, FV = 7500, and solve for PMT = -$654.23.

13. e. $PV = PMT/i = \$100/0.12 = \$833.33.$

14. b. $PV = \$2,000/1.12 + \$2,000/1.12^2 + \$2,000/1.12^3 + \$3,000/1.12^4 - \$4,000/1.12^5$
$= \$4,440.50.$

With a financial calculator, using the cash flow register, CF_j, input 0; 2000; 2000; 2000; 3000; and -4000. Enter I = 12 and solve for NPV = \$4,440.51.

15. c. $EAR = (1 + i_{Nom}/m)^m - 1.0$
$= (1 + 0.12/12)^{12} - 1.0$
$= (1.01)^{12} - 1.0$
$= 1.1268 - 1.0$
$= 0.1268 = 12.68\%.$

With a financial calculator, enter P/YR = 12 and NOM% = 12, and then solve for EFF% = 12.68%.

16. d. Here we want to have the same effective annual rate on the credit extended as on the bank loan that will be used to finance the credit extension.

First, we must find the EAR = EFF% on the bank loan. With a financial calculator, enter P/YR = 12, NOM% = 18, and press EFF% to get EAR = 19.56%.

Because 4 months of credit is being given there are 3 credit periods in a year, so enter P/YR = 3, EFF% = EAR = 19.56, and press NOM% to find the nominal rate of 18.41%. Therefore, if Martha charges an 18.41% nominal rate and gives credit for 4 months, she will cover the cost of her bank loan.

Alternative solution: First, we need to find the effective annual rate charged by the bank:

$EAR = (1 + i_{Nom}/m)^m - 1$
$= (1 + 0.18/12)^{12} - 1$
$= (1.0150)^{12} - 1 = 19.56\%.$

Now, we can find the nominal rate Martha must quote her customers so that her financing costs are exactly covered:

$19.56\% = (1 + i_{Nom}/3)^3 - 1$
$1.1956 = (1 + i_{Nom}/3)^3$
$1.0614 = 1 + i_{Nom}/3$
$0.0614 = i_{Nom}/3$
$\qquad i_{Nom} = 18.41\%.$

17. a.

Year	Payment	Interest	Repayment on Principal	Remaining Principal Balance
1	$7,047.55	$6,000.00	$1,047.55	$58,952.45
2	7,047.55	5,895.25	1,152.30	57,800.15

18. d. Currently: $FV_n = \$1,000(1+0.16)^2 = \$1,000(1.3456) = \$1,345.60.$

With a financial calculator, input N = 2, I = 16, PV = -1000, PMT = 0, and solve for FV = $1,345.60.

New account: $FV_n = \$1,000(1 + i_{Nom}/m)^{mn} = \$1,000(1.3686) = \$1,368.60.$

With a financial calculator, input N = 8, I = 4, PV = -1000, PMT = 0, and solve for FV = $1,368.57.

Thus, the new account will be worth $1,368.60 − $1,345.60 = $23.00 more after 2 years. With a financial calculator, the new account will be worth $22.97 more after 2 years.

PV of difference = $23(PVIF$_{4\%,8}$) = $23 $(1/(1+0.04)^8)$ = $23(0.7307) = $16.81.

With a financial calculator, input N = 8, I = 4, PMT = 0, FV = 22.97, and solve for PV = −$16.78.

Therefore, the most you should be willing to pay the finder for locating the new account is $16.81.

19. e. $\$11,958.20 = \$2,000(PVIF_{12\%,1}) + CF_2(PVIF_{12\%,2})$
         $+ \$4,000(PVIF_{12\%,3}) + \$4,000(PVIF_{12\%,4})$
         $\$11,958.20 = \$2,000(1/1.12) + CF_2(1/1.12^2) + \$4,000(1/1.12^3) + \$4,000(1/1.12^4)$
         $\$11,958.20 = \$2,000(0.8929) + CF_2(0.7972) + \$4,000(0.7118) + \$4,000(0.6355)$
         $\$11,958.20 = \$7,175.00 + (0.7972)CF_2$
         $(0.7972)CF_2 = \$4,783.20$
         $CF_2 = \$6,000.00.$

With a financial calculator, input cash flows into the cash flow register, using -11,958.20 as the cash flow for time 0 (CF$_0$), and using 0 as the value for the unknown cash flow, input I = 12, and then press the NPV key to solve for the present value of the unknown cash flow, $4,783.29. This value should be compounded by $(1.12)^2$, so that $4,783.29(1.2544) = $6,000.16.

20. b. First, how much must you accumulate on your 18th birthday?

$PVA_n = \$4,000(PVIFA_{12\%,4}) = \$4,000[(1-[1/(1+i)^n])/i] = \$4,000[(1-[1/(1+0.12)^4])/0.12]$
$PVA_n = \$4,000(3.0373) = \$12,149.20.$
Present birthday = ?

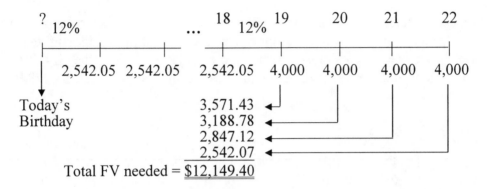

Using a financial calculator (with the calculator set for an ordinary annuity), enter N = 4, I = 12, PMT = 4000, FV = 0, and solve for PV = -$12,149.40. This is the amount (or lump sum) that must be present in your bank account on your 18th birthday in order for you to be able to withdraw $4,000 at the end of each year for the next 4 years.

Now, how many payments of $2,542.05 must you make to accumulate $12,149.20?

Using a financial calculator, enter I = 12, PV = 0, PMT = -2542.05, FV = 12149.40, and solve for N = 4. Therefore, if you make payments at 18, 17, 16, and 15, you are now 14.

21. c. This can be done with a calculator by specifying an interest rate of 4 percent per period for 40 periods.

N = 20 x 2 = 40.
I = 8/2 = 4.
PV = -50000.
FV = 0.
PMT = $2,526.17.

Set up an amortization table:

Period	Beginning Balance	Payment	Interest	Payment of Principal	Ending Balance
1	$50,000.00	$2,526.17	$2,000.00	$526.17	$49,473.83
2	49,473.83	2,526.17	1,978.95		
			$3,978.95		

You can really just work the problem with a financial calculator using the amortization function. Find the interest in each 6-month period, sum them, and you have the answer. Even simpler, with some calculators such as the HP-17B, just input 2 for periods and press INT to get the interest during the first year, $3,978.95.

22. e.

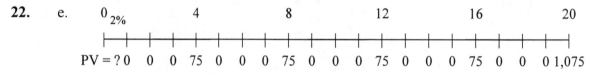

Input the cash flows in the cash flow register, input I = 2, and solve for NPV = $970.51.

Alternatively, find the equivalent annual interest rate: $I=(1+.02)^4=0.08243=8.243\%$. Now use your financial calculator: N = 5, I = 8.243, PMT = 75, FV = 1000, and solve for PV =

23. a. Input N = 5, I = 7, PV = -500000, and FV = 0 to solve for PMT = $121,945.35.

Year	Beginning Balance	Payment	Interest	Payment of Principal	Ending Balance
1	$500,000.00	$121,945.35	$35,000.00	$86,945.35	$413,054.65
2	413,054.65	121,945.35	28,913.83	93,031.52	320,023.13

The fraction that is principal is $93,031.52/$121,945.35 = 76.29%.

24. b. Start with a time line to picture the situation:

Bank: 14% nominal; EAR = 14.93%.

```
0   1   2   3   4   5   6   7   8   9   10  11  12
├───┼───┼───┼───┼───┼───┼───┼───┼───┼───┼───┼───┤
```

Insurance company: EAR = 14.93%; Nominal = 14.16%.

```
0           1           2           3           4
├───────────┼───────────┼───────────┼───────────┤
```

Here we must find the EAR on the bank loan and then find the quarterly nominal rate for that EAR. The bank loan amounts to a nominal 14 percent, monthly compounding.

Using the interest conversion feature of the calculator, or the EAR formula, we must find the EAR on the bank loan. Enter P/YR = 12 and NOM% = 14, and then press the EFF% key to find EAR bank loan = 14.93%.

Now, we can find the nominal rate with quarterly compounding that also has an EAR of 14.93 percent. Enter P/YR = 4 and EFF% = 14.93, and then press the NOM% key to get 14.16%. If the insurance company quotes a nominal rate of 14.16%, with quarterly compounding, then the bank and insurance company loans would be equivalent in the sense that they both have the same effective annual rate, 14.93%.

Alternative solution:

$$EAR = (1 + i_{Nom}/12)^{12} - 1$$
$$= (1 + 0.14/12)^{12} - 1$$
$$= 14.93\%.$$

$$14.93\% = (1 + i_{Nom}/4)^4 - 1$$
$$1.1493 = (1 + i_{Nom}/4)^4$$
$$1.0354 = 1 + i_{Nom}/4$$
$$0.0354 = i_{Nom}/4$$
$$i_{Nom} = 14.16\%.$$

25.   e.   Inflation = 3%.

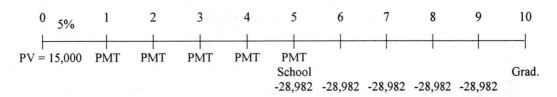

Fixed income = $25,000(1.03)^5 = $28,981.85.

1. Find the FV of $25,000 compounded for 5 years at 3 percent; that FV, $28,981.85, is the amount you will need each year while you are in school. (Note: Your real income will decline.)

2. You must have enough in 5 years to make the $28,981.85 payments to yourself. These payments will begin as soon as you start school, so we are dealing with a 5-year, 5 percent interest rate *annuity due*. Set the calculator to "BEG" mode, because we are dealing with an annuity due, and then enter N = 5, I = 5, PMT = -28981.85, and FV = 0. Then press the PV key to find the PV, $131,750.06. This is the amount you must have in your account 5 years from today. (Do not forget to switch the calculator back to "END" mode.)

3. You now have $15,000. It will grow at 5 percent to $19,144.22 after 5 years. Enter N = 5, I = 5, PV = -15000, and PMT = 0, to solve for FV = $19,144.22. You can subtract this amount to determine the FV of the amount you must save: $131,750.06 − $19,144.22 = $112,605.84.

4. Therefore, you must accumulate an additional $112,605.84 by saving PMT per year for 5 years, with the first PMT being deposited at the end of this year and earning a 5 percent interest rate. Now we have an ordinary annuity, so be sure you returned your calculator to "END" mode. Enter N = 5, I = 5, PV = 0, FV = 112605.84, and then press PMT to find the required payments, -$20,378.82.

26. c. Find the EAR on the TV dealer's credit. Use the interest conversion feature of your calculator. First, though, note that if you are charged a 15 percent nominal rate, you will have to pay interest of 15%/4 = 3.75% after 3 months. The dealer then has the use of the interest, so he can earn 3.75 percent on it for the next three months, and so forth. Thus, we are dealing with quarterly compounding. The nominal rate is 15 percent, quarterly compounding.

Enter NOM% = 15, P/YR = 4, and then press EFF% to get EAR = 15.8650%. You should be indifferent between the dealer credit and the bank loan if the bank loan has an EAR of 15.8650 percent. The bank is using monthly compounding, or 12 periods per year. To find the nominal rate at which you should be indifferent, enter P/YR = 12, EFF% = 15.8650, and then press NOM% to get NOM% = 14.8163%.

Conclusion: A loan that has a 14.8163 percent nominal rate with monthly compounding is equivalent to a 15 percent nominal rate loan with quarterly compounding. Both have an EAR of 15.8650 percent.

Alternative Solution

$$EAR = (1 + i_{Nom}/4)^4 - 1$$
$$= (1 + 0.15/4)^4 - 1$$
$$= (1.0375)^4 - 1$$
$$= 15.8650\%.$$

$$15.8650\% = (1 + i_{Nom}/12)^{12} - 1$$
$$1.15865 = (1 + i_{Nom}/12)^{12}$$
$$1.012347 = 1 + i_{Nom}/12$$
$$i_{Nom} = 14.8163\%.$$

27.   a.   Information given:

1. Will save for 20 years, then receive payments for 25 years.

2. Wants payments of $75,000 per year in today's dollars for first payment only. Real income will decline. Inflation will be 4 percent. Therefore, to find the inflated fixed payments, we have this time line:

Enter N = 20, I = 4, PV = -75000, PMT = 0, and press FV to get FV = $164,334.24.

3. He now has $200,000 in an account which pays 7 percent, annual compounding. We need to find the FV of $200,000 after 20 years. Enter N = 20, I = 7, PV = -200000, PMT = 0, and press FV to get FV = $773,936.89.

4. He wants to withdraw, or have payments of, $164,334.24 per year for 25 years, with the first payment made at the beginning of the first retirement year. So, we have a 25-year annuity due with PMT = $164,334.24, at an interest rate of 7 percent. (The interest rate is 7 percent annually, so no adjustment is required.) Set the calculator to "BEG" mode, then enter N = 25, I = 7, PMT = -164334.24, FV = 0, and press PV to get PV = $2,049,138.53. This amount must be on hand to make the 25 payments.

5. Since the original $200,000, which grows to $773,936.89, will be available, he must save enough to accumulate $2,049,138.53 − $773,936.89 = $1,275,201.64.

6. The $1,275,201.64 is the FV of a 20-year ordinary annuity. The payments will be deposited in the bank and earn 7 percent interest. Therefore, set the calculator to "END" mode and enter N = 20, I = 7, PV = 0, FV = 1275201.64, and press PMT to find PMT = $31,105.90.

CHAPTER 9
BONDS AND THEIR VALUATION

OVERVIEW

This chapter presents a discussion of the key characteristics of bonds, and then uses time value of money concepts to determine bond values. Bonds are one of the most important types of securities to investors, a major source of financing for corporations and governments.

The value of any financial asset is the present value of the cash flows expected from that asset. Therefore, once the cash flows have been estimated, and a discount rate determined, the value of the financial asset can be calculated.

A bond is valued as the present value of the stream of interest payments (an annuity) plus the present value of the par value which is received by the investor on the bond's maturity date. Depending on the relationship between the current interest rate and the bond's coupon rate, a bond can sell at its par value, at a *discount*, or at a *premium*. The total rate of return on a bond is comprised of two components: *interest yield* and *capital gains yield.*

The bond valuation concepts developed earlier in the chapter are used to illustrate interest rate and reinvestment rate risk. In addition, default risk, various types of corporate bonds, bond ratings, and bond markets are discussed.

OUTLINE

A bond is a long-term contract under which a borrower agrees to make payments of interest and principal, on specific dates, to the holders of the bond. There are four main types of bonds: Treasury, corporate, municipal, and foreign. Each type differs with respect to expected return and degree of risk.

■ *Treasury bonds*, sometimes referred to as government bonds, are issued by the Federal government and are not exposed to default risk.

■ *Corporate bonds* are issued by corporations and are exposed to default risk. Different corporate bonds have different levels of default risk, depending on the issuing company's characteristics and on the terms of the specific bond.

■   *Municipal bonds* are issued by state and local governments. The interest earned on most municipal bonds is exempt from federal taxes, and also from state taxes if the holder is a resident of the issuing state.

■   *Foreign bonds* are issued by foreign governments or foreign corporations. These bonds are not only exposed to default risk, but are also exposed to an additional risk if the bonds are denominated in a currency other than that of the investor's home currency.

Differences in contractual provisions, and in the underlying strength of the companies backing the bonds, lead to major differences in bonds' risks, prices, and expected returns. It is important to understand both the key characteristics, which are common to all bonds, and how differences in these characteristics affect the values and risks of individual bonds.

■   The *par value* is the stated face value of a bond, usually $1,000. This is the amount of money that the firm borrows and promises to repay on the maturity date.

■   The *coupon interest payment* is the dollar amount that is paid annually to a bondholder by the issuer for use of the $1,000 loan. This payment is a fixed amount, established at the time the bond is issued. The *coupon interest rate* is obtained by dividing the coupon payment by the par value of the bond.

    ❑   In some cases, a bond's coupon payment may vary over time. These bonds are called *floating rate,* or *indexed, bonds.* Floating rate debt is popular with investors because the market value of the debt is stabilized. It is advantageous to corporations because firms can issue long-term debt without committing themselves to paying a historically high interest rate for the entire life of the loan.

    ❑   *Zero coupon bonds* pay no coupons at all, but are offered at a substantial discount below their par values, and hence, provide capital appreciation rather than interest income.

    ❑   In general, any bond originally offered at a price significantly below its par value is called an *original issue discount bond (OID).*

■   The *maturity date* is the date on which the par value must be repaid. Most bonds have *original maturities* of from 10 to 40 years, but any maturity is legally permissible.

■   Most bonds contain a *call provision*, which gives the issuing corporation the right to call the bonds for redemption. The call provision generally states that if the bonds are called, the company must pay the bondholders an amount greater than the par value, which is a *call premium.*

    ❑   Bonds are often not callable until several years after they are issued. This is known as a *deferred call*, and the bonds are said to have *call protection*.

    ❑   A call provision is valuable to the firm but potentially detrimental to investors. Investors lose when interest rates go up, but don't reap the gains when rates fall. To

induce an investor to take this type of risk a new issue of callable bonds must provide a higher interest rate than an otherwise similar issue of noncallable bonds.
- ❑ The process of using the proceeds of a new low-rate bond issue to retire a high-rate issue and reduce the firm's interest expense is called a *refunding operation*.

- ■ Bonds that are *redeemable at par* at the holder's option protect the holder against a rise in interest rates.
  - ❑ *Event risk* is the risk that some sudden action, such as an LBO, will occur and increase the credit risk of the company, hence lower the firm's bond rating and the value of its outstanding bonds.
  - ❑ In an attempt to control debt costs, a new type of protective covenant devised to minimize event risk was developed. This covenant, called a *super poison put*, enables a bondholder to turn in, or "put" a bond back to the issuer at par in the event of a takeover, merger, or major recapitalization.

- ■ A *sinking fund provision* facilitates the orderly retirement of a bond issue. This can be achieved in one of two ways, and the firm will choose the least-cost method.
  - ❑ The company can call in for redemption (at par value) a certain percentage of bonds each year.
  - ❑ The company may buy the required amount of bonds on the open market.

- ■ *Convertible bonds* are securities that are convertible into shares of common stock, at a fixed price, at the option of the bondholder.
  - ❑ Convertibles have a lower coupon rate than nonconvertible debt, but they offer investors a chance for capital gains in exchange for the lower coupon rate.

- ■ Bonds issued with *warrants* are similar to convertibles. Warrants are options which permit the holder to buy stock for a stated price, thereby providing a capital gain if the stock price rises.
  - ❑ Like convertibles, they carry lower coupon rates than straight bonds.

- ■ *Income bonds* pay interest only if the interest is earned. These securities cannot bankrupt a company, but from an investor's standpoint they are riskier than "regular" bonds.

- ■ The interest rate of an *indexed, or purchasing power, bond* is based on an inflation index such as the consumer price index (CPI), so the interest paid rises automatically when the inflation rate rises, thus protecting the bondholders against inflation.

The value of any financial asset is simply the present value of the cash flows the asset is expected to produce. The cash flows from a specific bond depend on its contractual features.

■ A bond represents an annuity plus a lump sum, and its value is found as the present value of this payment stream:

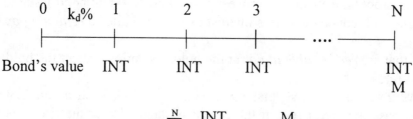

$$\text{Bond value} = \sum_{t=1}^{N} \frac{\text{INT}}{(1+k_d)^t} + \frac{M}{(1+k_d)^N}$$

$$= \text{INT} \left(\frac{1 - \dfrac{1}{(1+k_d)^N}}{k_d} \right) + \frac{M}{(1+k_d)^N}$$

$$= \text{INT}\left(\text{PVIFA}_{k_d,N}\right) + M\left(\text{PVIF}_{k_d,N}\right).$$

■ Here INT = dollars of interest paid each year, M = par, or maturity, value, which is typically $1,000, k_d = interest rate on the bond, and N = number of years until the bond matures.

■ For example, consider a 15-year, $1,000 bond paying $150 annually, when the appropriate interest rate, k_d, is 15 percent. Utilizing the formula above, we find:

$$V_B = \$150 \left(\frac{1 - \dfrac{1}{(1+0.15)^{15}}}{0.15} \right) + \frac{\$1,000}{(1+0.15)^{15}}$$

$$= \$150(5.8474) + \$1,000(0.1229)$$
$$= \$877.11 + \$122.90$$
$$= \$1,000.01 \approx \$1,000.$$

❏ Using a financial calculator, enter N = 15, k_d = I = 15, PMT = 150, and FV = 1000, and then press the PV key for an answer of -$1,000.

❏ Excel and other spreadsheet software packages provide specialized functions for bond prices.

■ A *new issue* is the term applied to a bond that has just been issued. At the time of issue, the coupon payment is generally set at a level that will force the market price of the bond to equal its par value. Once the bond has been on the market for a while, it is classified as an outstanding bond, or a *seasoned issue*.

■ Bond prices and interest rates are *inversely* related; that is, they tend to move in the opposite direction from one another.

   ❑ A fixed-rate bond will sell at par when its coupon interest rate is equal to the going rate of interest, k_d.

   ❑ When the going rate of interest is above the coupon rate, a fixed-rate bond will sell at a *discount* below its par value.

   ❑ If current interest rates are below the coupon rate, a fixed-rate bond will sell at a *premium* above its par value.

   ❑ Your percentage rate of return on a bond consists of an *interest yield*, or *current yield*, plus a *capital gains yield*.

The expected interest rate on a bond, also called its "yield," can be calculated in three different ways.

■ The rate of return earned on a bond if it is held until maturity is known as the *yield to maturity (YTM)*. The YTM for a bond that sells at par consists entirely of an interest yield, but if the bond sells at a price other than its par value, the YTM consists of the interest yield plus a positive or negative capital gains yield.

   ❑ The yield to maturity can also be viewed as the bond's *promised rate of return*, which is the return that investors will receive if all the promised payments are made.

   ❑ The yield to maturity equals the expected rate of return only if (1) the probability of default is zero and (2) the bond cannot be called.

■ If current interest rates are well below an outstanding bond's coupon rate, then a *callable bond* is likely to be called, and investors should estimate the most likely rate of return on the bond as the *yield to call (YTC)* rather than as the yield to maturity. To calculate the YTC, solve this equation for k_d:

$$\text{Price of bond} = \sum_{t=1}^{N} \frac{\text{INT}}{(1+k_d)^t} + \frac{\text{Call price}}{(1+k_d)^N}.$$

■ The *current yield* is the annual interest payment divided by the bond's current price. The current yield provides information about the cash income a bond will generate in a given year, but since it does not take account of capital gains or losses that will be realized if the bond is held until maturity (or call), it does not provide an accurate measure of the total expected return.

The bond valuation model must be adjusted when interest is paid semiannually:

$$V_B = \sum_{t=1}^{2N} \frac{INT/2}{(1+k_d/2)^t} + \frac{M}{(1+k_d/2)^{2N}}$$

$$= (INT/2)\left(\frac{1 - \dfrac{1}{(1+k_d/2)^{2N}}}{k_d/2}\right) + \frac{M}{(1+k_d/2)^{2N}}$$

$$= (INT/2)\left(PVIFA_{k_d/2,2N}\right) + M\left(PVIF_{k_d/2,2N}\right).$$

Interest rates fluctuate over time.

- People or firms who invest in bonds are exposed to risk from changing interest rates, or *interest rate risk*. The longer the maturity of the bond, the greater the exposure to interest rate risk.
  - To induce an investor to take this extra risk, long-term bonds must have a higher expected rate of return than short-term bonds. This additional return is the *maturity risk premium*.

- The shorter the maturity of the bond, the greater the risk of a decrease in interest rates. The risk of a decline in income due to a drop in interest rates is called *reinvestment rate risk*.

- Interest rate risk relates to the *value* of the bonds in a portfolio, while reinvestment rate risk relates to the *income* the portfolio produces. No fixed-rate bond can be considered totally riskless. Bond portfolio managers try to balance these two risks, but some risk always exists in any bond.

Another important risk associated with bonds is default risk. If the issuer defaults, investors receive less than the promised return on the bond. Default risk is affected by both the financial strength of the issuer and the terms of the bond contract, especially whether collateral has been pledged to secure the bond.

- The greater the default risk, the higher the bond's yield to maturity.

- A corporation can affect default risk by the terms of the bond contract.
  - An *indenture* is a legal document that spells out the rights of both bondholders and the issuing corporation.
  - A *trustee* is an official who represents the bondholders and makes sure the terms of the indenture are carried out.

- ❑ *Restrictive covenants* are typically included in the indenture and cover such points as the conditions under which the issuer can pay off the bonds prior to maturity, the level at which the issuer's TIE ratio must be maintained if the company is to issue additional debt, and restrictions against the payment of dividends unless earnings meet certain specifications.

- ■ Corporations can affect the default risk of their bonds by changing the type of bonds they issue.
  - ❑ Under a *mortgage bond*, the corporation pledges certain assets as security for the bond.
  - ❑ A *debenture* is an unsecured bond, and as such, it provides no lien against specific property as security for the obligation. Debenture holders are, therefore, general creditors whose claims are protected by property not otherwise pledged.
  - ❑ *Subordinated debentures* have claims on assets, in the event of bankruptcy, only after senior debt as named in the subordinated debt's indenture has been paid off. Subordinated debentures may be subordinated to designated notes payable or to all other debt.
  - ❑ Some companies may be in a position to benefit from the sale of either *development bonds* or *pollution control bonds*. State and local governments may set up both industrial development agencies and pollution control agencies. The agencies are allowed, under certain circumstances, to sell *tax-exempt bonds*, then to make the proceeds available to corporations for specific uses deemed by Congress to be in the public interest.

- ■ Municipalities can have their bonds insured. An insurance company guarantees to pay the coupon and principal payments should the issuer default.
  - ❑ This reduces risk to investors, who will thus accept a lower coupon rate for an insured bond vis-a-vis an uninsured one.

- ■ Bond issues are normally assigned quality ratings by major rating agencies, such as Moody's Investors Service and Standard & Poor's Corporation. These ratings reflect the probability that a bond will go into default. Aaa (Moody's) and AAA (S&P) are the highest ratings.
  - ❑ Rating assignments are based on qualitative and quantitative factors including the firm's debt/assets ratio, current ratio, and coverage ratios.
  - ❑ Bond ratings are important both to firms and to investors.
  - ❑ Because a bond's rating is an indicator of its default risk, the rating has a direct, measurable influence on the bond's interest rate and the firm's cost of debt capital.
  - ❑ Most bonds are purchased by institutional investors rather than individuals, and many institutions are restricted to *investment-grade* securities, securities with ratings of Baa/BBB or above.
  - ❑ Changes in a firm's bond rating affect both its ability to borrow long-term capital and the cost of that capital. Rating agencies review outstanding bonds on a periodic

basis, occasionally upgrading or downgrading a bond as the issuer's circumstances change. Also, if a company issues more bonds, this will trigger a review by the rating agencies.

■ *Junk bonds* are high-risk, high-yield bonds issued to finance leveraged buyouts, mergers, or troubled companies.

　❑ The emergence of junk bonds as an important type of debt is another example of how the investment banking industry adjusts to and facilitates new developments in capital markets.

　❑ The development of junk bond financing has done much to reshape the U. S. financial scene. The existence of these securities has led directly to the loss of independence of some companies, and has led to major shake-ups in other companies.

Corporate bonds are traded primarily in the over-the-counter market. Most bonds are owned by and traded among the large financial institutions, and it is relatively easy for the over-the-counter bond dealers to arrange the transfer of large blocks of bonds among the relatively few holders of the bonds.

■ Information on bond trades in the over-the-counter market is not published, but a representative group of bonds is listed and traded on the bond division of the NYSE.

SELF-TEST QUESTIONS

Definitional

1.　A(n) _____ is a long-term contract under which a borrower agrees to make payments of interest and principal on specific dates.

2.　_____ bonds are issued by state and local governments, and the _____ earned on these bonds is exempt from federal taxes.

3.　The stated face value of a bond is referred to as its _____ value and is usually set at $_____.

4.　The "coupon interest rate" on a bond is determined by dividing the _____ _____ by the _____ _____ of the bond.

5.　The date at which the par value of a bond is repaid to each bondholder is known as the _____ _____.

6. A(n) _____ _____, or _____, bond is one whose interest rate fluctuates with shifts in the general level of interest rates.

7. A(n) _____ _____ bond is one that pays no annual interest but is sold at a discount below par, thus providing compensation to investors in the form of capital appreciation.

8. The legal document setting forth the terms and conditions of a bond issue is known as the _____.

9. In meeting its sinking fund requirements, a firm may _____ the bonds or purchase them on the _____ _____.

10. Except when the call is for sinking fund purposes, when a bond issue is called, the firm must pay a(n) _____ _____, which is an amount in excess of the _____ value of the bond.

11. A bond with annual coupon payments represents an annuity of INT dollars per year for N years, plus a lump sum of M dollars at the end of N years, and its value, V_B, is the _____ _____ of this payment stream.

12. At the time a bond is issued, the coupon interest rate is generally set at a level that will cause the _____ _____ and the _____ _____ of the bond to be approximately equal.

13. Market interest rates and bond prices move in _____ directions from one another.

14. The rate of return earned by purchasing a bond and holding it until maturity is known as the bond's _____ ____ _____.

15. To adjust the bond valuation formula for semiannual coupon payments, the _____ _____ and _____ _____ must be divided by 2, and the number of _____ must be multiplied by 2.

16. A bond secured by real estate is known as a(n) _____ bond.

17. _____ bonds are issued by the Federal government and are not exposed to default risk.

18. _____ bonds pay interest only if the interest is earned.

19. The interest rate of a(n) _____, or _____ _____, bond is based on an inflation index, so the interest paid rises automatically when the inflation rate rises, thus protecting the bondholders against inflation.

20. Any bond originally offered at a price significantly below its par value is called a(n) _____ _____ _____ bond.

21. Once a bond has been on the market for a while, it is classified as an outstanding bond, or a(n) _____ _____.

22. The _____ _____ is the annual interest payment divided by the bond's current price.

23. Bonds are often not callable until several years after they are issued. This is known as a(n) _____ _____, and the bonds are said to have _____ _____.

24. To induce investors to take on the risk of a callable bond, a new issue of callable bonds must provide a(n) _____ interest rate than an otherwise similar issue of noncallable bonds.

25. _____ are options sold with bonds which permit the holder to buy stock for a stated price, thereby providing a capital gain if the stock price rises.

26. _____ risk is the risk that some sudden action, such as an LBO, will occur and increase the credit risk of the company, hence lower the firm's bond rating and the value of its outstanding bonds.

27. To induce an investor to take on the extra risk of investing in long-term bonds, they must have a higher expected rate of return than short-term bonds. The additional return is the _____ _____ _____.

28. A(n) _____ is an official who represents the bondholders and makes sure the terms of the indenture are carried out.

29. _____ bonds are high-risk, high-yield bonds issued to finance leveraged buyouts, mergers, or troubled companies.

Conceptual

30. Changes in economic conditions cause interest rates and bond prices to vary over time.

    a. True   b. False

31. If the appropriate rate of interest on a bond is greater than its coupon rate, the market value of that bond will be above par value.

    a. True   b. False

32. A 20-year, annual coupon bond with one year left to maturity has the same interest rate risk as a 10-year, annual coupon bond with one year left to maturity. Both bonds are of equal risk, have the same coupon rate, and the prices of the two bonds are equal.

    a. True   **b.** False

33. There is a direct relationship between bond ratings and the required rate of return on bonds; that is, the higher the rating, the higher is the required rate of return.

    a. True   **b.** False

34. The "penalty" for having a low bond rating is less severe when the Security Market Line is relatively steep than when it is not so steep.

    a. True   **b.** False

35. Which of the following statements is *false*? In all of the statements, assume that "other things are held constant."

    a. Price sensitivity—that is, the change in price due to a given change in the required rate of return—increases as a bond's maturity increases.
    b. For a given bond of any maturity, a given percentage point increase in the going interest rate (k_d) causes a *larger* dollar capital loss than the capital gain stemming from an identical decrease in the interest rate.
    c. For any given maturity, a given percentage point increase in the interest rate causes a *smaller* dollar capital loss than the capital gain stemming from an identical decrease in the interest rate.
    d. From a borrower's point of view, interest paid on bonds is tax deductible.
    e. A 20-year zero-coupon bond has less reinvestment rate risk than a 20-year coupon bond.

36. Which of the following statements is most correct?

    a. Ignoring interest accrued between payment dates, if the required rate of return on a bond is less than its coupon interest rate, and k_d remains below the coupon rate until maturity, then the market value of that bond will be below its par value until the bond matures, at which time its market value will equal its par value.
    b. Assuming equal coupon rates, a 20-year original maturity bond with one year left to maturity has more interest rate risk than a 10-year original maturity bond with one year left to maturity.
    c. Regardless of the size of the coupon payment, the price of a bond moves in the same direction as interest rates; for example, if interest rates rise, bond prices also rise.
    d. For bonds, price sensitivity to a given change in interest rates generally increases as

years remaining to maturity increases.

e. Because short-term interest rates are much more volatile than long-term rates, you would, in the real world, be subject to more interest rate risk if you purchased a 30-*day* bond than if you bought a 30-*year* bond.

37. Which of the following statements is most correct?

a. Bonds C and Z both have a $1,000 par value and 10 years to maturity. They have the same default risk, and they both have an effective annual rate (EAR) = 8%. If Bond C has a 15 percent annual coupon and Bond Z a zero coupon (paying just $1,000 at maturity), then Bond Z will be exposed to more *interest rate risk*, which is defined as the *percentage* loss of value in response to a given increase in the going interest rate.

b. If the words "interest rate risk" were replaced by the words "reinvestment rate risk" in Statement a, then the statement would be true.

c. The interest rate paid by the state of Florida on its debt would be lower, other things held constant, if interest on the debt were not exempt from federal income taxes.

d. Given the conditions in Statement a, we can be sure that Bond Z would have the higher price.

e. Statements a, b, c, and d are all false.

38. If a company's bonds are selling at a *discount*, then:

a. The YTM is the return investors probably expect to earn.

b. The YTC is probably the expected return.

c. Either a or b could be correct, depending on the yield curve.

d. The current yield will exceed the expected rate of return.

e. The after-tax cost of debt to the company will have to be less than the coupon rate on the bonds.

SELF-TEST PROBLEMS

1. Delta Corporation has a bond issue outstanding with an annual coupon rate of 7 percent and 4 years remaining until maturity. The par value of the bond is $1,000. Determine the current value of the bond if present market conditions justify a 14 percent required rate of return. The bond pays interest annually.

    a. $1,126.42   **b.** $1,000.00   **c.** $796.06   **d.** $791.00   **e.** $536.42

2. Refer to Self-Test Problem 1. Suppose the bond had a semiannual coupon. Now what would be its current value?

    a. $1,126.42   **b.** $1,000.00   **c.** $796.06   **d.** $791.00   **e.** $536.42

3. Refer to Self-Test Problem 1. Assume an annual coupon but 20 years remaining to maturity. What is the current value under these conditions?

    a. $1,126.42   **b.** $1,000.00   **c.** $796.06   **d.** $791.00   **e.** $536.42

4. Refer to Self-Test Problem 3. What is the bond's current yield?

    a. 12.20%   **b.** 13.05%   **c.** 13.75%   **d.** 14.00%   **e.** 14.50%

5. Acme Products has a bond issue outstanding with 8 years remaining to maturity, a coupon rate of 10 percent with interest paid annually, and a par value of $1,000. If the current market price of the bond issue is $814.45, what is the yield to maturity, k_d?

    a. 12%   **b.** 13%   **c.** 14%   **d.** 15%   **e.** 16%

6. You have just been offered a bond for $863.73. The coupon rate is 8 percent, payable annually, and interest rates on new issues with the same degree of risk are 10 percent. You want to know how many more interest payments you will receive, but the party selling the bond cannot remember. If the par value is $1,000, how many interest payments remain?

    a. 10   **b.** 11   **c.** 12   **d.** 13   **e.** 14

7. Bird Corporation's 12 percent coupon rate, semiannual payment, $1,000 par value bonds which mature in 20 years are callable at a price of $1,100 five years from now. The bonds sell at a price of $1,300, and the yield curve is flat. Assuming that interest rates in the economy are expected to remain at their current level, what is the best estimate of Bird's *nominal interest rate* on the new bonds? (Hint: You will need a financial calculator to work this problem.)

    a. 8.46%   **b.** 6.16%   **c.** 9.28%   **d.** 6.58%   **e.** 8.76%

8. The Graf Company needs to finance some new R&D programs, so it will sell new bonds for this purpose. Graf's currently outstanding bonds have a $1,000 par value, a 10 percent coupon rate, and pay interest semiannually. The outstanding bonds have 25 years remaining to maturity, are callable after 5 years at a price of $1,090, and currently sell at a price of $700. The yield curve is expected to remain flat. On the basis of these data, what is the best estimate of Graf's *nominal interest rate* on the new bonds it plans to sell?

(Hint: You will need a financial calculator to work this problem.)

    a. 21.10%   **b.** 14.48%   **c.** 15.67%   **d.** 16.25%   **e.** 18.29%

9.   Suppose Hadden Inc. is negotiating with an insurance company to sell a bond issue. Each bond has a par value of $1,000, it would pay 10 percent per year in quarterly payments of $25 per quarter for 10 years, and then it would pay 12 percent per year ($30 per quarter) for the next 10 years (Years 11-20). The $1,000 principal would be returned at the end of 20 years. The insurance company's alternative investment is in a 20-year mortgage which has a nominal rate of 14 percent and which provides monthly payments. If the mortgage and the bond issue are equally risky, how much should the insurance company be willing to pay Hadden for each bond? (Hint: You will need a financial calculator to work this problem.)

    a. $750.78   **b.** $781.50   **c.** $804.65   **d.** $710.49   **e.** $840.97

ANSWERS TO SELF-TEST QUESTIONS

1.	bond	**16.**	mortgage
2.	Municipal; interest	**17.**	Treasury
3.	par; 1,000	**18.**	Income
4.	coupon payment; par value	**19.**	indexed; purchasing power
5.	maturity date	**20.**	original issue discount
6.	floating rate; indexed	**21.**	seasoned issue
7.	zero coupon	**22.**	current yield
8.	indenture	**23.**	deferred call; call protection
9.	call; open market	**24.**	higher
10.	call premium; par	**25.**	Warrants
11.	present value	**26.**	Event
12.	market price; par value	**27.**	maturity risk premium
13.	opposite	**28.**	trustee
14.	yield to maturity	**29.**	Junk
15.	coupon payment; interest rate; years		

30.   a. For example, if inflation increases, the interest rate (or required return) will increase, resulting in a decline in bond price.

31.   b. It will sell at a discount.

32.   a. Both bonds are valued as 1-year bonds regardless of their original issue dates, and since they are of equal risk and have the same coupon rate, their prices must be equal.

33. b. The relationship is inverse. The higher the rating, the lower is the default risk and hence the lower is the required rate of return. Aaa/AAA is the highest rating, and as we go down the alphabet, the ratings are lower.

34. b. A steeper SML implies a higher risk premium on risky securities and thus a greater "penalty" on lower-rated bonds.

35. b. Statements a, d, and e are all true. To determine which of the remaining statements is false, it is best to use an example. Assume you have a 10-year, 10 percent annual coupon bond which sold at par. If interest rates increase to 13 percent, the value of the bond decreases to $837.21, while if interest rates decrease to 7 percent, the value of the bond increases to $1,210.71. Thus, the capital gain is greater than the capital loss and statement b is false.

36. d. Statement a is false because the bond would have a premium and thus sell above par value. Statement b is false because both bonds would have the same interest rate risk because they both have one year left to maturity. Statement c is false because the price of a bond moves in the opposite direction as interest rates. Statement e is false because the 30-year bond would have more interest rate risk than the 30-day bond. Statement d is correct. As years to maturity increase for a bond, the number of discount periods used in finding the current bond value also increases. Therefore, bonds with longer maturities will have more price sensitivity to a given change in interest rates.

37. a. Statement a is correct. Bond C has a high coupon (hence its name), so bondholders get cash flows right away. Bond Z has a zero coupon, so its holders will get no cash flows until the bond matures. Since all of the cash flows on Z come at the end, a given increase in the interest rate will cause this bond's value to fall sharply relative to the decline in value of the coupon bond.

You could also use the data in the problem to find the value of the two bonds at two different interest rates, and then calculate the percentage change. For example, at k_d = 15%, V_C = $1,000 and V_Z = $247.18. At k_d = 20%, V_C = $790.38 and V_Z = $161.51. Therefore, Bond Z declines in value by 34.66 percent, while Bond C declines by only 20.96 percent. Note that Bond Z is exposed to *less* reinvestment rate risk than Bond C.

38. a. When bonds sell at a discount, the going interest rate (k_d) is above the coupon rate. If a company called the old discount bonds and replaced them with new bonds, the new coupon would be above the old coupon. This would increase a firm's interest cost; hence, the company would not call the discount bonds. Therefore, the YTM would be the expected rate of return. The shape of the yield curve would have no effect in the situation described in this question, but if the bonds had been selling at a premium, making the YTC the relevant yield, then the yield curve in a sense would have an effect. The YTC would be below the cost if the company were to sell new long-term bonds, if the yield curve were steeply upward sloping. Statement d is false because the expected rate of return would include a current yield component and a capital gains component (because the bond's price will rise from its current discounted price to par as maturity approaches). Therefore, the current yield will *not* exceed the expected rate of return. The after-tax cost of debt is the expected rate adjusted for taxes, $k_d(1 - T)$. Because the bonds are selling at a discount, the coupon rate could be quite low, even zero, so we know that statement e is false. Therefore, statement a is correct.

SOLUTIONS TO SELF-TEST PROBLEMS

1. c. $V_B = INT(PVIFA_{k_d,N}) + M(PVIF_{k_d,N})$
    $= \$70(PVIFA_{14\%,4}) + \$1,000(PVIF_{14\%,4})$
    $= \$70 [(1-1/1.14^4)/0.14] + \$1000 (1/1.14^4)$
    $= \$70(2.9137) + \$1,000(0.5921) = \$796.06.$

    Calculator solution: Input N = 4, I = 14, PMT = 70, FV = 1000, and solve for PV = -\$796.04.

2. d. $V_B = (INT/2)(PVIFA_{k_d/2,2N}) + M(PVIF_{k_d/2,2N})$
    $= \$35(PVIFA_{7\%,8}) + \$1,000(PVIF_{7\%,8})$
    $= \$35 [(1-1/1.07^8)/0.07] + \$1000 (1/1.07^8)$
    $= \$35(5.9713) + \$1,000(0.5820) = \$791.00.$

    Calculator solution: Input N = 8, I = 7, PMT = 35, FV = 1000, and solve for PV = -\$791.00.

3. e. $V_B = INT(PVIFA_{k_d,N}) + M(PVIF_{k_d,N})$
    $= \$70(PVIFA_{14\%,20}) + \$1,000(PVIF_{14\%,20})$
    $= \$70 [(1-1/1.14^{20})/0.14] + \$1000 (1/1.14^{20})$
    $= \$70(6.6231) + \$1,000(0.0728) = \$536.42.$

    Calculator solution: Input N = 20, I = 14, PMT = 70, FV = 1000, and solve for PV = -\$536.38.

4.   b.   From Self-Test Problem 3 we know that the current price of the bond is $536.38.

Therefore, the current yield $= \dfrac{\text{Annual Interest}}{\text{Current Price}}$

$$= \dfrac{\$70}{\$536.38}$$

$$= 13.05\%.$$

5.   c. $V_B = INT(PVIFA_{k_d,N}) + M(PVIF_{k_d,N})$

$814.45 = \$100(PVIFA_{k_d,8}) + \$1,000(PVIF_{k_d,8})$.

$814.45 = \$100 \, [(1-1/(1+k_d)^8)/k_d] + \$1000 \, (1/(1+k_d)^8)$

Now use trial and error techniques. Try $I = k_d = 12\%$:

$814.45 = \$100(4.9676) + \$1,000(0.4039) = \$900.66$.

Since $814.45 < \$900.66$, the yield to maturity is not 12 percent. The calculated value is too large. Therefore, increase the value of I to 14 percent to lower the calculated value: $814.45 = \$100(4.6389) + \$1,000(0.3506) = \$814.49$. This is close enough to conclude that $k_d =$ yield to maturity $= 14\%$.

Calculator solution: Input N = 8, PV = -814.45, PMT = 100, FV = 1000, and solve for $I = k_d = 14.00\%$.

6.   c. $V_B = INT(PVIFA_{k_d,N}) + M(PVIF_{k_d,N})$

$863.73 = \$80(PVIFA_{10\%,N}) + \$1,000(PVIF_{10\%,N})$

$863.73 = \$80 \, [(1-1/(1+0.10)^N)/0.10] + \$1000 \, (1/(1+0.10)^N)$

Now use trial and error to find the value of N for which the equality holds. For N = 12, $80(6.8137) + \$1,000(0.3186) = \$863.70$. Or using a financial calculator, input I = 10, PV = -863.73, PMT = 80, FV = 1000, and solve for N = 12.

7.   d.   The bond is selling at a large premium, which means that its coupon rate is much higher than the going rate of interest. Therefore, the bond is likely to be called—it is more likely to be called than to remain outstanding until it matures. Thus, it will probably provide a return equal to the YTC rather than the YTM. So, there is no point in calculating the YTM; just calculate the YTC. Enter these values: N = 10, PV = -1300, PMT = 60, and FV = 1100. The periodic rate is 3.29 percent, so the nominal YTC is 2(3.29%) = 6.58%. This would be close to the going rate, and it is about what Bird would have to pay on new bonds.

8. b. Investors would expect to earn either the YTM or the YTC, and the expected return on the old bonds is the cost Graf would have to pay in order to sell new bonds.

YTM: Enter $N = 2(25) = 50$; PV = -700; PMT = 100/2 = 50; and FV = 1000. Press I to get $I = k_d/2 = 7.24\%$. Multiply 7.24%(2) = 14.48% to get the YTM.

YTC: Enter $N = 2(5) = 10$, PV = -700, PMT = 50, FV = 1090, and then press I to get I=10.55%. Multiply by 2 to get YTC = 21.10%.

Would investors expect the company to call the bonds? Graf currently pays 10 percent on its debt (the coupon rate). New debt would cost at least 14.48 percent. Because $k_d > 10\%$ coupon rate, it would be stupid for the company to call, so investors would not expect a call. Therefore, they would expect to earn 14.48 percent on the bonds. This is k_d, so 14.48 percent is the rate Graf would probably have to pay on new bonds.

9. a. Time line:

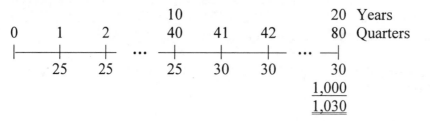

1. You could enter the time line values into the cash flow register, but one element is missing: the interest rate. Once we have the interest rate, we could press the NPV key to get the value of the bond.

2. We need a *periodic* interest rate, and it needs to be a quarterly rate, found as the annual nominal rate divided by 4: $k_{Per} = k_{Nom}/4$. So, we need to find k_{Nom} so that we can find k_{Per}.

3. The insurance company will insist on earning at least the same effective annual rate on the bond issue as it can earn on the mortgage. The mortgage pays 14 percent monthly, which is equivalent to an EAR = 14.93%. Using a financial calculator, enter NOM% = 14, P/YR = 12, and press EFF% to obtain 14.93%. So, the bond issue will have to have a k_{Nom}, with quarterly payments, which translates into an EAR of 14.93 percent.

4. EAR = 14.93% is equivalent to a quarterly nominal rate of 14.16 percent; that is, a nominal rate of 14.16 percent with quarterly compounding has an EAR of 14.93 percent. You can find this by entering EFF% = 14.93, P/YR = 4, and pressing the NOM% key to get NOM% = 14.16%. If this nominal rate is set on the bond issue, the insurance company will earn the same effective rate as it can get on the

mortgage. (Don't forget to set your calculator back to P/YR = 1.)

5. The periodic rate for a 14.16 percent nominal rate, with quarterly compounding, is 14.16%/4 = 3.54%. This 3.54% is the rate to use in the time line calculations.

With an HP-10B calculator, enter the following data:
$CF_0 = 0$, $CF_j = 25$; $N_j = 40$; $CF_j = 30$; $N_j = 39$; $CF_j = 1030$; $I = 3.54$.
Solve for NPV = $750.78 = Value of each bond.

With an HP-17B calculator, enter the following data:
Flow(0) = 0 Input; Flow(1) = 25 Input; # Times = 40 Input; Flow(2) = 30 Input; # Times = 39 Input; Flow(3) = 1030 Input; # Times = 1 Input; Exit; Calc; I = 3.54.
Solve for NPV = $750.78 = Value of each bond.

If each bond is priced at $750.78, the insurance company will earn the same effective rate of return on the bond issue as on the mortgage.

CHAPTER 10
STOCKS AND THEIR VALUATION

OVERVIEW

Common stock constitutes the ownership position in a firm. As owners, common stockholders have certain rights and privileges, including the right to control the firm through election of directors and the right to the firm's residual earnings.

Firms generally begin corporate life as closely held companies, with all the common stock held by the founding managers. Then, as the company grows, it is often necessary to sell stock to the general public (that is, to go public) to raise more funds. Eventually, the firm may choose to list its stock on one of the organized exchanges.

A common stock is valued as the present value of its expected future dividend stream. The total rate of return on a stock is comprised of a dividend yield plus a capital gains yield. If a stock is in equilibrium, its total expected return must equal the average investor's required rate of return.

Preferred stock is a hybrid—it is similar to bonds in some respects and to common stock in others. The value of a share of preferred stock which is expected to pay a constant dividend forever is found as the dividend divided by the required rate of return.

OUTLINE

The corporation's common stockholders are the owners of the corporation, and as such, they have certain rights and privileges.

- Common stockholders have control of the firm through their election of the firm's directors, who in turn elect officers who manage the business.
  - In a large, publicly owned firm, neither the managers nor any individual shareholders normally have the 51 percent necessary for absolute control of the company.
  - Thus, stockholders must vote for directors, and the voting process is regulated by both state and federal laws.
  - Stockholders who are unable to attend annual meetings may still vote by means of a *proxy*. Proxies can be solicited by any party seeking to control the firm.

- If earnings are poor and stockholders are dissatisfied, an outside group may solicit the proxies in an effort to overthrow management and take control of the business. This is known as a *proxy fight*.
- A *takeover* is an action whereby a person or group succeeds in ousting a firm's management and taking control of the company.
- A *poison pill* makes a possible acquisition unattractive and wards off hostile takeover attempts.

■ The *preemptive right* gives the current shareholders the right to purchase any new shares issued in proportion to their current holdings.
- The preemptive right may or may not be required by state law.
- When granted, the preemptive right enables current owners to maintain their proportionate share of ownership and control of the business.
- It also prevents the sale of shares at low prices to new stockholders, which would dilute the value of the previously issued shares.

Special classes of common stock are sometimes created by a firm to meet special needs and circumstances. If two classes of stock were desired, one would normally be called "Class A" and the other "Class B."

■ Class A might be entitled to receive dividends before dividends can be paid on Class B stock.

■ Class B might have the exclusive right to vote.
- Note that Class A and Class B have no standard meanings.

■ *Founders' shares* are stock owned by the firm's founders that have sole voting rights but restricted dividends for a specified number of years.

■ The right to vote is often a distinguishing characteristic between different classes of stock. As you would expect, the stock with voting rights would be more valuable.

Some companies are so small that their common stocks are not actively traded; they are owned by only a few people, usually the companies' managers. Such firms are said to be closely held corporations. In contrast, the stocks of most larger companies are owned by a large number of investors, most of whom are not active in management. Such companies are said to be publicly owned corporations. Larger, publicly owned companies generally apply for listing on an organized security exchange, and they and their stocks are said to be listed.
■ Stock market transactions may be separated into three distinct categories.
- The *secondary market* deals with trading in previously issued, or outstanding, shares of established, publicly owned companies. The company receives no new money when sales are made in the secondary market.

- ❑ The *primary market* handles additional shares sold by established, publicly owned companies. Companies can raise additional capital by selling in this market.
- ❑ The primary market also handles new public offerings of shares in firms that were formerly closely held. Capital for the firm can be raised by *going public*, and this market is often termed the *initial public offering (IPO) market*.

■ Initial offerings are generally *oversubscribed*, which means that the demand for shares at the offering price exceeds the number of shares issued. Investors can buy the stock in the after-market, but evidence suggests that if you do not get in on the ground floor, the average IPO underperforms the overall market over the longer run.

Common stocks are valued by finding the present value of the expected future cash flow stream.

■ People typically buy common stock expecting to earn *dividends* plus a *capital gain* when they sell their shares at the end of some holding period. The capital gain may or may not be realized, but most people expect a gain or else they would not buy stocks.

■ The expected dividend yield on a stock during the coming year is equal to the expected dividend, D_1, divided by the current stock price, P_0. $(\hat{P}_1 - P_0)/P_0$ is the expected capital gains yield. The expected dividend yield plus the expected capital gains yield equals the expected total return. *expected total return = Capital gain + dividend*

■ The value of the stock today is calculated as the present value of an infinite stream of dividends. For any investor, cash flows consist of dividends plus the expected future sales price of the stock. This sales price, however, depends on dividends expected by future investors:

$$\text{Value of stock} = \hat{P}_0 = \text{PV of expected dividends}$$

$$= \frac{D_1}{(1+k_s)^1} + \frac{D_2}{(1+k_s)^2} + \cdots + \frac{D_\infty}{(1+k_s)^\infty}$$

$$= \sum_{t=1}^{\infty} \frac{D_t}{(1+k_s)^t}.$$

Here k_s is the discount rate used to find the present value of the dividends.

■ Dividends are not expected to remain constant in the future, and dividends are harder to predict than bond interest payments. Thus, stock valuation is a more complex task than bond valuation.

■ If expected dividend growth is zero (g = 0), the value of the stock is found as follows: $\hat{P}_0 = D/k_s$. Since a zero growth stock is expected to pay a constant dividend, it can be thought of as a *perpetuity*. The expected rate of return is simply the dividend yield: $\hat{k}_s = D/P_0$.

■ For many companies, earnings and dividends are expected to grow at some normal, or constant, rate. Dividends in any future Year t may be forecasted as $D_t = D_0(1 + g)^t$, where D_0 is the last dividend paid and g is the expected growth rate. For a company which last paid a $2.00 dividend and which has an expected 6 percent constant growth rate, the estimated dividend one year from now would be $D_1 = \$2.00(1.06) = \$2.12$; D_2 would be $\$2.00(1.06)^2 = \$2.25$, and the estimated dividend 4 years hence would be $D_t = D_0(1 + g)^t = \$2.00(1.06)^4 = \$2.525$. Using this method of estimating future dividends, the current price, P_0, is determined as follows:

$$\hat{P}_0 = D_0 \sum_{t=1}^{\infty} \frac{(1+g)^t}{(1+k_s)^t} = \frac{D_0(1+g)}{k_s - g} = \frac{D_1}{k_s - g}.$$

■ This equation for valuing a constant growth stock, the *constant growth model*, is often called the *Gordon Model*, after Myron J. Gordon, who developed it.
   ❑ If growth is zero, this is simply a special case of constant growth.
   ❑ A necessary condition is that k_s must be greater than g.
   ❑ Growth in dividends occurs primarily as a result of growth in earnings per share. Earnings growth results from a number of factors including (1) inflation, (2) the amount of earnings the company retains and reinvests, and (3) the rate of return the company earns on its equity (ROE).

■ A number of professors and consulting firms have used actual company data to show that over 80 percent of a typical company's stock price is due to cash flows expected to occur more than five years in the future.
   ❑ If most of a stock's value is due to long-term cash flows, why do so many managers and analysts focus so much attention on quarterly earnings? While the quarterly earnings itself may not be terribly important, the information it conveys about future prospects might be quite important.
   ❑ Another reason many managers focus on short-term earnings is that some firms pay managerial bonuses on the basis of current earnings rather than stock prices (which reflect future earnings).

■ For all stocks, the total expected return is composed of an expected dividend yield plus an expected capital gains yield. For a constant growth stock, the formula for the total expected return can be written as:

$$\hat{k}_s = \frac{D_1}{P_0} + g.$$

❑ For a *constant growth stock*, the following conditions must hold:
  • The dividend is expected to grow forever at a constant rate, g.
  • The stock price is expected to grow at that same rate.
  • The expected dividend yield is a constant.
  • The expected capital gains yield is also a constant, and it is equal to g.
  • The expected total return, $\hat{k}_s$, is equal to the expected dividend yield plus the expected growth rate.

■ Firms typically go through periods of nonconstant growth, after which time their growth rate settles to a rate close to that of the economy as a whole. The value of such a firm is equal to the present value of its expected future dividends. To find the value of such a stock, we proceed in three steps:
  ❑ Find the present value of the dividends during the period of nonconstant growth.
  ❑ Find the price of the stock at the end of the nonconstant growth period, at which point it has become a constant growth stock, and discount this price back to the present.
  ❑ Add these two components to find the stock's present value.

The relationship between a stock's required and expected rates of return determines the equilibrium price level where buying and selling pressures will just offset each other.

■ If the expected rate of return is less than the required rate, investors will desire to sell the stock; there will also be a tendency for the price to decline.

■ When the expected rate of return is greater than the required rate, investors will try to purchase shares of the stock; this will drive the price upward.

■ Only at the equilibrium price, where the expected and required rates are equal, will the stock be stable.

■ *Equilibrium* will generally exist for a given stock because security prices, especially those of large companies, adjust rapidly to new information.

- Changes in the equilibrium price can be brought about by (1) a change in risk aversion, (2) a change in the risk-free rate, (3) a change in the stock's beta coefficient, or (4) a change in the stock's expected growth rate.

- The *Efficient Markets Hypothesis (EMH)* holds that stocks are always in equilibrium and that it is impossible for an investor to consistently "beat the market."
  - The *weak-form* of the EMH states that all information contained in past price movements is fully reflected in current market prices.
  - The *semistrong-form* of the EMH states that current market prices reflect all *publicly available* information. If this is true, no abnormal returns can be gained by analyzing stocks. Another implication of semistrong-form efficiency is that whenever information is released to the public, stock prices will respond only if the information is different from what had been expected.
  - The *strong-form* of the EMH states that current market prices reflect all pertinent information, whether publicly available or privately held (inside information). If this form holds, even insiders would find it impossible to earn abnormal returns in the stock market.

- In general, stocks are neither overvalued nor undervalued—they are fairly priced and in equilibrium.

- Empirical tests have shown that EMH is, in its weak and semistrong forms, valid.

Anyone who has ever invested in the stock market knows that there can be, and generally are, large differences between expected and realized prices and returns.

- Investors always expect positive returns from stock investments or else they would not buy them. However, in some years negative returns are actually earned.

- Even in bad years, some individual stocks do well, and the "name of the game" in security analysis is to pick the winners. Financial managers are trying to take those actions that will help put their companies in the winners' column, but they don't always succeed.

- When investing overseas, you are making two bets: (1) that foreign stocks will increase in their local markets and (2) that the currencies in which you will be paid will rise relative to the dollar.
  - Foreign investments improve diversification.

Preferred stock is a hybrid—it is similar to bonds in some respects and to common stock in other respects.

■ Preferred dividends are similar to interest payments on bonds in that they are fixed in amount and generally must be paid before common stock dividends can be paid.

■ If the preferred dividend is not earned, the directors can omit (or "pass") it without throwing the company into bankruptcy. So, although preferred stock has a fixed payment like bonds, a failure to make this payment will not lead to bankruptcy.

■ Most preferred stocks entitle their owners to regular fixed dividend payments. If the payments last forever, the issue is a *perpetuity* whose value, V_{ps}, is found as follows:

$$V_{ps} = \frac{D_{ps}}{k_{ps}}.$$

❑ Here D_{ps} is the dividend to be received in each year and k_{ps} is the required rate of return on the preferred stock.

SELF-TEST QUESTIONS

Definitional

1. One of the fundamental rights of common stockholders is to elect a firm's __directors__ , who in turn elect the firm's operating management.

2. If a stockholder cannot vote in person, participation in the annual meeting is still possible through a(n) __proxy__ .

3. The preemptive right protects stockholders against loss of __control__ of the corporation as well as __dilution__ of market value from the sale of new shares below market value.

4. Firms may find it desirable to separate the common stock into different __classes__ . Generally, this classification is designed to differentiate stock in terms of the right to receive __dividends__ and the right to __vote__ .

5. A(n) __closely held__ corporation is one whose stock is held by a small group, normally its management.

6. The trading of previously issued shares of a corporation takes place in the __secondary__ market, while new issues are offered in the __primary__ market.

7. __Going public__ refers to the sale of shares of a closely held business to the general public.

8. Securities traded on the organized exchanges are known as ___listed___ securities.

9. Like other financial assets, the value of common stock is the ___present___ value of a future stream of income.

10. The income stream expected from a common stock consists of a(n) ___dividend___ yield and a(n) ___capital___ ___gains___ yield.

11. If the future growth rate of dividends is expected to be ___zero___, the rate of return is simply the ___dividend___ yield.

12. Investors always expect a(n) ___positive___ return on stock investments, but in some years ___negative___ returns may actually be earned.

13. Preferred stock is referred to as a hybrid because it is similar to ___debt___ in some respects and to ___common stock___ in others.

14. If earnings are poor and stockholders are dissatisfied, an outside group may solicit the votes of stockholders unable to attend the annual meeting in an effort to overthrow management and take control of the business. This is known as a(n) ___proxy fight___.

15. A(n) ___takeover___ is an action whereby a person or group succeeds in ousting a firm's management and taking control of the company.

16. A(n) ___poison pill___ makes a possible acquisition unattractive and wards off hostile takeover attempts.

17. The market where capital is raised for firms that were formerly closely held companies is often termed the ___initial public offering___ market.

18. ___oversubscribed___ is the term used when the demand for shares at the offering price exceeds the number of shares issued.

19. A zero growth stock can be thought of as a(n) ___perpetuity___.

20. If the expected rate of return on a stock is less than its required rate of return, investors will desire to ___sell___ the stock; there will also be a tendency for the stock's price to ___decline___.

21. Only at the ___equilibrium___ price, where the expected and required rates of return are equal, will the stock's price be stable.

22. The _efficient_ _market_ _hypothes_ holds that stocks are always in equilibrium and that it is impossible for an investor to consistently "beat the market."

23. The _weak_-form of the EMH states that all information contained in past price movements is fully reflected in current market prices.

24. When investing overseas, you are making two bets: (1) that foreign stock prices will _increase_ in their local markets and (2) that the currencies in which you will be paid will _increase_ relative to the dollar.

25. Growth in dividends occurs primarily as a result of growth in _earnings_ _per_ _share_.

26. Most of a stock's value is due to _long_-term cash flows.

27. Although preferred stock has a fixed payment like bonds, a failure to make this payment will not lead to _bankruptcy_

Conceptual

28. According to the valuation model developed in this chapter, the value that an investor assigns to a share of stock is independent of the length of time the investor plans to hold the stock.

    a. True   **b.** False

29. Which of the following assumptions would cause the constant growth stock valuation model to be invalid? The constant growth model is given below:

$$\hat{P}_0 = \frac{D_0(1+g)}{k_s - g}.$$

    a. The growth rate is negative.
    b. The growth rate is zero.
    c. The growth rate is less than the required rate of return.
    d. The required rate of return is above 30 percent.
    e. None of the above assumptions would invalidate the model.

30. Assume that a company's dividends are expected to grow at a rate of 25 percent per year for 5 years and then to slow down and to grow at a constant rate of 5 percent thereafter. The required (and expected) total return, k_s, is expected to remain constant at 12 percent. Which of the following statements is most correct?

    a. The dividend yield will be higher in the early years and then will decline as the annual capital gains yield gets larger and larger, other things held constant.

    b. Right now, it would be easier (require fewer calculations) to find the dividend yield expected in Year 7 than the dividend yield expected in Year 3.

    c. The stock price will grow each year at the same rate as the dividends.

    d. The stock price will grow at a different rate each year during the first 5 years, but its average growth rate over this period will be the same as the average growth rate in dividends; that is, the average stock price growth rate will be $(25 + 5)/2$.

    e. Statements a, b, c, and d are all false.

31. Which of the following statements is most correct?

    a. According to the text, the constant growth model is especially useful in situations where g is greater than 15 percent and k_s is 10 percent or less.

    b. According to the text, the constant growth model can be used as one part of the process of finding the value of a stock which is expected to experience a very rapid rate of growth for a few years and then to grow at a constant ("normal") rate.

    c. According to the text, the constant growth model cannot be used unless g is greater than zero.

    d. According to the text, the constant growth model cannot be used unless the constant g is greater than k.

    e. Statements a, b, c, and d are all true.

32. When stockholders assign their right to vote to another party, this is called

    a. A privilege.

    b. A preemptive right.

    c. An ex right.

    d. A proxy.

    e. A takeover.

SELF-TEST PROBLEMS

1. Stability Inc. has maintained a dividend rate of $4 per share for many years. The same rate is expected to be paid in future years. If investors require a 12 percent rate of return on similar investments, determine the present value of the company's stock.

    a. $15.00   **b.** $30.00   **c.** $33.33   **d.** $35.00   **e.** $40.00

2. Your sister-in-law, a stockbroker at Invest Inc., is trying to sell you a stock with a current market price of $25. The stock's last dividend (D_0) was $2.00, and earnings and dividends are expected to increase at a constant growth rate of 10 percent. Your required return on this stock is 20 percent. From a strict valuation standpoint, you should:

    a. Buy the stock; it is fairly valued.
    b. Buy the stock; it is undervalued by $3.00.
    c. Buy the stock; it is undervalued by $2.00.
    d. Not buy the stock; it is overvalued by $2.00.
    e. Not buy the stock; it is overvalued by $3.00.

3. Lucas Laboratories' last dividend was $1.50. Its current equilibrium stock price is $15.75, and its expected growth rate is a constant 5 percent. If the stockholders' required rate of return is 15 percent, what is the expected dividend yield and expected capital gains yield for the coming year?

    a. 0%; 15%   **b.** 5%; 10%   **c.** 10%; 5%   **d.** 15%; 0%   **e.** 15%; 15%

4. The Canning Company has been hard hit by increased competition. Analysts predict that earnings (and dividends) will decline at a rate of 5 percent annually into the foreseeable future. If Canning's last dividend (D_0) was $2.00, and investors' required rate of return is 15 percent, what will be Canning's stock price *in 3 years*?

    a. $8.15   **b.** $9.50   **c.** $10.00   **d.** $10.42   **e.** $10.96

(The following data apply to the next three Self-Test Problems.)

The Club Auto Parts Company has just recently been organized. It is expected to experience no growth for the next 2 years as it identifies its market and acquires its inventory. However, Club will grow at an annual rate of 5 percent in the third year and, beginning with the fourth year, should attain a 10 percent growth rate which it will sustain thereafter. The first dividend (D_1) to be paid at the end of the first year is expected to be $0.50 per share. Investors require a 15 percent rate of return on Club's stock.

5.   What is the current equilibrium stock price?

   a. $5.00   **b.** $8.75   **c.** $9.56   **d.** $12.43   **e.** $15.00

6.   What will Club's stock price be at the end of the first year $\left(\hat{P_1} \right)$?

   a. $5.00   **b.** $8.75   **c.** $9.56   **d.** $12.43   **e.** $15.00

7.   What dividend yield and capital gains yield should an investor in Club expect for the first year?

   a. 7.5%; 7.5%   **b.** 4.7%; 10.3%   **c.** 5.7%; 9.3%   **d.** 10.5%; 4.5%   **e.** 11.5%; 3.5%

8.   Johnson Corporation's stock is currently selling at $45.83 per share. The last dividend paid (D_0) was $2.50. Johnson is a constant growth firm. If investors require a return of 16 percent on Johnson's stock, what do they think Johnson's growth rate will be?

   a. 6%   **b.** 7%   **c.** 8%   **d.** 9%   **e.** 10%

9.   Assume that the average firm in your company's industry is expected to grow at a constant rate of 7 percent and its dividend yield is 8 percent. Your company is about as risky as the average firm in the industry, but it has just successfully completed some R&D work which leads you to expect that its earnings and dividends will grow at a rate of 40 percent [$D_1 = D_0(1 + g) = D_0(1.40)$] this year and 20 percent the following year, after which growth should match the 7 percent industry average rate. The last dividend paid (D_0) was $1. What is the current value per share of your firm's stock?

   a. $22.47   **b.** $24.15   **c.** $21.00   **d.** $19.48   **e.** $22.00

10. Assume that as investment manager of Maine Electric Company's pension plan (which is exempt from income taxes), you must choose between Exxon bonds and GM preferred stock. The bonds have a $1,000 par value; they mature in 20 years; they pay $35 each 6 months; they are callable at Exxon's option at a price of $1,150 after 5 years (ten 6-month periods); and they sell at a price of $815.98 per bond. The preferred stock is a perpetuity; it pays a dividend of $1.50 each quarter, and it sells for $75 per share. Assume interest rates do not change. What is the most likely *effective annual rate of return (EAR)* on the *higher* yielding security? (Hint: You will need a financial calculator to work this problem.)

   a. 9.20%   **b.** 8.24%   **c.** 9.00%   **d.** 8.00%   **e.** 8.50%

11. Chadmark Corporation is expanding rapidly, and it currently needs to retain all of its earnings, hence it does not pay any dividends. However, investors expect Chadmark to begin paying dividends, with the first dividend of $0.75 coming 2 years from today. The dividend should grow rapidly, at a rate of 40 percent per year, during Years 3 and 4. After Year 4, the company should grow at a constant rate of 10 percent per year. If the required return on the stock is 16 percent, what is the value of the stock today?

   a. $16.93   **b.** $17.54   **c.** $15.78   **d.** $18.87   **e.** $16.05

12. Some investors expect Endicott Industries to have an irregular dividend pattern for several years, and then to grow at a constant rate. Suppose Endicott has $D_0 = \$2.00$; no growth is expected for 2 years ($g_1 = 0$); then the expected growth rate is 8 percent for 2 years; and finally the growth rate is expected to be constant at 15 percent thereafter. If the required return is 20 percent, what will be the value of the stock?

   a. $28.53   **b.** $25.14   **c.** $31.31   **d.** $21.24   **e.** $23.84

ANSWERS TO SELF-TEST QUESTIONS

1.	directors	**15.**	takeover
2.	proxy	**16.**	poison pill
3.	control; dilution	**17.**	initial public offering
4.	classes; dividends; vote	**18.**	Oversubscribed
5.	closely held	**19.**	perpetuity
6.	secondary; primary	**20.**	sell; decline
7.	Going public	**21.**	equilibrium
8.	listed	**22.**	Efficient Markets Hypothesis
9.	present	**23.**	weak
10.	dividend; capital gains	**24.**	increase; increase
11.	zero; dividend	**25.**	earnings per share
12.	positive; negative	**26.**	long
13.	debt; common stock	**27.**	bankruptcy
14.	proxy fight		

28. a. The model considers all future dividends. This produces a current value which is appropriate for all investors independent of their expected holding period.

29. e. The model would be invalid, however, if the growth rate *exceeded* the required rate of return.

30. b. Statement b is correct. We know that after Year 5, the stock will have a constant growth rate, and the capital gains yield will be equal to that growth rate. We also know that the total return is expected to be constant. Therefore, we could find the expected dividend yield in Year 7 simply by subtracting the growth rate from the total return: yield = 12% – 5% = 7% in Year 7.

The other statements are all false. This could be confirmed by thinking about how the dividend growth rate starts high, ends up at the constant growth rate, and must lie between these two rates and be declining between Years 1 and 5. The average growth rate in dividends during Years 1 through 5 will be (25 + 5)/2 = 15%, which is above k_s = 12%, so statements c and d must be false.

31. b. Statement b is correct. In the case of a nonconstant growth stock which is expected to grow at a constant rate after Year N, we would find the value of D_{N+1} and use it in the constant growth model to find P_N. The other statements are all false. Note that the constant growth model can be used for g = 0, g < 0, and g < k.

32. d. Recently, there has been a spate of proxy fights, whereby a dissident group of stockholders solicits proxies in competition with the firm's management. If the dissident group gets a majority of the proxies, then it can gain control of the board of directors and oust existing management.

SOLUTIONS TO SELF-TEST PROBLEMS

1. c. This is a zero-growth stock, or perpetuity: $\hat{P}_0 = D / k_s = \$4.00 / 0.12 = \$33.33$.

2. e. $\hat{P}_0 = \dfrac{D_0(1+g)}{k_s - g} = \dfrac{\$2.00(1.10)}{0.20 - 0.10} = \$22.00$.

Since the stock is currently selling for $25.00, the stock is not in equilibrium and is overvalued by $3.00.

3. c. $\dfrac{\text{Dividend}}{\text{yield}} = \dfrac{D_1}{P_0} = \dfrac{D_0(1+g)}{P_0} = \dfrac{\$1.50(1.05)}{\$15.75} = 0.10 = 10\%$.

$\dfrac{\text{Capital}}{\text{gains yield}} = \dfrac{\hat{P}_1 - P_0}{P_0} = \dfrac{P_0(1+g) - P_0}{P_0} = \dfrac{\$16.54 - \$15.75}{\$15.75} = g = 5\%$.

4. a. $\hat{P}_0 = \dfrac{D_0(1+g)}{k_s - g} = \dfrac{\$2.00(0.95)}{0.15 - (-0.05)} = \dfrac{\$1.90}{0.20} = \$9.50$.

$\hat{P}_3 = \hat{P}_0(1+g)^3 = \$9.50(0.95)^3 = \$9.50(0.8574) = \$8.15$.

The Gordon model can also be used:

$\hat{P}_3 = \dfrac{D_4}{k_s - g} = \dfrac{D_0(1+g)^4}{0.15 - (-0.05)} = \dfrac{\$2.00(0.95)^4}{0.20} = \dfrac{\$2.00(0.8145)}{0.20} = \$8.15$.

5. b. To calculate the current value of a nonconstant growth stock, follow these steps:

1. Determine the expected stream of dividends during the nonconstant growth period. Also, calculate the expected dividend at the end of the first year of constant growth that will be used later to calculate stock price.

$$D_1 = \$0.50.$$
$$D_2 = D_1(1 + g) = \$0.50(1 + 0.0) = \$0.50.$$
$$D_3 = D_2(1 + g) = \$0.50(1.05) \quad = \$0.525.$$
$$D_4 = D_3(1 + g) = \$0.525(1.10) \quad = \$0.5775.$$

2. Discount the expected dividends during the nonconstant growth period at the investor's required rate of return to find their present value.

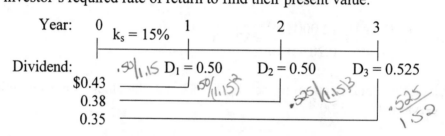

3. Calculate the expected stock price at the end of the final year of nonconstant growth. This occurs at the end of Year 3. Use the Gordon model for this calculation.

$$\hat{P}_3 = \frac{D_4}{k_s - g} = \frac{\$0.5775}{0.15 - 0.10} = \$11.55.$$

Then discount this stock price back 3 periods at the investor's required rate of return to find its present value.

$$PV = \$11.55(1/1.15^3) = \$11.55(0.6575) = \$7.59.$$

4. Add the present value of the stock price expected at the end of Year 3 plus the dividends expected in Years 1, 2, and 3 to find the present value of the stock, P_0.

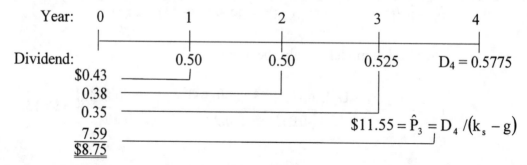

Alternatively, input 0, 0.5, 0.5, 12.075 (0.525 + 11.55 = 12.075) into the cash flow register, input I = 15, and then solve for NPV = \$8.75.

6. c. To calculate the expected stock price at the end of Year 1, $\hat{P}_1$, follow the same procedure you did to find the value of the nonconstant growth stock in Self-Test Problem 5. However, discount values to Year 1 instead of Year 0. Also, remember that the dividend in Year 1, D_1, is not included in the valuation because it has already been paid and therefore adds nothing to the wealth of the investor buying the stock at the end of Year 1.

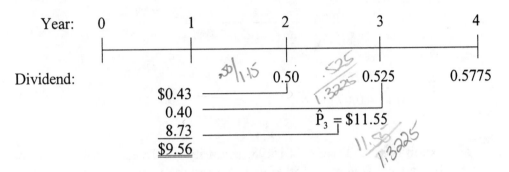

Alternatively, input 0, 0.5, 12.075 (0.525 + 11.55) into the cash flow register, input I = 15, and then solve for NPV = $9.57.

7. c.
$$\frac{\text{Dividend}}{\text{yield}} = \frac{D_1}{P_0} = \frac{\$0.50}{\$8.75} = 5.7\%.$$

$$\frac{\text{Capital}}{\text{gains yield}} = \frac{\hat{P}_1 - P_0}{P_0} = \frac{\$9.56 - \$8.75}{\$8.75} = 9.3\%.$$

The Total yield = Dividend yield + Capital gains yield = 5.7% + 9.3% = 15%. The total yield must equal the required rate of return. Also, the capital gains yield is not equal to the growth rate during the nonconstant growth phase of a nonconstant growth stock. Finally, the dividend and capital gains yields are not constant until the constant growth state is reached.

8. e.
$$P_0 = \frac{D_0(1+g)}{k_s - g}$$

$$\$45.83 = \frac{\$2.50(1+g)}{0.16 - g}$$

$$\$7.33 - \$45.83g = \$2.50 + \$2.50g$$

$$\$48.33g = \$4.83$$

$$g = 0.0999 \approx 10\%.$$

9. d. $D_0 = \$1.00$; $k_s = 8\% + 7\% = 15\%$; $g_1 = 40\%$; $g_2 = 20\%$; $g_n = 7\%$.

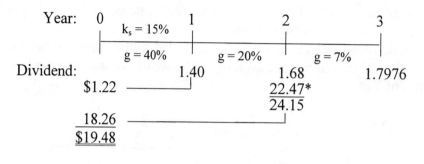

$$* \hat{P}_2 = \frac{\$1.7976}{0.15 - 0.07} = \$22.47.$$

10. a. Exxon bonds: Price = \$815.98, Maturity = 20 years, PMT = \$35 per 6 months, and they are callable at \$1,150 after 10 periods (5 years).

Will the bond's YTM or YTC be applicable? The bond is selling at a discount, so k_d > Coupon interest rate. Therefore, the bond is not likely to be called, so calculate the YTM.

Input N = 40, PV = -815.98, PMT = 35, FV = 1000, and solve for I = $k_d/2$ = 4.5%. EAR = $(1.045)^2 - 1 = 9.2\%$.

Preferred: D = \$1.50 per quarter and P_0 = \$75.
$k_{ps} = \$1.50/\$75 = 2\% = $ periodic rate. EAR = $(1.02)^4 - 1 = 8.24\%$.

Thus, the Exxon bonds provide the higher effective annual rate of return.

11. a. To calculate Chadmark's current stock price, follow the following steps: (1) Determine the expected stream of dividends during the nonconstant growth period. You will need to calculate the expected dividend at the end of Year 5, which is the first year of constant growth. This dividend will be used in the next step to calculate the stock price. (2) Calculate the expected stock price at the end of the final year of nonconstant growth. This occurs at the end of Year 4. Use the Gordon model for this calculation. (3) Add the value obtained in Step 2 to the dividend expected in Year 4. (4) Put the values obtained in the prior steps on a time line and discount them at the required rate of return to find the present value of Chadmark's stock. These steps are shown below.

$D_0 = \$0$; $D_1 = \$0$; $D_2 = \$0.75$; $D_3 = \$0.75(1.4) = \$1.05$; $D_4 = \$0.75(1.4)^2 = \$1.47$; $D_5 = \$0.75(1.4)^2(1.10) = \$1.617$.

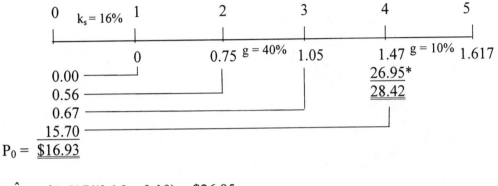

$$* \hat{P}_4 = \$1.617/(0.16 - 0.10) = \$26.95.$$

$CF_0 = 0$; $CF_1 = 0$; $CF_2 = 0.75$; $CF_3 = 1.05$; $CF_4 = 28.42$.

Alternatively, using a financial calculator you could input the cash flows as shown above into the cash flow register, input I = 16, and press NPV to obtain the stock's value today of $16.93.

12. c. First, set up the time line as follows. Note that D_5 is used to find $\hat{P}_4$, which is treated as part of the cash flow at t = 4:

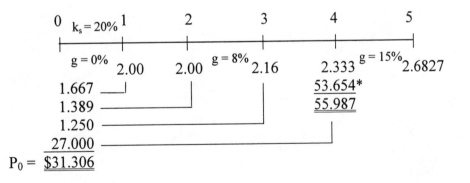

$$* \hat{P}_4 = \$2.6827/(0.20 - 0.15) = \$53.654.$$

Enter the time line values into the cash flow register, with I = 20, to find NPV = $31.31. Be sure to enter $CF_0 = 0$. Note that $\hat{P}_4$ is the PV, at t = 4, of dividends from t = 5 to infinity; that is, the PV of the dividends after the stock is expected to become a constant growth stock.

CHAPTER 11
THE COST OF CAPITAL

OVERVIEW

When companies issue stocks or bonds, they are raising capital that can be invested in various projects. Capital is a necessary factor of production, and like any other factor, it has a cost. This cost is equal to the marginal investor's required return on the security in question.

The key to understanding the capital budgeting process is to recognize (1) that investors provide managers with the necessary funds, or capital, to undertake projects and (2) managers, if they are good stewards of the money entrusted to them, invest only in projects that can produce a rate of return at least as high as the return investors could get elsewhere. The return investors could get elsewhere is their opportunity cost of capital.

Recall that the firm's primary financial objective is to maximize shareholder value. Companies can increase shareholder value by investing in projects that earn more than the cost of capital. For this reason, the cost of capital is sometimes referred to as a hurdle rate: For a project to be accepted, it must earn more than its hurdle rate.

Although its most important use is in capital budgeting, the cost of capital is also used for at least four other purposes: (1) It is a key input required for determining a firm's or division's economic value added (EVA). (2) Managers estimate and use the cost of capital when deciding if they should lease or purchase assets. (3) The cost of capital is a key factor in decisions relating to the use of debt versus equity capital. And, (4) the cost of capital has also been important over time in the regulation of electric, gas, and telephone companies.

The same factors that affect required rates of return on securities by investors also determine a firm's cost of capital, so exactly the same models are used by investors and by corporate treasurers.

OUTLINE

To implement projects for growth, corporations must raise capital from investors. The projects must earn a high enough rate of return to compensate the investors for their capital.

■ Most firms employ several types of capital, called *capital components*, with common and preferred stock, along with debt, being the three most frequently used types.

■ The required rate of return on each capital component is called its *component cost*, and the cost of capital used to analyze capital budgeting decisions should be a *weighted average* of the various components' costs.
   ❑ This weighted average is the *weighted average cost of capital*, or *WACC*.

■ Most firms set target percentages for the different financing sources. This is called the *target capital structure*.

■ Firms try to stay close to their target capital structures; however, they frequently deviate from them in the short run for several reasons.
   ❑ Market conditions may be more favorable in one market than another at a particular time.
   ❑ The second, and probably more important, reason for deviations relates to *flotation costs*, which are the costs that a firm must incur to issue securities.

■ Managers should view companies as ongoing concerns, and calculate their costs of capital as weighted averages of the various types of funds they use, regardless of the specific source of financing employed in a particular year.

The cost of each capital component can be determined as follows:

■ The after-tax cost of debt, $k_d(1 - T)$, is defined as the interest rate on new debt, k_d, less the tax savings that result because interest is tax deductible.
   ❑ If a firm has issued debt in the past, and it is publicly traded, the market price can be used to find either the YTM or YTC (whichever is appropriate). This will provide a good estimate of k_d.
   ❑ If a firm has no publicly traded debt, yields on publicly traded debt of similar firms should provide a reasonable estimate of k_d.
   ❑ If a firm has a tax rate of 40 percent and can borrow at a rate of 11 percent, then its after-tax cost of debt is $k_d = 11\%(1 - 0.40) = 11\%(0.60) = 6.6\%$.
   ❑ Since interest payments are deductible, the government in effect pays part of the total cost.
      • k_d is the marginal cost of new debt to be raised during the planning period.

■ The component cost of preferred stock, k_{ps}, is the preferred dividend, D_{ps}, divided by the net issuing price of the preferred stock, P_n: $k_{ps} = D_{ps}/P_n$.
  ❑ P_n is the price the firm receives after deducting flotation costs.
  ❑ No tax adjustments are made when calculating k_{ps} because preferred dividends, unlike interest expense on debt, are not deductible, and hence there are no tax savings.

■ Companies can raise common equity in two ways: (1) by issuing new shares and (2) by retaining earnings.
  ❑ Companies must earn more than k_s on new shares because it incurs flotation costs to issue new stock.
  ❑ In addition, an increase in the supply of stock will put pressure on the stock price, forcing the company to sell new stock at a lower price than existed before the new issue was announced.
  ❑ The combined effects of flotation costs and price pressure inhibit companies from issuing additional common stock.

■ The most important way companies raise new common equity is to reinvest earnings.
  ❑ If some of a firm's earnings are reinvested, stockholders incur an *opportunity cost*—the earnings could have been paid out as dividends.
  ❑ The firm should earn on its reinvested earnings at least as much as its stockholders themselves could earn on alternative investments of equivalent risk.

■ k_s is the cost of common equity raised by reinvesting earnings.

■ There are three methods used to estimate k_s:
  ❑ The Capital Asset Pricing Model (CAPM) works as follows:
    ● Estimate the risk-free rate, k_{RF}, generally taken to be a long-term U. S. Treasury bond rate.
    ● Estimate the stock's beta coefficient as an index of risk.
    ● Estimate the current expected rate of return on the market, or on an "average" stock, k_M.
    ● Substitute the preceding values into the CAPM equation, $k_s = k_{RF} + (k_M - k_{RF})b$, to estimate the required rate of return on the stock in question.
    ● Thus, if $k_{RF} = 8\%$, $k_M = 14\%$, and the beta is 1.1, then $k_s = 8\% + (14\% - 8\%)1.1 = 14.6\%$.
  ❑ The *bond-yield-plus-risk-premium approach* estimates k_s by adding a judgmental risk premium of three to five percentage points to the interest rate on the firm's own long-term debt. Thus, k_s = Bond yield + Risk premium.
    ● If the firm uses a risk premium of 4 percentage points, and its bond rate is 11 percent, then $k_s = 11\% + 4\% = 15\%$.

- Because the risk premium is a judgmental estimate, this method is not likely to produce a precise cost of equity; however, it does get us "into the right ballpark."
- The required rate of return, k_s, may also be estimated by the *discounted cash flow (DCF) approach*. This approach combines the expected dividend yield, D_1/P_0, with the expected future growth rate, g, of earnings and dividends, or

$$k_s = \hat{k}_s = \frac{D_1}{P_0} + \text{Expected g.}$$

- The DCF approach assumes that stocks are normally in equilibrium and that growth is expected to be at a constant rate. If growth is not constant, then a nonconstant growth model must be used.
- The expected growth rate may be based on projections of past growth rates, if they have been relatively stable, or on expected future growth rates as projected by security analysts.
- Another method for estimating g is called the *retention growth rate method*. First, the firm's average future dividend payout ratio and its complement, the *retention rate*, are forecasted, and then the retention rate is multiplied by the company's expected future rate of return on equity (ROE):

  g = (Retention rate)(ROE) = (1.0 – Payout rate)(ROE).

- If the firm's next expected dividend is $2.40, its expected growth rate is 7 percent per year, and its stock is selling for $32 per share, then

$$k_s = \hat{k}_s = \frac{\$2.40}{\$32} + 7.0\% = 14.5\%.$$

- When faced with the task of estimating a company's cost of equity, we generally use all three methods and then choose among them on the basis of our confidence in the data used for each in the specific case at hand.

The target proportions of debt, preferred stock, and common equity, along with the component costs of capital, are used to calculate the firm's weighted average cost of capital (WACC).

- The weighted average cost of capital calculation is shown below for a firm which finances 30 percent with debt, 10 percent with preferred stock, and 60 percent with common equity and which has the following after-tax component costs:

Component	Weight	×	After-tax Cost	=	Weighted Cost
Debt	0.3	×	6.6%	=	1.98%
Preferred	0.1	×	10.3	=	1.03
Common	0.6	×	14.7	=	8.82
				WACC =	11.83%

- In more general terms, and in equation format,

$$WACC = w_d k_d (1 - T) + w_{ps} k_{ps} + w_{ce} k_s.$$

- The WACC is the weighted average cost of each new, or *marginal*, dollar of capital.
  - We are primarily interested in obtaining a cost of capital for use in capital budgeting, and for this purpose the cost of the new money that will be invested is the relevant cost.

- The percentage capital components, called weights, could be based on (1) accounting values as shown on the balance sheet (book values), (2) current market values of the capital components, or (3) management's target capital structure, which is presumably an estimate of the firm's optimal capital structure.
  - The correct weights are those based on the firm's target capital structure, since this is the best estimate of how the firm will, on average, raise money in the future.

The weighted average cost of capital is affected by a variety of factors.

- The two most important factors which are beyond the firm's direct control are the level of interest rates and taxes.
  - If interest rates in the economy rise, the cost of debt increases because firms will have to pay bondholders a higher interest rate. Higher interest rates also increase the cost of common and preferred equity capital.
  - Tax rates are used in the calculation of the cost of debt for use in the WACC, and there are other less apparent ways in which tax policy affects the cost of capital. For example, lowering the capital gains tax rate relative to the rate on ordinary income would make stocks more attractive, which would reduce the cost of equity relative to that of debt. That would lead to a change in a firm's optimal capital structure.

- A firm can affect its cost of capital through its capital structure policy, its dividend policy, and its investment (capital budgeting) policy.
  - The firm can change its capital structure, and such a change can affect its cost of capital. If a firm decides to use more debt and less common equity, this change in the

weights in the WACC equation will tend to lower the WACC. However, an increase in the use of debt will increase the riskiness of both debt and equity, and increases in component costs will tend to offset the effects of the change in the weights.

❑ The percentage of earnings paid out in dividends may affect a stock's required rate of return, k_s. Also, if a firm's payout ratio is so high that it must issue new stock to fund its capital budget, this will force it to incur flotation costs, and this too will affect its cost of capital.

❑ When we estimate the cost of capital, we use as the starting point the required rate of return on the firm's outstanding stock and bonds. Those cost rates reflect the riskiness of the firm's existing assets. Therefore, we have implicitly been assuming that new capital will be invested in assets of the same type and with the same degree of risk as is embedded in the existing assets. This assumption would be incorrect if the firm dramatically changed its investment policy.

The cost of capital is a key element in the capital budgeting process. A project should be accepted if and only if its estimated return exceeds its cost of capital. For this reason, the cost of capital is sometimes referred to as a "hurdle rate"—project returns must jump the "hurdle" to be accepted.

■ Investors require higher returns for riskier investments. Consequently, a company that is raising capital to take on risky projects will have a higher cost of capital than a company that is investing in safer projects.

■ The hurdle rate for each project should reflect the risk of the project itself, not necessarily the risk associated with the firm's average project as reflected in its composite WACC.

■ Applying a specific hurdle rate to each project ensures that every project will be evaluated properly.

■ If a company has different divisional costs of capital, then it would be incorrect to use the company's overall cost of capital to find the NPV of all the company's projects.

Three separate and distinct types of risk can be identified: (1) stand-alone risk, (2) corporate (within-firm) risk, and (3) market (beta) risk.

■ Stand-alone risk is the risk an asset would have if it were a firm's only asset. It is measured by the variability of the project's expected returns.

■ *Corporate risk* is the project's risk to the corporation, giving consideration to the fact that the project represents only one of the firm's portfolio of assets. It is measured by a project's impact on uncertainty about the firm's future earnings.

■ *Market risk* is the riskiness of the project as seen by a well-diversified stockholder who recognizes that the project is only one of the firm's assets and that the firm's stock is but one part of the investor's total portfolio. It is measured by the project's effect on the firm's beta coefficient.

■ Taking on a project with a high degree of either stand-alone or corporate risk will not necessarily affect the firm's beta. However, if the project has highly uncertain returns, and if those returns are highly correlated with returns on the firm's other assets and with most other assets in the economy, then the project will have a high degree of all types of risk.

■ Of the three measures, market risk is theoretically the most relevant measure because of its direct effect on stock prices. Unfortunately, the market risk for a project is also the most difficult to estimate.

  ❑ In practice, most decision-makers consider all three risk measures in a judgmental manner, and then they classify projects into subjective risk categories.
  ❑ *Risk-adjusted costs of capital* are developed for each category using the composite WACC as a starting point.

■ Risk adjustments are necessarily subjective and somewhat arbitrary. Unfortunately, there is no completely satisfactory way to specify exactly how much higher or lower we should go in setting risk-adjusted costs of capital.

Many firms use the CAPM to estimate the cost of capital for specific projects or divisions.

■ The required rate of return on equity, k_s, is equal to the risk-free rate of return, k_{RF}, plus a risk premium equal to the market risk premium, $k_M - k_{RF}$, times the firm's beta coefficient, b:

$$k_s = k_{RF} + (k_M - k_{RF})b.$$

  ❑ This is the Security Market Line (SML) equation that expresses the risk/return relationship.
  ❑ For example, if a firm has a beta of 1.1, $k_M = 12\%$, and $k_{RF} = 8\%$, then its required rate of return would be $k_s = 8\% + (12\% - 8\%)1.1 = 12.4\%$. Stockholders would be willing to let the firm invest their money if the firm could earn 12.4 percent on their equity capital.

- The acceptance of a particular capital budgeting project may cause a firm's overall beta to rise or fall, causing a change in the required rate of return.
  - The impact of any one project on a firm's beta will depend upon the size of the project relative to the firm's existing "portfolio" of projects.
  - The beta of any portfolio is a weighted average of the betas of its individual assets.
  - An increase in a firm's beta coefficient will cause the stock price to decline unless the increased beta is offset by a higher expected rate of return.

- If the beta coefficient for each project could be determined, then a *project cost of capital* for each individual project could be found as follows:

$$k_{Project} = k_{RF} + (k_M - k_{RF})b_{Project}.$$

High beta, or high-risk, projects will have a relatively high cost of equity capital, while low beta projects will have a correspondingly low cost of equity capital.

- If the expected rate of return on a given capital project lies above the SML, the expected rate of return on the project is more than enough to compensate for its risk, and the project should be accepted. Conversely, if the project's rate of return lies below the SML, it should be rejected.

- The discount rate applied in capital budgeting is the firm's weighted average cost of capital. When debt financing is used, the project's cost of equity must be combined with the cost of debt to obtain the *project's overall cost of capital*.

The estimation of project betas is even more difficult than that for stocks. However, two approaches have been used to estimate individual asset's betas: the pure play method and the accounting beta method.

- In the *pure play method*, the company tries to find several single-product companies in the same line of business as the project being evaluated, and it then averages those companies' betas to determine the cost of capital for its own project.
  - The pure play approach can only be used for major assets such as whole divisions.

- In the *accounting beta method*, a company's return on assets (ROA) is regressed against the average ROA for a large sample of firms, say the S&P 400. The resulting accounting beta is then used as a proxy for the market beta.
  - In practice, accounting betas are normally calculated for divisions or other large units, not for single assets, and divisional betas are then used for the division's projects.

Flotation costs can increase the cost of capital.

- Let F denote the percentage of the proceeds from a debt issue that must be paid as a flotation cost. M is the par value of the bond, INT is the interest payment, T is the tax rate, k_d is the cost of debt, and N is the number of payments. Assuming annual payments, the cost of debt with flotation costs is found by solving for k_d in the following equation:

$$M(1-F) = \sum_{t=1}^{N} \frac{INT}{(1+k_d)^t} + \frac{M}{(1+k_d)^N}$$

- The required rate of return for externally raised common equity, k_e, may be estimated by the DCF approach. This approach combines the expected dividend yield, D_1/P_0, with the expected future growth rate, g, of earnings and dividends, or

$$k_e = \frac{D_1}{P_0(1-F)} + g.$$

A number of difficult issues relating to the cost of capital are listed below. These topics are covered in advanced finance courses.

- As a general rule, the same principles of cost of capital estimation apply to both *privately held* and publicly owned firms, but the problems of obtaining input data are somewhat difficult for each.

- One cannot overemphasize the practical difficulties encountered when one actually attempts to estimate the cost of equity. As a result, we can never be sure just how accurate our estimated cost of capital is.

- It is difficult to assign risk-adjusted discount rates to capital budgeting projects of differing degrees of riskiness.

- Establishing the target capital structure is a major task in itself.

Managers and students often make four common mistakes when estimating the cost of capital. Here are four common mistakes to avoid:

- Do not use the coupon rate on a firm's existing debt as the pre-tax cost of debt.

- When applying the CAPM method, never use the historical average return on stocks with the current risk-free rate to estimate $(k_M - k_{RF})$.

■   If you don't know the target capital structure weights, use weights based on current market values instead of weights based on current book values to calculate WACC.

■   Do not include accounts payable and accruals as components in the calculation of WACC. If it's not a source of funding from an investor, then it's not a capital component.

SELF-TEST QUESTIONS

Definitional

1.   The firm should calculate its cost of capital as a(n) _weighted_ _average_ of the after-tax costs of the various types of funds it uses.

2.   There are _3_ methods that can be used to determine the cost of common equity.

3.   Assigning a cost to reinvested earnings is based on the _opportunity_ _cost_ principle.

4.   Companies must earn more than k_s on new shares because they incur _flotation_ _cost_ to issue new stock.

5.   Using the Capital Asset Pricing Model (CAPM), the required rate of return on common stock is found as a function of the _risk_ - _free_ _rate_, the firm's _beta coefficient_, and the required rate of return on an average _stock_ .

6.   The cost of common equity may also be found by adding a(n) _risk_ _premium_ to the interest rate on the firm's own long-term debt.

7.   The required rate of return on common equity may also be estimated as the expected _dividend yield_ on the common stock plus the expected future _growth rate_ of the dividends.

8.   The proportions of _debt_, _Preferred Stock_, and _Common Equity_ in the target capital structure should be used to calculate the _average weight_ cost of capital.

9. The component cost of preferred stock is calculated as the _preferred_ _dividend_ divided by the _net_ _issuing_ _price_ of preferred stock.

10. One method for estimating g involves multiplying the _retention_ _rate_ by the company's expected future rate of return on equity (ROE).

11. The two most important factors that affect the cost of capital and which are beyond the firm's direct control are the level of _interest_ rates and _taxes_ .

12. A firm can affect its cost of capital through its _Capital_ _Structure_ policy, its _dividend_ policy, and its _investment_ (capital budgeting) policy.

13. The cost of capital is sometimes referred to as the _hurdle_ rate because projects must jump over it to be accepted.

14. The hurdle rate for each project should reflect the _risk_ of the project itself, not necessarily those associated with the firm's _average_ project as reflected in the firm's composite WACC.

15. Three separate and distinct types of risk can be identified: _Stand - alone_ risk, _Market_ risk, and _Corporate_ risk.

16. Of the three risk measures, _Market_ risk is theoretically the most relevant measure because of its direct effect on stock prices.

17. If the expected rate of return on a given capital project lies _above_ the SML, the expected rate of return on the project is more than enough to compensate for its risk, and the project should be accepted.

18. _Stand -alone_ risk is the risk an asset would have if it were a firm's only asset.

19. Two approaches have been developed for estimating project betas: the _pure_ _play_ and the _accounting beta_ methods.

20. Projects are classified into subjective risk categories and then _risk - adjusted_ _cost of capital_ are developed for each category using the composite WACC as a starting point.

21. _Capital budgeting_ analysis is a similar process to the corporate valuation model, except that it focuses on proposed new projects rather than on the firm's existing assets.

22. Most firms employ several types of capital, called _Capital Components_ , with common and preferred stock, along with debt, being the three most frequently used types.

23. k_d is the _marginal_ cost of new debt to be raised during the planning period.

24. The combined effects of _flotation costs_ and _price pressure_ inhibit companies from issuing additional common stock.

25. The correct weights to use in the WACC calculation are those based on the firm's _target_ capital structure, since this is the best estimate of how the firm will, on average, raise money in the future.

26. For many firms, _depreciation_ is the largest source of funds as shown in their statement of cash flows and is available to support the capital budget.

27. The opportunity cost of depreciation is the _weighted average cost of capital_.

Conceptual

28. Funds acquired by the firm through preferred stock have a cost to the firm equal to the preferred dividend divided by the net issuing price, P_n, the price the firm receives on preferred after deducting flotation costs.

    a. True   b. False

    $$P_s = \frac{d_o}{n_o}$$

29. Which of the following statements could be true concerning the costs of debt and equity?

    a. The cost of debt for Firm A is greater than the cost of equity for Firm A.
    b. The cost of debt for Firm A is greater than the cost of equity for Firm B.
    c. The cost of reinvested earnings for Firm A is less than its cost of new equity.
    d. The cost of reinvested earnings for Firm A is less than its cost of debt.
    e. Statements b and c could both be true.

30. Which of the following statements is most correct?

    a. If Congress raised the corporate tax rate, this would lower the effective cost of debt but probably would also reduce the amount of earnings available to reinvest, so the effect on the marginal cost of capital is uncertain.
    b. For corporate investors, 70 percent of the dividends received on both common and preferred stocks is exempt from taxes. However, neither preferred nor common dividends may be deducted by the issuing company. Therefore, the dividend exclusion has no effect on a company's cost of capital, so its WACC would probably not change at all if the dividend exclusion rule were rescinded by Congress.

c. The calculation for a firm's WACC includes an adjustment to the cost of debt for taxes, since interest is deductible, and includes the cost of short-term debt.
d. Each of the above statements is true.
e. Each of the above statements is false.

SELF-TEST PROBLEMS

1. Roland Corporation's next expected dividend (D_1) is $2.50. The firm has maintained a constant payout ratio of 50 percent during the past 7 years. Seven years ago its EPS was $1.50. The firm's beta coefficient is 1.2. The required return on an average stock in the market is 13 percent, and the risk-free rate is 7 percent. Roland's A-rated bonds are yielding 10 percent, and its current stock price is $30. Which of the following values is the most reasonable estimate of Roland's cost of common equity, k_s?

   a. 10%   b. 12%   c. 14%   d. 20%   e. 26%

2. The director of capital budgeting for See-Saw Inc., manufacturers of playground equipment, is considering a plan to expand production facilities in order to meet an increase in demand. He estimates that this expansion will produce a rate of return of 11 percent. The firm's target capital structure calls for a debt/equity ratio of 0.8. See-Saw currently has a bond issue outstanding which will mature in 25 years and has a 7 percent annual coupon rate. The bonds are currently selling for $804. The firm has maintained a constant growth rate of 6 percent. See-Saw's next expected dividend is $2 and its current stock price is $40. Its tax rate is 40 percent. Should it undertake the expansion? (Assume that there is no preferred stock outstanding and that any new debt will have a 25-year maturity.)

   a. No; the expected return is 2.5 percentage points lower than the cost of capital.
   b. No; the expected return is 1.0 percentage point lower than the cost of capital.
   c. Yes; the expected return is 0.5 percentage point higher than the cost of capital.
   d. Yes; the expected return is 1.0 percentage point higher than the cost of capital.
   e. Yes; the expected return is 2.5 percentage points higher than the cost of capital.

3. The management of Florida Phosphate Industries (FPI) is planning next year's capital budget. The company's earnings and dividends are growing at a constant rate of 5 percent. The last dividend, D_0, was $0.90; and the current equilibrium stock price is $7.73. FPI can raise new debt at a 14 percent before-tax cost. FPI is at its optimal capital structure, which is 40 percent debt and 60 percent equity, and the firm's marginal tax rate is 40 percent. FPI has the following independent, indivisible, and equally risky investment opportunities:

Project	Cost	Rate of Return
A	$15,000	17%
B	15,000	16
C	12,000	15
D	20,000	13

What is FPI's optimal capital budget?

a. $62,000   **b.** $42,000   **c.** $30,000   **d.** $15,000   **e.** $0

4. Gator Products Company (GPC) is at its optimal capital structure of 70 percent common equity and 30 percent debt. GPC's WACC is 14 percent. GPC has a marginal tax rate of 40 percent. Next year's dividend is expected to be $2.00 per share, and GPC has a constant growth in earnings and dividends of 6 percent. The cost of common equity used in the WACC is based on retained earnings, while the before-tax cost of debt is 12 percent. What is GPC's current equilibrium stock price?

a. $12.73   **b.** $17.23   **c.** $18.33   **d.** $20.37   **e.** $23.70

(The following data apply to the next four Self-Test Problems.)

Sun Products Company (SPC) uses only debt and equity. It can borrow unlimited amounts at an interest rate of 12 percent so long as it finances at its target capital structure, which calls for 45 percent debt and 55 percent common equity. Its last dividend was $2.40, its expected constant growth rate is 5 percent, and its stock sells for $24. SPC's tax rate is 40 percent. Four projects are available: Project A has a cost of $240 million and a rate of return of 13 percent, Project B has a cost of $125 million and a rate of return of 12 percent, Project C has a cost of $200 million and a rate of return of 11 percent, and Project D has a cost of $150 million and a rate of return of 10 percent. All of the company's potential projects are independent and equally risky.

5. What is SPC's cost of common equity?

a. 15.50%   **b.** 13.40%   **c.** 7.20%   **d.** 12.50%   **e.** 16.00%

6. What is SPC's weighted average cost of capital? In other words, what WACC cost rate should it use to evaluate capital budgeting projects (these four projects plus any others that might arise during the year, provided the WACC remains as it is currently)?

a. 12.05%   **b.** 13.40%   **c.** 11.77%   **d.** 12.50%   **e.** 10.61%

7. What is SPC's optimal capital budget (in millions)?

a. $240   **b.** $325   **c.** $365   **d.** $565   **e.** $715

8. Assume now that all four projects are independent; however, Project A has been judged a very risky project, while Projects C and D have been judged low-risk projects. Project B remains an average-risk project. If SPC adjusts its WACC by 2 percentage points up or down to account for risk, what is its optimal capital budget (in millions) now?

   a. $365   **b.** $390   **c.** $440   **d.** $475   **e.** $715

(The following data apply to the next two Self-Test Problems.)

On January 1, the total market value of the Haberdasher Company was $20 million. During the year, the company plans to raise and invest $10 million in new projects. The firm's present market value capital structure, shown below, is considered to be optimal. Assume that there is no short-term debt.

Debt	$10,000,000
Common equity	10,000,000
Total capital	$20,000,000

New bonds will have a 7 percent coupon rate, and they will be sold at par. Common stock is currently selling at $25 a share. Stockholder's required rate of return is estimated to be 13 percent, consisting of a dividend yield of 5 percent and an expected constant growth rate of 8 percent. (The next expected dividend is $1.25, so $1.25/$25 = 5%.) The marginal corporate tax rate is 40 percent.

9. To maintain the present capital structure, how much of the new investment (in millions) must be financed by common equity?

   a. $1.75   **b.** $2.25   **c.** $3.45   **d.** $5.00   **e.** $10.00

10. Assume that there is sufficient cash flow such that Haberdasher can maintain its target capital structure without issuing additional shares of equity. What is the WACC?

   a. 7.0%   **b.** 8.6%   **c.** 9.2%   **d.** 10.1%   **e.** 13.0%

(The following data apply to the next two Self-Test Problems.)

The following tabulation gives earnings per share figures for Gustafson Manufacturing during the preceding 10 years. The firm's common stock, 100,000 shares outstanding, is now selling for $40 a share, and the expected dividend for the coming year (1999) is 40 percent of EPS for the year. Investors expect past trends to continue, so g may be based on the historical earnings growth rate.

1989	$1.60
1990	1.73
1991	1.86
1992	2.02
1993	2.18
1994	2.35
1995	2.54
1996	2.74
1997	2.96
1998	3.20

The current interest rate on new debt is 7.5 percent. The firm's marginal federal-plus-state tax rate is 40 percent. The firm's market value capital structure, considered to be optimal, is as follows:

Debt	$2,400,000
Common equity	5,600,000
Total capital	$8,000,000

11. What is the firm's after-tax cost of new debt and common equity, assuming new equity comes only from reinvested cash flow? Calculate the cost of equity assuming constant growth; that is, $\hat{k}_s = D_1 / P_0 + g = k_s$.

   a. 4.5%; 11.5% **b.** 4.8%; 11.5% **c.** 4.5%; 12.3% **d.** 4.8%; 12.3% **e.** 4.0%; 11.5%

12. What is the firm's WACC, assuming no new common stock is sold?

   a. 8.05% **b.** 8.75% **c.** 9.40% **d.** 9.80% **e.** 10.05%

(The following data apply to the next two Self-Test Problems.)

Suppose the Williamson Company has this *book value* balance sheet:

Current assets	$45,000,000	Notes payable	$ 15,000,000
Fixed assets	75,000,000	Long-term debt	45,000,000
		Common equity:	
		Common stock (1.5 million shares)	1,500,000
		Retained earnings	58,500,000
Total assets	$120,000,000	Total claims	$120,000,000

The interest rate on the notes payable is 10 percent, the same as the rate on new bank loans. The long-term debt consists of 45,000 bonds, each of which has a par value of $1,000, carries an annual coupon interest rate of 6 percent, and matures in 20 years. The going rate of interest on new long-term debt, k_d, is 10 percent, and this is the present yield to maturity on the bonds. The common stock sells at a price of $30 per share.

13. What is the market value of the firm's long-term debt?

   a. $24,231,145 **b.** $29,675,585 **c.** $30,148,667 **d.** $32,498,885 **e.** $33,415,625

14. What is the market value weight of common equity in the firm's capital structure, if short-term debt is included?

   a. 25.00%   **b.** 38.75%   **c.** 42.45%   **d.** 50.18%   **e.** 63.00%

ANSWERS TO SELF-TEST QUESTIONS

1. weighted average
2. three
3. opportunity cost
4. flotation costs
5. risk-free rate (k_{RF}); beta coefficient (b); stock (k_M)
6. risk premium
7. dividend yield; growth rate
8. debt; preferred stock; common equity; weighted average
9. preferred dividends; net issuing price
10. retention rate
11. interest; taxes
12. capital structure; dividend; investment
13. hurdle

14. risk; average
15. stand-alone; corporate (within-firm); market (beta)
16. market
17. above
18. Stand-alone
19. pure play; accounting beta
20. risk-adjusted costs of capital
21. Capital budgeting
22. capital components
23. marginal
24. flotation costs; price pressure
25. target
26. depreciation
27. weighted average cost of capital

28. a. This statement is true.

29. e. If Firm A has more business risk than Firm B, Firm A's cost of debt could be greater than Firm B's cost of equity. Also, the cost of reinvested earnings is less than the cost of new equity because of flotation costs.

30. a. Statement a is correct. If Congress were to raise the tax rate, this would lower the cost of debt; however, a bigger chunk of the firm's earnings would go to Uncle Sam. The effect on the WACC would depend on which had the greater effect on the WACC. Statement b is false. Preferred stock generally has a lower before-tax cost than debt due to the dividend exclusion; however, if the dividend exclusion were omitted, preferred stock would have an increased before-tax cost. Statement c is false because short-term debt is not considered in the calculation of WACC.

SOLUTIONS TO SELF-TEST PROBLEMS

1. c. Use all three methods to estimate k_s.

CAPM: $k_s = k_{RF} + (k_M - k_{RF})b = 7\% + (13\% - 7\%)1.2 = 14.2\%$.

Risk Premium: k_s = Bond yield + Risk premium = $10\% + 4\% = 14\%$.

DCF: $k_s = D_1/P_0 + g = \$2.50/\$30 + g$, where g can be estimated as follows:
$$\$0.75 = \$2.50(PVIF_{k,7})$$
$$PVIF_{k,7} = \$0.75/\$2.50 = 0.3000.$$

Thus k, which is the compound growth rate, g, is about 19%, or, using a calculator, 18.8%. Therefore, $k_s = 0.083 + 0.188 = 27.1\%$.

Roland Corporation has apparently been experiencing supernormal growth during the past 7 years, and it is not reasonable to assume that this growth will continue. The first two methods yield a k_s of about 14 percent, which appears reasonable.

2. e. Cost of equity = $k_s = \$2/\$40 + 0.06 = 0.11 = 11\%$.

Cost of debt = k_d = Yield to maturity on outstanding bonds based on current market price.

$$V_B = INT(PVIFA_{k_d,25}) + M(PVIF_{k_d,25}),$$
$$\$804 = \$70(PVIFA_{k_d,25}) + \$1,000(PVIF_{k_d,25}).$$

Solving by trial and error gives $k_d = 9\%$.

Alternatively, with a financial calculator: Input N = 25, PV = -804, PMT = 70, FV = 1000, and solve for I = $k_d = 9\%$.

In determining the capital structure weights, note that Debt/Equity = 0.8 or, for example, 4/5. Therefore, Debt/Assets is

$$\frac{D}{A} = \frac{Debt}{Debt + Equity} = \frac{4}{4+5} = \frac{4}{9},$$

and Equity/Assets = 5/9. Hence, the weighted average cost of capital is calculated as follows:

$$WACC = k_d(1 - T)(D/A) + k_s(1 - D/A)$$
$$= 0.09(1 - 0.4)(4/9) + 0.11(5/9)$$
$$= 0.024 + 0.061 = 0.085 = 8.5\%.$$

The cost of capital is 8.5 percent, while the expansion project's rate of return is 11.0 percent. Since the expected return is 2.5 percentage points higher than the cost, the expansion should be undertaken.

3.   b.   The cost of common equity is as follows:

$$k_s = \frac{D_0(1+g)}{P_0} + g = \frac{\$0.90(1.05)}{\$7.73} + 0.05 = 0.1723 = 17.23\%.$$

Now, determine the weighted average cost of capital.

$$\begin{aligned} \text{WACC} &= w_d(k_d)(1-T) + w_{ce}(k_s) \\ &= 0.4(14\%)(0.6) + 0.6(17.23\%) = 13.70\%. \end{aligned}$$

To determine FPI's optimal capital budget, we must determine those projects whose rate of return > WACC. (Note that all projects being considered are independent.) Since Projects A, B, and C all have rates of return > WACC, they should be accepted. Therefore, the optimal capital budget is $42,000.

4.   c.   GPC's WACC = 14%. Therefore,

$$\begin{aligned} 14\% &= w_d(k_d)(1-T) + w_{ce}(k_s) \\ 14\% &= 0.3(12\%)(0.6) + 0.7(k_s) \\ k_s &= 16.91\%. \end{aligned}$$

Now, at equilibrium:

$$\hat{k}_s = k_s = \frac{D_1}{P_0} + g$$

$$0.1691 = \frac{\$2.00}{P_0} + 0.06$$

$$0.1091 = \frac{\$2.00}{P_0}$$

$$P_0 = \$18.33.$$

5.   a. $k_s = [\$2.40(1.05)]/\$24 + 5\% = 0.1050 + 0.05 = 0.1550 = 15.50\%.$

6.   c. $k_d = 12\%$; $k_d(1 - T) = 12\%(0.6) = 7.2\%$.

        $k_s = [\$2.40(1.05)]/\$24 + 5\% = 15.50\%$.

        WACC $= 0.45(7.2\%) + 0.55(15.50\%) = 11.77\%$.

7.   c.   Since all projects are equally risky and are independent, those projects whose rate of return > WACC should be chosen. Projects A and B have returns > 11.77%; therefore, the firm's optimal capital budget is $365 million.

8.   d.

Project	Cost (Millions)	Return	Risk Level	Risk-Adjusted Cost of Capital
A	$240	13%	High	13.77%
B	125	12	Average	11.77
C	200	11	Low	9.77
D	150	10	Low	9.77

From Self-Test Problem 6 we know that SPC's WACC is 11.77%. We adjust the firm's WACC up by 2% for risky projects and lower it by 2% for low-risk projects. Note that once the WACC is risk-adjusted, Projects B, C, and D are acceptable as their returns are greater than the risk-adjusted WACC. Therefore, the firm's optimal capital budget is $475 million.

9.   d.   Common equity needed:

        $0.5(\$10,000,000) = \$5,000,000$.

10.   b.   Cost using k_s:

	Percent	×	After-tax Cost	=	Product
Debt	0.50		4.2%*		2.1%
Common equity	0.50		13.0		6.5%
				WACC =	8.6%

        $*7\%(1 - T) = 7\%(0.6) = 4.2\%$.

11. a. After-tax cost of new debt = $k_d(1 - T)$:

$k_d(1 - T) = 0.075(1 - 0.4) = 0.045 = 4.5\%$.

Cost of common equity = k_s:

$k_s = D_1/P_0 + g$.

Using the point-to-point technique, $g = 8.01\%$. Thus,

$k_s = \$3.20(0.4)(1.08)/\$40.00 + 8\% = 3.5\% + 8\% = 11.5\%$.

12. c. WACC calculation:

Component	% Capital Structure	×	After-tax Cost	=	Component Cost
Debt	0.30		4.5%		1.35%
Common equity	0.70		11.5		8.05
	1.00				WACC = 9.40%

13. b. The bonds have a value of

$V_B = \$60(PVIFA_{10\%, 20}) + \$1,000(PVIF_{10\%, 20}) = \$60(8.5136) + \$1,000(0.1486)$
$= \$510.82 + \$148.60 = \$659.42$.

Alternatively, using a financial calculator, input N = 20, I = 10, PMT = 60, and FV = 1000 to arrive at a PV = $659.46.

The total market value of the long-term debt is 45,000($659.46) = $29,675,585.

14. d. The book and market value of the current liabilities are both $15,000,000.

There are 1.5 million shares of stock outstanding, and the stock sells for $30 per share. Therefore, the market value of the equity is $30(1,500,000) = $45,000,000. From Self-Test Problem 13 we know that the market value of the bonds is $29,675,585.

The market value capital structure is thus:

Short-term debt	$15,000,000	16.73%
Long-term debt	29,675,585	33.09
Common equity	45,000,000	50.18
Total capital	$89,675,585	100.00%

CHAPTER 12
PUTTING THE PIECES TOGETHER: CORPORATE VALUATION AND VALUE-BASED MANAGEMENT

OVERVIEW

How does one value a corporation that pays no dividends? Or how does one value a division of a company? This chapter presents the corporate valuation model which calculates a firm's value as the present value of its expected future free cash flows from operations discounted at its cost of capital, plus the value of its nonoperating assets. Managers can use the corporate valuation model to determine whether proposed actions will increase the company's value. When a company systematically uses this principle to guide its actions, it is called value-based management

The set of rules used to motivate managers to act in the best interests of shareholders is called corporate governance. These include provisions in the corporate charter that make it easier for someone to take over a poorly performing firm and replace its managers, the strength of the board of directors relative to the CEO, and the compensation system for managers.

OUTLINE

The corporate valuation model can be used to value (1) companies that don't pay dividends, (2) privately held businesses, and (3) individual divisions of a company.

■ A firm's value is determined by its ability to generate cash flow, both now and in the future.

■ To apply the corporate valuation model, one must forecast the projected financial statements for enough years until the company's free cash flows begin to grow at a constant rate. This is called the forecast horizon, at period N. The value of the firm's operations at the horizon, N, can be calculated as:

$$V_{op\,(at\,time\,N)} = \frac{FCF_N\,(1+g)}{WACC-g}.$$

- A company's *horizon, value* is its value of operations at the end of the forecast horizon. This is also called its *continuing value*, or is *terminal value*.

- A firm's value of operations is the present value of its expected future free cash flows (FCF) from operations during the forecast period and its horizon value, discounted at its weighted average cost of capital, WACC.

- A firm's total value is its value of operations plus the value of its nonoperating, or financial, assets.

- Debtholders and preferred stockholders have the first claim on the total value of a company. The remaining value belongs to the equity holders. Thus, the value of equity is:

    Value of equity = Total value – debt – preferred stock.

- The price per share is the value of equity divided by the number of shares of stock.

- Even if a company is paying steady dividends much can be learned from the corporate value model, so many analysts today use it for all types of valuations.
    - The process of projecting the future financial statements can reveal quite a bit about the company's operations and financing needs.

Value-based management is the systematic application of the corporate valuation model to decision-making.

- The four value drivers are growth in sales (g), operating profitability (OP), capital requirements (CR), and the weighted average cost of capital.
    - OP = NOPAT / Sales.
    - CR = Operating capital / Sales.

- A company's expected return on invested capital (EROIC) is its forecasted NOPAT divided by its current amount of capital:
    $$EROIC_N = NOPAT_{N+1} / Capital_N.$$

If a company's expected ROIC is greater than its WACC, then it is creating value.

Corporate governance is the set of rules to ensure that managers act in the interests of shareholders.

- Managers are entrenched when they don't have to worry about being replaced if they perform poorly.
    - Barriers to hostile takeovers allow managers to remain entrenched.

❑ Effective monitoring by a strong board of directors prevents managerial entrenchment.

■ Compensation plans can help align managerial interests with shareholder interests.
  ❑ Stock options allow a manager to reap rewards when the company's stock goes up.
  ❑ Employee stock ownership plans (ESOPs) help all employees when the stock goes up.

SELF-TEST QUESTIONS

Definitional

1. The _____ _____, or _____, _____ model can be used to value companies that don't pay dividends, privately held businesses, and particular divisions that a company may want to sell.

2. A firm's value is determined by its ability to generate _____ _____, both now and in the future.

3. A firm's _____ _____ can be calculated as the present value of its expected future free cash flows from operations, discounted at its cost of capital, plus the value of its nonoperating assets.

4. The company's _____, or _____, value is its value at the end of the forecast period.

5. A company's _____ _____ is NOPAT divided by sales.

6. A company's _____ _____ is its operating capital divided by sales.

7. A company's expected _____ ___ _____ _____ is its projected NOPAT divided by its current operating capital.

8. _____-_____ _____ is the systematic application of the corporate valuation model to decisions.

·9. _____ _____ is the set of rules to ensure that managers act in the interests of shareholders.

Conceptual

10.   Managerial entrenchment occurs when there is very little chance that poorly performing managers will be replaced.

    a. True   **b.** False

11.   A nonpecuniary benefit is a barrier to a hostile takeover.

    a. True   **b.** False

12.   An ESOP is an employee stock option plan.

    a. True   **b.** False

13.   If a stock underperforms the market, then a stock option will be worthless.

    a. True   **b.** False

14.   Which of the following is *not* a value driver in the corporate valuation model?

    a. Sales growth.
    b. The weighted average cost of capital.
    c. Earnings per share.
    d. Capital requirements.
    e. Operating profitability.

15.   Which of the following is *not* a barrier to a hostile takeover?

    a. Targeted share repurchases.
    b. Shareholder rights provision.
    c. Restricted voting rights.
    d. Executive stock option plan.
    f. Interlocking board of directors.

SELF-TEST PROBLEMS

1.   HBT Corporation has never paid a dividend. Its current free cash flow is $1,200,000 and is expected to grow at a constant rate of 4 percent. The weighted average cost of capital is 10 percent. What is HBT's value of operations (in millions)?

   a. $22.00   **b.** $20.80   **c.** $12.48   **d.** $20.00   **e.** $10.00

   (The following data apply to the next two Self-Test Problems.)

   Cane Enterprises has never paid a dividend. Free cash flow is projected to be $40,000 and $50,000 for the next two years, and after the second year it is expected to grow at a constant rate of 6 percent. The company's weighted average cost of capital is 11%.

2.   What is the terminal, or horizon, value of operations (in millions)? (Hint: First find the value of all free cash flows beyond Year 2 discounted back to Year 2.)

   a. $0.363   **b.** $0.848   **c.** $1.000   **d.** $1.060   **e.** $1.500

3.   What is the value of Cane's operations?

   a. $848,492   **b.** $936,937   **c.** $1,136,617   **d.** $1,500,000   **e.** $1,724,898

4. Given the following information, what is Garret Starr Inc.'s free cash flow for 1999?

Income Statement:

	1999	1998
Net sales	$1,590.0	$1,500.0
Costs (except depreciation)	1,200.0	1,140.0
Depreciation	90.0	75.0
Total operating costs	$1,290.0	$1,215.0
EBIT	300.0	285.0
Less interest	69.0	63.0
EBT	$ 231.0	$ 222.0
Taxes (40%)	92.4	88.8
Net income	$ 138.6	$ 133.2

Balance sheet:

	1999	1998
Assets		
Cash	$ 84.0	$ 81.0
Marketable securities	207.0	198.0
Accounts receivable	252.0	240.0
Inventories	336.0	318.0
Total current assets	$ 879.0	$ 837.0
Net plant and equipment	843.0	795.0
Total assets	$1,722.0	$1,632.0
Liabilities and Equity		
Accounts payable	$ 168.0	$ 156.0
Notes payable	414.0	390.0
Accruals	84.0	84.0
Total current liabilities	$ 666.0	$ 630.0
Long-term bonds	$ 519.0	$ 492.0
Common stock	300.0	300.0
Retained earnings	237.0	210.0
Common equity	$ 537.0	$ 510.0
Total liabilities and equity	$1,722.0	$1,632.0

a. $276 **b.** $399 **c.** $420 **d.** $180 **e.** $111

(The following data apply to the next three Self-Test Problems.)

Alday Corporation is a fast growing supplier of office products. Analysts project the following free cash flows (FCF) during the next three years, after which FCF is expected to grow at a constant 5 percent rate. Alday's weighted average cost of capital is 12%.

Time	1	2	3
Free cash flow ($ millions)	-$10	$15	$20

5.   What is Alday's terminal, or horizon, value (in millions)? (Hint: Find the value of all free cash flows beyond Year 3 discounted back to Year 3.)

   a. $300   **b.** $167   **c.** $420   **d.** $266   **e.** $500

6.   What is the current value of operations (in millions) for Alday?

   a. $175.60   **b.** $230.80   **c.** $300.00   **d.** $420.00   **e.** $489.98

7.   Suppose Alday has $5 million in marketable securities, $50 million in debt, and 5 million shares of stock. What is the price per share?

   a. $40.50   **b.** $33.00   **c.** $28.95   **d.** $43.79   **e.** $37.16

ANSWERS TO SELF-TEST QUESTIONS

1.   total company; corporate; valuation
2.   cash flow
3.   total value
4.   terminal; horizon
5.   operating profitability (OP)

6.   capital requirements (CR)
7.   return on invested capital
8.   Value-based management
9.   Corporate governance

10.   a.   True.

11.   a.   False.

12.   a.   False. It is a stock ownership plan, not a stock option plan.

13.   a.   False.

14.   c.   Earnings per share.

SOLUTIONS TO SELF-TEST PROBLEMS

1. b. Value of operations = V_{op} = PV of expected future free cash flow.

$$V_{op} = \frac{FCF(1+g)}{WACC-g} = \frac{\$1,200,000(1.04)}{0.10-0.04} = \$20,800,000.$$

2. d. $$V_{op2} = \frac{\$50,000(1.06)}{0.11-0.06} = \$1,060,000.$$

3. b.

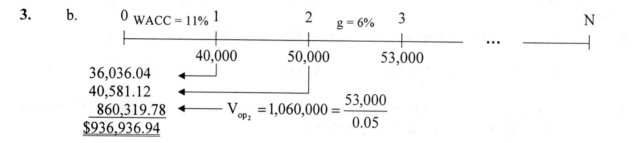

4. e. NOPAT = EBIT(1 – T)
        = $300(1 – 0.4) = $180.

    Net operating WC_{98} = ($81 + $240 + $318) – ($156 + $84)
            = $639 – $240 = $399.

    Operating capital$_{98}$ = $399 + $795 = $1,194.

    Net operating WC_{99} = ($84 + $252 + $336) – ($168 + $84)
            = $672 – $252 = $420.

    Operating capital$_{99}$ = $420 + $843 = $1,263.

    FCF = NOPAT – Net investment in operating capital
        = $300(0.6) – ($1,263 – $1,194)
        = $111.

5.   a. $V_{op_3} = \dfrac{\$20(1.05)}{0.12 - 0.05} = \$300.$

6.   b.

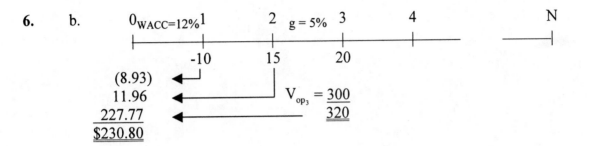

7.   e.   Total value$_{t = 0}$ = \$230.80 + \$5.0 = \$235.80.

Value of common equity = \$235.80 – \$50 = \$185.80.

Price per share = $\dfrac{\$185.80}{5.0} = \$37.16.$

OVERVIEW

Capital budgeting is similar in principle to security valuation in that future cash flows are estimated, risks are appraised and reflected in a cost of capital discount rate, and all cash flows are evaluated on a present value basis. Six primary methods can be used to determine which projects should be included in a firm's capital budget: (1) payback, (2) discounted payback, (3) Net Present Value (NPV), (4) Internal Rate of Return (IRR), (5) Modified IRR (MIRR), and (6) Profitability Index (PI).

Both payback methods have deficiencies, and thus should not be used as the sole criterion for making capital budgeting decisions. The NPV, IRR, PI, and MIRR methods all lead to the same accept/reject decisions on independent projects. However, the methods may conflict when ranking mutually exclusive projects which differ in scale or timing. Under these circumstances, the NPV method should be used to make the final decision.

When comparing two projects with unequal lives, replacement chains should be used. A project should be operated only for its economic life, and not necessarily for its full physical life.

OUTLINE

The capital budget is an outline of planned investments in fixed assets, and capital budgeting is the process of planning expenditures on assets whose cash flows are expected to extend beyond one year.

- A number of factors combine to make capital budgeting perhaps the most important function financial managers and their staffs must perform. Since the results of capital budgeting decisions continue for many years, the firm loses some of its flexibility. Also, a firm's capital budgeting decisions define its strategic direction. Timing is also important since capital assets must be put in place when they are needed.

■ The same general concepts that are used in security valuation are also involved in capital budgeting; however, whereas a set of stocks and bonds exists in the securities market from which investors select, capital budgeting projects are created by the firm.

■ Analyzing capital expenditure proposals has a cost, so firms classify projects into different categories to help differentiate the level of analysis required:
   ❑ Replacement: maintenance of business
   ❑ Replacement: cost reduction
   ❑ Expansion of existing products or markets
   ❑ Expansion into new products or markets
   ❑ Safety and/or environmental projects
   ❑ Research and development
   ❑ Other miscellaneous projects

■ Normally, a more detailed analysis is required for cost-reduction replacements, expansion, and new product decisions than for simple replacement and maintenance decisions. Also, projects requiring larger investments will be analyzed more carefully than smaller projects.

■ Once a potential capital budgeting project has been identified, its evaluation involves the same steps that are used in security analysis.
   ❑ The cost of the project must be determined.
   ❑ Cash flows from the project are estimated.
   ❑ The riskiness of these projected cash flows is determined.
   ❑ Given the riskiness of the projected cash flows, the appropriate cost of capital is determined at which cash flows are to be discounted.
   ❑ Cash flows are discounted to their present value to obtain an estimate of the asset's value to the firm.
   ❑ The present value of the expected cash flows is compared with the required outlay, or cost. If the PV of the cash flows exceeds the cost, the project should be accepted; otherwise, it should be rejected. (Alternatively, if the expected rate of return on the project exceeds its cost of capital, the project is accepted.)

Six key methods are currently used to rank projects and to decide whether or not they should be accepted for inclusion in the capital budget: (1) payback, (2) discounted payback, (3) Net Present Value (NPV), (4) Internal Rate of Return (IRR), (5) Modified Internal Rate of Return (MIRR), and (6) Profitability Index (PI). The MIRR and PI are discussed in later sections.

■ The *payback period* is defined as the expected number of years required to recover the original investment in the project, and it was the first formal method used to evaluate capital budgeting projects. Payback is a type of "breakeven" calculation in the sense that if cash flows come in at the expected rate until the payback year, then the project will break even.

- ❏ The payback method's flaws are that cash flows beyond the payback period are ignored and it does not take into account the cost of capital.
- ❏ Although the payback method has some serious faults as a project-ranking criterion, it does provide information on how long funds will be tied up in a project. Thus, the shorter the payback period, other things held constant, the greater the project's *liquidity*.
- ❏ Also, since cash flows expected in the distant future are generally riskier than near-term cash flows, the payback is often used as one indication of a project's *riskiness*.

- ■ A variant of the regular payback, the *discounted payback period* discounts the expected cash flows by the project's cost of capital, thus taking into account the effects of capital costs. Thus, the discounted payback period is defined as the number of years required to recover the investment from discounted net cash flows.

- ■ The *Net Present Value (NPV)* method of evaluating investment proposals is a discounted cash flow (DCF) technique that accounts for the time value of all cash flows from a project.
  - ❏ To implement the NPV, proceed as follows: (a) Find the present value of each cash flow, discounted at the project's cost of capital, (b) sum these discounted cash flows to obtain the project's NPV, and (c) accept the project if the NPV is positive.
  - ❏ The NPV is defined as follows:

$$NPV = \sum_{t=0}^{n} \frac{CF_t}{(1+k)^t}.$$

    Here, CF_t is the expected net cash flow in Period t and k is the project's cost of capital. Cash outflows are treated as negative cash flows.
  - ❏ If the NPV is positive, the project should be accepted; if negative, it should be rejected. If two projects are *mutually exclusive* (that is, only one can be accepted), the one with the higher NPV should be chosen, assuming that the NPV is positive. If both projects have negative NPVs, neither should be chosen.
  - ❏ Finding the NPV with a financial calculator is efficient and easy. Simply enter the different cash flows into the "cash flow register" along with the value of k = I, and then press the NPV key for the solution.
  - ❏ Financial analysts generally use spreadsheets when dealing with capital budgeting projects. Once a spreadsheet has been set up, it is easy to change input values to see what would happen as inputs are changed.
  - ❏ There is a direct relationship between NPV and EVA. NPV is equal to the present value of the project's future EVAs. Therefore, accepting positive NPV projects should result in a positive EVA for the company, and in a positive MVA.

- ❑ A reward system that compensates managers for producing positive EVA will encourage the use of NPV for making capital budgeting decisions.

- ■ The *Internal Rate of Return (IRR)* is defined as the discount rate which equates the present value of a project's expected cash inflows to the present value of its costs.
  - ❑ The equation for calculating the IRR is shown below:

$$\sum_{t=0}^{n} \frac{CF_t}{(1+IRR)^t} = 0.$$

  This equation has one unknown, the IRR, and we can solve for the value of the IRR that will make the equation equal to zero. The solution value of IRR is defined as the internal rate of return.
  - ❑ The IRR formula is simply the NPV formula solved for the particular discount rate that causes the NPV to equal zero.
  - ❑ The IRR can be found by trial and error, but most financial calculators and computers with financial analysis software can easily calculate IRRs and NPVs.
  - ❑ To find the IRR with a financial calculator, simply enter the different cash flows into the cash flow register, making sure to input the t = 0 cash flow, and then press the IRR key for the solution.
  - ❑ The IRR rule indicates that a project with an IRR greater than its cost of capital, or hurdle rate, should be accepted.
  - ❑ If the internal rate of return exceeds the cost of the funds used to finance the project, a surplus remains after paying for the capital, and this surplus accrues to the firm's stockholders. Therefore, taking on a project whose IRR exceeds its cost of capital increases shareholders' wealth.
  - ❑ Its "breakeven" characteristic makes the IRR useful in evaluating capital projects.

- ■ The same basic equation is used for both the NPV and the IRR methods, but in the NPV method, the discount rate, k, is specified and the NPV is found, whereas in the IRR method, the NPV is specified to equal zero, and the value of IRR that forces this equality is determined.

- ■ In many respects the NPV method is better than the IRR method. However, the IRR is widely used in business. Therefore, it is important to understand the IRR method including its problems.

- ■ A *net present value profile* is a graph which plots a project's NPV against different discount rates.
  - ❑ The NPV profile crosses the Y-axis at the *undiscounted* NPV, while it crosses the X-axis at the IRR.
  - ❑ The *crossover rate* is the discount rate at which the NPV profiles of two projects cross and, thus, at which the projects' NPVs are equal.

❑ If an *independent* project is being evaluated, then the NPV and IRR criteria always lead to the same accept/reject decision.

❑ If two *mutually exclusive* projects have NPV profiles which intersect in the upper right-hand quadrant, then there may be a conflict in rankings between NPV and IRR methods. A conflict between the NPV and IRR decision rules exists for mutually exclusive projects if the cost of capital is less than the crossover rate. Two basic conditions can lead to conflicts between NPV and IRR:

- *Project size* (or *scale*) differences exist; that is, the cost of one project is larger than that of the other.

- *Timing differences* exist such that cash flows from one project come in the early years and most of the cash flows from the other project come in the later years.

❑ The critical issue in resolving conflicts between mutually exclusive projects is to determine how useful it is to generate cash flows earlier rather than later. Thus, the value of early cash flows depends on the rate at which we can reinvest these cash flows.

- The NPV method implicitly assumes that project cash flows are reinvested at the project's cost of capital.

- The IRR method implicitly assumes that project cash flows are reinvested at the project's IRR.

- The opportunity cost of a project's cash flows is the project's cost of capital. If these cash flows were not available to the firm and if the firm needed capital to invest in new projects, then the funds would be obtained from the firm's capital suppliers; the cost would be the overall cost of capital. Thus, the assumption of reinvestment at the cost of capital is the best *reinvestment rate assumption*, and NPV is the preferred method.

❑ In summary, when projects are independent, the NPV and IRR methods both make exactly the same accept/reject decision. However, when evaluating mutually exclusive projects, especially those that differ in scale and/or timing, the NPV method should be used.

Multiple IRRs can result when the IRR criterion is used with a project that has nonnormal cash flows. Projects with nonnormal cash flows call for a large cash outflow either sometime during or at the end of its life. In such cases, the NPV criterion can be easily applied, and this method leads to conceptually correct capital budgeting decisions.

Business executives often prefer to work with percentage rates of return, such as IRR, rather than dollar amounts of NPV when analyzing investments. To overcome some of the IRR's limitations a Modified IRR, or MIRR, has been devised.

■ The MIRR is defined as the discount rate which forces PV costs = PV terminal value, where *terminal value (TV)* is the future value of the inflows compounded at the project's cost of capital. Thus,

$$\sum_{t=0}^{n} \frac{COF_t}{(1+k)^t} = \frac{\sum_{t=0}^{n} CIF_t (1+k)^{n-t}}{(1+MIRR)^n}$$

$$PV\ costs = \frac{TV}{(1+MIRR)^n} .$$

■   Most spreadsheets have a function for finding the MIRR.

■   MIRR assumes that cash flows are reinvested at the cost of capital rather than the project's own IRR, making it a better indicator of a project's true profitability.

■   NPV and MIRR will lead to the same project selection decision if the two projects are of equal size. However, conflicts can still occur when projects differ in scale, and in this case, NPV should be used.

■   MIRR also avoids the problem of multiple IRRs, which can arise when a project has nonnormal cash flows or has negative cash flows after the project has gone into operation. NPV can be easily applied to such situations; however, MIRR can also overcome the multiple IRR problem because there is only one MIRR for any set of cash flows.

Another method used to evaluate projects is the Profitability Index (PI).

■   The equation for the *profitability index* is:

$$PI = \frac{PV\ future\ cash\ flows}{Intial\ cost} = \frac{\sum_{t=0}^{n} \frac{CF_t}{(1+k)^t}}{CF_0} .$$

■   The PI shows the relative profitability of any project, or the present value of future cash flows per dollar of initial cost.

■   A project is acceptable if its PI is greater than 1.0, and the higher the PI, the higher the project's ranking.

■   Mathematically, the NPV, IRR, MIRR, and PI methods will always lead to the same accept/reject decisions for independent projects; however, these methods can give conflicting rankings for mutually exclusive projects.

In making the accept/reject decision, each of the six capital budgeting decision methods provides decision makers with a somewhat different piece of relevant information.

■ Payback and discounted payback provide an indication of both the risk and the liquidity of a project.

■ NPV is important because it gives a direct measure of the dollar benefit (on a present value basis) of the project to shareholders, so it is regarded as the best single measure of profitability.

■ IRR also measures profitability, but expressed as a percentage rate of return, which many decision makers prefer. Further, IRR contains information regarding a project's "safety margin."

■ The modified IRR has all the virtues of the IRR, but it incorporates a better reinvestment rate assumption, and it avoids the multiple rate of return problem.

■ The PI measures profitability relative to the cost of a project—it shows the "bang per buck." Like the IRR, it gives an indication of the project's risk, for a high PI means that cash flows could fall quite a bit and the project would still be profitable.

■ Quantitative methods such as NPV and IRR should be considered as an aid to informed decisions but not as a substitute for sound managerial judgment.

■ In a perfectly competitive economy, there would be no positive NPV projects—all companies would have the same opportunities, and competition would quickly eliminate any positive NPV.

■ Positive NPV projects must be due to some imperfection in the marketplace, and the longer the life of the project, the longer that imperfection must last. Therefore, managers should be able to identify the imperfection and explain why it will persist before accepting that a project will really have a positive NPV.
  ❑ If you can't identify the reason a project has a positive projected NPV, then its actual NPV will probably not be positive.
  ❑ Positive NPV projects don't just happen—they result from hard work to develop some competitive advantage.
  ❑ Some competitive advantages last longer than others, with their durability depending upon competitors' ability to replicate them.

A number of studies regarding firms' use of capital budgeting methods have been published. The general conclusion one can reach from these studies is that large firms should and do use the procedures we recommend, and that managers of small firms, especially managers with aspirations for future growth, should at least understand DCF

procedures well enough to make rational decisions about using or not using them. Moreover, as computer technology makes it easier and less expensive for small firms to use DCF methods, and as more and more of their competitors begin using these methods, survival will necessitate increased DCF usage.

An important aspect of the capital budgeting process is the post-audit, which involves comparing actual results with those predicted by the project's sponsors and explaining why any differences occurred. The results of the post-audit help to improve forecasts, increase efficiency of the firm's operations, and identify abandonment/termination opportunities.

- The post-audit is not a simple process—a number of factors can cause complications.
  - Each element of the cash flow forecast is subject to uncertainty, so a percentage of all projects undertaken by any reasonably aggressive firm will necessarily go awry.
  - Projects sometime fail to meet expectations for reasons beyond the control of the operating executives and for reasons that no one could realistically be expected to anticipate.
  - It is often difficult to separate the operating results of one investment from those of a larger system.
  - It is often hard to hand out blame or praise, because the executives who were responsible for launching a given long-term investment may have moved on by the time the results are known.

- The results of post-audits often conclude that (1) the actual NPVs of most cost reduction projects exceed their expected NPVs by a slight amount, (2) expansion projects generally fall short of their expected NPVs by a slight amount, and (3) new product and new market projects fall short by relatively large amounts.

- The best-run and most successful organizations put great emphasis on post-audits.

The techniques developed in this chapter can help managers make a number of different types of decisions.

- Two examples of decisions which use capital budgeting techniques are evaluating corporate mergers and deciding whether to downsize personnel or to sell off particular assets or divisions.

- Most decisions should be based on whether they contribute to shareholder value, and that, in turn, can be determined by estimating the net present value of a set of cash flows.

If two mutually exclusive projects have significantly different lives, the analysis must include an adjustment using the replacement chain method.

■ The *replacement chain (common life) method* extends one, or both, projects until an equal life is achieved.

    ❑ Suppose two mutually exclusive projects are being considered: Project A with a 2-year life, and Project B with a 3-year life. The projects' lives would be extended to a 6-year common life.

    ❑ Project A would have an extended NPV equal to NPV_A plus NPV_A discounted for 2 years at the project's cost of capital, plus NPV_A discounted for 4 years at the project's cost of capital. Project B would have an extended NPV equal to NPV_B plus NPV_B discounted for 3 years at the project's cost of capital.

    ❑ The project with the highest extended NPV would be chosen.

    ❑ This method assumes that the project can be repeated and that there is no change in cash flows.

■ As a general rule, the unequal life issue does not arise for independent projects. Also, common life techniques can only be applied when the shorter-life project is actually expected to be replicated.

■ A serious weakness of the analysis techniques discussed is that changing revenues and/or costs have not been considered. These complications are handled by building the new revenue/cost estimates directly into the cash flow estimates and then using the replacement chain approach.

Thus far, all the capital budgeting examples have been based on a well-defined economic life. However, in most situations, the economic life, or that life which maximizes the project's NPV, is shorter than the project's physical, or engineering, life.

SELF-TEST QUESTIONS

Definitional

1. A firm's _____ _____ outlines its planned expenditures on fixed assets.

2. The number of years necessary to return the original investment in a project is known as the _____ _____.

3. The primary advantage of payback analysis is its _____.

4. One important weakness of payback analysis is the fact that _____ _____ beyond the payback period are _____.

5.   The Net Present Value (NPV) method of evaluating investment proposals is a(n) _____ cash flow technique.

6.   A capital investment proposal should be accepted if its NPV is _____.

7.   If two projects are _____ _____, the one with the _____ positive NPV should be selected.

8.   In the IRR approach, a discount rate is sought which makes the NPV equal to _____.

9.   A net present value profile plots a project's _____ against different _____ _____.

10. If an independent project's _____ is greater than the project's cost of capital, it should be accepted.

11. If two mutually exclusive projects are being evaluated and one project has a higher NPV while the other project has a higher IRR, the project with the higher _____ should be preferred.

12. The NPV method implicitly assumes reinvestment at the project's _____ ____ _____, while the IRR method implicitly assumes reinvestment at the _____ _____ ____ _____.

13. The MIRR method assumes reinvestment at the _____ ____ _____, making it a better indicator of a project's profitability than IRR.

14. The process of comparing a project's actual results with its projected results is known as a(n) _____-_____.

15. The objective of the post-audit is to improve _____, _____, and identify _____ and _____ opportunities.

16. The internal rate of return (IRR) is the _____ rate that equates the present value of the _____ _____ with the present value of the _____ _____.

17. The MIRR is defined as the discount rate which forces the present value of costs to equal the present value of the _____ _____.

18. The shorter the payback period, other things held constant, the greater the project's _____.

19.   The NPV profile crosses the Y-axis at the _____ NPV, while it crosses the X-axis at the _____.

20.   If a(n) _____ project is being evaluated, then the NPV and IRR criteria always lead to the same accept/reject decisions.

21.   Two basic conditions can lead to conflicts between NPV and IRR: _____ and _____ differences.

22.   _____ _____ can result when the IRR criterion is used with a project that has nonnormal cash flows.

23.   In addition to measuring a project's liquidity, the payback is often used as one indication of a project's _____.

24.   There is a direct relationship between NPV and _____. NPV is equal to the present value of the project's future _____.

25.   The _____ _____ is the discount rate at which the NPV profiles of two projects cross and, thus, at which the projects' NPVs are equal.

26.   The _____ _____ shows the relative profitability of any project, or the present value of future cash flows per dollar of initial cost.

27.   _____ contains information regarding a project's safety margin.

28.   _____ gives a direct measure of the dollar benefit of the project to shareholders.

29.   The ____ shows the "bang per buck."

30.   A conflict between the NPV and IRR decision rules exist for mutually exclusive projects if the cost of capital is _____ than the crossover rate.

31.   If two projects are _____, the fact that they have unequal lives will not affect the analysis.

32.   If two mutually exclusive projects have unequal lives, the _____ _____ method may be used for the analysis.

Conceptual

33.   The NPV of a project with cash flows that accrue relatively slowly is *more sensitive* to changes in the discount rate than is the NPV of a project with cash flows that come in more rapidly.

     a. True   **b.** False

34.   The NPV method is preferred over the IRR method because the NPV method's reinvestment rate assumption is better.

     a. True   **b.** False

35.   When you find the yield to maturity on a bond, you are finding the bond's net present value (NPV).

     a. True   **b.** False

36.   Other things held constant, a decrease in the cost of capital (discount rate) will cause an *increase* in a project's IRR.

     a. True   **b.** False

37.   The IRR method can be used in place of the NPV method for all independent projects.

     a. True   **b.** False

38.   The NPV and MIRR methods lead to the same decision for mutually exclusive projects regardless of the projects' relative sizes.

     a. True   **b.** False

39.   Projects with nonnormal cash flows sometimes have multiple MIRRs.

     a. True   **b.** False

40.   Projects A and B each have an initial cost of $5,000, followed by a series of positive cash inflows. Project A has total undiscounted cash inflows of $12,000, while B has total undiscounted inflows of $10,000. Further, at a discount rate of 10 percent, the two projects have identical NPVs. Which project's NPV will be *more sensitive* to changes in the discount rate? (Hint: Projects with steeper NPV profiles are more sensitive to discount rate changes.)

    a. Project A.

    b. Project B.

    c. Both projects are equally sensitive to changes in the discount rate since their NPVs are equal at all costs of capital.

    d. Neither project is sensitive to changes in the discount rate, since both have NPV profiles which are horizontal.

    e. The solution cannot be determined unless the timing of the cash flows is known.

41. Which of the following statements is most correct?

    a. The IRR of a project whose cash flows accrue relatively rapidly is more sensitive to changes in the discount rate than is the IRR of a project whose cash flows come in more slowly.

    b. There are many conditions under which a project can have more than one IRR. One such condition is where an otherwise normal project has a negative cash flow at the end of its life.

    c. The phenomenon called "multiple internal rates of return" arises when two or more mutually exclusive projects which have different lives are being compared.

    d. The modified IRR (MIRR) method has wide appeal to professors, but most business executives prefer the NPV method to either the regular or modified IRR.

    e. Each of the above statements is false.

42. Which of the following statements is most correct?

    a. If a project has an IRR greater than zero, then taking on the project will increase the value of the company's common stock because the project will make a positive contribution to net income.

    b. If a project has an NPV greater than zero, then taking on the project will increase the value of the firm's stock.

    c. Assume that you plot the NPV profiles of two mutually exclusive projects with normal cash flows and that the cost of capital is greater than the rate at which the profiles cross one another. In this case, the NPV and IRR methods will lead to contradictory rankings of the two projects.

    d. For independent (as opposed to mutually exclusive) normal projects, the NPV and IRR methods will generally lead to conflicting accept/reject decisions.

    e. Statements b, c, and d are all true.

43. Which of the following statements is most correct?

    a. Underlying the MIRR is the assumption that cash flows can be reinvested at the firm's cost of capital.

    b. Underlying the IRR is the assumption that cash flows can be reinvested at the firm's cost of capital.

    c. Underlying the NPV is the assumption that cash flows can be reinvested at the firm's cost of capital.

    d. The discounted payback method always leads to the same accept/reject decisions as the NPV method.

    e. Statements a and c are both correct.

44. Terminating a project before the end of its useful physical life may result in a higher NPV for the project.

    a. True   b. False

SELF-TEST PROBLEMS

1. Your firm is considering a fast-food concession at the World's Fair. The cash flow pattern is somewhat unusual since you must build the stands, operate them for 2 years, and then tear the stands down and restore the sites to their original conditions. You estimate the net cash flows to be as follows:

Time	Expected Net Cash Flows
0	($800,000)
1	700,000
2	700,000
3	(400,000)

What is the approximate IRR of this venture?

    a. 5%   b. 15%   c. 25%   d. 35%   e. 45%

(The following data apply to the next four Self-Test Problems.)

Toya Motors needs a new machine for production of its new models. The financial vice president has appointed you to do the capital budgeting analysis. You have identified two different machines that are capable of performing the job. You have completed the cash flow analysis, and the expected net cash flows are as follows:

| | Expected Net Cash Flows | |
Year	Machine B	Machine O
0	($5,000)	($5,000)
1	2,085	0
2	2,085	0
3	2,085	0
4	2,085	9,677

2. What is the payback period for Machine B?

   a. 1.0 year   **b.** 2.0 years   **c.** 2.4 years   **d.** 2.6 years   **e.** 3.0 years

3. The cost of capital is uncertain at this time, so you construct NPV profiles to assist in the final decision. The profiles for Machines B and O cross at what cost of capital?

   a. 6%   **d.** 24%
   b. 10%   **e.** They do not cross in the upper righthand quadrant.
   c. 18%

4. If the cost of capital for both projects is 14 percent at the time the decision is made, which project would you choose?

   a. Project B; it has the higher positive NPV.
   b. Project O; it has the higher positive NPV.
   c. Neither; both have negative NPVs.
   d. Either; both have the same NPV.
   e. Project B; it has the higher IRR.

5. If the cost of capital is 14 percent, what is the profitability index for Machine A?

   a. 0.750   **b.** 0.995   **c.** 1.150   **d.** 1.215   **e.** 1.333

(The following data apply to the next eight Self-Test Problems.)

The director of capital budgeting for Giant Inc. has identified two mutually exclusive projects, L and S, with the following expected net cash flows:

Year	Expected Net Cash Flows Project L	Project S
0	($100)	($100)
1	10	70
2	60	50
3	80	20

Both projects have a cost of capital of 10 percent.

6. What is the payback period for Project S?

    a. 1.6 years   **b.** 1.8 years   **c.** 2.1 years   **d.** 2.5 years   **e.** 2.8 years

7. What is Project L's NPV?

    a. $50.00   **b.** $34.25   **c.** $22.64   **d.** $18.79   **e.** $10.06

8. What is Project L's IRR?

    a. 18.1%   **b.** 19.7%   **c.** 21.4%   **d.** 23.6%   **e.** 24.2%

9. What is Project L's PI?

    a. 0.955   **b.** 1.050   **c.** 1.188   **d.** 1.215   **e.** 1.346

10. What is Project S's PI?

    a. 0.875   **b.** 0.964   **c.** 1.000   **d.** 1.100   **e.** 1.200

11. What is Project L's MIRR?

    a. 15.3%   **b.** 16.5%   **c.** 16.9%   **d.** 17.1%   **e.** 17.4%

12. What is Project S's MIRR?

    a. 15.3%   **b.** 16.5%   **c.** 16.9%   **d.** 17.1%   **e.** 17.4%

13. Plot the NPV profiles for the two projects. Where is the crossover point?

    a. 6.9%   **b.** 7.8%   **c.** 8.7%   **d.** 9.6%   **e.** 9.9%

14. Your company is considering two mutually exclusive projects, X and Y, whose costs and cash flows are shown below:

Year	Project X	Project Y
0	($2,000)	($2,000)
1	200	2,000
2	600	200
3	800	100
4	1,400	100

The projects are equally risky, and their cost of capital is 10 percent. You must make a recommendation, and you must base it on the modified IRR. What is the MIRR of the better project?

    a. 11.50%   **b.** 12.00%   **c.** 11.70%   **d.** 12.50%   **e.** 13.10%

15. A company is analyzing two mutually exclusive projects, S and L, whose cash flows are shown below:

Year	Project S	Project L
0	($2,000)	($2,000)
1	1,800	0
2	500	500
3	20	800
4	20	1,600

The company's cost of capital is 9 percent, and it can get an unlimited amount of capital at that cost. What is the regular IRR (not MIRR) of the better project? (Hint: Note that the better project may or may not be the one with the higher IRR.)

    a. 11.45%   **b.** 11.74%   **c.** 13.02%   **d.** 13.49%   **e.** 12.67%

16. The stock of Barkley Inc. and "the market" provided the following returns over the last 5 years:

Year	Barkley	Market
1994	-5%	-3%
1995	21	10
1996	9	4
1997	23	11
1998	31	15

Barkley finances only with retained earnings, and it uses the CAPM with a historical beta to determine its cost of equity. The risk-free rate is 7 percent, and the market risk premium is 5 percent. Barkley is considering a project which has a cost at t = 0 of $2,000 and which is expected to provide cash inflows of $1,000 per year for 3 years. What is the project's MIRR?

    a. 23.46%   **b.** 18.25%   **c.** 22.92%   **d.** 20.95%   **e.** 21.82%

17.   CDH Worldwide's stock returns versus the market were as follows, and the same relative volatility is expected in the future:

Year	CDH	Market
1995	12%	15%
1996	-6	-3
1997	25	19
1998	18	12

The T-bond rate is 6 percent; the market risk premium is 7 percent; CDH finances only with equity from retained earnings; and it uses the CAPM to estimate its cost of capital. Now CDH is considering two alternative trucks. Truck S has a cost of $12,000 and is expected to produce cash flows of $4,500 per year for 4 years. Truck L has a cost of $20,000 and is expected to produce cash flows of $7,500 per year for 4 years. By how much would CDH's value rise if it buys the better truck, and what is the MIRR of the better truck?

a. $803.35; 17.05%   **d.** $1,338.91; 16.06%
b. $1,338.91; 17.05%   **e.** $803.35; 14.41%
c. $1,896.47; 16.06%

18.   Assume that your company has a cost of capital of 14 percent and that it is analyzing the following project:

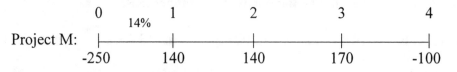

What are the project's IRR and MIRR?

a. 24.26%; 16.28%   **d.** 24.26%; 17.19%
b. 23.12%; 17.19%   **e.** None of the above.
c. 23.12%; 16.28%

19. Buckeye Foundries builds railroad cars and then leases them to railroads and shippers. The company has some old boxcars which it plans to convert into specialized carriers. Its analysts foresee demand in two areas—cars to carry coal and cars to carry livestock. Each type of car will cost $50,000 per car to convert. Because of the greater weight they will carry, the coal cars will last only 10 years but will provide an after-tax cash flow of $9,500 per year. The livestock cars will last for 15 years, and their annual after-tax cash flow is estimated at $8,140. Buckeye's cost of capital is 10 percent. At the end of each car's original life, it can be rebuilt into "like new" condition at a cost expected to equal the original conversion cost. Also, since Buckeye has only a limited number of cars to convert, regard the two types of cars as being mutually exclusive. Using the replacement chain method of evaluation, find the adjusted NPV for each alternative.

   a. $8,373; $11,913   c. $8,373; $16,212   e. $12,846; $14,765
   b. $8,373; $14,765   d. $12,846; $11,913

20. Central City Electric is considering two alternative ways to meet demand: It can build a coal-fired plant (Project C) at a cost of $1,000 million. This plant would have a 20-year life and would provide net cash flows of $120 million per year over its life. Alternatively, the company can build a gas-fired plant (Project G) that would cost $400 million and would produce net cash flows of $68 million per year for 10 years, after which the plant would have to be replaced. The power will be needed for exactly 20 years; the cost of capital for either plant is 10 percent; and inflation and productivity gains are expected to offset one another so as to leave expected costs and cash flows constant over time. What is the NPV of the better project, that is, how much (in millions) will the better project add to Central City's total value?

   a. $17.83   b. $21.63   c. $20.03   d. $24.70   e. $19.57

21. A firm is considering a project with a cost of $5,000 and operating cash flows of $2,000 for 3 years. The expected abandonment cash flows for Years 0, 1, 2, and 3 are $5,000, $3,500, $2,000, and $0, respectively. If the firm's cost of capital is 10 percent, what should the firm do?

   a. Do not accept the project.
   b. Abandon after Year 1; NPV is $0.
   c. Abandon after Year 2; NPV is $56.
   d. Abandon after Year 2; NPV is $124.
   e. Continue the project until the end of its 3-year physical life.

22. Wild West Air is considering two alternative planes. Plane A has an expected life of 5 years, will cost $200, and will produce net cash flows of $60 per year. Plane B has a life of 10 years, will cost $245, and will produce net cash flows of $48 per year. Wild West plans to serve the route for 10 years. Inflation in operating costs, airplane costs, and fares is expected to be zero, and the company's cost of capital is 14 percent. Assume all costs are in millions. By how much (in millions) would the value of the company increase if it accepted the better project (plane)?

    a. $12.76   **b.** $9.78   **c.** $5.37   **d.** $6.65   **e.** $9.09

ANSWERS TO SELF-TEST QUESTIONS

1.	capital budget		**17.**	terminal value
2.	payback period		**18.**	liquidity
3.	simplicity		**19.**	undiscounted; IRR
4.	cash flows; ignored		**20.**	independent
5.	discounted		**21.**	scale; timing
6.	positive		**22.**	Multiple IRRs
7.	mutually exclusive; higher		**23.**	riskiness
8.	zero		**24.**	EVA; EVAs
9.	NPV; discount rates		**25.**	crossover rate
10.	IRR		**26.**	profitability index (PI)
11.	NPV		**27.**	IRR
12.	cost of capital; internal rate of return		**28.**	NPV
13.	cost of capital		**29.**	PI
14.	post-audit		**30.**	less
15.	forecasts; operations; abandonment; termination		**31.**	independent
			32.	replacement chain (common life)
16.	discount; cash inflows; cash outflows (or initial cost)			

33. a. The more the cash flows are spread over time, the greater is the effect of a change in discount rate. This is because the compounding process has a greater effect as the number of years increases.

34. a. Project cash flows are substitutes for outside capital. Thus, the opportunity cost of these cash flows is the firm's cost of capital, adjusted for risk. The NPV method uses this cost as the reinvestment rate, while the IRR method assumes reinvestment at the IRR.

35.   b.   The yield to maturity on a bond is the bond's IRR.

36.   b.   The computation of IRR is independent of the project's cost of capital.

37.   a.   Both the NPV and IRR methods lead to the same accept/reject decisions for independent projects. Thus, the IRR method can be used as a proxy for the NPV method when choosing independent projects.

38.   b.   NPV and MIRR may not lead to the same decision when the projects differ in scale.

39.   b.   Multiple IRRs occur in projects with nonnormal cash flows, but there is only one MIRR for each project.

40.   a.   If we were to begin graphing the NPV profiles for each of these projects, we would know two of the points for each project. The Y-intercepts for Projects A and B would be $7,000 and $5,000, respectively, and the crossover rate would be 10 percent. Thus, from this information we can conclude that Project A's NPV profile would have the steeper slope and would be more sensitive to changes in the discount rate.

41.   b.   Statement a is false because the IRR is independent of the discount rate. Statement b is true; the situation identified is that of a project with nonnormal cash flows, which has multiple IRRs. Statement c is false; multiple IRRs occur with projects with nonnormal cash flows, not with mutually exclusive projects with different lives. Statement d is false; business executives tend to prefer the IRR because it gives a measure of the project's safety margin.

42.   b.   Statement b is true; the others are all false. Note that IRR must be greater than the cost of capital; that conflicts arise if the cost of capital is to the left of the crossover rate; and that for some projects with nonnormal cash flows there are two IRRs, so NPV and IRR could lead to conflicting accept/reject decisions, depending on which IRR we examine.

43.   e.   Statement e is correct, because both statements a and c are true. The IRR assumes reinvestment at the IRR, and since the discounted payback ignores cash flows beyond the payback period, it could lead to rejections of projects with high late cash flows and hence NPV > 0.

44.   a.   The NPV of a project may be maximized by terminating it at some point, thus making the economic life of the project shorter than the physical life.

SOLUTIONS TO SELF-TEST PROBLEMS

1.   c.   Unless you have a calculator that performs IRR calculations, the IRR must be obtained by trial and error or graphically. (Calculator solution: Input CF_0 = -800000, CF_{1-2} = 700000, CF_3 = -400000. Output: IRR = 25.48%.) Note that this project actually has multiple IRRs, with a second IRR at about -53 percent.

2.   c.   After Year 1, there is $5,000 – $2,085 = $2,915 remaining to pay back. After Year 2, only $2,915 – $2,085 = $830 is remaining. In Year 3, another $2,085 is collected. Assuming that the Year 3 cash flow occurs evenly over time, then payback occurs $830/$2,085 = 0.4 of the way through Year 3. Thus, the payback period is 2.4 years.

3.   b.   To solve graphically, construct the NPV profiles:

The Y-intercept is the NPV when k = 0%. For B, 4($2,085) – $5,000 = $3,340. For O, $9,677 – $5,000 = $4,677.   The X-intercept is the discount rate when NPV = $0, or the IRR. For B, N = 4, PV = -5000, PMT = 2085, FV = 0, which gives I = 24.14, so IRR ≈ 24%. For O, N = 4, PV = -5000, PMT = 0, FV = 9677, which gives I = 17.95, so IRR ≈ 18%. The graph is an approximation since we are only using two points to plot lines that are curvilinear. However, it

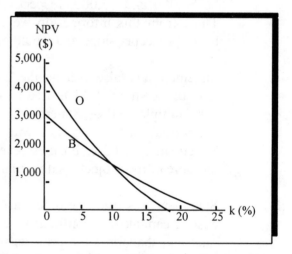

shows that there is a crossover point and that it occurs somewhere in the vicinity of k = 10%. (Note that other data points for the NPV profiles could be obtained by calculating the NPVs for the two projects at different discount rates.)

Alternatively,

Year	B	O	Project Δ (B ⅃ O)
0	($5,000)	($5,000)	$ 0
1	2,085	0	2,085
2	2,085	0	2,085
3	2,085	0	2,085
4	2,085	9,677	(7,592)

The IRR of Project Δ, 10.00 percent, is the crossover point.

4.   a.   Refer to the NPV profiles. When k = 14%, we are to the right of the crossover point and Project B has the higher NPV. You can verify this fact by calculating the NPVs. When k = 14%, NPV_B = $1,075 and NPV_O = $730. Note that Project B also has the higher IRR. However, the NPV method should be used when evaluating mutually exclusive projects. Note that had the project cost of capital been 8 percent, then Project O would be chosen on the basis of the higher NPV.

5.   d. $PI_A = \dfrac{\text{PV future cash flows}}{\text{PV initial cost}} = \dfrac{\$6,075.09}{\$5,000} = 1.215.$

6.   a.   After the first year, there is only $30 remaining to be repaid, and $50 is received in Year 2. Assuming an even cash flow throughout the year, the payback period is 1 + $30/$50 = 1.6 years.

7.   d. NPV_L = -$100 + $10/1.10 + $60/(1.10)^2$ + $80/(1.10)^3$ = -$100 + $9.09 + $49.59 + $60.11 = $18.79. Financial calculator solution: Input the cash flows into the cash flow register, I = k = 10, and solve for NPV = $18.78.

8.   a.   Input the cash flows into the cash flow register and solve for IRR = 18.1%.

9.   c. $PI_L = \dfrac{\text{PV future cash flows}}{\text{PV initial cost}} = \dfrac{\$118.78}{\$100} = 1.188.$

10.   e. $PI_S = \dfrac{\text{PV future cash flows}}{\text{PV initial cost}} = \dfrac{\$119.98}{\$100} = 1.200.$

11. b.
$$\sum_{t=0}^{n} \frac{COF_t}{(1+k)^t} = \frac{\sum_{t=0}^{n} CIF_t(1+k)^{n-t}}{(1+MIRR)^n}.$$

$$PV \; cost = \frac{TV}{(1+MIRR)^n}$$

$$\$100 = \frac{\$10(1.10)^2 + \$60(1.10)^1 + \$80(1.10)^0}{(1+MIRR)^3}$$

$$= \frac{\$12.10 + \$66.00 + \$80.00}{(1+MIRR)^3}$$

$$= \frac{\$158.10}{(1+MIRR)^3}$$

$$MIRR = 16.50\%.$$

Alternatively, input N = 3, PV = -100, PMT = 0, FV = 158.10, and solve for I = MIRR = 16.50%.

12. c.
$$\$100 = \frac{\$70(1.10)^2 + \$50(1.10)^1 + \$20(1.10)^0}{(1+MIRR)^3}$$

$$= \frac{\$84.70 + \$55.00 + \$20.00}{(1+MIRR)^3}$$

$$= \frac{\$159.70}{(1+MIRR)^3}$$

$$MIRR_S = 16.89\% \approx 16.9\%.$$

Alternatively, input N = 3, PV = -100, PMT = 0, FV = 159.70, and solve for I = MIRR = 16.89%.

13. c. The NPV profiles plot as follows:

k	NPV_L	NPV_S
0%	$50	$40
5	33	29
10	19	20
15	7	12
20	(4)	5
25	(13)	(2)

By looking at the graph, the approximate crossover point is 8 to 9 percent. Now, to find the precise crossover point, determine the cash flows for Project Δ, which is the difference between the two projects' cash flows:

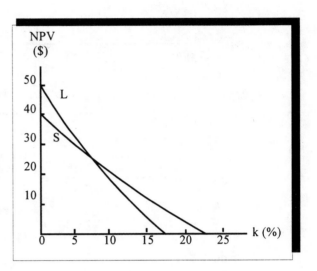

Year	L	S	Project Δ (L - S)
0	($100)	($100)	$ 0
1	10	70	(60)
2	60	50	10
3	80	20	60

The crossover point is the IRR of Project Δ, or 8.7 percent.

14.   e.   Project X:

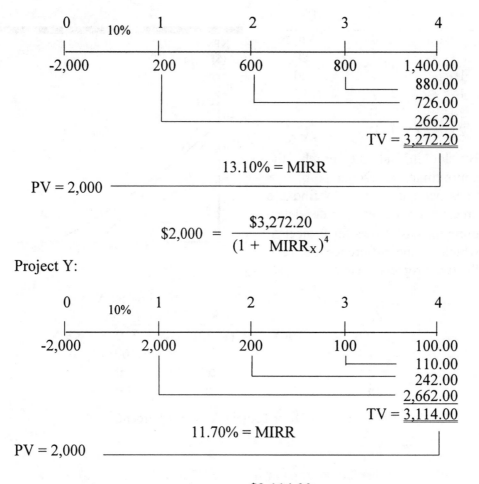

$$\$2,000 \;=\; \frac{\$3,272.20}{(1 + \; MIRR_X)^4}$$

Project Y:

$$\$2,000 \;=\; \frac{\$3,114.00}{(1 + \; MIRR_Y)^4}$$

Project X has the higher MIRR; $MIRR_X = 13.10\%$.

Alternate step: You could calculate NPVs, see that X has the higher NPV, and just calculate $MIRR_X$. $NPV_X = \$234.96$ and $NPV_Y = \$126.90$.

15.   b.   Put the cash flows into the cash flow register, and then calculate NPV at 9% and IRR:
Project S: $NPV_S = \$101.83$; $IRR_S = 13.49\%$.

Project L: $NPV_L = \$172.07$; $IRR_L = 11.74\%$.

Because $NPV_L > NPV_S$, it is the better project. $IRR_L = 11.74\%$.

16. d. First, calculate the beta coefficient. Barkley's stock has been exactly twice as volatile as the market; thus, beta = 2.0. This can be calculated as $[21 - (-5)]/[10 - (-3)]$ = 26/13 = 2.0. (Alternatively, you could use a calculator with statistical functions to determine the beta.)

Next, enter the known values in the CAPM equation to find the required rate of return, or the cost of equity capital. Since the company finances only with equity, this is the cost of capital:

$$CAPM = k_{RF} + (k_M - k_{RF})b = 7\% + (5\%)b = 7\% + 5\%(2.0) = 17\% = k_s.$$

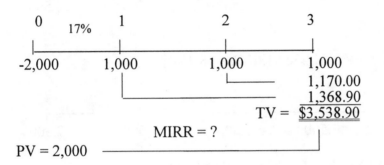

Find TV: N = 3; I = 17; PV = 0; PMT = -1000; FV = $3,538.90.

Find MIRR: N = 3; PV = -2000; PMT = 0; FV = 3538.90; I = MIRR = 20.95%.

17.   b.   First, we must find the cost of capital. Run a regression between the market and CDH stock returns to get beta = 1.31. Then apply the SML:

$$k_{CDH} = 6\% + (7\%)1.31 = 15.17\%.$$

(1) Now set up the time lines, insert the proper data into the cash flow register of the calculator, and find the NPVs and IRRs for the trucks.

Truck S: NPV = $803.35; IRR = 18.45%.

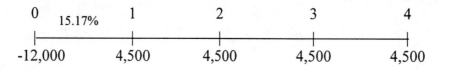

0	1	2	3	4
15.17%				
-12,000	4,500	4,500	4,500	4,500

Truck L: NPV = $1,338.91; IRR = 18.45%.

0	1	2	3	4
15.17%				
-20,000	7,500	7,500	7,500	7,500

$NPV_L > NPV_S$, thus Truck$_L$ is the better truck.

(2) To find Truck L's MIRR, compound its cash inflows at 15.17 percent to find the TV, then find the MIRR = I that causes PV of TV = $20,000:

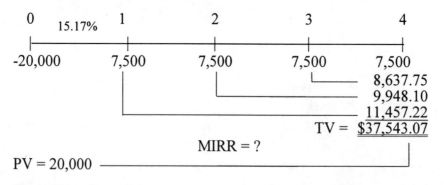

Find TV: Enter N = 4; I = 15.17; PV = `0; PMT = -7500; and solve for FV = $37,543.07.

Find MIRR: Enter N = 4; PV = -20000; PMT = 0; FV = 37543.07; and solve for I = MIRR = 17.05%.

It is interesting to note that both trucks have the same IRR and MIRR; however, the NPV rule should be used so Truck L is the better truck. This problem shows that the NPV method is superior when choosing among competing projects that differ in size.

18.   d.   IRR = 24.26%; MIRR = 17.19%.

To calculate the IRR, enter the given values into the cash flow register and press the IRR key to get IRR = 24.26%.

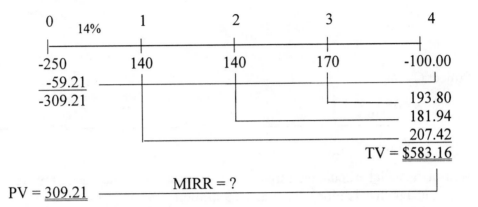

Enter N = 4; PV = -309.21; PMT = 0; FV = 583.16; and solve for MIRR = I = 17.19%.

19.   e.   First, find each car's original NPV as follows:

NPV_C: N = 10, I = 10, PMT = -9500, FV = 0; so PV = $58,373. NPV_C = $58,373 - $50,000 = $8,373.

NPV_L: N = 15, I = 10, PMT = -8140, FV = 0; so PV = $61,913. NPV_L = $61,913 - $50,000 = $11,913.

Now look at the projects at a common life of 30 years:

Adjusted NPV_C = $8,373 + $8,373(1/1.10^{10}) + $8,373(1/1.10^{20}) = $12,846.
Adjusted NPV_L = $11,913 + $11,913(1/1.10^{15}) = $14,765.

Alternatively, once you've found the original NPV of each car, then the replication of the cars can be shown on the time line.

Coal:

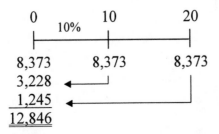

Livestock:

```
    0           15          30
        10%
    ├────────────┼───────────┤
  11,913       11,913
   2,852    ◄──────┘
  14,765
```

20. d. Project C:

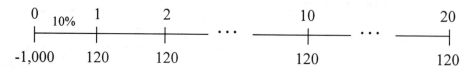

With a financial calculator, input the cash flows into the cash flow register, input I = 10, and then solve for NPV = $21.63 million.

Project G:

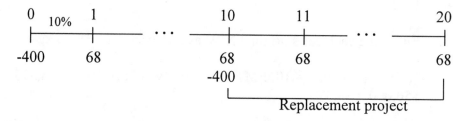

With a financial calculator input the cash flows for the first replication of the project into the cash flow register, input I = 10, and then solve for NPV = $17.83 million. However, this NPV must be adjusted for a 20-year common life. The NPV for the next replication can be calculated by inputting N = 10, I = 10, PMT = 0, FV = 17.83, and then solving for PV = $6.87. Thus, the extended NPV for Project G = $17.83 + $6.87 = $24.70 million:

$$\text{Extended NPV}_G = \$17.83 + \$17.83 \, (1/1.10^{10})$$
$$= \$17.83 + \$6.87 = \$24.70 \text{ million.}$$

21.   d.   Initial Investment &Abandonment

Year	Operating Cash Flow	Value in Year t
0	($5,000)	$5,000
1	2,000	3,500
2	2,000	2,000
3	2,000	0

NPV of project:
$-\$5,000 + \$2,000/(1.10)^1 + \$2,000/(1.10)^2 + \$2,000/(1.10)^3 = -\$26.30.$

NPV of project if abandoned after Year 1:
$-\$5,000 + \$2,000/(1.10)^1 + \$3,500/(1.10)^1 = \$0.$

NPV of project if abandoned after Year 2:
$-\$5,000 + \$2,000/(1.10)^1 + \$2,000/(1.10)^2 + \$2,000/(1.10)^2 = \$124.$

22.   e.   Plane A: Expected life = 5 years; Costs = $200; NCF = $60; WACC = 14%.

Plane B: Expected life = 10 years; Costs = $245; NCF = $48; WACC = 14%.

A:

0 14% 1	2	3	4	5	6	7	8	9	10
-200	60	60	60	60	60	60	60	60	60

-200
-140

Enter these values into the cash flow register: $CF_0 = -200$; $CF_1 = 60$, 4 times; $CF_2 = -140$; $CF_3 = 60$, 5 times. Then enter I = 14, and press the NPV to get $NPV_A = \$9.0932 \approx \$9.09.$

B:

0 14% 1	2	3	4	5	6	7	8	9	10
-245	48	48	48	48	48	48	48	48	48

Enter these values into the cash flow register, along with the interest rate, and press the NPV key to get $NPV_B = \$5.3736 \approx \$5.37.$

Project A is the better project and will increase the company's value by $9.09.

CHAPTER 14
CASH FLOW ESTIMATION AND RISK ANALYSIS

OVERVIEW

One of the most critical steps in capital budgeting analysis is *cash flow estimation.* The key to correct cash flow estimation is to consider only *incremental cash flows.* However, the process is complicated by such factors as sunk costs, opportunity costs, externalities, and salvage values. Adjustments to the analysis must be made for the effects of inflation.

The analysis of project risk focuses on three issues: (1) the effect of a project on the firm's beta coefficient (market risk), (2) the project's effect on the probability of bankruptcy (corporate risk), and (3) the risk of the project independent of both the firm's other projects and investors' diversification (stand-alone risk). Market risk directly affects the value of the firm's stock. Corporate risk affects the financial strength of the firm, and this, in turn, influences its ability to use debt, and to maintain smooth operations over time. Stand-alone risk is measured by the variability of a project's expected returns. Techniques for measuring stand-alone risk include sensitivity analysis, scenario analysis, and Monte Carlo simulation.

OUTLINE

The most important, and also the most difficult, step in the analysis of a capital project is estimating its cash flows—the investment outlays and the annual net cash inflows after a project goes into operation. Two key concepts in the process are important to recognize: (1) capital decisions must be based on cash flows, not accounting income, and (2) only incremental cash flows are relevant to the accept/reject decision.

■ *Relevant cash flows* are the specific set of cash flows that should be considered in the decision at hand. The relevant cash flow for a project is the additional free cash flow that the company expects if it implements the project.

■ There are four major ways that project cash flows differ from accounting income:
   ❏ *Costs of fixed assets.* This is a negative project cash flow; however, accountants do not show the purchase of fixed assets as a deduction from accounting income. Instead, they deduct a depreciation expense each year throughout the asset's life.

    ❑ *Noncash charges*. In calculating net income, accountants usually subtract some noncash charges from revenues. One example is depreciation. Depreciation is added back when estimating project cash flow.

    ❑ *Changes in net operating working capital*. The difference between the required increase in current assets and the spontaneous increase in current liabilities is the change in net operating working capital. If this change is positive, then additional financing, over and above the cost of fixed assets, will be needed.

    ❑ *Interest expenses are not included in project cash flows*. In calculating accounting income, interest expenses are subtracted because accountants attempt to measure the profit available for stockholders. Project cash flow is the cash flow available for all investors, so interest expenses are not subtracted.

■ In evaluating a capital project, we focus on those cash flows that result directly from the project. These *incremental cash flows* represent the change in the firm's total cash flow that occurs as a direct result of accepting the project. Three special problems in determining incremental cash flows follow:

    ❑ A *sunk cost* is an outlay that has already occurred or has been committed, and hence is not affected by the decision under consideration. Sunk costs are not incremental, and hence should not be included in the analysis.

    ❑ *Opportunity costs*, which are cash flows that could be generated from assets the firm already owns provided they are not used for the project in question, must be included in the analysis.

    ❑ *Externalities* involve the effects of a project on other parts of the firm, and their effects need to be considered in the incremental cash flows. For example, *cannibalization* occurs when the introduction of a new product causes sales of existing products to decline. This is an externality that must be considered in the analysis.

■ We must account properly for the timing of cash flows.

    ❑ In most cases, we simply assume that all cash flows occur at the end of every year.

Tax effects can have a major impact on cash flows, and the improper treatment of taxes can have serious consequences. Therefore, it is critical that taxes be dealt with properly when a project's cash flows are being analyzed.

■ For tax purposes, an asset's depreciation expense is calculated using the *Modified Accelerated Cost Recovery System (MACRS)*.

    ❑ Assets are categorized into one of several MACRS class lives. Then the depreciation expense in each year is found by multiplying the asset's depreciable basis by the appropriate allowance percentage. Here are the allowance percentages for personal property:

	MACRS Class			
Year	3-Year	5-Year	7-Year	10-Year
1	33%	20%	14%	10%
2	45	32	25	18
3	15	19	17	14
4	7	12	13	12
5		11	9	9
6		6	9	7
7			9	7
8			4	7
9				7
10				6
11				3

❑ Under MACRS, the assumption is generally made that property is placed in service in the middle of the first year. Then, the remaining half-year's depreciation is taken at the end. Thus, a 3-year class life asset is depreciated over 4 years, and so on.

❑ The *depreciable basis* is the purchase price of the asset, plus any shipping and installation costs. Note that, under MACRS, the depreciable basis is *not* reduced by the asset's expected salvage value.

■ When a depreciable asset is sold, the actual sales price (the realized salvage value) minus the then-existing book value is multiplied by the tax rate to determine the applicable taxes. The net salvage value, salvage value minus the applicable taxes, is then added to after-tax operating income.

A project creates value for the firm's shareholders if and only if the net present value of its incremental cash flows is positive.

■ In general, incremental cash flows from a project can be classified in one of three ways:
   ❑ Initial investment outlay
   ❑ Operating cash flows over the project's life
   ❑ Terminal year cash flows

■ For each year of the project's economic life, the net cash flow is determined as the sum of the cash flows from each of the three categories.

Two types of capital budgeting decisions are (1) expansion project analysis and (2) replacement project analysis.

■ An expansion project is one that calls for the firm to invest in new facilities to increase sales. Steps in the capital budgeting analysis for an expansion project include:

- ❑ Summarize the investment outlays required for the project. Increases in net operating working capital should be included as an outflow here; however, Decreases in new operating working capial should be considered as an inflow at the end of the project.
- ❑ Forecast the operating cash flows that will occur once production begins, including effects of depreciation and any changes in net operating working capital.
- ❑ Estimate the cash flows generated by salvage values.
- ❑ Summarize the data by combining all the net cash flows on a time line and evaluate the project by payback period, IRR, MIRR, and NPV (at the appropriate cost of capital).
- ❑ The cost of capital may need to be increased if the project is deemed riskier than the firm's average project.

- ■ Capital budgeting decisions are actually based on both quantitative factors plus qualitative, subjective factors such as the firm's strategic long-run plans.

- ■ The cash flows and cost of capital estimates used to develop the NPV are based on a number of assumptions, and if those assumptions turn out to be incorrect, then the actual NPV can turn out to be quite different from the forecasted NPV.

- ■ Replacement project analysis is similar to that of an expansion project, except that cash flows from disposal of the old asset must be considered in addition to those from the new assets.

When inflation occurs, the analysis must either explicitly adjust for inflation or treat all variables in real terms.

- ■ Investors recognize that inflation erodes purchasing power; they demand an inflation premium in addition to the real required rate of return, and hence they consider expected inflation rates when setting required rates of return. Thus, a firm's market-determined overall cost of capital is a nominal rate.
  - ❑ Inflation can be explicitly considered in capital budgeting analysis by expressing all cash flows in nominal terms (NCF_t) and then by using the nominal cost of capital (k_n):

$$NPV = \sum_{t=0}^{n} \frac{NCF_t}{(1+k_n)^t}.$$

  - ❑ The same result can be obtained by expressing all cash flows in real terms (RCF_t) and then by using the real cost of capital (k_r):

$$NPV = \sum_{t=0}^{n} \frac{RCF_t}{(1 + k_r)^t}.$$

■ Occasionally, the procedures set forth above are violated; that is, real, or constant dollar, cash flows that are not adjusted for inflation are used with the nominal cost of capital. If this occurs, the calculated NPV will be biased downward.

■ In practice, it is best to express the cash flows in nominal dollars; that is, to include inflation effects in the cash flow estimates and then to discount by the nominal cost of capital. This procedure is preferred because it allows various cash flow components to be adjusted at differing inflation rates.

Three separate and distinct types of risk can be identified in capital budgeting: (1) stand-alone risk, (2) corporate (within-firm) risk, and (3) market (beta) risk.

■ *Stand-alone risk* is the risk an asset would have if it were a firm's only asset. It is measured by the variability of the asset's expected returns.

■ *Corporate risk* is the project's risk to the corporation, giving consideration to the fact that the project represents only one of the firm's portfolio of assets. It is measured by a project's impact on uncertainty about the firm's future earnings.
  ❑ Corporate risk is important for three reasons.
    ● Undiversified stockholders are more concerned about corporate risk than about market risk.
    ● Empirical studies generally find that both market and corporate risk affect stock prices.
    ● The firm's stability is important to its managers, workers, customers, suppliers, and creditors, as well as to the community in which it operates.

■ *Market risk* is the riskiness of the project as seen by a well-diversified stockholder who recognizes that the project is only one of the firm's assets and that the firm's stock is but one small part of the investor's total portfolio. It is measured by the project's effect on the firm's beta.

Stand-alone risk is by far the easiest to measure and may be done so in a number of ways. Because all three types of risk are usually highly correlated, stand-alone risk is generally a good proxy for hard-to-measure corporate and market risk. Three techniques for assessing a project's stand-alone risk are: (1) sensitivity analysis, (2) scenario analysis, and (3) Monte Carlo simulation.

■ *Sensitivity analysis* is a technique which indicates how much a project's NPV will change in response to a given change in an input variable, other things held constant.

    ❑ The analysis begins with expected values for unit sales, sales price, fixed costs, and variable costs to give an expected, or *base case*, NPV. A series of "what if" questions may then be asked to find the change in NPV, given a change in one of the input variables.

    ❑ Each variable is changed by several specific percentage points above and below the expected value, holding other things constant. The resulting set of NPVs is plotted against the variable that was changed.

    ❑ The steeper the slope, the more sensitive NPV is to changes in each of the inputs.

    ❑ When comparing two projects, the one with the steeper sensitivity lines would be regarded as riskier, because for that project a relatively small error in estimating the input variable would produce a large error in the project's expected NPV.

    ❑ Sensitivity analysis can provide useful insights into the riskiness of a project.

    ❑ Spreadsheet computer models are ideally suited for performing sensitivity analysis.

■ *Scenario analysis* provides a more complete analysis, because in addition to the sensitivity of NPV to changes in key variables, it considers the range of likely values of these variables.

    ❑ Worst case and best case scenarios are estimated and the input values from these scenarios are used to find the worst case NPV and the best case NPV.

    ❑ Probabilities can be assigned to the best, worst, and base case NPVs to obtain the expected NPV.

    ❑ The project's coefficient of variation can be compared to the coefficient of variation of the firm's "average" project to determine the relative stand-alone riskiness of the project.

    ❑ Scenario analysis is limited in that it only considers a few discrete outcomes, even though there are an infinite number of possibilities.

■ *Monte Carlo simulation*, which ties together sensitivities and input variable probability distributions, requires a computer along with an efficient financial planning software package.

    ❑ The computer repeatedly selects a random value for each uncertain variable based on its specified probability distribution, along with values for fixed factors. The end result is a continuous NPV probability distribution with its own expected value and standard deviation.

    ❑ A simulation is more comprehensive than scenario analysis because it considers an infinite number of possible outcomes.

    ❑ In spite of its obvious appeal, Monte Carlo simulation has not been as widely used in industry as one might expect. The major problem is specifying each uncertain variable's probability distribution and the correlations among the distributions.

■ A problem with both scenario and simulation analysis is that even when the analysis has been completed, no clear-cut decision rule emerges.

❑ The analysis provides no criterion to indicate whether a project's profitability as measured by its expected NPV is sufficient to compensate for its risk as measured by σ_{NPV} or CV_{NPV}.

❑ In addition, scenario and simulation analysis both focus on a project's stand-alone risk—they ignore the effects of diversification, both among projects within the firm and by investors in their personal investment portfolios.

■ Managers, not computers, make the final decision on whether to accept or reject projects. Unlike computers, managers bring qualitative judgment into the decision process, and the stand-along risk profile of a project can provide some extremely valuable insights.

SELF-TEST QUESTIONS

Definitional

1. An increase in net operating working capital would show up as a cash _____ at time 0 and then again as a cash _____ at the _____ of the project's life.

2. A(n) _____ _____ is a cash outlay which has already occurred or has been committed.

3. A(n) _____ cash flow represents the change in the firm's total cash flow that occurs as a direct result of project acceptance.

4. If the cash flows are real, but the cost of capital is nominal, there will be a(n) _____ bias to the calculated NPV.

5. _____ _____, which are cash flows that could be generated from assets the firm already owns, provided they are not used for the project in question, must be included in the analysis.

6. _____ involve the effects of a project on other parts of the firm, and their effects need to be considered in the incremental cash flows.

7. _____ occurs when the introduction of a new product causes sales of existing products to decline. This is an externality that must be considered in the analysis.

8. In dealing with inflation in capital budgeting, cash flows and cost of capital must both be in _____ terms or both be in _____ terms.

9. The _____ cash flow for a project is the additional free cash flow that the company expects if it implements the project.

10. For tax purposes, an asset's depreciation expense is calculated using the _____ _____ _____ _____ _____.

11. The _____ _____ is the purchase price of the asset, plus any shipping and installation costs.

12. In general, incremental cash flows from a project can be classified in one of three ways: _____ _____ _____, _____ cash flows, and _____ year cash flows.

13. Three separate and distinct types of risk can be identified in capital budgeting: market risk, _____-_____ risk, and _____ risk.

14. A commonly used method of risk analysis is based on constructing optimistic, pessimistic, and expected value estimates for the key variables. This method is called _____ _____.

15. In project analysis, changing one key variable at a time and determining the effect on its NPV is known as _____ _____.

16. One purpose of sensitivity analysis is to determine which of the _____ have the greatest influence on the project's NPV.

17. _____-_____ risk is the risk an asset would have if it were a firm's only asset.

18. _____ risk is the riskiness of the project as seen by a well-diversified stockholder who recognizes that the project is only one of the firm's assets and that the firm's stock is but one small part of the investor's total portfolio.

19. _____ _____ _____ ties together sensitivities and input variable probability distributions, and requires a computer along with an efficient financial planning software package.

Conceptual

20.   In general, the value of land currently owned by a firm is irrelevant to a capital budgeting decision because the cost of that property is a sunk cost.

   a. True   **b.** False

21.   McDonald's is planning to open a new store across from the student union. Annual revenues are expected to be $5 million. However, opening the new location will cause annual revenues to drop by $3 million at McDonald's existing stadium location. The relevant sales revenues for the capital budgeting analysis are $2 million per year.

   a. True   **b.** False

22.   A problem with both scenario and simulation analysis is that even when the analysis has been completed, no clear-cut decision rule emerges.

   a. True   **b.** False

23.   Two corporations are formed. They are identical in all respects except for their methods of depreciation. Firm A uses MACRS depreciation, while Firm B uses the straight line method. Both plan to depreciate their assets for tax purposes over a 5-year life (6 calendar years), which is equal to the useful life, and both pay a 35 percent tax rate. (Note: The half-year convention will apply, so the firm using the straight line method will take 10 percent depreciation in Year 1 and 10 percent in Year 6.) Which of the following statements is *false*?

   a. Firm A will generate higher cash flows from operations in the first year than B.
   b. Firm A will pay more Federal corporate income taxes in the first year than B.
   c. If there is no change in tax rates over the 6-year period, and if we disregard the time value of money, the total amount of funds generated from operations by these projects for each corporation will be the same over the 6 years.
   d. Firm B will pay the same amount of federal corporate income taxes, over the 6-year period, as A.
   e. Firm A could, if it chose to, use straight line depreciation for stockholder reporting even if it used MACRS for tax purposes.

24. A company owns a building, free and clear, which had a cost of $100,000. The building is currently unoccupied, but it can be sold at a net price of $50,000, after taxes. Now the company is thinking of using the building for a new project. Which of the following statements is most correct?

   a. The building is unoccupied, and its cost was incurred in the past, and hence, is a sunk cost. Therefore, no cost for the building should be charged to the new project.
   b. A cost should be charged to the new project, and that cost should be $100,000.
   c. A cost should be charged to the new project, and that cost should be $50,000.
   d. The cost charged to the building would vary depending on the expected profitability of the new project and hence on the new project's ability to help carry the corporation's overhead.
   e. A cost for the building should be charged to the new project only if the NPV on the new project without considering the building is less than zero.

25. Which of the following statements is most correct?

   a. Since capital budgeting involves fixed assets, current assets (also called "working capital") should never be reflected in a capital budgeting analysis.
   b. If Congress changed the tax law such that depreciation allowances were reduced in the early years of an asset's life and then were increased in later years, this would increase net income in the early years and lower it in the later years. Such a change would stimulate investment in the economy because, other things held constant, it would raise projects' NPVs and IRRs.
   c. Sunk costs should not be included in a capital budgeting analysis.
   d. If expected inflation is ignored when cash flows are estimated, this will generally cause the calculated NPV, IRR, and MIRR to be overstated, and that could cause projects which should be rejected to be accepted.
   e. Both statements c and d are correct.

SELF-TEST PROBLEMS

1. The capital budgeting director of National Products Inc. is evaluating a new project that would decrease operating costs by $30,000 per year without affecting revenues. The project's cost is $50,000. The project will be depreciated using the MACRS method over its 3-year class life. It will have a *zero salvage value* after 3 years. The marginal tax rate of National Products is 35 percent, and the project's cost of capital is 12 percent. What is the project's NPV?

   a. $7,068   b. $8,324   c. $10,214   d. $11,010   e. $12,387

2. Your firm has a marginal tax rate of 40 percent and a cost of capital of 14 percent. You are performing a capital budgeting analysis on a new project that will cost $500,000. The project is expected to have a useful life of 10 years, although its MACRS class life is only 5 years. The project is expected to increase the firm's net income by $61,257 per year and to have a salvage value of $35,000 at the end of 10 years. What is the project's NPV?

    a. $95,356   **b.** $108,359   **c.** $135,256   **d.** $162,185   **e.** $177,902

3. The Board of Directors of National Brewing Inc. is considering the acquisition of a new still. The still is priced at $600,000 but would require $60,000 in transportation costs and $40,000 for installation. The still has a useful life of 10 years but will be depreciated over its 5-year MACRS life. It is expected to have a salvage value of $10,000 at the end of 10 years. The still would increase revenues by $120,000 per year and increase yearly operating costs by $20,000 per year. Additionally, the still would require a $30,000 increase in net working capital. The firm's marginal tax rate is 40 percent, and the project's cost of capital is 10 percent. What is the NPV of the still?

    a. $18,430   **b.** -$12,352   **c.** -$65,204   **d.** -$130,961   **e.** -$203,450

4. As financial vice president, you are evaluating a potential new project. The VP-manufacturing and VP-sales have provided the following real revenue, operating cost, and depreciation data, all stated in constant Year 0 dollars:

Year	Revenue	Cost	Depreciation
0	$ 0	$90,000	$ 0
1	40,000	10,000	30,000
2	40,000	10,000	30,000
3	40,000	10,000	30,000

    The cost of capital to the firm is 14 percent, including the current inflation premium. You estimate that the reported real costs will escalate by 10 percent per year over the project's life, starting at t = 0, while revenues will increase by only 5 percent per year. The firm's marginal tax rate is 40 percent. The $90,000 cost in Year 0 is the net after-tax cost of the project, while the $40,000 annual revenues and $10,000 annual costs are before tax. The project has no salvage value and does not require a change in net working capital. What is the project's NPV?

    a. $10,593   **b.** $3,297   **c.** -$5,586   **d.** -$17,689   **e.** -$20,351

(The following data apply to the next three Self-Test Problems.)

The Carlisle Corporation is considering a proposed project for its capital budget. The company estimates that the project's NPV is $5 million. This estimate assumes that the economy and market conditions will be average over the next few years. The company's CFO, however, forecasts that there is only a 40 percent chance that the economy will be average. Recognizing this uncertainty, she has also performed the following scenario analysis:

Economic Scenario	Probability of Outcome	(NPV)
Recession	0.05	($28 million)
Below Average	0.25	(10 million)
Average	0.40	5 million
Above Average	0.25	8 million
Boom	0.05	15 million

5. What is the project's expected NPV (in millions)?

   a. $0.25   b. $0.85   c. $1.20   d. $1.50   e. $2.00

6. What is the project's standard deviation?

   a. $10.04   b. $12.78   c. $15.65   d. $21.37   e. $29.43

7. What is the project's coefficient of variation?

   a. 5.02   b. 2.75   c. 6.39   d. 1.25   e. 11.81

ANSWERS TO SELF-TEST QUESTIONS

1. outflow; inflow; end
2. sunk cost
3. incremental
4. downward
5. Opportunity costs
6. Externalities
7. Cannibalization
8. nominal; real
9. relevant
10. Modified Accelerated Cost Recovery System (MACRS)
11. depreciable basis
12. initial investment outlay; operating; terminal
13. stand-alone; corporate (within-firm)
14. scenario analysis
15. sensitivity analysis
16. variables
17. Stand-alone
18. Market
19. Monte Carlo simulation

20.   b.   The net market value of land currently owned is an opportunity cost of the project. If the project is not undertaken, the land could be sold to realize its current market value less any taxes and expenses. Thus, project acceptance means forgoing this cash inflow.

21.   a.   Incremental revenues, which are relevant in a capital budgeting decision, must consider the effects on other parts of the firm.

22.   a.   This statement is true. Neither provides any criterion to indicate whether a project's profitability as measured by its expected NPV is sufficient to compensate for its risk as measured by σ_{NPV} or CV_{NPV}.

23.   b.   Statement a is true; MACRS is an accelerated depreciation method, so Firm A will have a higher depreciation expense than Firm B. We are also given that both firms are identical except for depreciation methods used. Net cash flow is equal to net income plus depreciation. In Year 1, Firm A's depreciation expense is twice as great as Firm B's; however, Firm A's lower net income is more than compensated for by the addition of depreciation (which is twice as high as Firm B's). Thus, in Year 1, Firm A's net cash flow is greater than Firm B's. Statement b is false; because Firm A's depreciation expense is larger, its earnings before taxes will be lower, and thus it will pay less income taxes than Firm B. Statements c, d, and e are all true.

24.   c.   Statement c is correct. The opportunity cost of the building should be assessed against the new project, and that cost is what the company could get for the building, $50,000. All of the other statements are incorrect.

25.   c.   Statement c is correct. Statement a is incorrect because the required investment in working capital is often reflected in capital budgeting decision analyses. Statement b is incorrect because higher early depreciation reduces taxes, increases cash flows, and thus leads to higher NPVs and IRRs. Statement d is incorrect because generally considering inflation will increase projected cash flows and thus increase the NPV.

SOLUTIONS TO SELF-TEST PROBLEMS

1. **d.** Cash flow = Net income + Depreciation. The first step is to set up the income statement for Years 1 through 3. (Note that a reduction in operating costs increases revenues.)

	1	2	3
Revenues	$30,000	$30,000	$30,000
Depreciation[a]	16,500	22,500	7,500
EBT	$13,500	$ 7,500	$22,500
Taxes (35%)	4,725	2,625	7,875
Net income	$ 8,775	$ 4,875	$14,625
Depreciation	16,500	22,500	7,500
	$25,275	$27,375	$22,125
SV tax savings[b]			1,225
Net cash flow	$25,275	$27,375	$23,350

[a]Depreciation schedule: Cost basis = $50,000.

Year	Allowance Percentage	Depreciation	Ending Book Value
1	0.33	$16,500	$33,500
2	0.45	22,500	11,000
3	0.15	7,500	3,500
4	0.07	3,500	0
		$50,000	

[b]At the end of Year 3, the project's book value is $3,500; however, its salvage value is zero. Thus, National can reduce its taxable income by $3,500, producing a 0.35($3,500) = $1,225 tax savings.

The project's cash flows are then placed on a time line as follows and discounted at the project's cost of capital:

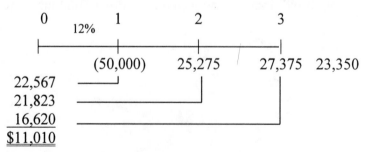

Alternatively, input the cash flows into the cash flow register, input I = 12, and then solve for NPV = $11,010.

2.   e.   In this case, the *net income* of the project is $61,257. Net cash flow = Net income + Depreciation = $61,257 + Depreciation. The depreciation allowed in each year is calculated as follows:

Dep_1 = $500,000(0.20) = $100,000.
Dep_2 = $500,000(0.32) = $160,000.
Dep_3 = $500,000(0.19) = $95,000.
Dep_4 = $500,000(0.12) = $60,000.
Dep_5 = $500,000(0.11) = $55,000.
Dep_6 = $500,000(0.06) = $30,000.
Dep_{7-10} = $0.

In the final year (Year 10), the firm receives $35,000 from the sale of the machine. However, the book value of the machine is $0. Thus, the firm would have to pay 0.4($35,000) = $14,000 in taxes; and the net salvage value is $35,000 - $14,000 = $21,000. The time line is as follows:

0 14%	1	2	3	4	5	6	7	8	9	10
(500,000)	61,257	61,257	61,257	61,257	61,257	61,257	61,257	61,257	61,257	61,257
	100,000	160,000	95,000	60,000	55,000	30,000				21,000
(500,000)	161,257	221,257	156,257	121,257	116,257	91,257	61,257	61,257	61,257	82,257

The project's NPV can be found by discounting each of the cash flows at the firm's 14 percent cost of capital. The project's NPV, found by using a financial calculator, is $177,902.

3.   d.   Cash flow = Net income + Depreciation. The first step to this problem is to set up the income statement for Years 1 through 10. (Note that the return of NWC is not shown in the income statement here, but is shown on the time line that follows.)

	1	2	3	4	5	6	7-9	10
Revenues	120,000	120,000	120,000	120,000	120,000	120,000	120,000	120,000
Operating costs	20,000	20,000	20,000	20,000	20,000	20,000	20,000	20,000
Depreciation[a]	140,000	224,000	133,000	84,000	77,000	42,000		
EBT	(40,000)	(124,000)	(33,000)	16,000	23,000	58,000	100,000	100,000
Taxes (40%)	(16,000)	(49,600)	(13,200)	6,400	9,200	23,200	40,000	40,000
Net income	(24,000)	(74,400)	(19,800)	9,600	13,800	34,800	60,000	60,000
Depreciation	140,000	224,000	133,000	84,000	77,000	42,000		
	116,000	149,600	113,200	93,600	90,800	76,800	60,000	60,000
SV (AT)[b]								6,000
Cash flow	116,000	149,600	113,200	93,600	90,800	76,800	60,000	66,000

[a]Depreciation schedule:

Cost basis = Price + Transportation + Installation = $600,000 + $60,000 + $40,000
    = $700,000.

Year	Allowance Percentage	Depreciation	Ending Book Value
1	0.20	$140,000	$560,000
2	0.32	224,000	336,000
3	0.19	133,000	203,000
4	0.12	84,000	119,000
5	0.11	77,000	42,000
6	0.06	42,000	0
		$700,000	

[b]At the end of Year 10 the still has a salvage value of $10,000; however, it has been fully depreciated so the firm must pay taxes of 0.4($10,000) = $4,000. Therefore, the still's after-tax salvage value is $10,000 - $4,000 = $6,000.

The still's cash flows are then placed on a time line as follows and discounted at the project's cost of capital:

0	10%	1	2	3	4	5	6	7	8	9	10
(700,000)		116,000	149,600	113,200	93,600	90,800	76,800	60,000	60,000	60,000	66,000
(30,000)*											+30,000*
(730,000)		116,000	149,600	113,200	93,600	90,800	76,800	60,000	60,000	60,000	96,000

*An increase in net working capital is required in Year 0, so this must be added back to the cash flow at the end of the project's life.

At a 10% cost of capital, the still's NPV is -$130,961.

4. d. The first step is to recast the given data in nominal terms since the cost of capital is nominal:

Year	Revenue	Cost	Depreciation
0	$ 0	$90,000	$ 0
1	42,000	11,000	30,000
2	44,100	12,100	30,000
3	46,305	13,310	30,000

Now apply standard capital budgeting procedures. The initial investment is $90,000. The operating cash flows are 0.6($42,000 – $11,000) = $18,600 for Year 1, 0.6($44,100 – $12,100) = $19,200 for Year 2, and 0.6($46,305 – $13,310) = $19,797 for Year 3. The tax savings from depreciation is 0.4($30,000) = $12,000 in Years 1 through 3. Now putting this on a time line gives the following:

```
   0     14%        1              2              3
   |-----------------|--------------|--------------|
-90,000           18,600         19,200         19,797
                  12,000         12,000         12,000
                  30,600         31,200         31,797
 26,842  ◄──────────┘              │              │
 24,007  ◄─────────────────────────┘              │
 21,462  ◄────────────────────────────────────────┘
($17,689)
```

5. b. E(NPV) = 0.05(-$28) + 0.25(-$10) + 0.40($5) + 0.25($8) + 0.05($15)

= -$1.40 + -$2.50 + $2.00 + $2.00 + $0.75

= $0.85 million.

6. a. $\sigma = [0.05(-\$28 - \$0.85)^2 + 0.25(-\$10 - \$0.85)^2 + 0.40(\$5 - \$0.85)^2 + 0.25(\$8 - \$0.85)^2 + 0.05(\$15 - \$0.85)^2]^{1/2}$

$\sigma = [\$41.62 + \$29.43 + \$6.89 + \$12.78 + \$10.01]^{1/2}$

$\sigma = [\$100.73]^{1/2}$

$\sigma = \$10.04.$

7. e. $CV = \dfrac{\$10.04}{\$0.85}$

$CV = 11.81.$

CHAPTER 15
OPTION PRICING WITH APLICATIONS TO REAL OPTIONS

OVERVIEW

Real options allow managers to intervene and make changes in a project after it has been implemented, in response to changing market conditions. Real options increase a project's expected cash flows and change the project's risk. Therefore, real options add value to a project.

It is important to understand financial options, because many of their features also apply to real options.

OUTLINE

Discounted cash flow techniques were developed for passive investments, but many projects give managers the opportunity to intervene if conditions change after the project has been implemented. These opportunities have option value.

A financial option is a contract which gives its holder the right to buy (or sell) an asset at some predetermined price within a specified period of time.

- The *strike*, or *exercise, price* is the price that must be paid for a share of common stock when an option is exercised.

- The seller of an option is called the *option writer*.

- An investor who "writes" call options against stock held in his or her portfolio is said to be selling *covered options*. Options sold without the stock to back them up are called *naked options*.

- When the exercise price exceeds the current stock price, a call option is said to be *out-of-the-money*. When the exercise price is below the current price of the stock, a call option is *in-the-money*.

- An option which gives you the right to sell a stock at a specified price within some future period is called a *put option*.

■ Options can be used to create *hedges* which protect the value of an individual stock or portfolio.

■ Conventional options are generally written for 6 months or less, but a new type of option called a *Long-Term Equity Anticipation Security* (LEAPS) has been trading in recent years.
  ❑ Like conventional options, LEAPS are listed on exchanges and are tied both to individual stocks and to stock indexes.
  ❑ LEAPS are long-term options, having maturities of up to 2 1/2 years.

■ Corporations on whose stocks options are written have nothing to do with the option market.

■ There are at least three factors which affect a call option's value.
  ❑ For a given strike price, the higher the stock's market price in relation to the strike price, the higher will be the call option price.
  ❑ For a given stock price, the higher the strike price, the lower the call option price.
  ❑ The longer the option period, the higher will be the option price, because the longer the time before expiration, the greater the chance that the stock price will climb substantially above the exercise price.

■ A call option's *exercise value* is equal to the current stock price less the strike price.
  ❑ Realistically, the minimum "true" value of an option is zero, because no one would exercise an out-of-the-money option.
  ❑ The actual market price of the option lies above the exercise value at each price of the common stock, although the premium declines as the price of the stock increases.
    • Options enable individuals to gain a high degree of personal leverage when buying securities.
    • The leverage effect and loss protection feature of options decline at high stock prices.

■ In addition to the stock price and the exercise price, the price of an option depends on three other factors: (1) the option's term to maturity, (2) the variability of the stock price, and (3) the risk-free rate.
  ❑ The longer a call option has to run, the greater its value and the larger its premium.
  ❑ An option on an extremely volatile stock is worth more than one on a very stable stock. If the stock price rarely moves, then there is only a small chance of a large gain. stock underlying the call option provides no dividends or other distributions during the life of the option.
  ❑ The value of the option is the present value of an expected future payoff. The higher the discount rate used to find the PV, the lower the value of the call option.

The Black-Scholes Model is a widely used but complex option pricing model. Some basic principles that will help you to understand the model are listed below.

- All option pricing models are based on the concept of a *riskless hedge*.
  - An investor buys a stock and simultaneously sells a call option on that stock. If the stock's price goes up, the investor will earn a profit, but the holder of the option will exercise it, and that will cost the investor money. If the stock goes down, the investor will lose on his or her investment in the stock, but gain from the option (which will expire worthless if the stock price declines.)
  - It is possible to set things up such that the investor will end up with a riskless position—regardless of what the stock does, the value of the investor's portfolio will remain constant.
  - A riskless investment must, in equilibrium, yield the risk-free rate. If it offered a higher rate of return, arbitrageurs would buy it and in the process push the rate of return down and vice versa.

- Given the price of the stock, its potential volatility, the option's exercise price, the life of the option, and the risk-free rate, there is but one price for the option if it is to meet the equilibrium conditions.

The Black-Scholes Option Pricing Model (OPM) is widely used by option traders to estimate the value of a call option.

- The assumptions made in the OPM are:
  - The stock underlying the call option provides no dividends or other distributions during the life of the option.
  - There are no transaction costs for buying or selling either the stock or the option.
  - The short-term, risk-free interest rate is known and is constant during the life of the option.
  - Any purchaser of a security may borrow any fraction of the purchase price at the short-term, risk-free interest rate.
  - Short selling is permitted, and the short seller will receive immediately the full cash proceeds of today's price for a security sold short.
  - The call option can be exercised only on its expiration date.
  - Trading in all securities takes place continuously, and the stock price moves randomly.

- The Black-Scholes model consists of the following three equations:

$$V = P[N(d_1)] - X e^{-k_{RF}t}[N(d_2)].$$

$$d_1 = \frac{\ln(P/X) + [k_{RF} + (\sigma^2/2)]t}{\sigma\sqrt{t}}.$$

$$d_2 = d_1 - \sigma\sqrt{t}.$$

   - V = current value of the call option.
   - P = current price of the underlying stock.
   - $N(d_i)$ = probability that a deviation less than d_i will occur in a standard normal distribution. Thus, $N(d_1)$ and $N(d_2)$ represent areas under a standard normal distribution function.
   - X = exercise, or strike, price of the option.
   - $e \approx 2.7183$.
   - k_{RF} = risk-free interest rate.
   - t = time until the option expires (the option period).
   - $\ln(P/X)$ = natural logarithm of P/X.
   - σ^2 = variance of the rate of return on the stock.

Traditional capital budgeting theory says nothing about actions that can be taken after the project has been accepted and placed in operation that might cause the cash flows to change.

- Chance plays a continuing role throughout the life of the project and managers can respond to changing market conditions and to competitors' actions.

- Opportunities to respond to changing circumstances are called *managerial options* because they give managers the option to influence the outcome of a project.
   - They are also called *strategic options* because they are often associated with large, strategic projects rather than routine maintenance projects.
   - They are also called *real options* and are differentiated from financial options because they involve real, rather than financial, assets.

Real options can add value to a project. Managers should be able to identify any real options embedded in projects. These include investment timing options, growth options, abandonment options, and flexibility options.

- *Investment timing options* allow a manager to defer making a decision on whether or not to accept a project
   - These are valuable during periods of volatile interest rates, since the ability to wait can allow firms to raise capital for projects when interest rates are lower. They are

also valuable when demand is very uncertain, since waiting might resolve this uncertainty.

❑ The option to delay is valuable only if it more than offsets any harm that might come from delaying.

■ *Growth options* allow a company to increase capacity to meet changing market conditions.

❑ Some projects give a company an *option to expand* capacity of an existing product line.

❑ Some projects give a company an *option to expand into a new geographical market*.

❑ Some projects give a company an *option to add a new product.* A company might accept negative NPV projects if they have embedded in them the option to add complementary projects, or successive "generations" of the original product.

■ The *abandonment option* allows the firm to discontinue a project.

❑ Some options allow a company to *reduce capacity* or *temporarily suspend operations*, rather than completely abandon them.

■ The *flexibility option* allows managers to switch inputs or outputs in a manufacturing process.

There are five possible procedures to evaluate real options: (1) use DCF analysis and ignore the real option by assuming is value is zero; (2) use DCF analysis and include a qualitative assessment of the real option's value; (3) use decision tree analysis; (4) use a standard model for a financial option; and (5) develop a unique, project-specific model using financial engineering techniques.

■ Using DCF analysis and ignoring the real option is a poor choice, since it incorrectly assumes that the real option has no value.

■ A qualitative assessment of a real option's value recognizes that:

❑ Real options are more valuable if the project is very volatile.

❑ Real options are more valuable if there is a long time until the option must be exercised.

❑ Real options are more valuable when the current value of the underlying project is relatively high compared with the cost to exercise the real option (i.e., the real option is in-the-money).

❑ Real options are more valuable when interest rates are high.

■ Projects with real options can be structured as *decision trees*.

❑ A decision tree defines the possible outcome as a *branch* on the tree; sometimes the point where the tree branches is called a *node*.

❑ *Decision nodes* are the points at which management can respond to new information.

- ❑ The decision tree also shows the probabilities of moving into each branch that leaves a node.
- ❑ Complex decision trees are used to analyze projects. Even more important, they are used to help structure projects and to help identify any real options that might be embedded in the projects.
- ❑ In general, DCF techniques will not give perfectly accurate estimates of the value of a real option, because real options change a project's risk and resulting cost of capital. Therefore, one should always use sensitivity analysis with respect to the cost of capital when using a decision tree.

- ■ Some projects can be structured so that they resemble a standard financial option. For example, growth options and investment timing options often resemble call options.

- ■ Some projects don't resemble standard financial option. For those projects, financial engineering techniques, such as the ones described in the Web/CD Extension to the chapter, must be used.

When using a standard financial option to value a real option, the analyst must identify the inputs to the financial option model. If the model is the Black-Scholes Option Pricing model, the inputs are: (1) exercise cost, (2) time until the option expires, (3) the risk-free rate, (4) price, and (5) variance.

- ■ The input for exercise cost is the cost to implement the real option.

- ■ The input for time is the amount of time, in years, until the option must be exercised.

- ■ The input for the risk-free rate is the rate on a government security with a maturity approximately equal to the time until the option expires.

- ■ The input for price is current value of the underlying asset. In general, this is the present value of the project's expected future cash flows, discounted at the cost of capital. These are the expected future cash flows, and do not include the exercise cost or the impact of any decisions (i.e., they are the cash flows that would be expected if there were no real option).

- ■ The input for variance is the variance of the underlying project's expected rate of return. (Notice that this is not the same as the variance of the project's NPV.) In general, this is the variance of the rate of return one would expect if the project had no real option. There are three ways to estimate this input: (1) use judgment, (2) use the decision tree to directly estimate the returns and their variance, and (3) use an indirect formula from the theory of financial option pricing.
  - ❑ When estimating variance by judgment, start with the variance of the company's stock return. For the typical company, this is about 12 percent. Individual projects

should have higher variances, since the company's variance reflects the diversification that occurs by having projects that are not perfectly correlated. Therefore, the analyst should scale up the company's stock return variance to reflect the additional risk of the project.

❑ Using the direct approach with the decision tree, it is possible to estimate the value of the project as of the time the option must be exercised for each branch, or scenario. Given the estimate of the current value of the project, it is possible to estimate the rate of return for each branch, and then the variance of these returns.

❑ Using the indirect approach, the theory of financial option pricing assumes that the variance of the project's rate of return is related to its coefficient of variation at the time the option expires (recall that the coefficient of variation is the ratio of the standard deviation of the expected value of the project to the project's expected value). If CV is the coefficient of variation and t is the time until the option expires, then the variance of the rate of return is:

$$\sigma^2 = \frac{\ln(CV^2 + 1)}{t}.$$

SELF-TEST QUESTIONS

Definitional

1. If an investment is riskless, it must, in equilibrium yield the _____-_____ _____.

2. All option pricing models are based on the concept of a _____ _____.

3. When the exercise price exceeds the current stock price a call option is said to be _____-_____-_____-_____; however, when the exercise price is less than the current price of the underlying stock, a call option is _____-_____-_____.

4. In addition to the stock price and the exercise price, the price of an option depends on three other factors: (1) the option's _____ ____ _____, (2) the _____ of the stock price, and (3) the risk-free rate.

5. The _____-_____ _____ _____ _____ is widely used by option traders to estimate the value of a call option.

6. A(n) _____ is a contract which gives its holder the right to buy (or sell) an asset at some predetermined price within a specified period of time.

7. The _____, or _____, price is the price that must be paid for a share of common stock when an option price is exercised.

8. The seller of an option is called the option _____.

9. An investor who writes call options against stock held in his or her portfolio is said to be selling _____ options.

10. Options sold without the stock to back them up are called _____ options.

11. An option which gives you the right to sell a stock at a specified price within some future period is called a(n) _____ option.

12. Conventional options are generally written for 6 months or less, but a new type of option called a(n) _____-_____ _____ _____ Security has a maturity of up to 2½ years.

13. A call option's _____ _____ is equal to the current price less the strike price.

14. Opportunities to respond to changing circumstances are called _____ _____ because they give managers the option to influence the outcome of a project.

15. Projects that can be structured to permit a sequence of decisions can be evaluated using _____ _____.

16. In general, DCF techniques will not give perfectly accurate estimates of the value of a(n) _____ _____, because it changes a project's risk and resulting cost of capital.

17. Real options often add considerable value to projects, so ignoring them could lead to _____-biased NPVs and systematic _____.

Conceptual

18. Which of the following statements about real options is *false*?

   a. The more volatile the underlying source of risk, the more valuable the option.
   b. In general, the longer before a real option must be exercised, the more valuable it is.
   c. If interest rates fall, the values of real options will increase.
   d. Real options often add considerable value to projects, so ignoring them could lead to downward-biased NPVs and systematic underinvestment.
   e. While sometimes it is not possible to quantify the value of a project with real options, managers should still think about real options in the framework of this equation: True NPV = NPV without options + NPV of options.

SELF-TEST PROBLEMS

1. A call option on the stock of Heuser Enterprises has a market price of $15. The stock sells for $38 a share, and the option has an exercise price of $30 a share. What is the exercise value of the call option?

   a. $5.00   **b.** $6.25   **c.** $7.00   **d.** $7.50   **e.** $8.00

2. Refer to Self-Test Problem 1. What is the premium on the option?

   a. $5.00   **b.** $6.25   **c.** $7.00   **d.** $7.50   **e.** $8.00

3. Assume you have been given the following information on Detweiler Industries:

   Current stock price = $27.50   Option's exercise price = $27.50
   Time to maturity of option = 3 months   Risk-free rate = 8%
   Variance of stock price = 0.14 $d_1 = 0.20045$
   $d_2 = 0.01336$ $N(d_1) = 0.57942$
   $N(d_2) = 0.50533$

   Using the Black-Scholes Option Pricing Model, what would be the option's value?

   a. $2.00   **b.** $2.31   **c.** $2.73   **d.** $3.18   **e.** $3.75

(The following data apply to the next three Self-Test Problems.)

The San Francisco Yacht Company (SFYC), a prominent sailboat builder in San Francisco, may design a new 30-foot sailboat based on the "winged" keels first introduced on the 12-meter yachts that raced for the America's Cup.

   First, SFYC would have to invest $20,000 at t = 0 for the design and model tank testing of the new boat. SFYC's managers believe that there is a 55 percent probability that this phase will be successful and the project will continue. If Stage 1 is not successful, the project will be abandoned with zero salvage value.

   The next stage, if undertaken, would consist of making the molds and producing two prototype boats. This would cost $1,000,000 at t = 1. If the boats test well, SFYC would go into production. If they do not, the molds and prototypes could be sold for $200,000. The managers estimate that the probability is 75 percent that the boats will pass testing, and that Stage 3 will be undertaken.

   Stage 3 consists of converting an unused production line to produce the new design. This would cost $2,000,000 at t = 2. If the economy is strong at this point, the new value of sales would be $6,000,000, while if the economy is weak, the net value would be $3,000,000. Both net values occur at t = 3, and each state of the economy has a probability of 0.5. SFYC's corporate cost of capital is 13 percent.

4.   What is the project's expected NPV?

     a. $94,298   **b.** $117,779   **c.** $155,189   **d.** $184,291   **e.** $203,471

5.   What is the project's standard deviation of NPV?

     a. $445,060   **b.** $575,011   **c.** $617,050   **d.** $731,295   **e.** $819,647

6.   What is the project's coefficient of variation (CV) of NPV?

     a. 1.50   **b.** 5.28   **c.** 2.75   **d.** 4.45   **e.** 3.89

ANSWERS TO SELF-TEST QUESTIONS

1.	risk-free rate	**10.**	naked
2.	riskless hedge	**11.**	put
3.	out-of-the-money; in-the-money	**12.**	Long-Term Equity Anticipation
4.	term to maturity; variability	**13.**	exercise value
5.	Black-Scholes Option Pricing Model	**14.**	managerial options
6.	option	**15.**	decision trees
7.	strike; exercise	**16.**	real option
8.	writer	**17.**	downward; underinvestment
9.	covered		

18.   c.   If interest rates rise, the values of real options will increase.

SOLUTIONS TO SELF-TEST PROBLEMS

1.   e.   Exercise value = Current stock price – Strike price
                      = $38 – $30
                      = $8.

2.   c.   Premium = Option's market price – Exercise value
                = $15 – $8
                = $7.

3.   b. $V = P[N(d_1)] - Xe^{-k_{RF}t}[N(d_2)]$

$= \$27.50(0.57942) - \$27.50e^{-0.02}[0.50533]$

$= \$15.93 - \$13.62$

$= \$2.31.$

4.   c.   The resulting decision tree is:

t = 0	t = 1	t = 2	t = 3	P	NPV	NPV Product
			$6,000,000	0.20625	$1,687,052	$347,954
		($2,000,000) P = 0.5				
		P = 0.75 $3,000,000		0.20625	(392,099)	(80,870)
	($1,000,000)		P = 0.5			
	P = 0.55	$200,000		0.1375	(748,326)	(102,895)
($20,000)		P = 0.25				
		0		0.45	(20,000)	(9,000)
	P = 0.45			1.00	Exp. NPV = (@ 13%)	$155,189

The NPV of the top path is:

$$\frac{\$6,000,000}{(1.13)^3} - \frac{\$2,000,000}{(1.13)^2} - \frac{\$1,000,000}{(1.13)^1} - \$20,000 = \$1,687,052.$$

Using a financial calculator, input the following: $CF_0 = -20000$, $CF_1 = -1000000$, $CF_2 = -2000000$, $CF_3 = 6000000$, and $I = 13$ to solve for NPV = $\$1,687,051.85 \approx \$1,687,052$.

The other NPVs were determined in the same manner. If the project is of average risk, it should be accepted because the expected NPV of the total project is positive.

5.   e. $\sigma^2_{NPV} = 0.20625(\$1,687,052 - \$155,189)^2 + 0.20625(-\$392,099 - \$155,189)^2$

$+ 0.1375(-\$748,326 - \$155,189)^2 + 0.45(-\$20,000 - \$155,189)^2$

$= 671,821,678,595.$

$\sigma_{NPV} = \$819,647.$

6.   b. $CV_{NPV} = \dfrac{\$819,647}{\$155,189} = 5.2816.$

CHAPTER 16
CAPITAL STRUCTURE DECISIONS: THE BASICS

OVERVIEW

One of the most perplexing issues facing financial managers is the relationship between *capital structure*, which is the mix of debt and equity financing, and stock prices. Should different industries and different firms within industries have different capital structures, and, if so, what factors lead to these differences.

In Chapters 16 and 17, we will discuss both the theories that underlie capital structure decisions and more pragmatic approaches to the problem. Although the optimal capital structure decision is complex and far from precise, an understanding of Chapters 16 and 17 will help you deal with the issues involved.

OUTLINE

Capital structure policy involves a tradeoff between risk and return: Using more debt raises the riskiness of the firm's earnings stream and the risk borne by stockholders; however, a higher debt ratio generally leads to a higher expected rate of return.

- The *target capital structure* is the mix of debt, preferred stock, and common equity with which the firm plans to raise capital. This target may change over time as conditions change. A firm's target capital structure is generally set equal to the estimated optimal capital structure.

- The *optimal capital structure* is the one that strikes the optimal balance between risk and return and thereby maximizes the firm's stock price.

- Five primary factors influence capital structure decisions:
  - *Business risk* is the riskiness inherent in the firm's operations if no debt is used. The greater the firm's business risk, the lower its optimal debt ratio.
  - A major reason for using debt is that interest is tax deductible, which lowers the effective cost of debt.
    - The higher a firm's tax rate, the more advantageous debt is to the firm.

❑ *Financial flexibility*, which is the ability to raise capital on reasonable terms under adverse conditions, is another consideration. The potential future availability of funds and the consequences of a funds shortage influence the target capital structure.

   ● The greater the probable future need for capital, and the worse the consequences of a capital shortage, the stronger the balance sheet should be.

❑ *Managerial conservatism or aggressiveness* influences the target capital structures firms actually establish.

❑ Firms with more *growth options* cannot support as much debt and require greater financial flexibility than firms whose value is comprised mostly of assets in place.

■ Operating conditions can cause the actual capital structure to vary from the target.

Business risk in a stand-alone sense is a function of the uncertainty inherent in projections of a firm's return on invested capital (ROIC). ROIC is defined as net operating profit after taxes divided by the firm's capital.

■ Return on invested capital (ROIC) is calculated as follows:

■ $$ROIC = \frac{NOPAT}{Capital} = \frac{\text{Net income to common stockholders} + \text{After-tax interest payments}}{Capital}.$$

❑ At zero debt ROIC = ROE.

■ The business risk of a leverage-free firm can be measured by the standard deviation of its ROE.

■ Business risk varies from one industry to another and also among firms in a given industry. It can also change over time.

■ Business risk depends on a number of factors, the more important ones are listed below:
   ❑ Demand variability
   ❑ Sales price variability
   ❑ Input cost variability
   ❑ Ability to adjust output prices for changes in input costs
   ❑ Ability to develop new products in a timely, cost-effective manner
   ❑ Foreign risk exposure
   ❑ Extent to which costs are fixed: operating leverage

■   Each of these factors is determined partly by the firm's industry characteristics, but each is also controllable to some extent by management.

    ❑   Many firms use hedging techniques to reduce business risk.

■   Operating leverage is the extent to which a firm uses fixed costs in its operations.

    ❑   High operating leverage means that a relatively small change in sales will result in a large change in operating income.

    ❑   The higher a firm's degree of operating leverage, the higher its operating breakeven point tends to be.

        ●   The *operating breakeven point* is defined as the output quantity at which ROE = 0, hence when EBIT = 0.

        ●   The breakeven point is calculated as fixed costs divided by the difference in sales price and variable cost per unit: $Q_{BE} = F/(P - V)$.

    ❑   The higher a firm's operating leverage, the higher its business risk (as measured by variability of EBIT and ROE), other things held constant.

    ❑   In general, holding other factors constant, the higher the degree of operating leverage, the greater the firm's business risk.

    ❑   Technology limits control over the amount of fixed costs and operating leverage. However, firms do have some control over the type of production processes they employ, and so the firm's capital budgeting decisions will have an impact on its operating leverage and business risk.

Financial leverage refers to the firm's use of fixed-income securities such as debt and preferred stock in the firm's capital structure, and financial risk is the additional risk placed on the common stockholders as a result of the decision to finance with debt.

■   The degree to which a firm employs financial leverage will affect its expected earnings per share (EPS) and the riskiness of these earnings. Financial leverage will cause EPS to rise; however, the degree of risk associated with the firm will also increase as leverage increases.

The optimal capital structure is the one that maximizes the price of the firm's stock, and this generally calls for a debt ratio that is lower than the one that maximizes expected EPS.

■   At first, EPS will rise as the use of debt increases. Interest charges rise, but the number of outstanding shares will decrease as equity is replaced by debt. At some point EPS will peak. Beyond this point interest rates will rise so fast that EPS is depressed in spite of the fact that the number of shares outstanding is decreasing.

■   Risk, as measured by the coefficient of variation of EPS, rises continuously as the use of debt increases.

■ Managers should choose the capital structure that maximizes the firm's stock price. The capital structure that maximizes the stock price is also the one that minimizes the WACC.

■ An increase in the debt/assets ratio raises the costs of both debt and equity.
   ❑ Bondholders recognize that if a firm has a higher debt ratio, this increases the risk of financial distress, and more risk leads to higher interest rates.
   ❑ Sophisticated financial managers use their forecasted ratios to predict how bankers and other lenders will judge their firms' risks and thus determine their cost of debt. Thus, they can judge quite accurately the effects of capital structure on the cost of debt.

■ An increase in the debt ratio also increases the risk faced by shareholders, and this has an effect on the cost of equity, k_s.
   ❑ It has been demonstrated, both theoretically and empirically, that beta increases with financial leverage.

■ The *Hamada equation* specifies the effect of financial leverage on beta:

■ $b = b_U[1 + (1 - T)(D/E)]$.

   ❑ The Hamada equation shows how increases in the debt/equity ratio increase beta.
   ❑ b_U is the firm's unlevered beta coefficient, the beta it would have if it has no debt.

■ Beta is the only variable under management's control in the CAPM cost of equity equation.
   ❑ Beta is determined by the firm's operating decisions and by its capital structure decisions as reflected in its debt/assets (or debt/equity) ratio.

■ Once b_U is determined, the Hamada equation can be used to estimate how changes in the debt/equity ratio would affect the leveraged beta and the cost of equity.

■ $k_s = k_{RF}$ + Premium for business risk + Premium for financial risk.

■ Although the component cost of equity is generally higher than that of debt, using only lower-cost debt would not maximize value because this lower cost would be more than offset by the fact that using more debt would raise the costs of both debt and equity.

■ The expected stock price will at first increase with financial leverage, will then reach a peak, and finally will decline as financial leverage becomes excessive due to the importance of potential bankruptcy costs.

■ The financial structure that maximizes EPS usually has more debt than the one that results in the highest stock price.

Modern capital structure theory began in 1958, when Professors Franco Modigliani and Merton Miller (MM) published what has been called the most influential finance article ever written.

■ MM proved, under a very restrictive set of assumptions, that a firm's value is unaffected by its capital structure. MM's results suggest that it doesn't matter how a firm finances its operations, hence capital structure is irrelevant. Their theory produces what is often referred to as the "irrelevance result."

■ By indicating the conditions under which capital structure is irrelevant, MM provided us with some clues about what is required for capital structure to be relevant and hence to have an effect on a firm's value. Consequently, MM's work was only the beginning of capital structure research.
  ❑ Subsequent research has focused on relaxing the MM assumptions in order to develop a more realistic theory of capital structure.

■ MM published a follow-up paper in 1963 in which they relaxed the assumption that there are no corporate taxes. MM demonstrated that if all of their other assumptions hold, the asymmetry of the tax deductibility of interest versus the non-deductibility of dividend payments leads to a situation that calls for 100 percent debt financing.

■ Merton Miller then analyzed the effects of personal taxes. While an increase in the corporate tax rate makes debt look better to corporations, an increase in the personal tax rate encourages additional equity financing.
  ❑ All income from bonds is generally interest, which is taxed as personal income at rates going up to 39.6 percent.
  ❑ Income from stocks generally comes partly from dividends and partly from capital gains.
    ● Long-term capital gains are taxed at a rate of 20 percent.
    ● Capital gains tax is deferred until the stock is sold and the gain realized.
    ● If stock is held until the owner dies, no capital gains tax must be paid.
  ❑ On balance, returns on common stocks are taxed at lower effective rates than returns on debt.

- The deductibility of interest favors the use of debt financing, but the more favorable tax treatment of income from stocks lowers the required rate of return on stock and thus favors the use of equity financing.
    - It is difficult to say what the net effect of these two factors is. Most observers believe that interest deductibility has the stronger effect, hence that our tax system still favors the corporate use of debt. However, that effect is certainly reduced by the lower long-term capital gains tax rate.

- Bankruptcy-related problems are more likely to arise when a firm includes more debt in its capital structure. Therefore, bankruptcy costs discourage firms from pushing their use of debt to excessive levels.
    - Bankruptcy-related costs have two components: the probability of their occurrence and the costs they would produce given that financial distress has arisen.
    - Firms whose earnings are more volatile, all else equal, face a greater chance of bankruptcy and, therefore, should use less debt than more stable firms.
    - Firms with high operating leverage, and thus greater business risk, should limit their use of financial leverage.
    - Likewise, firms that would face high costs in the event of financial distress should rely less heavily on debt.

- The *trade-off theory of leverage* recognizes that firms trade off the *benefits* of debt financing (favorable corporate tax treatment) against the *costs* of debt financing (higher interest rates and bankruptcy costs).

- Many large, successful firms use far less debt than the trade-off theory suggests. This led to the development of signaling theory.

- *Signaling theory* recognizes the fact that investors and managers do *not* have the same information regarding a firm's prospects, as was assumed by the trade-off theory. This is called *asymmetric information,* and it has an important effect on the optimal capital structure.
    - *Symmetric information* is the situation in which investors and managers have identical information about firms' prospects.
    - Because of asymmetric information one would expect a firm with very favorable prospects to try to avoid selling stock and to attempt to raise any required new capital by other means, including using debt beyond the normal target capital structure.
    - The announcement of a stock offering by a mature firm that seems to have financing alternatives is taken as a *signal* that the firm's prospects as seen by its management are not bright. This, in turn, suggests that when a firm announces a new stock offering, more often than not, the price of its stock will decline.

❑   The implication of the signaling theory for capital structure decisions is that firms should, in normal times, maintain a *reserve borrowing capacity* that can be used in the event that some especially good investment opportunity comes along. This means that firms should, in normal times, use more equity and less debt than is suggested by the tax benefit/bankruptcy cost trade-off model.

■   Agency conflicts are particularly likely when the firm's managers have too much cash at their disposal. Managers with limited *free cash flow* are less able to make wasteful expenditures. Firms can reduce excess cash flow in a variety of ways:
   ❑   Funnel cash back to shareholders through higher dividends or stock repurchases.
   ❑   Shift the capital structure toward more debt in the hope that higher debt service requirements will force managers to become more disciplined.
      •   *A leveraged buyout (LBO)* is one way to achieve this. An LBO *bonds* free cash flow by placing constraints on the cash flow.

■   Increasing debt and reducing excess cash flow has its downside: It increases the risk of bankruptcy, which can be costly.

■   Firms with poor investment opportunities should use high levels of debt and have high interest payments to constrain managers from wasting money on poor investments.

■   In practice, capital structure decisions must be made using a combination of judgment and numerical analysis.

The following factors will all have some influence on the firm's choice of a target capital structure.

■   *Sales stability.* If sales are stable, a firm will be more likely to take on increased debt and higher fixed charges than a company with unstable sales.

■   *Asset structure.* Firms whose assets can readily be pledged as collateral for loans will tend to operate with a higher degree of financial leverage.

■   *Operating leverage.* Lower operating leverage generally permits a firm to employ more debt.

■   *Growth rate.* Firms that are growing rapidly generally need large amounts of external capital. The flotation costs associated with debt are generally less than those for common stock, so rapidly growing firms tend to use more debt. At the same time, however, rapidly growing firms often face greater uncertainty, which tends to reduce their willingness to use debt.

- *Profitability.* A high degree of profitability would indicate an ability to carry a high level of debt. However, many profitable firms are able to meet most of their financing needs with retained earnings, and do so.

- *Taxes.* Interest charges are tax deductible, while dividend payments are not. This factor favors the use of debt over equity for firms in high tax brackets.

- *Control.* Management control issues such as voting, job security, and fear of takeover, all influence the capital structure of a firm in various ways.

- *Management attitudes.* Managements vary in their attitudes toward risk. More conservative managers will use stock rather than debt for financing, while less conservative managers will use more debt.

- *Lender and rating agency attitudes.* This factor will penalize firms that go beyond the average for their industry in the use of financial leverage.

- *Market conditions.* At any point in time, securities markets may favor either debt or equity.

- *Firm's internal conditions.* Expected future earnings patterns and internal factors will influence management's choice of debt versus equity.

- *Financial flexibility.* Most treasurers have as a goal to always be in a position to raise the capital needed to support operations, even under bad conditions. Therefore, they want to always maintain some reserve borrowing capacity.

There are wide variations in the use of financial leverage both among industries and among individual firms within each industry. The times-interest-earned ratio is a good tool to gauge the degree of financial leverage used by a particular firm. It gives a measure of how safe the debt is and how vulnerable the company is to financial distress. TIE ratios depend on three factors: (1) the percentage of debt, (2) the interest rate on debt, and (3) the company's profitability.

SELF-TEST QUESTIONS

Definitional

1. The _____ capital structure is the one that strikes the balance between _____ and _____ and thereby maximizes the firm's _____ _____ .

2. A firm's _____ capital structure is generally set equal to the estimated optimal structure.

3. _____ _____ in a stand-alone sense is a function of the uncertainty inherent in projections of a firm's return on invested capital.

4. Some of the factors that influence a firm's business risk include: (1) _____ variability, (2) sales price variability, and (3) _____ leverage.

5. Business risk represents the riskiness of the firm's operations if it uses no _____ ; financial risk represents the additional risk borne by common stockholders as a result of using _____ .

6. Common stockholders are compensated for bearing financial risk by a higher _____ _____ .

7. Expected EPS generally _____ as the debt/assets ratio increases.

8. As financial leverage increases, the stock price will first begin to rise, but it will then decline as financial leverage becomes excessive because potential _____ _____ become increasingly important.

9. _____ _____ refers to the use of debt financing.

10. Debt has a(n) _____ advantage over equity in that _____ is a deductible expense while _____ are not.

11. Management may prefer additional _____ as opposed to common stock in order to help maintain _____ of the company.

12. _____ _____ is the ability to raise capital on reasonable terms under adverse conditions.

13.   The _____ _____ _____ is defined as the output quantity at which ROE = 0, hence when EBIT = 0.

14.   The _____-_____ theory of leverage recognizes that firms trade off the benefits of debt financing against the costs of debt financing.

15.   _____ theory recognizes the fact that investors and managers do not have the same information regarding a firm's prospects.

16.   The fact that investors and managers do not have the same information regarding a firm's prospects is called _____ information.

17.   The implication of the signaling theory for capital structure decisions is that firms should, in normal times, maintain a(n) _____ _____ _____ that can be used in the event that some especially good investment opportunity comes along.

18.   The _____-_____-_____ ratio gives a measure of how safe the debt is and how vulnerable the company is to financial distress.

19.   TIE ratios depend on three factors: (1) the _____ of debt, (2) the _____ _____ on debt, and (3) the company's _____.

20.   _____ ____ _____ _____ is defined as net operating profit after taxes divided by the firm's capital.

21.   _____ _____ is the extent to which a firm uses fixed costs in its operations.

22.   The higher the degree of operating leverage, the _____ the firm's business risk.

23.   The optimal capital structure is the one that maximizes the price of the firm's stock, and this generally calls for a debt ratio that is _____ than the one that maximizes expected EPS.

24.   _____, as measured by the coefficient of EPS, rises continuously as the use of debt increases.

25.   The capital structure that maximizes the stock price is also the one that _____ the WACC.

26.   The _____ _____ specifies the effect of financial leverage on beta.

27.   Beta is determined by the firm's _____ decisions and by its _____ _____ decisions as reflected in its debt/assets (or debt/equity) ratio.

28.   MM's results suggest that it doesn't matter how a firm finances its operations, hence capital structure is _____.

29.   _____ _____ is the situation in which investors and managers have identical information about firms' prospects.

30.   _____ _____ are likely when the firm's managers have too much cash at their disposal.

Conceptual

31.   Firm A has a higher degree of business risk than Firm B. Firm A can offset this by increasing its operating leverage.

        a. True   **b.** False

32.   Two firms operate in different industries, but they have the same expected EPS and the same standard deviation of expected EPS. Thus, the two firms must have the same financial risk.

        a. True   **b.** False

33.   Two firms could have identical financial and operating leverage yet have different degrees of business risk.

        a. True   **b.** False

34.   As a general rule, the capital structure that maximizes stock price also

        a. Maximizes the weighted average cost of capital.
        b. Maximizes EPS.
        c. Maximizes bankruptcy costs.
        d. Minimizes the weighted average cost of capital.
        e. Minimizes the required rate of return on equity.

35. A decrease in the debt ratio will normally have no effect on

    a. Financial risk.   **d.** Systematic risk.
    b. Total risk.   **e.** Firm-unique risk.
    c. Business risk.

36. Which of the following statements is most correct?

    a. If a firm is exposed to a high degree of business risk as a result of its high operating leverage, then it probably should offset this risk by using a larger-than-average amount of financial leverage. This follows because debt has a lower after-tax cost than equity.
    b. Financial risk can be reduced by replacing common equity with preferred stock.
    c. The Hamada equation specifies the effect of financial leverage on beta. It shows how increases in the debt/equity ratio lowers beta.
    d. In the text it was stated that the capital structure that minimizes the WACC also maximizes the firm's stock price and its total value, but generally not its expected EPS. One reason given for why debt is beneficial is that it shelters operating income from taxes, while it was stated that a disadvantage of excessive debt has to do with costs associated with bankruptcy and financial distress generally.
    e. All of the above statements are false.

SELF-TEST PROBLEMS

1. The Fisher Company will produce 50,000 10-gallon aquariums next year. Variable costs will equal 40 percent of dollar sales, while fixed costs total $100,000. At what price must each aquarium be sold for the firm's EBIT to be $90,000?

    a. $5.00   **b.** $5.33   **c.** $5.50   **d.** $6.00   **e.** $6.33

2. The Diamond Company has identified two methods of producing playing cards. One method involves using a machine having a fixed cost of $20,000 and variable costs of $1.00 per deck. The other method would use a less expensive machine having a fixed cost of $5,000, but it would require variable costs of $2.00 per deck. If the selling price per deck will be the same under each method, at what level of output would the two methods produce the same net operating income (EBIT)?

    a. 5,000   **b.** 10,000   **c.** 15,000   **d.** 20,000   **e.** 25,000

3. Brown Products is a new firm just starting operations. The firm will produce backpacks which will sell for $22.00 each. Fixed costs are $500,000 per year, and variable costs are $2.00 per unit of production. The company expects to sell 50,000 backpacks per year, and its effective federal-plus-state tax rate is 40 percent. Brown needs $2 million to build facilities, obtain working capital, and start operations. If Brown borrows part of the money, the interest charges will depend on the amount borrowed as follows:

Amount Borrowed	Percentage of Debt in Capital Structure	Interest Rate on Total Amount Borrowed
$ 200,000	10%	9.00%
400,000	20	9.50
600,000	30	10.00
800,000	40	15.00
1,000,000	50	19.00
1,200,000	60	26.00

Assume that stock can be sold at a price of $20 per share on the initial offering, regardless of how much debt the company uses. Then after the company begins operating, its price will be determined as a multiple of its earnings per share. The multiple (or the P/E ratio) will depend upon the capital structure as follows:

Debt/Assets	P/E	Debt/Assets	P/E
0.0%	12.5×	40.0%	8.0×
10.0	12.0	50.0	6.0
20.0	11.5	60.0	5.0
30.0	10.0		

What is Brown's optimal capital structure, which maximizes stock price, as measured by the debt/assets ratio?

a. 10%   b. 20%   c. 30%   d. 40%   e. 50%

4. Hairston Industries has $25 million in assets, which is financed with $5 million of debt and $20 million in equity. If Hairston's beta is currently 1.75 and its tax rate is 40 percent, what is its unlevered beta, b_U?

a. 0.7564   b. 1.0000   c. 1.2525   d. 1.5217   e. 2.0125

5. The Hampton Hardware Company is trying to estimate its optimal capital structure. Hampton's current capital structure consists of 20 percent debt and 80 percent equity; however, management believes the firm should use more debt. The risk-free rate, k_{RF}, is 7 percent, the market risk premium, $k_M - k_{RF}$, is 5 percent, and the firm's tax rate is 35 percent. Currently, Hampton's cost of equity is 16 percent, which is determined on the basis of the CAPM. What would be Hampton's estimated cost of equity if it were to change its capital structure from its present capital structure to 40 percent debt and 60 percent equity?

    a. 14.93%   **b.** 15.45%   **c.** 18.10%   **d.** 19.25%   **e.** 20.33%

6. Backroads Sporting Goods is trying to determine its optimal capital structure, which now consists of only debt and common equity. The firm does not currently use preferred stock in its capital structure, and it does not plan to do so in the future. To estimate how much its debt would cost at different debt levels, the company's treasury staff has consulted with investment bankers and, on the basis of those discussions, has created the following table:

Debt-to-Assets Ratio (w_d)	Equity-to-Assets Ratio (w_c)	Debt-to-Equity Ratio (D/E)	Bond Rating	Before-Tax Cost of Debt (k_d)
0.0	1.0	0.00	A	6.5%
0.2	0.8	0.25	BBB	7.5
0.4	0.6	0.67	BB	9.5
0.6	0.4	1.50	C	11.5
0.8	0.2	4.00	D	14.5

    Backroads uses the CAPM to estimate its cost of common equity, k_s. The company estimates that the risk-free rate is 6 percent, the market risk premium is 5 percent, and its tax rate is 40 percent. Backroads estimates that if it had no debt, its "unlevered" beta, b_U, would be 1.25. On the basis of this information, what would the weighted average cost of capital be at the optimal capital structure?

    a. 9.56%   **b.** 10.48%   **c.** 11.13%   **d.** 11.45%   **e.** 12.25%

(The following data apply to the next six Self-Test Problems.)

United Producers (UP), an unleveraged firm, has a total market value of $10 million, consisting of 500,000 shares of common stock selling at $20 per share. Management is considering issuing $2 million of debt at a before-tax cost of 12 percent, and using the proceeds to repurchase stock at the new equilibrium market price. If the plan is carried out, the required rate of return on equity will increase by 2 percentage points to 16 percent. UP's marginal tax rate is 40 percent, and it pays out all earnings as dividends.

7.   What are UP's earnings before interest and taxes (EBIT) in millions of dollars?

   a. $1.4   **b.** $2.3   **c.** $3.0   **d.** $3.6   **e.** $4.2

8.   Regardless of your answer to Self-Test Problem 7, assume that UP's EBIT is $2,800,000. What is the value of the firm in millions of dollars if the restructuring occurs?

   a. $9.76   **b.** $10.00   **c.** $10.56   **d.** $11.00   **e.** $11.60

9.   Suppose a tax law change occurs which causes UP's marginal tax rate to decline to 30 percent. UP's EBIT remains at $2.8 million. Under these conditions, what is the value of the firm in millions of dollars at zero debt?

   a. $10   **b.** $11   **c.** $12   **d.** $13   **e.** $14

10.   Under the conditions of Self-Test Problem 9, what is the value of the firm in millions of dollars if restructuring occurs?

   a. $13.2   **b.** $14.0   **c.** $14.2   **d.** $14.6   **e.** $14.8

11.   Disregard the tax change in Self-Test Problem 9 and refer to the data in the original problem. Assume these data are correct, including an assumed EBIT of $2.8 million, except that use of financial leverage will increase the required rate of return on equity to only 15 percent, rather than 16 percent. What is the value of the firm in millions of dollars if the restructuring occurs?

   a. $9.4   **b.** $10.0   **c.** $12.2   **d.** $13.0   **e.** $13.1

12.   Under the conditions of Self-Test Problem 11, what will be the new number of shares outstanding if the restructuring occurs? (Hint: $P_1 = [V_1 - D_0]/n_0$.)

   a. 500,000   **b.** 478,642   **c.** 438,231   **d.** 418,301   **e.** 396,547

(The following data apply to the next four Self-Test Problems.)

Union Brick Inc. (UBI) has a total market value of $200 million, consisting of 2 million shares of common stock selling for $50 per share and $100 million of 10 percent perpetual bonds currently selling at par. UBI pays out all earnings as dividends, and its marginal tax rate is 40 percent. The firm's earnings before interest and taxes (EBIT) are $30 million. Management is considering increasing UBI's debt to $140 million. The additional funds will be used to repurchase stock at the new equilibrium price. At a debt level of $140 million UBI's cost of debt is estimated at 12 percent and its cost of equity is estimated to be 15 percent.

13.   What is UBI's required rate of return on equity at its current debt level of $100 million?

    a. 11.0%   **b.** 12.0%   **c.** 13.0%   **d.** 14.0%   **e.** 15.0%

14.   Assume that UBI will increase its outstanding debt by calling in the old debt and issuing new debt, resulting in a debt level of $140 million. What would be UBI's new firm value in millions of dollars?

    a. $52.8   **b.** $100.0   **c.** $140.0   **d.** $192.8   **e.** $200.0

15.   Refer to Self-Test Problem 14. What would be UBI's new stock price? (Hint: $P_1 = [V_1 - D_0]/n_0$.)

    a. $40.00   **b.** $46.40   **c.** $50.00   **d.** $50.40   **e.** $52.60

16.   Now assume that UBI will increase its outstanding debt by issuing $40 million of new debt—the debt outstanding will not be called. What would be UBI's new stock price? (Hint: $P_1 = [V_1 - D_0]/n_0$.)

    a. $40.00   **b.** $46.40   **c.** $50.00   **d.** $50.40   **e.** $52.60

(The following data apply to the next four Self-Test Problems.)

Tapley Dental Supplies Inc. is in a stable, no-growth situation. Its $1,000,000 of debt consists of perpetuities which have a 10 percent coupon and sell at par. Tapley's EBIT is $500,000, its cost of equity is 15 percent, it has 100,000 shares of common stock outstanding that sell for $16 per share, all earnings are paid out as dividends, and its federal-plus-state tax rate is 40 percent. Tapley could borrow an additional $500,000 at an interest rate of 13 percent without having to retire the original debt, and it would use the proceeds to repurchase stock at the new equilibrium price. The increased risk from the additional leverage will raise the cost of equity to 17 percent.

17.   What is the firm's current value in millions of dollars at a debt level of $1 million?

     a. $1.6   **b.** $2.0   **c.** $2.6   **d.** $1.8   **e.** $2.3

18.   What is the firm's new value in millions of dollars at a debt level of $1.5 million, assuming that the original debt is not retired?

     a. $2.25   **b.** $2.45   **c.** $2.68   **d.** $1.75   **e.** $1.18

19.   If the recapitalization takes place, what is Tapley's new stock price?   (Hint: $P_1 = [V_1 - D_0]/n_0$.)

     a. $16.50   **b.** $16.23   **c.** $17.10   **d.** $16.82   **e.** $17.45

20.   After the recapitalization takes place, how many shares of common stock will remain?

     a. 70,273   **b.** 69,697   **c.** 70,760   **d.** 71,347   **e.** 69,193

ANSWERS TO SELF-TEST QUESTIONS

1.	optimal; risk; return; stock price	10.	tax; interest; dividends
2.	target	11.	debt; control
3.	Business risk	12.	Financial flexibility
4.	demand; operating	13.	operating breakeven point
5.	debt; debt	14.	trade-off
6.	expected return	15.	Signaling
7.	increases	16.	asymmetric
8.	bankruptcy costs	17.	reserve borrowing capacity
9.	Financial leverage	18.	times-interest-earned

19.	percentage; interest rate; profitability	**25.**	minimizes
20.	Return on invested capital	**26.**	Hamada equation
21.	Operating leverage	**27.**	operating; capital structure
22.	greater	**28.**	irrelevant
23.	lower	**29.**	Symmetric information
24.	Risk	**30.**	Agency conflicts

31. b. Increasing operating leverage will increase Firm A's business risk; therefore, Firm A should use less operating leverage.

32. b. The two firms would have the same total risk. However, they could have different combinations of business and financial risk.

33. a. Business risk consists of several elements in addition to operating leverage, for example, sales variability, and it does not depend on financial risk at all.

34. d. The optimal capital structure balances risk and return to maximize the stock price. The structure that maximizes stock price also minimizes the firm's cost of capital.

35. c. Business risk measures the riskiness of a firm's operations assuming no debt is used.

36. d. Statement a is false; if a firm is exposed to a high degree of business risk this implies that it should offset this risk by using a lower amount of financial leverage. Statement b is false; preferred stock is a fixed-income security, and as such, would increase financial risk. Statement c is false; an increase in the debt/equity ratio increases beta. Statement d is the correct choice.

SOLUTIONS TO SELF-TEST PROBLEMS

1. e. $$EBIT = PQ - VQP - F$$
$$\$90,000 = P(50,000) - 0.4(50,000)P - \$100,000$$
$$30,000P = \$190,000$$
$$P = \$6.33.$$

2. c. For the first method: EBIT = PQ – $1.00Q – $20,000.

For the second method: EBIT = PQ – $2.00Q – $5,000.

Now, equate the EBITs:
PQ – $1.00Q – $20,000 = PQ – $2.00Q – $5,000; $1.00Q = $15,000; Q = 15,000.

3. b. The first step is to calculate EBIT:

Sales in dollars [50,000($22)]	$1,100,000
Less: Fixed costs	500,000
Variable costs [50,000($2)]	100,000
EBIT	$ 500,000

The second step is to calculate the EPS at each debt/assets ratio using the formula:

$$EPS = \frac{(EBIT - I)(1 - T)}{\text{Shares outstanding}}.$$

Recognize (1) that I = Interest charges = (Dollars of debt)(Interest rate at each D/A ratio), and (2) that shares outstanding = (Assets – Debt)/Initial price per share = ($2,000,000 – Debt)/$20.00.

D/A	EPS	D/A	EPS
0%	$3.00	40%	$3.80
10	3.21	50	3.72
20	3.47	60	2.82
30	3.77		

Finally, the third step is to calculate the stock price at each debt/assets ratio using the following formula: Price = (P/E)(EPS).

D/A	Price	D/A	Price
0%	$37.50	40%	$30.40
10	38.52	50	22.32
20	39.91	60	14.10
30	37.70		

Thus, a debt/assets ratio of 20 percent maximizes stock price. This is the optimal capital structure.

4.   d. From the Hamada Equation, $b = b_U[1 + (1 - T)(D/E)]$, we can calculate b_U as $b_U = b/[1 + (1 - T)(D/E)]$.

$b_U = 1.75/[1 + (1 - 0.4)(\$5,000,000/\$20,000,000)]$
$b_U = 1.75/[1 + 0.15]$
$b_U = 1.5217$.

5.   c. Facts as given: Current capital structure: 20%D, 80%E; $k_{RF} = 7\%$; $k_M - k_{RF} = 5\%$; $T = 35\%$; $k_s = 16\%$.

Step 1:   Determine the firm's current beta.
$k_s = k_{RF} + (k_M - k_{RF})b$
$16\% = 7\% + (5\%)b$
$9\% = 5\%b$
$1.8 = b$.

Step 2:   Determine the firm's unlevered beta, b_U.
$b_U = b/[1 + (1 - T)(D/E)]$
$b_U = 1.8/[1 + (1 - 0.35)(0.20/0.80)]$
$b_U = 1.8/1.1625$
$b_U = 1.5484$.

Step 3:   Determine the firm's beta under the new capital structure.
$b = b_U[1 + (1 - T)(D/E)]$
$b = 1.5484[1 + (1 - 0.35)(0.4/0.6)]$
$b = 1.5484(1.4333)$
$b = 2.2194$.

Step 4:   Determine the firm's new cost of equity under the changed capital structure.
$k_s = k_{RF} + (k_M - k_{RF})b$
$k_s = 7\% + (5\%)2.2194$
$k_s = 18.1\%$.

6. c. Tax rate = 40% k_{RF} = 6.0%
   b_U = 1.25 $k_M - k_{RF}$ = 5.0%

From data given in the problem and table we can develop the following table:

D/A	E/A	D/E	k_d	$k_d(1 - T)$	Leveraged beta[a]	k_s[b]	WACC[c]
0.00	1.00	0.0000	6.5%	3.90%	1.2500	12.2500%	12.25%
0.20	0.80	0.2500	7.5	4.50	1.4375	13.1875	11.45
0.40	0.60	0.6667	9.5	5.70	1.7500	14.7500	11.13
0.60	0.40	1.5000	11.5	6.90	2.3750	17.8750	11.29
0.80	0.20	4.0000	14.5	8.70	4.2500	27.2500	12.41

Notes:
[a] These beta estimates were calculated using the Hamada equation:
$b = b_U[1 + (1 - T)(D/E)]$.
[b] These k_s estimates were calculated using the CAPM: $k_s = k_{RF} + (k_M - k_{RF})b$.
[c] These WACC estimates were calculated with the following equation:
$WACC = w_d(k_d)(1 - T) + (w_c)(k_s)$.

The firm's optimal capital structure is that capital structure which minimizes the firm's WACC. Backroads' WACC is minimized at a capital structure consisting of 40% debt and 60% equity. At that capital structure, the firm's WACC is 11.13%.

7. b. $V_0 = S_0 = 500,000(\$20) = \$10,000,000$.

$$S_0 = \frac{(EBIT - k_dD)(1 - T)}{k_s}$$

$$S_0 = \frac{EBIT(1 - T)}{k_s}.$$

$$\$10,000,000 = \frac{EBIT(0.6)}{0.14}$$
$$0.6(EBIT) = \$1,400,000$$
$$EBIT = \$2,333,333.$$

8.   e. $S_1 = \dfrac{(EBIT - k_d D)(1 - T)}{k_s}$

$S_1 = \dfrac{[\$2,800,000 - 0.12(\$2,000,000)]0.6}{0.16} = \$9,600,000.$

$V_1 = D_1 + S_1 = \$2,000,000 + \$9,600,000 = \$11,600,000.$

9.   e. $S_0 = \dfrac{(EBIT - k_d D)(1 - T)}{k_s}$

$S_0 = \dfrac{(\$2,800,000 - \$0)(0.7)}{0.14} = \$14,000,000 = V_0.$

Now, less money is paid in taxes, more remains for the shareholders, and the value of the firm is higher.

10.   a. $S_1 = \dfrac{(EBIT - k_d D)(1 - T)}{k_s}$

$S_1 = \dfrac{[\$2,800,000 - 0.12(\$2,000,000)]0.7}{0.16} = \$11,200,000.$

$V_1 = D_1 + S_1 = \$2,000,000 + \$11,200,000 = \$13,200,000.$

11.   c. $S_1 = \dfrac{(EBIT - k_d D)(1 - T)}{k_s}$

$S_1 = \dfrac{[\$2,800,000 - 0.12(\$2,000,000)]0.6}{0.15} = \$10,240,000.$

$V_1 = D_1 + S_1 = \$2,000,000 + \$10,240,000 = \$12,240,000.$

12. d. First, find the equilibrium stock price:

$$P_1 = \frac{V_1 - D_0}{n_0} = \frac{\$12,240,000 - \$0}{500,000} = \$24.48.$$

Then, find the number of shares repurchased:

$$\text{Shares repurchased} = \frac{\$2,000,000}{\$24.48} = 81,699.$$

Finally, determine the shares remaining:

Shares remaining = 500,000 − 81,699 = 418,301.

13. b. $k_s = \dfrac{(\text{EBIT} - k_d D)(1 - T)}{S} = \dfrac{[\$30 - 0.10(\$100)]0.6}{\$100} = 12.0\%.$

14. d. $S_1 = \dfrac{(\text{EBIT} - k_d D)(1 - T)}{k_s} = \dfrac{[\$30 - 0.12(\$140)]0.6}{0.15} = \$52.8 \text{ million.}$

$V_1 = D_1 + S_1 = \$140 + \$52.8 = \$192.8 \text{ million.}$

15. b. $P_1 = \dfrac{V_1 - D_0}{n_0} = \dfrac{\$192.8 - \$100}{2} = \$46.40.$

Note that stock price decreases with the increase in leverage. Thus, the change should not be made.

16.   d. $S_1 = \dfrac{(EBIT - k_d D - k_{d_1} D_1)(1 - T)}{k_s}$

$S_1 = \dfrac{[\$30 - 0.10(\$100) - 0.12(\$40)]0.6}{0.15} = \$60.8$ million.

$V_1 = S_1 + D_0 + D_1.$

But the value of the old debt, D_0, decreases because its riskiness has increased:

$D_0 = \dfrac{0.1(\$100)}{0.12} = \$83.33$ million.

Thus, $V_1 = \$60.8 + \$83.33 + \$40 = \$184.13$ million. Finally,

$P_1 = \dfrac{V_1 - D_0}{n_0} = \dfrac{\$184.13 - \$83.33}{2} = \$50.40.$

Note that the change should be made under these circumstances. Here some of the wealth of the old bondholders is being transferred to the shareholders.

17.   c. $S_0 = \dfrac{(EBIT - k_d D)(1 - T)}{k_s} = \dfrac{(\$500,000 - \$100,000)(0.6)}{0.15} = \$1.6$ million.

$V_0 = S_0 + D_0 = \$1.6$ million + \$1.0 million = \$2.6 million.

18.   b. $S_1 = \dfrac{(EBIT - k_d D - k_{d_1} D_1)(1 - T)}{k_s}$

$S_1 = \dfrac{[\$500,000 - \$100,000 - \$65,000](0.6)}{0.17} = \$1,182,353.$

$V_1 = S_1 + D_0 + D_1$

$D_0 = 0.1(\$1,000,000)/0.13 = \$769,231.$

$V_1 = \$1,182,353 + \$769,231 + \$500,000 = \$2,451,584.$

19.   d. $P_1 = (\$2,451,584 - \$769,231)/100,000 = \$16.82$.

20.   a.   Shares remaining $= 100,000 - \$500,000/\$16.82 = 70,273$.

CHAPTER 17
CAPITAL STRUCTURE DECISIONS: EXTENSIONS

OVERVIEW

Chapter 16 presented some basic material necessary to understand capital structure concepts, including a brief introduction to capital structure theory. We saw that debt financing concentrates a firm's business risk on its stockholders, but debt also increases the expected return on equity. We also saw that there is some optimal level of debt that maximizes a company's stock price, but that it is next to impossible to identify that optimal capital structure. In this chapter, we go into more detail on capital structure theory. This will give you a deeper under-standing of the benefits and costs associated with debt financing.

OUTLINE

Beginning in 1958, Modigliani and Miller (MM) addressed the capital structure issue in a rigorous, scientific fashion. The result is the well-known MM propositions.

■   MM began with a set of assumptions including constant debt costs, zero brokerage costs, perpetual cash flows, and zero growth. Initially, they also assumed zero taxes. MM used an arbitrage proof to develop two propositions.

 ❑   Proposition I:

$$V_L = V_U = EBIT/WACC = EBIT/k_{sU},$$

 ❑   where V_L = value of a leveraged firm, V_U = value of an unleveraged firm in the same risk class, and k_{sU} is the cost of stock for an unleveraged firm.

  ●   Proposition I tells us that the value of a firm is established by capitalizing the expected net operating income at the firm's weighted average cost of capital which is a constant equal to the cost of equity of an unleveraged (zero debt) firm. Thus, Proposition I implies that the value of a firm is independent of its leverage.

- Proposition I also implies (1) that a firm's WACC is completely independent of its capital structure, and (2) that the WACC for any firm, regardless of the amount of debt it uses, is equal to the cost of equity it would have if it used no debt.
  - ❏ Proposition II:

$$k_{sL} = k_{sU} + \text{Risk premium} = k_{sU} + (k_{sU} - k_d)(D/S).$$

- Here we see that the cost of equity to a leveraged firm, k_{sL}, is equal to the cost of equity to an unleveraged firm in the same risk class, k_{sU}, plus a risk premium whose size depends on both the differential between the costs of equity and debt to an unleveraged firm and the amount of leverage used.
- Proposition II states that as the firm's use of debt increases, its cost of equity also rises, and in a mathematically precise manner.

- Taken together, the two MM propositions imply that the inclusion of more debt in the capital structure will not increase a firm's value because the benefits of lower cost debt will be exactly offset by an increase in the riskiness, hence, in the cost of equity. Thus, the MM theory implies that in a world without taxes, both the value of a firm and its overall cost of capital are unaffected by its capital structure.

- MM used an *arbitrage proof* to support their propositions. They showed that, under their assumptions, if two companies differed only (1) in the way they are financed and (2) in their total market values, then investors would sell shares of the higher-valued firm, buy those of the lower-valued firm, and continue this process until the companies had exactly the same market value.
  - ❏ *Perfect arbitrage* occurs when you invest none of your own money, you have no risk, you have no future negative cash flows, but you end up with cash in your pocket.

MM reworked their theory in 1963 by adding corporate taxes. The result was two additional propositions. With corporate income taxes, they concluded that leverage will increase a firm's value. This occurs because interest on debt is a tax-deductible expense, hence more of a leveraged firm's operating income flows through to investors.

- Proposition I:

$$V_L = V_U + TD = EBIT(1 - T)/k_{sU} + TD.$$

  - ❏ Thus, the value of a leveraged firm is equal to the value of the unleveraged firm in the same risk class plus the gain from leverage, the value of the tax savings which equals the corporate tax rate times the amount of debt used.

- ❑ Note that for an unleveraged firm with perpetual cash flows, EBIT$(1 - T)$ = Net income = Total dividends. Thus, the value of the unleveraged firm is equal to the perpetual dividend divided by k_{sU}.
- ❑ Also note that the differential between V_U and V_L increases as the firm's use of debt increases, so a firm's value is maximized at virtually 100 percent debt financing.

■ Proposition II:

$$k_{sL} = k_{sU} + (k_{sU} - k_d)(1 - T)(D/S).$$

- ❑ Now, the cost of equity for a leveraged firm is still equal to the cost of equity for an unleveraged firm plus a risk premium, but the risk premium is reduced by the term $(1 - T)$.
- ❑ Thus, when corporate taxes are introduced, the cost of equity rises at a slower rate than it did in the absence of corporate taxes. Further, the cost of debt is reduced by the tax deductibility of interest payments. These two factors combine to produce the increase in firm value which is shown by Proposition I.
- ❑ MM's model with corporate taxes leads to the conclusion that firms should use almost 100 percent debt. Without taxes, both WACC and the firm's value (V) are constant. With corporate taxes, WACC declines and V rises as more and more debt is used, so the optimal capital structure, under MM with corporate taxes, is 100% debt. However, firms do not follow this prescription, and hence theorists have been searching for other models which better describe actual behavior.

In our discussion of business and financial risk, we focused on stand-alone risk. Now we shift our focus from a stand-alone risk to a market risk perspective.

■ Robert Hamada, using the Capital Asset Pricing Model (CAPM) and MM with corporate taxes model, developed an expression for the cost of equity to a leveraged firm:

$$k_{sL} = \text{Risk-free rate} + \text{Business risk premium} + \text{Financial risk premium}$$
$$= k_{RF} + (k_M - k_{RF})b_U + (k_M - k_{RF})b_U(1 - T)(D/S).$$

■ Equating the SML equation with Hamada's equation for k_{sL}, we ultimately obtain:

$$b = b_U[1 + (1 - T)(D/S)].$$

■ Thus, under the MM and CAPM assumptions, the equity beta of any firm is equal to the equity beta the firm would have if it used zero debt, adjusted upward by a factor that depends on (1) the corporate tax rate and (2) the amount of financial leverage employed.

■ The stock's market risk, which is measured by b, depends on both the firm's business risk as measured by b_U and its financial risk as measured by $b - b_U = b_U(1 - T)(D/S)$.

■ The Hamada relationship can be used to help estimate a company's or a division's cost of equity by leveraging up or down the betas of comparable proxy firms to reflect the firm's or division's capital structure and tax rate.

❑ The result is an estimate of the firm's or division's equity beta, given (1) its business risk as measured by the equity betas of other firms in the same line of business and (2) its financial risk as measured by its own capital structure and tax rate.

In 1976, Miller presented a capital structure model which included not only corporate taxes, but personal taxes as well.

■ The *Miller Model* takes this form:

$$V_U = \frac{EBIT(1 - T_c)(1 - T_s)}{k_{sU}}, \text{ and } V_L = V_U + \left[1 - \frac{(1 - T_c)(1 - T_s)}{(1 - T_d)}\right]D.$$

❑ Here T_c is the corporate tax rate, T_s is the personal tax rate on stock income, and T_d is the personal tax rate on income from debt.

❑ The term in brackets, multiplied by D, is the gain from leverage. The bracketed term replaces the factor $T = T_c$ in the MM model with corporate taxes.

❑ If all taxes are ignored, then $T_c = T_s = T_d = 0$, and the model reduces to the original MM model without taxes.

❑ If we ignore personal taxes, then $T_s = T_d = 0$, and the model reduces to the MM model with corporate taxes.

■ The gain from leverage in the Miller model depends on the values of T_c, T_s, and T_d as well as the amount of debt financing.

❑ Because taxes on capital gains are both lower than on ordinary income and can be deferred, the effective tax rate on stock income is normally less than that on bond income.

❑ When $T_s < T_d$, the bracketed term is less than T_c, and the value of financial leverage is less than it would be in the absence of personal taxes.

■ Thus, Miller's model confirms the earlier MM conclusion that the use of corporate debt increases the value of a firm, but the advantage is clearly less than TD, and hence personal taxes reduce the benefits of corporate debt. Note, however, that the Miller model still prescribes close to 100 percent debt as the value-maximizing capital structure.

❑ In his paper, Miller argued that firms in the aggregate would issue a mix of debt and equity securities such that the before-tax yields on corporate securities and the personal tax rates of the investors who bought these securities would adjust until an equilibrium was reached. At equilibrium, the tax advantage of debt to the firm would be exactly offset by personal taxation, and capital structure would have no effect on a firm's value or its cost of capital.

While the conclusions of the two MM models and the Miller model follow logically from the initial assumptions, these theories lack support because (1) their assumptions do not reflect actual market conditions, and (2) more important, their prescriptions are not followed. Some of the main objections include the following:

- Both MM and Miller assumed that personal and corporate leverage are perfect substitutes.
- Homemade leverage puts stockholders in greater danger of bankruptcy than does corporate leverage.

- Brokerage costs are assumed away, making the switch from leveraged to unleveraged costless.

- MM initially assumed that corporations and investors can borrow at the risk-free rate.

- Miller concluded that equilibrium would be reached, but to reach equilibrium the tax benefit from corporate debt must be the same for all firms, and it must be constant for an individual firm regardless of the amount of leverage used.

- MM and Miller assumed that there are no financial distress costs and they ignore agency costs.

- MM and Miller assume that all market participants have identical information about firms' prospects.

A potential problem with the MM and Miller models is that they ignore financial distress and agency costs. Quite a few firms go bankrupt every year, and the costs of financial distress, as well as agency costs, can be significant.

- Actual bankruptcy results in extraordinary costs such as forced sale of assets at below-market prices, deterioration of property, and court and administrative costs. The threat of financial distress also involves costs, since managers must spend more time on fending off bankruptcy than on making good operating decisions, as well as taking costly actions in attempts to ward off distress.

- In general, the probability of *financial distress* increases as more debt is used. The greater the use of debt financing, and the larger the fixed interest charges, the greater the probability that a decline in earnings will lead to financial distress, and hence the higher the probability that costs associated with financial distress will be incurred.

- ❑ An increase in the probability of future financial distress lowers the current value of a firm and raises its cost of capital.

- ❑ The effects of financial distress are also felt by a firm's bondholders. Firms experiencing financial distress have a higher probability of defaulting on debt payments, so the higher the probability of financial distress, the higher the required return on debt.

- ■ *Agency costs* also tend to increase as more and more debt is used.
  - ❑ Lost efficiency plus monitoring costs are agency costs that increase the cost of debt and thus reduces its advantage.

- ■ When these costs are considered, MM's Proposition I, with corporate taxes, becomes:

$$V_L = V_U + TD - \left(\begin{array}{c} \text{PV of expected} \\ \text{financial distress costs} \end{array} \right) - \left(\begin{array}{c} \text{PV of agency} \\ \text{costs} \end{array} \right).$$

- ■ This relationship is shown in Figure 1.

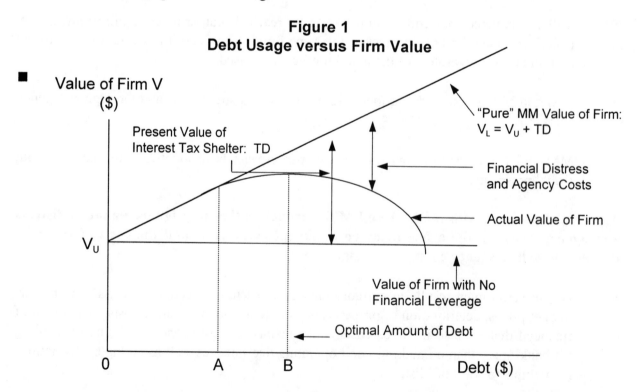

Figure 1
Debt Usage versus Firm Value

- ■ Here we see that the tax shelter effect dominates until debt reaches Point A. After Point A, the financial distress and agency costs begin to offset the tax advantages of debt financing. At Point B, the marginal tax benefits of debt are exactly offset by the marginal financial distress and agency costs, and beyond Point B, the disadvantages of using debt outweigh the benefits. However, the financial distress and agency costs cannot be estimated easily, and it is very difficult, if not impossible, to identify Point B in practice with any precision.

■ Note that financial distress and agency costs can also be added to the Miller model. When these are added, the relationship between value and debt is the same as when these costs are added to the MM with corporate taxes model. However, the "Pure" MM Value of Firm line would be less steep under Miller since the value of debt financing is reduced. Further, the Y intercept would be lowered because the addition of personal taxes reduces the value of the unleveraged firm.

Both the MM with corporate taxes and Miller models modified to include financial distress and agency costs are called trade-off models. That is, the optimal capital structure is found by balancing the tax shield benefits of leverage against the costs of leverage, and hence the costs and benefits are "traded off" against one another.

■ The trade-off models cannot be used to specify a firm's precise optimal capital structures, but they can enable us to make three statements about leverage:
  ❑ Firms with more business risk ought to use less debt than lower-risk firms, other things being equal, because the greater the business risk, the greater the probability of financial distress at any level of debt, hence the greater the expected costs of distress.
  ❑ Firms that have tangible, readily marketable assets can use more debt than firms whose value is derived primarily from intangible assets.
  ❑ Firms paying taxes at the highest rates gain the most benefit from debt financing and, hence, should carry more debt than firms in lower tax brackets.

■ Although the trade-off models present a logical framework for thought, empirical support for the trade-off models is not strong, suggesting that factors that are not incorporated into the models are at work.

The signaling, or asymmetric information, theory of capital structure was developed in an attempt to reconcile the MM/Miller theories with the pecking order method of financing observed by Professor Gordon Donaldson. By allowing that asymmetric (or different) information exists for different groups of market participants, certain actions may be implied for corporate financial policy.

■ Donaldson observed that there is a "pecking order" of financing, not the balanced approach that would result if the trade-off models accurately described real-world behavior.

■ The *signaling,* or *asymmetric information, theory* attempts to explain this "pecking order."
  ❑ Information asymmetries often exist between managers and investors.
  ❑ When such situations exist, a firm will issue new stock only when its stock price is overvalued by the market. If its stock is undervalued, the firm will issue debt.
  ❑ Because investors recognize all this, they tend to mark down a company's share price when it announces plans to issue new shares, since chances are that the announcement is signaling bad news, not good news.
  ❑ If managers believe that new stock sales will be regarded as negative signals, then they should maintain some "reserve borrowing capacity," so they can always issue debt on favorable terms if external financing is needed.

■ Industries which hold a significant amount of proprietary information, such as pharmaceutical or semiconductor industries, will have a higher degree of asymmetric information than retailing or trucking industries. Although signaling theory is applicable to all firms, its impact on managerial decisions varies from firm to firm.

■ Emerging firms with limited capital but good growth opportunities are recognized as having to use external financing, so the announcement of new stock offerings by a new company is not viewed with as much concern by investors as are offerings by mature firms with limited growth opportunities.

The great contribution of the trade-off models developed by MM and Miller is that these models identified the specific costs and benefits of using debt. Prior to these models, no capital structure theory existed, and we had no systematic approach to analyzing the effects of financial leverage.

■ The trade-off view is summarized graphically in Figure 2.

Figure 2

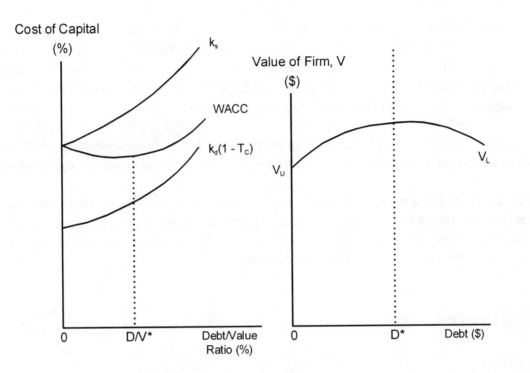

Effects of Debt Financing

❏ The left-hand graph shows the relationship between the debt ratio and capital costs. Both the cost of equity and cost of debt rise steadily with increasing leverage, but the rate of increase accelerates sharply at higher debt levels. The weighted average cost of capital first declines, then hits a minimum, and then begins to rise. Note, however, that the WACC curve is shallow, indicating the debt ratio does not have a pronounced effect on WACC over a fairly wide range of values.

❏ The right-hand graph shows that firm value first rises with debt usage, hits a peak, and then falls. Again, the relationship is such that small deviations from the optimal debt ratio do not have a large impact on value.

❏ Note in the figure that the same debt ratio that minimizes the cost of capital also maximizes firm value. Thus, the optimal capital structure can be defined in terms of either cost minimization or value maximization because the same capital structure does both.

■ Little disagreement exists in either business or academic circles that the general situation described above is correct. However, details can only be discovered by empirical testing. Unfortunately, firms which differ only in capital structure do not exist, and future earnings are not known with any certainty. Thus, empirical tests have not produced conclusive results.

■   We believe that there is a net benefit to debt financing, at least out to some point, but we also believe that firms should maintain a borrowing reserve. Thus, firms use debt on the basis of their tax rates, asset structures, and inherent riskiness, but they also try to maintain the ability to issue new debt at favorable rates if it becomes necessary to raise external capital when chaotic market conditions exist.

Wide variations in the use of financial leverage occur both across industries and among the individual firms in each industry. In addition, capital structures also change over time.

Firms should focus on market value capital structures and base their cost of capital calculations on target market value weights. Because market values do change, it would be impossible to keep the actual capital structure on target at all times, but this fact in no way detracts from the validity of market value targets.

SELF-TEST QUESTIONS

Definitional

1.   The addition of financial distress and agency costs leads to a WACC curve which first _____, then reaches a _____, and then _____.

2.   The optimal capital structure is that structure at which the marginal _____ of leverage equal the marginal _____.

3.   The signaling, or asymmetric information, theory relaxes the MM models' assumption that _____ _____ exists.

4.   By allowing for asymmetric information, Donaldson's _____ _____ method of financing can be explained.

5.   Difficulties in estimating the relationship between _____ ratios and the costs of _____ and _____ have made some managers reluctant to rely heavily on quantitative analysis to set the target capital structure.

6.   Conservative financial managers may try to maintain a target capital structure that is _____ than optimal.

7. External capital is particularly important to firms with high _____ _____.

8. Owner/managers may prefer additional _____ as opposed to common stock in order to maintain _____ of the company.

9. A firm's cost of capital should be based on _____ _____ _____ weights.

Conceptual

10. While signaling, or asymmetric information, theory applies to all firms, its impact on managerial decisions varies from firm to firm.

    a. True   **b.** False

11. As a general rule, the capital structure which *maximizes* stock price (firm value) also

    a. Maximizes earnings per share.
    b. Minimizes the probability of financial distress.
    c. Minimizes both the cost of equity and the cost of debt.
    d. Answers a, b, and c above are all correct.
    e. All the statements above are false.

12. Firms should use *more* debt if

    a. They are in a lower tax bracket.
    b. They have stable expected returns on their assets (low business risk).
    c. They employ standardized, tangible assets.
    d. Answers b and c above are correct.
    e. Answers a, b, and c above are correct.

13. If information asymmetries exist, then management is motivated to issue new stock only if the stock is

    a. Overvalued.
    b. Undervalued.
    c. Fairly valued.

14. Which of the following statements is most correct?

    a. The "pure MM" theory of capital structure, when income taxes are considered, suggests that the value of a firm rises as it uses more and more debt and that this increase is due to tax savings. Thus, the optimal capital structure under MM theory calls for 100 percent debt.

b. When the "pure MM" theory is modified to include bankruptcy costs, an optimal capital structure with some debt, but less than 100 percent debt, is found for the "typical" firm.

c. Under the signaling, or asymmetric information, theory the issuance of new common stock by a mature company is taken by investors as bad news. As a result, new stock issues depress the stock price. This implies that firms should, under normal conditions, use less debt than they otherwise might so as to have a reserve borrowing capacity which would enable them to avoid issuing stock under most conditions.

d. The above statements are all true.

e. The above statements are all false.

SELF-TEST PROBLEMS

(The following data apply to the next two Self-Test Problems.)

A firm with no debt financing has a firm value of $20 million. It has a corporate marginal tax rate of 34 percent. The firm's investors are estimated to have marginal tax rates of 31 percent on interest income and a weighted average of 28 percent on stock income. The firm is planning to change its capital structure by issuing $10 million in debt, and repurchasing $10 million of common stock.

1. According to the Modigliani-Miller view with corporate taxes, what is the value in millions of dollars of the leveraged firm?

   a. $20.00   **b.** $22.44   **c.** $23.40   **d.** $26.40   **e.** $30.00

2. According to the Miller view with corporate and personal taxes, what is the gain from leverage in millions of dollars?

   a. $0.00   **b.** $3.11   **c.** $4.65   **d.** $6.48   **e.** $8.50

(The following data apply to the next three Self-Test Problems.)

The Ensyder Trading Company (ETC) is a zero growth firm with an EBIT of $250,000 and a corporate tax rate of 40 percent. ETC uses $1 million of debt financing, and the cost of equity of an unleveraged firm in the same risk class is 15 percent. The personal tax rates of ETC's investors are 30 percent on interest income and 20 percent (on average) on income from common stocks.

3. What is the value of ETC according to MM with corporate taxes?

    a. $1,000,000   **b.** $1,114,000   **c.** $1,314,000   **d.** $1,400,000   **e.** $2,000,000

4. What is ETC's value rounded to the nearest thousand according to Miller (including personal taxes)?

    a. $1,000,000   **b.** $1,114,000   **c.** $1,314,000   **d.** $1,600,000   **e.** $2,000,000

5. Suppose that the present value of financial distress costs is estimated to be $800,000, and that, at a debt level of $1 million, ETC has a 20 percent probability of going bankrupt. Further, assume that the present value of agency costs are $50,000 at a $1,000,000 debt level. What is the firm's value rounded to the nearest thousand if these costs are added to the Miller model?

    a. $904,000   **b.** $1,114,000   **c.** $1,314,000   **d.** $1,600,000   **e.** $2,000,000

(The following data apply to the next five Self-Test Problems.)

Unleveraged Corporation (Firm U) has a total market value of $500,000, a tax rate of 40 percent, and earnings before interest and taxes (EBIT) of $100,000. Leveraged Corporation (Firm L) is identical in all respects to Firm U, but Firm L has $200,000 market (and book) value of debt outstanding. Firm L pays total annual interest of $16,000 on this debt. Both firms satisfy the MM assumptions.

6. What is the value of Firm L according to MM's Proposition I with corporate taxes?

    a. $500,000   **b.** $520,000   **c.** $540,000   **d.** $560,000   **e.** $580,000

7. What is Firm U's cost of equity?

    a. 10.00%   **b.** 10.34%   **c.** 11.00%   **d.** 12.00%   **e.** 13.26%

8. What is Firm L's cost of equity?

    a. 10.00%   **b.** 10.34%   **c.** 11.00%   **d.** 12.00%   **e.** 13.26%

9. What is Firm L's weighted average cost of capital?

    a. 10.00%   **b.** 10.34%   **c.** 11.00%   **d.** 12.00%   **e.** 13.26%

10. An alternative equation for a firm's cost of capital is

$$\text{WACC} = \frac{\text{EBIT}(1-T)}{V}.$$

What is Firm L's weighted average cost of capital according to this formula?

    a. 10.00%   **b.** 10.34%   **c.** 11.00%   **d.** 12.00%   **e.** 13.26%

ANSWERS TO SELF-TEST QUESTIONS

1. declines; minimum; rises
2. benefits; costs
3. perfect information
4. pecking order
5. debt; debt; equity

6. less
7. growth rates
8. debt; control
9. target market value

10. a. This statement is correct.

11. e. The capital structure which maximizes stock price also minimizes the firm's weighted average cost of capital. The probability of financial distress is minimized at zero debt. Also, note that neither the cost of debt nor the cost of equity is minimized at the optimal capital structure.

12. d. Firms gain the most benefits from using debt when they are in the highest tax bracket. Firms with highly variable expected returns and intangible, specialized assets should use lower levels of debt.

13. a. Management will want to issue new stock only if the excess value will benefit the existing stockholders and not be passed on to new investors.

14. d. Statements a, b, and c are all correct; therefore, statement d is the proper choice.

SOLUTIONS TO SELF-TEST PROBLEMS

1. c. $V_L = V_U + TD = \$20 + 0.34(\$10) = \$20 + \$3.4 = \$23.4$ million.

2. b. Gain from leverage $= \left[1 - \dfrac{(1 - T_c)(1 - T_s)}{(1 - T_d)}\right] D$

$$= \left[1 - \dfrac{(1 - 0.34)(1 - 0.28)}{(1 - 0.31)}\right]\$10$$

$$= [1 - 0.689]\$10 = 0.311(\$10) = \$3.11 \text{ million.}$$

Note that the gain from leverage is reduced when personal taxes are added.

3. d. $V_L = V_U + TD = \dfrac{EBIT(1 - T)}{k_{sU}} + TD$

$$= \dfrac{\$250,000(0.6)}{0.15} + 0.4(\$1,000,000)$$

$$= \$1,000,000 + \$400,000 = \$1,400,000.$$

4. b. $V_L = V_U + \left[1 - \dfrac{(1 - T_c)(1 - T_s)}{(1 - T_d)}\right] D$

$$= V_U + \left[1 - \dfrac{0.6(0.8)}{0.7}\right]\$1,000,000$$

$$= V_U + 0.3143(\$1,000,000) = V_U + \$314,286.$$

Now, the addition of personal taxes also reduces the value of V_U:

$$V_U = \dfrac{EBIT(1 - T_c)(1 - T_s)}{k_{sU}} = \dfrac{\$250,000(0.6)(0.8)}{0.15} = \$800,000.$$

Thus, $V_L = \$800,000 + \$314,286 = \$1,114,286 \approx \$1,114,000.$

5. a. $V_L = V_{Miller} - PV$ (Financial distress costs) $- PV$ (Agency costs)
   $= \$1,114,286 - 0.2(\$800,000) - \$50,000 = \$904,286 \approx \$904,000.$

6.   e. $V_L = V_U + TD = \$500,000 + 0.4(\$200,000) = \$500,000 + \$80,000 = \$580,000.$

7.   d. $V_U = \dfrac{EBIT(1-T)}{k_{sU}}; \$500,000 = \dfrac{\$100,000(0.6)}{k_{sU}}; \ k_{sU} = \dfrac{\$60,000}{\$500,000} = 12.0\%.$

8.   e.   First, note that Firm L's cost of debt is 8.0 percent:

$k_d = \$16,000/\$200,000 = 8.0\%.$

Next, note that $V_L = \$580,000$ and D = $200,000. Thus, Firm L's equity value is S = $580,000 – $200,000 = $380,000. Finally,

$$\begin{aligned}
k_{sL} &= k_{sU} + (k_{sU} - k_d)(1 - T)(D/S) \\
&= 12.0\% + (12.0\% - 8.0\%)(0.6)(\$200,000/\$380,000) \\
&= 12.0\% + 1.26\% = 13.26\%.
\end{aligned}$$

9.   b. $\begin{aligned}[t]
WACC &= w_d k_d(1 - T) + w_{ce}k_s \\
&= (\$200,000/\$580,000)(8.00\%)(0.6) + (\$380,000/\$580,000)(13.26\%) \\
&= 10.34\%.
\end{aligned}$

10.   b. $WACC = EBIT(1 - T)/V = \$100,000(0.6)/\$580,000 = 10.34\%.$

CHAPTER 18
DISTRIBUTIONS TO SHAREHOLDERS:
DIVIDENDS AND REPURCHASES

OVERVIEW

Income earned by companies can be reinvested in operating assets, used to acquire securities, used to retire debt, or distributed to stockholders. If the decision is made to distribute income to stockholders, three key issues arise: (1) What percentage should be distributed? (2) Should the distribution be as cash dividends, or should the cash be passed on to shareholders by buying back some of the stock? (3) How stable should the distribution be; that is, should the funds paid out from year to year be stable and dependable, which stock-holders would probably prefer, or be allowed to vary with the firm's cash flows and investment requirements, which would probably be better from the firm's standpoint? These three issues, as well as stock dividends and stock splits, are discussed in this chapter.

OUTLINE

Dividend policy involves the decision to pay out earnings versus retaining them for reinvestment in the firm.

■ The *target payout ratio* is defined as the percentage of net income to be paid out as cash dividends, and it should be based in large part on investors' preferences for dividends versus capital gains.

■ The constant growth stock model, $P_0 = D_1/(k_s - g)$, shows that paying out more dividends will increase stock price. However, if D_1 is raised then less money will be available for reinvestment, that will cause the expected growth rate to decline, and that would tend to lower the stock's price.

■ The firm's *optimal dividend policy* must strike a balance between current cash dividends and future growth so as to maximize the stock price.

A number of theories have been proposed to explain how factors interact to determine a firm's optimal dividend policy. These theories include: (1) the dividend irrelevance theory, (2) the bird-in-the-hand theory, and (3) the tax preference theory.

■ Modigliani and Miller (MM), the principal proponents of the *dividend irrelevance theory*, argue that the value of the firm depends only on the income produced by its assets, not on how this income is split between dividends and retained earnings.

   ❑ MM prove their proposition, but only under a set of restrictive assumptions including the absence of taxes and brokerage costs.

   ❑ Obviously, taxes and brokerage costs do exist, so the MM conclusions on dividend irrelevance may not be valid under real-world conditions. The validity of a theory must be judged by empirical tests, not by the realism of its assumptions.

■ The principal conclusion of MM's dividend irrelevance theory is that dividend policy does not affect the required rate of return on equity, k_s. Relaxing this assumption provides the basis for the *bird-in-the-hand theory*.

   ❑ Myron Gordon and John Lintner argue that k_s decreases as the dividend payout is increased because investors are less certain of receiving income from capital gains that presumably result from retained earnings than they are of receiving dividend payments.

   ❑ MM call the Gordon-Lintner argument the *bird-in-the-hand fallacy* because Gordon and Lintner believe that investors view dividends in the hand as being less risky than capital gains in the bush. In MM's view, however, most investors plan to reinvest their dividends in the stock of the same or similar firms, and the riskiness of the firm's cash flows to investors in the long run is determined by the riskiness of operating cash flows, not by dividend payout policy.

■ The *tax preference theory* states that investors may prefer to have companies retain most of their earnings because of various tax advantages. Investors then would be willing to pay more for low payout companies than for otherwise similar high payout companies. There are three tax-related reasons for thinking that investors might prefer a low dividend payout to a high payout.

   ❑ Long-term capital gains are taxed at a maximum rate of 20 percent. Therefore, wealthy investors might prefer to have companies retain and plow earnings back into the business. Earnings growth would presumably lead to higher stock prices, and thus lower-taxed capital gains would be substituted for higher-taxed dividends.

   ❑ Taxes are not paid on the gain until a stock is sold.

   ❑ If a stock is held by someone until he or she dies, no capital gains tax is due at all.

Empirical testing of the dividend theories has not produced definitive results regarding which theory is correct. Two reasons for this are: We cannot find a set of publicly owned firms that differ only in their dividend policies, nor can we obtain precise estimates of each sample firm's cost of equity.

- No one can establish a clear relationship between dividend policy and the cost of equity.
  - Investors cannot be seen to uniformly prefer either higher or lower dividends.
  - However, *individual* investors do have strong preferences.

- Both evidence and logic suggest that investors prefer firms which follow a *stable, predictable dividend policy*.

There are two other issues that have a bearing on optimal dividend policy: (1) the information content, or signaling, hypothesis and (2) the clientele effect.

- It has been observed that a dividend increase announcement is often accompanied by an increase in the stock price.
  - This might be interpreted by some to mean that investors prefer dividends to capital gains, thus supporting the Gordon-Lintner hypothesis.
  - However, MM argue that a dividend increase is a signal to investors that the firm's management forecasts good future earnings. Thus, MM argue that investors' reactions to dividend announcements do not necessarily show that investors prefer dividends to retained earnings. Rather, the fact that the stock price changes merely indicates that there is an important information content in dividend announcements. This is referred to as the *information content, or signaling, hypothesis*.

- MM also suggest that a *clientele effect* might exist.
  - Some stockholders (for example, retirees) prefer current income; therefore, they would want the firm to pay out a high percentage of its earnings as dividends.
  - Other stockholders have no need for current income (for example, doctors in their peak earning years) and they would simply reinvest any dividends received, after first paying income taxes on the dividend income. Therefore, they would want the firm to retain most of its earnings.
  - Thus, a firm establishes a dividend policy and then attracts a specific clientele that is drawn to this dividend policy. Those who do not like the dividend policy can simply sell their shares to those that do.

    ❑   To the extent that stockholders can switch firms, a firm can change from one dividend payout policy to another and then let stockholders who do not like the new policy sell to other investors who do. However, frequent switching would be inefficient because of brokerage costs, the likelihood that stockholders who are selling will have to pay capital gains taxes, and a possible shortage of investors who like the firm's newly adopted dividend policy.

Dividend stability is important.

■   Profits and cash flows vary over time, as do investment opportunities. Taken alone, this suggests that corporations should vary their dividends over time, increasing them when cash flows are large and the need for funds is low and lowering them when cash is in short supply relative to investment opportunities.

    ❑   However, many stockholders rely on dividends to meet expenses, and they would be seriously inconvenienced if the dividend stream were unstable.

    ❑   Reducing dividends to make funds available for capital investment could send incorrect signals to investors who may push down the stock price because they interpret the dividend cut to mean that the company's future earnings prospects have been diminished.

■   Dividend stability has two components.

    ❑   How dependable is the growth rate?

    ❑   Can we count on at least receiving the current dividend in the future?

■   The most stable policy, from an investor's standpoint, is that of a firm whose dividend growth rate is predictable.

    ❑   Such a company's total return (dividend yield plus capital gains yield) would be relatively stable over the long run, and its stock would be a good hedge against inflation.

■   The second most stable policy is where stockholders can be reasonably sure that the current dividend will not be reduced—it may not grow at a steady rate, but management will probably be able to avoid cutting the dividend.

■   Investors prefer stocks that pay more predictable dividends to stocks which pay the same average amount of dividends but in a more erratic manner. Thus, the cost of equity will be minimized, and the stock price maximized, if a firm stabilizes its dividends as much as possible.

When deciding how much cash should be distributed to stockholders, two points should be kept in mind: (1) The overriding objective is to maximize shareholder value, and (2) the firm's cash flows really belong to its shareholders, so management should refrain from retaining income unless it can be reinvested to produce returns higher than shareholders could themselves earn by investing the cash in investments of equal risk.

■ When establishing a dividend policy, one size does not fit all.

■ For a given firm, the optimal payout ratio is a function of four factors: (1) investors' preferences for dividends versus capital gains, (2) the firm's investment opportunities, (3) its target capital structure, and (4) the availability and cost of external capital.
   ❑ The last three elements are combined in the *residual dividend model*.

■ *Residual dividend policy* is based on the premise that investors prefer to have a firm retain and reinvest earnings rather than pay them out in dividends if the rate of return the firm can earn on reinvested earnings exceeds the rate of return investors can obtain for themselves on other investments of comparable risk. Further, it is less expensive for the firm to use retained earnings than it is to issue new common stock. A firm using the residual policy would follow these four steps:
   ❑ Determine the optimal capital budget.
   ❑ Determine the amount of equity needed to finance the optimal capital budget, given the firm's target capital structure.
   ❑ Use retained earnings to meet equity requirements to the extent possible.
   ❑ Pay dividends only if more earnings are available than are needed to support the optimal capital budget.

■ If a firm rigidly follows the residual dividend policy, then dividends paid in any given year can be expressed as follows:

■ Dividends = Net Income – [(Target Equity Ratio)(Total Capital Budget)].

■ Since investment opportunities and earnings will surely vary from year to year, strict adherence to the residual dividend policy would result in unstable dividends. Firms should use the residual policy to help set their *long-run target payout ratios*, but not as a guide to the payout in any one year.

■ Companies use the residual dividend model to help understand the determinants of an optimal dividend policy, but they typically use a computerized financial forecasting model when setting the target payout ratio.

❑ Most companies use the computer model to find a dividend pattern over the forecast period that will provide sufficient equity to support the capital budget without having to sell new common stock or move the capital structure ratio outside the optimal range.

■ Some companies, especially those in cyclical industries, have difficulty maintaining in bad times a dividend that is really too low in good times. Such companies set a very low "regular" dividend and then supplement it with an "extra" dividend when times are good. This is called a *low-regular-dividend-plus-extras* policy.

■ Dividends clearly depend more on cash flows, which reflect the company's ability to pay dividends, than on current earnings, which are heavily influenced by accounting practices and which do not necessarily reflect the ability to pay dividends.

Firms usually pay dividends on a quarterly basis in accordance with the following payment procedures:

■ *Declaration date*. This is the day on which the board of directors declares the dividend. At this time they set the amount of the dividend to be paid, the holder-of-record date, and the payment date.

■ *Holder-of-record date*. This is the date the stock transfer books of the corporation are closed. Those shareholders who are listed on the company's books on this date are the holders of record and they receive the announced dividend.

■ *Ex-dividend date*. This date is two days prior to the holder-of-record date. Shares purchased after the ex-dividend date are not entitled to the dividend. This practice is a convention of the brokerage business which allows sufficient time for stock transfers to be made on the books of the corporation.

■ *Payment date*. This is the day when dividend checks are actually mailed to the holders of record.

Firms should try to establish a rational dividend policy and then stick with it. Dividend policy can be changed, but this can cause problems because such changes can inconvenience the firm's existing stockholders, send unintended signals, and convey the impression of dividend instability, all of which can have negative implications for stock prices. Still, economic circumstances do change, and occasionally such changes dictate that a firm should alter its dividend policy.

Many firms have instituted dividend reinvestment plans (DRIPs) whereby stockholders can automatically reinvest dividends received in the stock of the paying corporation. Income taxes on the amount of the dividends must be paid even though stock rather than cash is received.

■ There are two types of DRIPs.
   ❑ Plans which involve only "old stock" that is already outstanding.
   ❑ Plans which involve newly issued stock.

■ Stockholders choose between continuing to receive dividend checks or having the company use the dividends to buy more stock in the corporation.

■ One interesting aspect of DRIPs is that they are forcing corporations to reexamine their basic dividend policies. A high participation rate in a DRIP suggests that stockholders might be better off if the firm simply reduced cash dividends, which would save stockholders some personal income taxes.

■ Some companies have expanded their DRIPs by moving to *open enrollment* whereby anyone can purchase the firm's stock directly and bypass brokers' commissions.

Dividend policy decisions are truly exercises in informed judgment, not decisions quantified based on rules. Regardless of the debate on the relevancy of dividend policy, it is possible to identify several factors that influence dividend policy. These factors are grouped into four broad categories.

■ Constraints: (1) Bond indentures, (2) preferred stock restrictions, (3) impairment of capital rule, (4) availability of cash, and (5) penalty tax on improperly accumulated earnings.

■ Investment opportunities: (1) Number of profitable investment opportunities and (2) possibility of accelerating or delaying projects.

■ Alternative sources of capital: (1) Cost of selling new stock, (2) ability to substitute debt for equity, and (3) control.

■ Effects of dividend policy on k_s: (1) Stockholders' desire for current versus future income, (2) perceived riskiness of dividends versus capital gains, (3) the tax advantage of capital gains over dividends, and (4) the information content of dividends (signaling).

Dividend policy decisions are exercises in informed judgment, not decisions that can be based on a precise mathematical model.

- Dividend policy is not an independent decision—the dividend decision is made jointly with capital structure and capital budgeting decisions. The underlying reason for this joint process is asymmetric information, which influences managerial actions in two ways.
  - In general, managers do not want to issue new common stock. Managers strongly prefer to use retained earnings as their primary source of new equity.
  - Dividend changes provide signals about managers' beliefs as to their firms' future prospects. Thus, dividend reductions, or worse yet, omissions, generally have a significant negative effect on a firm's stock price.

- In setting dividend policy, managers should begin by considering the firm's future investment opportunities relative to its projected internal sources of funds.

- Managers should use the residual dividend model to set dividends, but in a long-term framework.

- The current dollar dividend should be set so that there is an extremely low probability that the dividend, once set, will ever have to be lowered or omitted.

- In general, firms with superior investment opportunities should set lower payouts, hence retain more earnings, than firms with poor investment opportunities. The degree of uncertainty also influences the decision.
  - If there is a great deal of uncertainty in the forecasts of free cash flows, then it is best to be conservative and to set a lower current dollar dividend.
  - Firms with postponable investment opportunities can afford to set a higher dollar dividend, because, in times of stress, investments can be postponed for a year or two, thus increasing the cash available for dividends.
  - Firms whose cost of capital is largely unaffected by changes in the debt ratio can also afford to set a higher payout ratio, because they can, in times of stress, more easily issue additional debt to maintain the capital budgeting program without having to cut dividends to issue stock.

- Today's dividend decisions are constrained by policies that were set in the past, hence setting a policy for the next five years necessarily begins with a review of the current situation.

- Because dividend policy still remains one of the most judgmental decisions that firms must make, it is always set by the board of directors. The financial staff analyzes the situation and makes a recommendation, but the board makes the final decision.

Stock dividends and stock splits are often used to lower a firm's stock price and, at the same time, to conserve its cash resources.

■ The effect of a *stock split* is an increase in the number of shares outstanding and a reduction in the par, or stated, value of the shares. For example, if a firm had 1,000 shares of stock outstanding with a par value of $100 per share, a 2-for-1 split would reduce the par value to $50 and increase the number of shares to 2,000.

❑ The total net worth of the firm remains unchanged.

❑ The stock split does not involve any cash payment, only additional certificates representing new shares.

❑ Stock splits often occur due to the widespread belief that there is an *optimal price range* for each stock.

❑ Stock splits are generally used after a sharp price run-up to produce a large price reduction.

■ A *stock dividend* requires an accounting entry transfer from retained earnings to common stock.

❑ Again, no cash is involved with this "dividend." Net worth remains unchanged, and the number of shares is increased.

❑ Stock dividends used on a regular annual basis will keep the stock price more or less constrained.

■ From a pure economic standpoint, stock dividends and splits are just additional pieces of paper. However, they provide management with a relatively low-cost way of signaling that the firm's prospects look good.

❑ All in all, it probably makes sense to employ stock dividends/splits when a firm's prospects are favorable especially if the price of its stock has gone beyond the normal trading range.

Stock repurchases are an alternative to dividends for transmitting cash to stockholders.

■ There are two principal types of repurchases: (1) Situations where the firm has cash available for distribution to its stockholders and it distributes this cash by repurchasing shares rather than by paying cash dividends, and (2) situations where the firm concludes that its capital structure is too heavily weighted with equity, and then it sells debt and uses the proceeds to buy back its stock.

■ Stock repurchased by the issuing firm is called *treasury stock.*

- ■ Advantages of repurchases include:
  - ❑ The repurchase is often motivated by management's belief that the firm's shares are undervalued.
  - ❑ The stockholder is given a choice of whether or not to sell his stock to the firm.
  - ❑ The repurchase can remove a large block of stock overhanging the market.
  - ❑ If an increase in cash flow is temporary, the cash can be distributed to stockholders as a repurchase rather than as a dividend, which could not be maintained in the future.
  - ❑ The company has more flexibility in adjusting the total distribution than it would if the entire distribution were in the form of cash dividends, because repurchases can be varied from year to year without giving off adverse signals.
  - ❑ Repurchases can be used to produce large-scale changes in capital structures.
  - ❑ Companies that grant large numbers of options can repurchase stock and then reissue those shares when options are exercised, thus avoiding the dilution that would occur if new shares were sold to cover exercised options.

- ■ Disadvantages of repurchases include:
  - ❑ Repurchases are not as dependable as cash dividends; therefore, the stock price may benefit more from cash dividends.
  - ❑ Selling stockholders may not be aware of all the implications of the repurchase; therefore, repurchases are usually announced in advance.
  - ❑ If a firm pays too high a price for the repurchased stock, it is to the disadvantage of the remaining stockholders.

- ■ Increases in the size and frequency of repurchases in recent years suggest that companies are doing more repurchases and paying out less cash as dividends.

SELF-TEST QUESTIONS

Definitional

1. MM argue that a firm's dividend policy has ____ _____ on a stock's price.

2. Gordon and Lintner hypothesize that investors value a dollar of _____ more highly than a dollar of expected _____ _____.

3. A company may be forced to increase its _____ ratio in order to avoid a tax on retained earnings deemed to be unnecessary for the conduct of the business.

4. Some stockholders prefer dividends to _____ _____ because of a need for current _____.

5. If the _____ of a firm's stock increases with the announcement of an increase in dividends, it may be due to the _____ content in the dividend announcement rather than to a preference for dividends over capital gains.

6. A firm with _____ earnings is most appropriate for using the policy of "extra" dividends.

7. The stock transfer books of a corporation are closed on the _____-____-_____ date.

8. The ____-_____ date occurs two days prior to the _____-____-_____ date and provides time for stock transfers to be recorded on the firm's books.

9. Actual payment of a dividend is made on the _____ date as announced by the _____ ____ _____.

10. Many firms have instituted _____ _____ plans whereby stockholders can use their dividends to purchase additional shares of the company's stock.

11. A stock split involves a reduction in the _____ _____ of the common stock, but no accounting transfers are made between accounts.

12. The assumption that some investors prefer a high dividend payout while others prefer a low payout is called the _____ effect.

13. The residual dividend policy is based on the fact that new common stock is _____ _____ than retained earnings.

14. Stock repurchased by the firm which issued it is called _____ _____.

15. _____ _____ involves the decision to pay out earnings versus retaining them for reinvestment in the firm.

16. The _____ _____ _____ is defined as the percentage of net income to be paid out as cash dividends.

17. The _____ _____ theory states that investors may prefer to have companies retain most of their earnings because of various tax advantages.

18.   Dividend _____ has two components: (1) How dependable is the growth rate and (2) can we count on at least receiving the current dividend in the future?

19.   The _____ _____ _____ is based on the premise that investors prefer to have a firm retain and reinvest earnings rather than to pay them out in dividends, if the rate of return the firm can earn on reinvested earnings exceeds the rate of return investors can obtain for themselves on other investments of comparable risk.

20.   Some companies have expanded their DRIPs by moving to _____ _____ whereby anyone can purchase the firm's stock directly and bypass brokers' commissions.

21.   The dividend decision is made jointly with _____ _____ and _____ _____ decisions.

22.   _____ _____ are an alternative to dividends for transmitting cash to stockholders.

Conceptual

23.   An increase in cash dividends will always result in an increase in the price of the common stock because D_1 will increase in the stock valuation model.

       a. True   **b.** False

24.   A stock split will affect the amounts shown in which of the following balance sheet accounts?

       a. Common stock   **d.** Cash
       b. Pain-in capital   **e.** None of the above accounts.
       c. Retained earnings

25.   If investors prefer dividends to capital gains, then

       a. The required rate of return on equity, k_s, will not be affected by a change in dividend policy.
       b. The cost of capital will not be affected by a change in dividend policy.
       c. k_s will increase as the payout ratio is reduced.
       d. k_s will decrease as the retention rate increases.
       e. A policy conforming to the residual dividend model will maximize stock price.

26. Which of the following statements is most correct?

    a. Modigliani and Miller's theory of the effect of dividend policy on the value of a firm has been called the bird-in-the-hand theory, because MM argued that a dividend in the hand is less risky than a potential capital gain in the bush. After extensive empirical tests, this theory is now accepted by most financial experts.

    b. According to proponents of the dividend irrelevance theory, if a company's stock price rises after the firm announces a greater-than-expected dividend increase, the price increase occurs because of signaling effects, not because of investors' preferences for dividends over capital gains.

    c. Both statements a and b are correct.

    d. Both statements a and b are false.

27. Which of the following statements is most correct?

    a. The residual dividend policy calls for the establishment of a fixed, stable dividend (or dividend growth rate) and then for the level of investment each year to be determined as a residual equal to net income minus the established dividends.

    b. According to the residual dividend policy, if a firm has a large number of profitable investment opportunities this will tend to produce a lower optimal dividend payout ratio.

    c. According to the text, a firm would probably maximize its stock price if it established a specific dividend payout ratio, say 40 percent, and then paid that percentage of earnings out each year because stockholders would then know exactly how much dividend income to count on when they planned their spending for the coming year.

    d. If you buy a stock after the ex-dividend date but before the dividend has been paid, then you, and not the seller, will receive the next dividend check the company sends out.

    e. Each of the above statements is false.

28.   Which of the following statements is most correct?

    a. According to the asymmetric information, or signaling, theory of capital structure, the announcement of a new stock issue by a mature firm would generally lead to an *increase* in the price of the firm's stock.

    b. According to the asymmetric information, or signaling, theory of capital structure, the announcement of a new stock issue by a mature firm would generally lead to a *decrease* in the price of the firm's stock.

    c. If Firm A's managers believe in the asymmetric information theory, but Firm B's managers do not, then, other things held constant, Firm A would probably have the *higher* normal target debt ratio.

    d. There is no such thing as the asymmetric information theory of capital structure, at least according to the text.

    e. Statements b and c are both true.

29.   Which of the following statements is most correct?

    a. According to the tax preference theory, investors prefer dividends and, as a result, the higher the payout ratio, the higher the value of the firm.

    b. According to the bird-in-the-hand theory, investors prefer cash to paper (stock), so if a company announces that it plans to repurchase some of its stock, this causes the price of the stock to increase.

    c. According to the dividend irrelevance theory developed by Modigliani and Miller, stock dividends (but not cash dividends) are irrelevant because they "merely divide the pie into thinner slices."

    d. According to the information content, or signaling, hypothesis, the fact that stock prices generally increase when an increase in the dividend is announced demonstrates that investors prefer higher to lower payout ratios.

    e. According to the text, the residual dividend policy is more appropriate for setting a company's long-run target payout ratio than for determining the payout ratio on a year-to-year basis.

30.   Which of the following statements is most correct?

    a. Stock prices generally rise on the ex-dividend date, and that increase is especially great if the company increases the dividend.

    b. Dividend reinvestment plans are popular with investors because investors who do not need cash income can have their dividends reinvested in the company's stock and thereby avoid having to pay income taxes on the dividend income until they sell the stock.

c. In the past, stock dividends and stock splits were frequently used by corporations which wanted to lower the prices of their stocks to an "optimal trading range." However, recent empirical studies have demonstrated that stock dividends and stock splits generally cause stock prices to decline, so companies today rarely split their stock or pay stock dividends.

d. Statements a, b, and c are all false.

e. Statements a, b, and c are all true.

SELF-TEST PROBLEMS

1. Express Industries' expected net income for next year is $1 million. The company's target and current capital structure is 40 percent debt and 60 percent common equity. The optimal capital budget for next year is $1.2 million. If Express uses the residual theory of dividends to determine next year's dividend payout, what is the expected payout ratio?

   a. 0% **b.** 10% **c.** 28% **d.** 42% **e.** 56%

2. Amalgamated Shippers has a current and target capital structure of 30 percent debt and 70 percent equity. This past year Amalgamated, which uses the residual dividend model, had a dividend payout ratio of 47.5 percent and net income of $800,000. What was Amalgamated's capital budget?

   a. $400,000 **b.** $500,000 **c.** $600,000 **d.** $700,000 **e.** $800,000

3. The Aikman Company's optimal capital structure calls for 40 percent debt and 60 percent common equity. The interest rate on its debt is a constant 12 percent; its cost of common stock is 18 percent; and its federal-plus-state tax rate is 40 percent. Aikman has the following investment opportunities:

   Project A: Cost = $5 million; IRR = 22%.
   Project B: Cost = $5 million; IRR = 14%.
   Project C: Cost = $5 million; IRR = 11%.

   Aikman expects to have net income of $7 million. If Aikman bases its dividends on the residual policy, what will its payout ratio be?

   a. 22.62% **b.** 14.29% **c.** 31.29% **d.** 25.62% **e.** 18.75%

4.   Hiers Automotive Supply Inc.'s stock trades at $100 a share. The company is contemplating a 4-for-3 stock split. Assuming that the stock split will have no effect on the market value of its equity, what will be the company's stock price following the stock split?

    a. $50.00   b. $62.50   c. $70.00   d. $75.00   e. $80.00

5.   Ridgdill Corporation has net income of $8,000,000 and it has 1,000,000 shares of common stock outstanding. The company's stock currently trades at $30 a share. Ridgdill is considering a plan where it will use available cash to repurchase 15 percent of its shares in the open market. The repurchase is expected to have no effect on either net income or the company's P/E ratio. What will be its stock price following the stock repurchase?

    a. $35.29   b. $32.00   c. $36.89   d. $35.15   e. $31.43

ANSWERS TO SELF-TEST QUESTIONS

1.	no effect	12.	clientele
2.	dividends; capital gains	13.	more costly
3.	payout	14.	treasury stock
4.	capital gains; income	15.	Dividend policy
5.	price (value); information	16.	target payout ratio
6.	volatile (fluctuating)	17.	tax preference
7.	holder-of-record	18.	stability
8.	ex-dividend; holder-of-record	19.	residual dividend policy
9.	payment; board of directors	20.	open enrollment
10.	dividend reinvestment	21.	capital structure; capital budgeting
11.	par value	22.	Stock repurchases

23.   b. A dividend increase could be perceived by investors as signifying poor investment opportunities and hence lower growth in future earnings, thus reducing g in the DCF model. The net effect on stock price is uncertain.

24.   e. A stock split will affect the par value and number of shares outstanding. However, no dollar values will be affected.

25.   c. This is the Gordon-Lintner hypothesis. If investors view dividends as being less risky than potential capital gains, then the cost of equity is inversely related to the payout ratio.

26. b. Statement a is false; the proponents of this theory were Gordon and Lintner and empirical tests have not proven any of the dividend theories. Statement b is correct.

27. b. Statement a is false; the residual dividend policy calls for the determination of the optimal capital budget and then the dividend is established as a residual of net income minus the amount of retained earnings necessary for the capital budget. Statement b is correct. Statement c is false; a constant payout policy would lead to uncertainty of dividends due to fluctuating earnings. Statement d is false; if a stock is bought after the ex-dividend date the dividend remains with the seller of the stock.

28. b. The asymmetric information theory suggests that investors regard the announcement of a stock sale as bad news: If the firm had really good investment opportunities, it would use debt financing so that existing stockholders would get all the benefits from the good projects. Therefore, the announcement of a stock sale leads to a decline in the price of the firm's stock. In order to reduce the chances of having to issue stock, firms therefore set low target debt ratios, which give them "reserve borrowing capacity."

29. e. Statements a, b, c, and d are false, but statement e is true.

30. d. The statements are all false.

SOLUTIONS TO SELF-TEST PROBLEMS

1. c. The $1,200,000 capital budget will be financed using 40 percent debt and 60 percent equity. Therefore, the equity requirement will be 0.6($1,200,000) = $720,000. Since the expected net income is $1,000,000, $280,000 will be available to pay as dividends. Thus, the payout ratio is expected to be $280,000/$1,000,000 = 0.28 = 28%.

2. c. Of the $800,000 in net income, 0.475($800,000) = $380,000 was paid out as dividends. Thus, $420,000 was retained in the firm for investment. This is the equity portion of the total capital budget, or 70 percent of the total capital budget. Therefore, the total capital budget was $420,000/0.7 = $600,000.

3.   b.   WACC $= 0.4(12\%)(0.6) + 0.6(18\%) = 13.68\%$.

We see that the capital budget should be $10 million, since only Projects A and B have IRRs > WACC. We know that 60 percent of the $10 million should be equity. Therefore, the company should pay dividends of:

Dividends = NI − Needed equity = $7,000,000 − $6,000,000 = $1,000,000.

Payout ratio = $1,000,000/$7,000,000 = 0.1429 = 14.29%.

4.   d. $P_0 = \$100$; Split $= 4$ for 3; New $P_0 = ?$ $P_{0\,New} = \dfrac{\$100}{4/3} = \$75.00$.

5.   a.   NI = $8,000,000; Shares = 1,000,000; $P_0 = \$30$; Repurchase = 15%; New $P_0 = ?$

Repurchase $= 0.15 \times 1,000,000 = 150,000$ shares.

Repurchase amount $= 150,000 \times \$30.00 = \$4,500,000$.

$$EPS_{Old} = \frac{NI}{Shares} = \frac{\$8,000,000}{1,000,000} = \$8.00.$$

$$P/E = \frac{\$30}{\$8} = 3.75\times.$$

$$EPS_{New} = \frac{\$8,000,000}{1,000,000 - 150,000} = \frac{\$8,000,000}{850,000} = \$9.41.$$

$Price_{New} = EPS_{New} \times P/E = \$9.41 \times 3.75 = \$35.29$.

CHAPTER 19
INITIAL PUBLIC OFFERINGS, INVESTMENT BANKING, AND FINANCIAL RESTRUCTURING

OVERVIEW

In Chapters 9 and 10, the basics of bond and stock financing were discussed, as well as how they are valued. In this chapter additional topics related to long-term financing are discussed, including why firms sell equity to the public, how stocks and bonds are issued, the regulation of securities markets, and how bonds and preferred stocks are refunded.

OUTLINE

Most companies are originally financed by their owner/founders. As they grow, their first external financing is usually from a private placement of equity to an accredited individual investor called an angel.

■ Accredited investors include the firm's officers and directors, high wealth individuals, and institutional investors.

■ A private placement can only be made to accredited investors or a small number of non-accredited investors.

As the firm grows, it might sell equity to a venture capital fund.

"Going public" means selling some of a company's stock to outside investors and then letting the stock trade in public markets.

■ *Going public* has the following advantages:
   ❑ The original owners are able to *diversify* their holdings by selling some of their stock in a public offering.
   ❑ Public ownership *increases* the stock's *liquidity*.
   ❑ New corporate cash is more *easily raised* by a publicly owned company.
   ❑ Going public *establishes the firm's value* in the market place.
   ❑ Public companies have an easier time in merger negotiations, whether they are trying to acquire another company or if they are trying to sell themselves.

    ❑ Public companies often find it is easier to sell their products to new customers.

■ Going public has the following disadvantages:
    ❑ A publicly owned company must file quarterly and annual reports with various governmental agencies. These reports can be *costly*.
    ❑ Publicly owned firms must *disclose* operating and ownership data.
    ❑ The opportunities for owners/managers to engage in questionable, but legal, *self-dealings are reduced.*
    ❑ If a publicly held firm is very small, and if its shares will be *traded infrequently,* then its stock will not really be liquid, and the market price may be lower than the stocks' true value.
    ❑ Managers of publicly owned firms with *less than 50 percent* control must be concerned about tender offers and proxy fights. This sometimes leads to operating decisions that are not in the best long-run interests of the shareholders.

After deciding to go public, the company must select an investment banker.

■ The company must select an investment bank, called an underwriter, to help it go public.
    ❑ The firm and its investment banker must decide whether the banker will work on a "best efforts" basis or will "underwrite" the issue.

        • On a *best efforts basis*, the banker does not guarantee that the securities will be sold or that the company will get the cash it needs, only that it will put forth its best efforts to sell the issue.

        • On an *underwritten issue*, the company does get a guarantee. Essentially, the banker agrees to buy the entire issue from the company and then resells the securities to its customers at a higher price. The banker bears significant risks in underwritten offerings. Virtually all IPOs (except those of very small firms) are underwritten.

■ Because they are exposed to large potential losses, investment bankers typically do not handle the purchase and distribution of issues single-handedly unless the issue is a very small one. If the sum of money involved is large, investment bankers form *underwriting syndicates* in an effort to minimize the risk each banker faces. The banking house which sets up the deal is called the *lead*, or *managing, underwriter*.
    ❑ In addition to the underwriting syndicate, on larger offerings still more investment bankers are included in a *selling group*, which handles the distribution of securities to individual investors.

Once the company and its investment banker have decided how much money to raise, the type of securities to issue, and the basis for pricing the issue, they will prepare and file an Registration statement and a prospectus with the Securities and Exchange Commission (SEC).

- The SEC has jurisdiction over all interstate public offerings in amounts of $1.5 million or more.

- New issues (stocks and bonds) must be registered with the SEC at least 20 days before they are publicly offered.
  - The *registration statement* provides financial, legal, and technical information about the company to the SEC.
  - A *prospectus* summarizes this information for investors.
  - A preliminary, or "*red herring*," *prospectus* may be distributed to potential buyers during the 20-day waiting period, but no sales may be finalized during this time. It contains all the key information that will appear in the final prospectus except the price.

- If the registration statement or prospectus contains *misrepresentations or omissions* of material facts, any purchaser who suffers a loss may sue for damages.

Before the IPO, the company's senior managers and investment banker go on a roadshow.

- During the roadshow, the company will present its plans to dozens of institutional investors.

- Bookbuilding occurs when the investment banker builds a book by asking the institutional investors how many shares of stock they would like to purchase.

The first day of trading can be very wild, with large price swings.

- During the first day of trading, the average IPO increases in value by about 14 percent from the offering price to the closing price at the end of the day.

IPOs are very expensive.

- Investment bankers usually charge a 7 percent spread (the difference between the price the investor pays and the proceeds received by the issuing company.

- Other costs (such as legal fees, printing, etc.) may exceed several hundred thousand dollars.

- In addition to these costs, the difference between the offering price and the closing price is the amount of "money left on the table."

After the IPO, the stock trades in a public secondary market.

- For new issues involving small companies, the investment banker will normally *maintain a market* in the shares after the public offering. This is done in order to provide liquidity for the shares and to maintain a good relationship with both the issuer and the investors who purchased the shares.

- Not including the first day's return, the three-year return for the average IPO is less than that of similar companies. In other words, IPO stocks underperform in the long run.

Stocks traded on organized exchanges are called listed stocks. While the decision to go public is significant, the decision to list is not a major event. In order to have a listed stock, a company must apply to an exchange, pay a relatively small fee, and meet the exchange's minimum requirements.

- An exchange's minimum requirements relate to the following:
  - Size of the company's net income.
  - Number of shares outstanding and in the hands of outsiders.
  - Company must agree to disclose certain information to the exchange.

- The company will have to file a few new reports with an exchange.

- It will have to abide by the exchange's rules.

- Firms benefit from listing their stock by *gaining liquidity, status,* and *free publicity*.
  - By providing investors with these benefits, financial managers may be able to lower their
  - Due to improvements in telecommunications and computer technologies, the differences between the Nasdaq market and the physical exchanges have become less distinct.

Most participants in the securities markets, including the organized exchanges, brokers, investment bankers, and dealers, are regulated by the federal government through the Securities and Exchange Commission (SEC) and, to a lesser extent, by state governments.

- The SEC also regulates all national stock exchanges. Firms listed on these exchanges must file financial reports with both the SEC and the exchanges.

- The SEC also monitors the stock transactions of corporate *insiders*.

- The SEC has the power to prohibit *manipulation* by such devices as pools or wash sales.

- The SEC has control over the *proxy statement* and the way the company uses it to solicit votes.

- The Federal Reserve System controls credit used to buy securities.

- States also have some control over the issuance of new securities within their boundaries.
  - State laws relating to security sales are called *blue sky laws*, because they were put into effect to keep unscrupulous promoters from selling securities that offered the "blue sky" but which actually had little or no asset backing.

- The securities industry realizes the importance of stable markets, sound brokerage firms, and the absence of stock manipulation. Therefore, the various exchanges and trade organizations work closely with the SEC to police transactions and to maintain the integrity and credibility of the system.
  - The *National Association of Securities Dealers* (NASD) cooperates with the SEC to police trading in the OTC market.

- In general, government regulation of securities trading, as well as industry self-regulation, is designed to ensure (1) that investors receive information that is as accurate as possible, (2) that no one artificially manipulates the market price of a given stock, and (3) that corporate insiders do not take advantage of their position to profit in their companies' stocks at the expense of other stockholders.

An equity carve-out is a special type of IPO.

- When an existing company has more than one division or operating unit, it may decide to turn one of them into a separately traded subsidiary.

- If it sells new stock in the newly formed subsidiary, it is called an equity carve-out.

Investment banks also help firms that have already had an IPO raise additional debt and equity.

- Before raising capital, the firm makes some initial, preliminary decisions on its own.
  - The *dollar amount* of new capital required is established.
  - The *type of securities* to be offered is specified. Further, if common stock is to be issued, managers must decide whether a rights offering should be used.
  - The basis on which to deal with the investment bankers, either by a *competitive bid* or a *negotiated deal,* is determined.
  - Only about 100 of the largest firms listed on the NYSE, whose securities are already well known to the investment banking community, are in a position to use the competitive bidding process.
  - Except for the largest firms, offerings of stocks and bonds are generally on a negotiated basis.
  - Finally, the *investment banking firm* must be *selected.*

Additional equity or debt can be issued in a private placement.

■ In a *private placement*, securities are sold to one or a few investors, generally institutional investors. Private placements are most common with bonds, but they also occur with stocks.

    ❑ The primary advantages are lower flotation costs and greater speed, since the shares will not have to go through the SEC registration process.

    ❑ The most common type of private placement occurs when a company places securities directly with a financial institution.

    ❑ One particular type of private placement that is occurring with increasing frequency is where a large company makes an equity investment in a smaller supplier.

    ❑ The primary disadvantage of a private placement is that the securities generally do not go through the SEC registration process, so under SEC rules they cannot be sold except to another large, "sophisticated" purchaser in the event the original buyer wants to sell them.

Large well-known public companies which issue securities frequently may file *a master registration statement* with the SEC and then update it with a *short-form statement* just prior to each individual offering.

■ This procedure is known as a *shelf registration* because, in effect, the company puts its new securities "on the shelf," and then sells them to investors when it feels the market is "right".

■ Firms with less than $150 million in stock held by outside investors cannot use shelf registrations.

■ Shelf registrations have two advantages over standard registrations: (1) lower flotation costs and (2) more control over the timing of the issue.

If a company sells additional stock after its IPO, it is called a seasoned stock offering.

■ The sale of additional common stock may be perceived by investors as a *negative signal*, because managers may believe that the stock is not worth its current price (hence, selling additional stock at the current price is a good deal for the company). Therefore, the stock price usually falls when a seasoned equity offering is announced.

■ If stockholders have a preemptive right, or if the firm chooses to do so, it can sell the additional stock to existing stockholders as a *rights offering*.

    ❑ Each shareholder is issued an option to buy a certain number of new shares, and the terms of the option are listed on a certificate called a *stock purchase right*, or simply a *right*.

Some companies choose to go private, usually through a leveraged buyout (LBO).

■ In going private, a small group of investors, usually including the current management group, purchases all the stock of the company.

■ If the investor group borrows money to make the purchase, it is called a leveraged buyout.

■ There are several advantages to going private.
  ❑ Administrative costs, such as those associated with securities registration, annual reports, etc., are reduced.
  ❑ Managers, who now have a large ownership stake in the company, have greater incentives.
  ❑ Managers have increased flexibility since they do not have to report results to the public.
  ❑ The other investors have greater participation in decision making, since they typically have representatives on the board of directors who provide advice and monitor the managers.
  ❑ The increased use of financial leverage reduces taxes.

Firms must manage the maturity structure of their debt.

■ *Maturity matching* means that firms consider the *maturity of the assets being financed.*
  ❑ If a firm uses 30-year bonds to finance 10-year assets, the bond payments would continue long after the assets were retired.
  ❑ If a firm uses 10-year bonds to finance 30-year assets, it would have to "roll over" the debt after 10 years.
  ❑ Each of the above strategies involves significant risks. In general, the best all-around financing strategy is to match debt maturities with asset maturities.

■ *Current interest rate levels and forecasts of future interest rates* also play an important role in the financing decision.
  ❑ If current rates are high, and are expected to drop, it might be wise to use short-term financing until rates drop, and then lock in the lower rates with long-term financing.
  ❑ Conversely, if current rates are low and expected to rise, use long-term financing now to lock in the rates.
  ❑ However, interest rates are difficult, if not impossible, to forecast. Thus, pursuing one of the above strategies could prove to be disastrous if the forecasts were wrong.

■ Information asymmetry occurs when managers know more about the firm's future prospects than do investors.

- ❑ If managers know that the future prospects are better than investors expect, they will tend to issue short-term debt, and then refinance it with low-coupon rate long-term debt when investors recognize the true strength of their firm.

Some firms use zero coupon bonds to help manage the maturity structure of their debt.

- ■ *Zero coupon bonds*, pay no interest but are offered at a substantial discount below their par values and hence provide capital appreciation rather than interest income.
  - ❑ A new form of zeros was created from U. S. Treasury bonds, *zero coupon U. S. Treasury Trust Certificates*. Coupons were clipped off and the "stripped" bond was sold as itself with the coupons used as collateral.
    - In 1985 the Treasury Department began allowing investors to strip long-term U. S. Treasury bonds and directly register the newly created zero coupon bonds, called *STRIPs*, with the Treasury Department.
    - Now virtually all U. S. Treasury zeros are held in the form of STRIPs.
  - ❑ Zero coupon bonds are just one type of *original issue discount bond (OID)*. Any nonconvertible bond whose coupon rate is set below the going market rate at the time of its issue will sell at a discount, and it will be classified as an OID bond.
  - ❑ Corporate and municipal zeros are generally callable at the option of the issuer after some stated call protection period.
    - The call price is set at a premium over the accrued value at the time of the call.
    - Stripped U. S. Treasury bonds are not callable. Thus, Treasury zeros are completely protected against reinvestment risk.

Corporations that issue callable debt or preferred stock during high interest rate periods often replace the issue with a lower cost issue when interest rates drop. This operation is called refunding.

- ■ Refunding decisions involve two separate questions: (1) Is it profitable to call an outstanding issue in the current period and replace it with a new issue; and (2) even if refunding is currently profitable, would the value of the firm be increased even more if the refunding were postponed to a later date?

- ■ The decision to refund a security is analyzed in much the same way as a capital budgeting expenditure.
  - ❑ The costs of refunding (the investment outlays) are (1) the call premium paid for the privilege of calling the old issue, (2) the tax savings from writing off the unexpensed flotation costs on the old issue, and (3) the net interest that must be paid while both issues are outstanding.
  - ❑ The annual cash flows, in a capital budgeting sense, are the interest payments that are saved each year plus the net tax savings which the firm receives for amortizing the flotation expenses.

■ The *net present value method* is used to analyze the advantages of refunding.
  ❑ The future cash flows are discounted back to the present, and then this discounted value is compared with the cash outlays associated with the refunding.
  ❑ The firm should refund the bond only if the present value of the savings exceed the cost—that is, if the NPV of the refunding operation is positive.

■ In the discounting process, the *after-tax cost of the new debt* should be used as the discount rate.
  ❑ The reasons for this are (1) there is relatively little risk to the savings—cash flows in a refunding are known with relative certainty and (2) the cash outlay required to refund the old issue is generally obtained by increasing the amount of the new issue.

■ If the refunding operation is advantageous to the firm, it must be disadvantageous to bondholders.
  ❑ This points out the danger of the call provision to bondholders, and it also explains why bonds without a call provision command higher prices than callable bonds.

■ The mechanics of calculating the NPV of a refunding are simple, but the decision on when to refund is not a simple one at all, because it requires a forecast of future interest rates. Thus, refunding now versus waiting for a possibly more favorable future refunding is a judgmental decision.

■ Financial managers making bond refunding decisions can now use the values of derivative securities to estimate the value of the bond issue's *embedded call option*.
  ❑ If the call option is worth *more* than the NPV of refunding today, the issue should not be immediately refunded.
  ❑ The issuer should either delay the refunding to take advantage of the information obtained from the derivative market or actually create a derivative transaction to lock in the value of the call option.

Companies use various techniques to manage the risk structure of their debt. These include project financing and securitization, which permit a firm to tie a debt issue to a specific asset.

■ *Project financing* is another type of debt that has been used extensively in recent years.
  ❑ In project financing, the holders of the debt generally have claims only against the sponsor's equity in the project and the cash flows generated from the project, and not against the firm or firms that own the project (the sponsors).
  ❑ Project financings are generally characterized by large size and a high degree of complexity. However, since project financing is tied to a specific project, it can be tailored to meet the specific needs of both the creditors and the sponsors.

❑   Project financing offers several potential benefits over conventional debt financing.

-   Project financing usually restricts the usage of the project's cash flows, which means that the lenders, rather than the managers, can decide whether to reinvest excess cash flows or to use them to reduce the loan balance by more than the minimum required.

-   Conferring the above power on lenders reduces their risks.

❑   Project financings also have advantages for borrowers.

-   Because risks to the lenders are reduced, the interest rate built into a project financing deal may be relatively low.

-   Project financings insulate the firm's other assets from risks associated with the project being financed.

❑   Project financings increase the number and type of investment opportunities; hence they make capital markets "more complete."

❑   Project financings reduce the costs to investors of obtaining information and monitoring the borrower's operations.

❑   Project financings also permit firms whose earnings are below the minimum requirements specified in their existing bond indentures to obtain additional debt financing.

❑   Project financings increase the ability of a firm to maintain confidentiality.

❑   Project financings can improve incentives for key managers by enabling them to take direct ownership stakes in the operations under their control.

■   As the term is generally used, a *security* refers to a publicly traded financial instrument, as opposed to a privately placed instrument. Thus securities tend to have high liquidity. In recent years, procedures have been developed to securitize various types of debt instruments, thus *increasing their liquidity*, *lowering the cost of capital to borrowers*, and generally *increasing the efficiency of the financial markets*.

❑   Securitization has occurred in two ways.

-   Some debt instruments that were formerly rarely traded are now being actively traded. Examples are commercial paper and junk bonds.

-   In *asset securitization*, or the creation of *asset-backed securities*, individual assets are pledged as collateral, but then typically combined into pools to reduce risk. The oldest type of asset securitization is the mortgage-backed security, but today, such things as accounts receivable and automobile loans are also used as collateral.

❑   The process of securitization has, in general, *lowered costs* and *increased the availability of funds* to borrowers, *decreased risks* to lenders, and *created new investment opportunities* for many investors.

SELF-TEST QUESTIONS

Definitional

1. _____ _____ refers to the sale of shares of a closely held business to the general public.

2. Going public establishes the firm's _____ in the market place.

3. Securities traded on an organized exchange are known as _____ securities.

4. Before an interstate issue of stock amounting to $1.5 million or more can be sold to the public, it must be _____ with and approved by the _____.

5. In a(n) _____ _____ securities are sold to one or a few investors, generally institutional investors. The primary advantages are lower flotation costs and greater speed, since shares will not have to go through the SEC registration process.

6. Setting the _____ price for a stock issue may present a conflict of interest between the issuer and the _____ _____.

7. In order to spread the risk of underwriting a sizable common stock issue, investment bankers will form a(n) _____ _____.

8. On a(n) _____ _____ _____, the investment banker does not guarantee that the securities will be sold or that the company will get the cash it needs; while on a(n) _____ issue the company does get a guarantee.

9. _____ _____ _____ are offered at a substantial discount below their par values and pay no interest.

10. The oldest type of asset securitization is the _____-_____ _____.

11. The least risky financing strategy is to match the debt _____ with the asset _____.

12. It is very _____, if not _____, to forecast interest rates.

13. In _____ _____, the holders of the debt generally have claims only against the sponsor's equity in the project and the cash flows generated from the project, and not against the firm or firms that own the project.

Conceptual

14. A firm may go public, yet the firm itself may not receive any additional funds in the process.

    a. True   **b.** False

15. Flotation costs are generally higher for bond issues than for stock issues.

    a. True   **b.** False

16. When new shares are being sold, if it appears that the investment bankers will be unable to sell the entire issue at the initial offering price, the only way the entire issue can be sold is to lower the price.

    a. True   **b.** False

17. Which of the following statements is most correct?

    a. Stocks traded on organized exchanges are called listed stocks. Both the decision to go public and to list are major events for the firm.

    b. Whenever a publicly-owned firm decides to issue new common stock, it must register the stock with the SEC, and prospective stockholders must be given a copy of the prospectus. The SEC must approve the prospectus, and one key aspect of this approval is that the SEC must agree that the price at which the shares are to be offered is fair to investors.

    c. Once a company "goes public," it must file periodic statements with the SEC. These periodic statements are called prospectuses, or, sometimes, "red herring" prospectuses.

    d. One important recent innovation is "shelf registration," whereby large companies can register securities in advance, in effect putting them "on the shelf" of an investment banking house, which can then sell them at any time, in whole or in part, when the market is receptive to the securities. Theoretically, either stock or bonds could be sold through shelf registrations, but, because of the preemptive right, as a practical matter, only bonds are involved.

    e. All of the above statements are false.

18. Which of the following statements is most correct?

    a. Large companies such as IBM and Exxon are exempt from SEC listing requirements, but small companies (assets below $10 million) are not. Hence, small companies have listed stock, while large companies have unlisted stock.

    b. If a company's stock is publicly owned, and if its price has been established in the market and is quoted in a source such as *The Wall Street Journal*, then the price of any new issue of stock will be based on the current market price. However, if the stock is not traded, and if the company is going public for the first time, then the Securities and Exchange Commission (SEC) must approve the price at which the stock is to be offered to the public.

    c. In the United States, most new stock issues are sold through the commercial banks.

    d. The SEC must normally approve the prospectuses relating to new stock offerings by companies whose securities are listed on the New York Stock Exchange before the new stock can be sold to the public.

    e. Statements b and d are both correct.

19. Which of the following statements is most correct?

    a. A disadvantage to the issuer of long-term debt financing is that the cost of debt is fixed, so debtholders do not participate if profits soar.

    b. If current interest rates are high, and are expected to drop, it might be wise to use long-term financing until rates drop, and then lock in the lower rates with short-term financing.

    c. The primary advantage of zero coupon bonds to investors, especially to wealthy individual investors, is that the investor gets his or her returns in the form of capital gains rather than interest income. Since capital gains (1) are taxed at relatively low rates and (2) are deferred until the bond matures or is sold, zero coupon corporate bonds have a significant advantage over regular coupon bonds.

    d. The bond refunding decision is analyzed like a capital budgeting decision. The investment cost consists of the call premium plus the flotation cost on the new issue, and the cash flow benefits consist of the interest saved each year as a result of substituting low rate debt for high rate debt. Rational companies constantly monitor the situation, and they call callable bonds immediately if the NPV on the refunding decision is positive.

    e. The above statements are all false.

SELF-TEST PROBLEMS

1. J.C. Nickel is planning a zero coupon bond issue. The bond has a par value of $1,000, matures in 10 years, and will be sold at an 80 percent discount, or for $200. The firm's marginal tax rate is 40 percent. What is the annual after-tax cost of debt to Nickel on this issue? (Hint: You will need to use a financial calculator.)

   a. 10.48%   **b.** 10.00%   **c.** 11.62%   **d.** 14.79%   **e.** 17.46%

2. Assume that the City of Miami sold an issue of $1,000 maturity value, tax exempt (muni), zero coupon bonds 10 years ago. The bonds had a 30-year maturity when they were issued, and the interest rate built into the issue was a nominal 12 percent, but with semiannual compounding. The bonds are now callable at a premium of 12 percent over the accrued value. What effective annual rate of return would an investor who bought the bonds when they were issued and who still owns them earn if they are called today? (Hint: You will need to use a financial calculator.)

   a. 13.33%   **b.** 12.00%   **c.** 12.37%   **d.** 11.76%   **e.** 13.64%

3. The City of Tampa issued $1,000,000 of 12 percent coupon, 25-year, semiannual payment, tax-exempt muni bonds 10 years ago. The bonds had 10 years of call protection, but now Tampa can call the bonds if it chooses to do so. The call premium would be 11 percent of the face amount. New 15-year, 10 percent, semiannual payment bonds can be sold at par, but flotation costs on this issue would be 3 percent, or $30,000. What is the net present value of the refunding?

   a. $13,011   **b.** $12,262   **c.** $15,121   **d.** $13,725   **e.** $14,545

4. Assume that the Tennessee Valley Power Authority (which is exempt from income taxes) issued $100,000 of 30-year maturity, 10 percent coupon, semiannual payment, tax-exempt bonds on January 1, 1989. The bonds were callable after 10 years, or after January 1, 1999, at a price that is 10 percent above the bonds' par value. On January 1, 1999, the Power Authority learns that it can issue $100,000 of new 20-year, semiannual payment, 8 percent coupon bonds at par. Costs associated with selling the new issue will amount to $2,000. What is the NPV of the refunding decision?

   a. -$7,485.46   **b.** $9,285.48   **c.** -$4,334.60   **d.** $7,792.77   **e.** $6,982.74

5. Assume that the City of Pensacola has $10 million of 12 percent, 20-year, $1,000 par value, semiannual payment bonds outstanding that can be called at a price of $1,100 per bond. New 20-year, 10 percent, semiannual payment bonds can be sold at a flotation cost of $600,000, or 6 percent. What is the NPV of the refunding operation?

    a. $115,909   **b.** $120,606   **c.** $125,505   **d.** $130,707   **e.** $135,808

ANSWERS TO SELF-TEST QUESTIONS

1. Going public
2. value
3. listed
4. registered; SEC
5. private placement
6. offering; investment banker
7. underwriting syndicate

8. best efforts basis; underwritten
9. Zero coupon bonds
10. mortgage-backed security
11. maturity; maturity
12. difficult; impossible
13. project financings

14. a. An example, that of the Ford Foundation selling stock to the general public, is given in the text. Also, a firm may go public if its managers sell off a portion of their stock holdings. Then, the funds obtained go to the managers rather than the firm.

15. b. The investment banker normally must expend greater effort in selling stocks, thus must charge a higher fee. Also, a new common stock issue may lower stock price because of negative signaling effects and/or supply/demand price pressure.

16. b. The investment bankers may be able to increase the demand for the stock by promoting the issue. If not, then a price reduction may be required.

17. e. Statement a is false; while the decision to go public is a major event, the decision to list is not. Statement b is false; the SEC is responsible for making sure the information in the registration and prospectus is adequate; however, it does not determine the fairness of the offering price. Statement c is false; prospectuses accompany any sales solicitations. Statement d is false; shelf registrations are also applicable to common stock. Thus, statement e is the correct choice.

18. d. All companies are subject to the SEC's listing requirements, which makes statement a false. The SEC does not have to approve offering prices for initial public offerings. Therefore, statement b is false. Finally, statement c is false because commercial banks are barred from participating in investment bank activities at the present time.

19. e. Statement a is false; this is an advantage to the issuer. Statement b is false; the firm should use short-term financing until interest rates drop and then lock in the lower rates with long-term financing. Statement c is false; investors must impute interest income in each year on zero coupon bonds even though the interest is not received until maturity. The advantage to investors is that there is no reinvestment rate risk with zeros. Statement d is false; companies do not necessarily call callable bonds immediately if the NPV on the refunding decision is positive because if interest rates decrease further it may be beneficial to wait awhile. Therefore, the correct choice is statement e.

SOLUTIONS TO SELF-TEST PROBLEMS

1. a. Maturity $= N = 10$; Issue price $= PV = 200$; PMT $= 0$; Maturity value $= FV = 1000$; Corporate tax rate $= 40\%$.

Enter into a financial calculator: $N = 10$, $PV = -200$, $PMT = 0$, and $FV = 1000$, and then solve for $k_d = I = 17.46\%$. However, this is a before-tax cost of debt. $k_d(1 - T) = 17.46\%(1 - 0.4) = 10.48\%$.

Alternatively, set the analysis up on a time line:

	0	1	2	3	4	5	6	7	8	9	10 Years
Year-end accrued value[1]	200.00	234.92	275.94	324.12	380.71	447.18	525.25	616.96	724.69	851.22	1,000.00
Interest deduction[2]		34.92	41.02	48.18	56.59	66.47	78.07	91.71	107.73	126.53	148.78
Tax savings (40%)[3]		13.97	16.41	19.27	22.64	26.59	31.23	36.68	43.09	50.61	59.51
Cash flow[4]	200.00	13.97	16.41	19.27	22.64	26.59	31.23	36.68	43.09	50.61	-940.49

After-tax cost of debt: 10.48%.

Notes:
[1]Year-end accrued value = Issue price $\times (1 + k_d)^n$.
[2]Interest in Year n = Accrued value$_n$ – Accrued value$_{n-1}$.
[3]Tax savings = (Interest deduction)(T).
[4]Cash flow in Year 10 = Tax savings – Maturity value.

2. e.

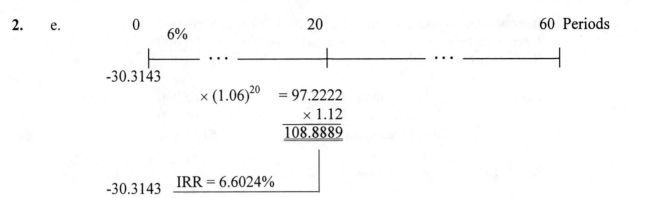

Periodic rate = 6.6024%.

$$EAR = (1.066024)^2 - 1 = 0.1364 = 13.64\%.$$

The solution to this problem requires three steps:

1. Solve for the PV of the original issue. Using a financial calculator, enter N = 60, I = 6, PMT = 0, and FV = 1000, and then solve for PV = $30.3143.

2. Determine the accrued value at the end of 20 periods, and multiply by the call premium.

$30.3143 \times (1.06)^{20} \times 1.12 = \$108.8889.$

3. Solve for the EAR to an investor if the bonds are called today. Using a financial calculator, enter N = 20, PV = -30.3143, PMT = 0, and FV = 108.8889, and then solve for $k_d/2$ = I = 6.6024%.

$$EAR = (1.066024)^2 - 1 = 0.1364 = 13.64\%.$$

3.   d.   Interest on old bond per 6 months: $120,000/2 = $ 60,000

           Interest on new bond per 6 months: $100,000/2 =   50,000

           Savings per six months $ 10,000

Cost:	Call premium = 11% =	$110,000
	Flotation cost = 3% =	30,000
	Total investment outlay	$140,000

$k_d/2 = 10\%/2 = 5\%$ per 6 months.

$$\text{NPV} = \sum_{t=1}^{30} \frac{\$10,000}{(1.05)^t} - \$140,000 = \$153,725 - \$140,000 = \$13,725.$$

Alternatively, input the cash flows into the cash flow register, enter I = 5, and then solve for NPV = $13,725.

4.   d.   Cost of refunding = Call premium + Flotation cost

                   = 0.10($100,000) + $2,000 = $12,000.

Savings each 6 months = Interest on old bonds − Interest on new bonds

                       = 0.05($100,000) − 0.04($100,000)

                       = $5,000 − $4,000 = $1,000.

$k_d/2 = 8.0\%/2 = 4.0\%$ = Discount rate for NPV.

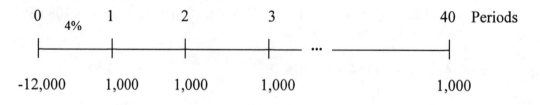

$$\text{NPV} = \sum_{t=1}^{40} \frac{\$1,000}{(1.04)^t} - \$12,000 = \$19,792.77 - \$12,000 = \$7,792.77.$$

5.   a.   Cost of refunding = Call premium + Flotation cost
$$= (\$1,100 - \$1,000)10,000 + \$600,000 = \$1,600,000.$$

Savings each 6 months = Interest on old bonds – Interest on new bonds
$$= 0.06(\$1,000)(10,000) - 0.05(\$1,000)(10,000)$$
$$= \$100,000.$$

Using a time line, the cash flows are shown below:

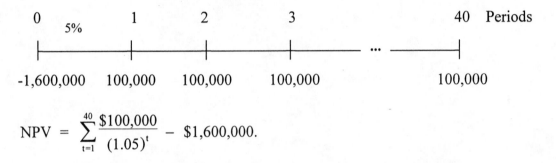

$$\text{NPV} = \sum_{t=1}^{40} \frac{\$100,000}{(1.05)^t} - \$1,600,000.$$

Using a financial calculator, input the cash flows into the cash flow register, enter I = 5, and then solve for NPV = \$115,908.64, or approximately \$115,909.

CHAPTER 20
LEASE FINANCING

OVERVIEW

Firms generally own fixed assets and report them on their balance sheets, but it is the use of the fixed assets that is important, not their ownership. One way to obtain the use of facilities and equipment is to buy them, but an alternative is to lease them. Prior to the 1950s, leasing was generally associated with real estate—land and buildings. Today, however, it is possible to lease virtually any kind of fixed asset, and currently over 30 percent of all new capital equipment is financed through lease arrangements.

OUTLINE

There are two parties to every lease agreement, and there are several different types of leases.

■ The *lessor* is the owner of the leased property. The lessor receives the tax benefit of ownership through depreciation tax savings.

■ The *lessee* buys the right to use the property in exchange for one or more *lease*, or *rental*, *payments* to the lessor.

■ Leasing takes several different forms, the four most important include:
   ❑ *Operating leases.* These leases are sometimes called *services leases* and generally provide for both financing and maintenance.
      ● Operating leases ordinarily require the lessor to maintain and service the leased equipment; the cost of the maintenance is built into the lease payments.
      ● Operating leases are not fully amortized. In other words, the rental payments required under the lease contract are not sufficient for the lessor to recover the full cost of the asset.
      ● The lease contract is written for less than the useful life of the equipment.

- The lessor expects to recover the cost of the equipment by subsequent renewal payments, by releasing the equipment to other lessees, or by sale of the equipment.
- Operating leases often contain a cancellation clause to protect the lessee against obsolescence.
- *Financial, or capital, leases.* These leases are fully amortized; they do not provide for maintenance; and they are not cancelable.
  - Equipment is purchased by the lessor from the manufacturer or distributor, and the lessee simultaneously executes an agreement to lease the equipment from the financial institution.
  - The terms of the lease generally call for full amortization of the lessor's investment, plus a rate of return on the unamortized balance which is close to the percentage rate the lessee would have paid on a secured loan.
  - The lessee generally pays the property taxes and insurance on the leased property. Since the lessor receives a return after, or net of, these payments, this type of lease is often called a "net, net" lease.
- *Sale and leaseback.* In this type of lease, a firm owning an asset sells the property to another firm and simultaneously leases it back for a stated period under specific terms.
  - The sale and leaseback is an alternative to a mortgage.
  - The seller immediately receives the purchase price, but retains the use of the property in exchange for rental payments.
  - The lease payments are sufficient to return the purchase price to the lessor plus provide a specified return on the investment.
  - A sale and leaseback may be thought of as a special type of financial lease.
- *Combination leases.* This type of lease combines features of both operating and financial leases.

Lease payments are deductible expenses for income tax purposes, provided the IRS agrees that the contract is a genuine lease and not an installment loan called a lease.

- A lease that complies with all IRS requirements is called a *guideline,* or *tax-oriented, lease.* The main provisions of the tax guidelines are as follows:
  - The lease term (including any extensions or renewals at a fixed rental rate) must not exceed 80 percent of the estimated useful life of the equipment at the commencement of the lease transaction.
  - The equipment's estimated residual value (in constant dollars without adjustment for inflation) at the expiration of the lease must equal at least 20 percent of its value at the start of the lease.

- ❑ Neither the lessee nor any related party can have the right to purchase the property at a predetermined fixed price at the lease's inception.
- ❑ Neither the lessee nor any related party can pay or guarantee payment of any part of the price of the leased equipment.
- ❑ The leased equipment must not be "limited use" property, defined as equipment that can only be used by the lessee or a related party at the end of the lease.

- ■ In a guideline lease, the tax benefits of ownership (depreciation and any investment tax credits) belong to the lessor.

- ■ A lease that does not meet the tax guidelines is called a *non-tax-oriented lease*.
  - ❑ For this type of lease, the lessee is (1) the effective owner of the leased property, (2) can depreciate it for tax purposes, and (3) can deduct only the interest portion of each lease payment.

Lease financing is financially comparable to debt financing because both subject the firm to a contractual series of payments and failure to make these payments could lead to bankruptcy.

- ■ Leasing is sometimes referred to as *off balance sheet financing* because, under certain conditions, neither the leased assets nor the lease liabilities appear directly on the firm's balance sheet.

- ■ A firm with extensive lease arrangements not appearing directly on the firm's balance sheet would have both its assets and its liabilities understated in comparison with a firm which borrowed to purchase the assets, and hence, the firm that leases would show a lower debt ratio. Note, however, that these lease obligations must be disclosed in the notes to the financial statements.

- ■ FASB Statement 13 requires firms to *capitalize* certain financial leases, and thus to restate their balance sheets to report the leased asset as a fixed asset and the present value of the future lease payments as a liability, if certain conditions exist.
  - ❑ The logic behind FASB Statement 13 is as follows. If a firm signs a financial lease, its obligation to make lease payments is just as binding as if it had signed a loan agreement—the failure to make lease payments can bankrupt a firm just as fast as the failure to make principal and interest payments on a loan.
  - ❑ For all intents and purposes, a financial lease is identical to a loan.

- ■ A lease is capitalized if one or more of the following conditions exist:
  - ❑ Ownership of the property is effectively transferred from the lessor to the lessee.

- ❑ The lessee can purchase the property at less than its true market value when the lease expires.
- ❑ The lease runs for a period equal to or greater than 75 percent of the asset's life.
- ❑ The present value of the lease payments is equal to or greater than 90 percent of the initial value of the asset.

- ■ Leases are regarded as debt for capital structure purposes, and they have the same effects as debt on k_d and k_s.
  - ❑ Therefore, leasing is not likely to permit a firm to use more financial leverage than could be obtained with conventional debt.

- ■ The lease decision is a *financing decision,* and not a capital budgeting decision. Thus, lease analysis is not generally conducted unless the decision has already been made to acquire the asset.

Leases must be evaluated by both the lessee and the lessor. For the lessee, the analysis focuses on whether leasing the asset is less costly than buying the asset, and the lessor must decide whether the lease payments provide a satisfactory return on the invested funds.

- ■ Whether or not to acquire the asset is *not* part of the typical lease analysis. In a lease analysis, we are concerned simply with whether to obtain the use of the asset by lease or by purchase.

- ■ The leasing analysis should compare the cost of leasing with the cost of debt financing regardless of how the asset purchase is actually financed.
  - ❑ The asset may be purchased with available cash if not leased, but since leasing is a substitute for debt financing, and has the same capital structure effect, the appropriate comparison would still be with debt financing.

- ■ In an NPV-type analysis, the lessee estimates the cost of leasing and the cost of owning, assuming that the asset is financed solely with debt. If the cost of leasing is less than the cost of owning, the asset should be leased.
  - ❑ All cash flows must reflect tax effects.
  - ❑ Since leasing is a substitute for debt financing, and since lease cash flows have approximately the same risk as debt cash flows, the *appropriate discount rate is the after-tax cost of debt.*
  - ❑ In a lease analysis, the PV cost of owning less the PV cost of leasing is called the *net advantage to leasing (NAL).*

■ A second method that lessees can use to evaluate leases focuses on the percentage cost of leasing and is analogous to the IRR method used in capital budgeting. The *percentage cost approach* is discussed in the Extensions to this chapter.

The lessor views the lease transaction as an investment, and hence, the lessor's analysis focuses on the return on the lease transaction.

■ Any potential lessor needs to know the rate of return on the capital invested in the lease, and this information is also useful to the prospective lessee: Lease terms on large leases are generally negotiated, so the lessee should know what return the lessor is earning.

■ The lessor's analysis involves:
  ❑ Determining the net cash outlay, which is usually the invoice price of the leased equipment less any lease payments made in advance.
  ❑ Determining the periodic cash inflows, which consist of the lease payments minus both income taxes and any maintenance expense the lessor must bear.
  ❑ Estimating the after-tax residual value of the property when the lease expires.
  ❑ Determining whether the rate of return on the lease exceeds the lessor's opportunity cost of capital or, equivalently, whether the NPV of the lease exceeds zero.

■ The lessor compares the return on the lease with the return available on alternative investments of similar risk. If the return expected on the lease is greater than that available on alternatives of similar risk, the lease should be written.

■ The analysis is similar to that of the lessee, in that the cash flows are laid out on a time line.
  ❑ All tax effects must be considered.
  ❑ If the lessor's NPV is positive, then the lease should be written.
  ❑ The lessor's IRR can also be examined, and if it is greater than the after-tax return on comparable investments, the lease transaction should be completed.

In large leases the parties generally sit down and work out an agreement on the size of the lease payments, with these payments being set so as to provide the lessor with some specific required rate of return.

■ In situations where the lease terms are not negotiated, the lessor must still go through an analysis, setting terms which provide a target rate of return, and then offering these terms to the potential lessee on a take-it-or-leave-it basis.

■ Leasing is not always a zero sum game, but if the inputs to the lessee and the lessor are identical, then a positive NAL to the lessee implies an equal but negative NPV to the lessor.

■ However, conditions are often such that leasing can provide net benefits to both parties.
   ❑ This situation arises because of differentials, generally in taxes, in estimated residual values, or in the ability to bear the residual value risk.

■ The lessor can, under certain conditions, increase the return on the lease by borrowing some of the funds used to purchase the leased asset. Such a lease is called a *leveraged lease*.
   ❑ Whether or not a lease is leveraged has no effect on the lessee's analysis, but it can have a significant effect on the cash flows to the lessor, hence on the lessor's expected return.
   ❑ Leveraged leases are discussed in the Extensions to this chapter.

Other issues often arise in leasing decisions.

■ The value of the asset at lease termination is called its *residual value*.
   ❑ Superficially, it might first appear that assets with large residual values would most likely be owned since the owner gets the residual value.
   ❑ However, competition among leasing companies forces lease contracts to fully recognize expected residual values. Thus, large residual value assets are not necessarily more suitable for buying than for leasing.

■ It is sometimes argued that firms which lease a significant portion of their assets can get more favorable debt terms than firms which do not.
   ❑ This premise rests upon the assumption that credit analysts do not recognize the full impact of leasing on a firm's financial strength.
   ❑ However, this contention is of *questionable validity* for firms with audited financial statements.
   ❑ Leasing can be a way to circumvent existing loan covenants. If restrictive covenants prohibit a firm from issuing more debt but fail to restrict lease payments, then the firm could effectively increase its leverage by leasing additional assets.
   ❑ Firms in very poor financial condition and facing possible bankruptcy may be able to obtain lease financing at a lower cost than comparable debt financing.
      • Lessors often have a more favorable position than lenders should the lessee actually go bankrupt.
      • Lessors that specialize in certain types of equipment may be in a better position to dispose of repossessed equipment than banks or other lenders.

■ Lease-versus-purchase analysis discussed here is just as applicable for real estate as for equipment.

■ Tax considerations are an important motive behind many nonoperating leases that are written today.
  ❑ A firm that is unprofitable, or that is expanding rapidly and generating large depreciation write-offs, cannot immediately use the full tax benefits of ownership.
  ❑ On the other hand, firms in the highest marginal tax bracket gain the most tax benefits from owning.
  ❑ Therefore, companies that make extensive use of lease financing are typically doing poorly and are unable to effectively use tax benefits, while lessors include highly profitable companies which can fully use the tax benefits.

■ The ability to structure leases that are advantageous to both lessor and lessee depends in large part on tax laws. The four major factors that influence leasing are (1) investment tax credits, (2) depreciation rules, (3) tax rates, and (4) alternative minimum taxes.
  ❑ The *investment tax credit (ITC)* is a direct reduction of taxes that occurs when a firm purchases new capital equipment. Current tax laws do not allow an ITC, but they once did, and it is possible they will do so again in the future.
  ❑ Owners recover their investments in capital assets through *depreciation*, which is tax deductible. Recent tax laws have tended to slow depreciation write-offs, thus reducing the value of ownership.
  ❑ The value of depreciation depends on the firm's *tax rate*, because the depreciation tax savings equals the amount of depreciation multiplied by the tax rate. Higher tax rates mean greater ownership tax savings, and hence more incentive for tax-driven leases.
  ❑ The *alternative minimum tax (AMT)* also impacts leasing activity.
    • Previously, some corporations were able to pay little or no taxes by using accelerated depreciation for tax purposes, and yet report high earnings to stockholders by using straight line depreciation. The AMT now requires companies to pay a minimum tax equal to approximately 20 percent of their reported earnings.
    • A company can reduce its reported income, and hence its AMT liability, by using short-term, fully amortized leases on long-term assets—such leases need not meet the requirements for ordinary tax deductibility.

In addition to tax motivations, there are many other reasons why firms might lease assets rather than purchase them.

- Many assets are leased, particularly through operating leases, because it is less risky for the firm to lease the asset than to commit to ownership.
  - Leasing provides *operating flexibility*.
  - Assets that face rapid and uncertain *technological obsolescence* are often leased. Lessees benefit because they are more easily able to acquire the most advanced equipment. Although the risk of obsolescence is passed to the lessor, lessors may be better able to bear this risk because of (1) diversification across a wide variety of assets and (2) being better able to assess residual values and market the used assets.
  - If the life of the project is in doubt, then it may be better to lease the asset, since it might be easier to dispose of the asset in the event of *premature termination* of the project.

- The leasing industry recently introduced a type of lease that transfers some of a project's operating risk from the lessee to the lessor.
  - In the health care industry, such leases are called *per-procedure leases*.
  - Instead of making a fixed rental payment, the lessee pays a fee each time the leased equipment is used. By using a per-procedure lease, the company is converting a fixed cost for the equipment into a variable cost, hence reducing the machine's operating leverage and breakeven point.

- Some companies also find leasing attractive because the lessor is able to provide servicing on favorable terms.

SELF-TEST QUESTIONS

Definitional

1. Conceptually, leasing is similar to _____, and it provides the same type of financial _____ .

2. Under a(n) _____ _____ _____ arrangement, the seller receives the purchase price of the asset but retains the _____ of the property.

3. _____ leases include both financing and maintenance arrangements.

4. A(n) _____, or _____, lease is similar to a sale and leaseback arrangement, but generally apply to the purchase of _____ equipment directly from the manufacturer.

5.	The IRS would disallow a "lease" which pays for the asset in a relatively _____ period, and then permits the lessee to retain the asset for a(n) _____ payment.

6.	If the IRS allows the lease, then the _____ _____ is fully deductible.

7.	FASB Statement 13 requires that firms _____ certain financial leases, and hence restate their _____ _____.

8.	Capitalizing a lease requires that the asset be listed under _____ _____, and that the _____ _____ of the future lease payments be shown as _____.

9.	The value of an asset at the end of the lease term is referred to as its _____ _____.

10.	_____ among leasing companies will tend to force leasing rates down to the point where _____ values are fully recognized in the lease rates.

11.	Since some leases do not appear on the _____ _____, a firm may be able to use more _____ than if it did not lease.

12.	The leasing decision is a(n) _____ decision rather than a(n) _____ _____ decision.

13.	_____ _____ are often an important motive behind financial leases.

14.	The _____ _____ _____ is designed to ensure that corporations reporting high earnings will pay some taxes.

15.	_____ leases contain features of both operating and financial leases.

16.	A lease that complies with all the IRS requirements for a genuine lease is called a(n) _____, or _____-_____, lease.

17.	Since leasing is a substitute for debt financing, and since lease cash flows have approximately the same risk as debt cash flows, the appropriate discount rate is the _____-_____ _____ ____ _____.

18.	Assets that face rapid and uncertain _____ _____ are often leased.

Conceptual

19. Capital leases typically include both financing and maintenance arrangements.

    a. True   b. False

20. When one is evaluating a lease proposal, cash flows should be discounted at a relatively high rate because lease flows are fairly certain.

    a. True   b. False

21. Generally, operating leases are fully amortized, and the lease is written for the expected life of the asset.

    a. True   b. False

22. A firm which uses extensive lease financing may have a substantially lower reported debt ratio than a firm which borrows to finance its assets.

    a. True   b. False

23. Firms may or may not capitalize a financial lease.

    a. True   b. False

24. The more stringent alternative minimum tax (AMT) has generated new leasing business.

    a. True   b. False

25. Which of the following statements is most correct?

    a. Some years ago leasing was called "off balance sheet financing" because the leased asset and the corresponding lease obligation did not appear directly on the balance sheet. Today, though, that situation has changed materially because all leases must be capitalized and reported on the balance sheet, along with the value of the leased asset.
    b. In a lease-versus-purchase analysis, cash flows should generally be discounted at the weighted average cost of capital (WACC).
    c. Each of the above statements is true.
    d. Each of the above statements is false.

SELF-TEST PROBLEMS

(The following data apply to the next four Self-Test Problems.)

Treadmill Trucking Company is negotiating a lease for five new tractor/trailer rigs with Leasing International. Treadmill has received its best offer from Betterbilt Trucks for a total price of $1 million. The terms of the lease offered by International Leasing call for a payment of $205,000 at the beginning of each year of the 5-year lease. As an alternative to leasing, the firm can borrow from a large insurance company and buy the trucks. The $1 million would be borrowed on a simple interest term loan at a 10 percent interest rate for 5 years. The trucks fall into the MACRS 5-year class and have an expected residual value of $100,000. Maintenance costs would be included in the lease. If the trucks are owned, a maintenance contract would be purchased at the beginning of each year for $10,000 per year. Treadmill plans to buy a new fleet of trucks at the end of the fifth year. Leasing International has a 40 percent federal-plus-state marginal tax rate, while Treadmill Trucking has a total tax rate of 20 percent.

1. What is Treadmill's present value of the cost of owning?

   a. $802,468   b. $805,265   c. $807,189   d. $817,197   e. $829,668

2. What is Treadmill's present value of the cost of leasing?

   a. $702,468   b. $705,265   c. $707,189   d. $729,668   e. $735,419

3. Treadmill should lease the trucks.

   a. True   b. False

4. Assume that the lessor's alternative to leasing is to invest in a 5-year certificate of deposit which pays 9 percent before taxes. The lessor should

   a. Write the lease; it has an IRR of 3 percent.
   b. Not write the lease; it has an IRR of 3 percent.
   c. Write the lease; its NPV is $78,625.
   d. Not write the lease; its NPV is -$78,625.
   e. Be indifferent between the lease and the alternative investment.

(The following data apply to the next four Self-Test Problems.)

Walton Publishing Company (WPC) is evaluating a potential lease agreement on a printing press that costs $250,000 and falls into the MACRS 3-year class. The firm can borrow at an 8 percent rate on a 4-year amortized loan, if WPC decided to borrow and buy rather than lease. The press has a 4-year economic life, and its estimated residual value is $25,000 at the end of Year 4. If WPC buys the press, it would purchase a maintenance contract which costs $5,000 per year, payable at the beginning of each year. The lease terms, which include maintenance, call for a $71,000 lease payment at the beginning of each year. WPC's tax rate is 40 percent. (Hint: Use a financial calculator.)

5. Should the firm lease or buy?

    a. Lease; it costs $842 less than buying.
    b. Lease; it costs $1,576 less than buying.
    c. Buy; it costs $1,576 less than leasing.
    d. Buy; it costs $842 less than leasing.
    e. Neither lease nor buy; the truck's NPV is negative.

6. Assume that the lessor is in the 40 percent tax bracket. Further, the lessor's investment alternatives of similar risk yield 8 percent before taxes. Should the lessor write the lease?

    a. Yes, its NPV is $1,577.   **d.** No, its NPV is -$842.
    b. No, its NPV is -$1,577.   **e.** The lessor is indifferent.
    c. Yes, its NPV is $842.

7. At what lease payment would the lessee be indifferent between owning and leasing?

    a. $42,178   **b.** $68,348   **c.** $69,572   **d.** $70,898   **e.** $70,296

ANSWERS TO SELF-TEST QUESTIONS

1. borrowing; leverage
2. sale and leaseback; use
3. Operating
4. financial; capital; new
5. short; small (nominal)
6. lease payment
7. capitalize; balance sheets

8. fixed assets; present value; debt (liability)
9. residual value
10. Competition; residual
11. balance sheet; leverage (debt)
12. financing; capital budgeting
13. Tax considerations
14. alternative minimum tax

15. Combination
16. guideline; tax-oriented

17. after-tax cost of debt
18. technological obsolescence

19. b. Operating leases include both financing and maintenance arrangements, while financial, or capital, leases typically do not provide maintenance services. However, many leases written today are combination leases, which combine some of the features of both operating and financial leases.

20. b. The cash flows are fairly certain, so they should be discounted at a relatively low rate, generally, the after-tax cost of debt.

21. b. Operating leases are not fully amortized. The lessor expects to recover all costs either in subsequent leases or through the sale of the used equipment at its residual value.

22. a. But analysts would recognize that leases are as risky as debt financing, and thus include the impact of lease financing on the firm's debt costs and capital structure.

23. b. FASB #13 spells out in detail the conditions under which leases must be capitalized.

24. a. Firms have been seeking ways to lower their AMT liability. Leasing for short periods and hence making high lease payments will reduce the company's reported earnings and meet this need.

25. d. Statement a is false; only certain leases that meet the FASB #13 criteria for capitalization have to be reported on the balance sheet. Statement b is false; the discount rate in a borrow-versus-lease decision is the after-tax cost of debt because the cash flows are fairly certain. Therefore, statement d is the correct choice.

SOLUTIONS TO SELF-TEST PROBLEMS

1.   d.   Place the cash flows associated with ownership on a time line:

	0 8%	1	2	3	4	5 Years
AT loan payments		-80,000	-80,000	-80,000	-80,000	-1,080,000
Dep. tax savings[a]		40,000	64,000	38,000	24,000	22,000
Maintenance (AT)[b]	-8,000	-8,000	-8,000	-8,000	-8,000	
Residual value (AT)[c]						92,000
	-8,000	-48,000	-24,000	-50,000	-64,000	-966,000

Notes:

[a]Depreciation schedule:

Year	Factor	Depreciation Expense	Tax Savings
1	0.20	$ 200,000	$ 40,000
2	0.32	320,000	64,000
3	0.19	190,000	38,000
4	0.12	120,000	24,000
5	0.11	110,000	22,000
6	0.06	60,000	12,000
		$1,000,000	$200,000

[b]After-tax maintenance cash flow = $10,000(1 – T) = $8,000.
[c]Net residual value = $100,000 – ($100,000 – $60,000)(T) = $92,000.
  PV cost of owning at the firm's 8 percent after-tax cost of debt is $817,197.

2.   c.   Place the cash flows associated with leasing on a time line:

	0 8%	1	2	3	4	5 Years
Lease payments (AT)[a]	-164,000	-164,000	-164,000	-164,000	-164,000	

Notes:
[a]$205,000(1 – T) = $164,000.

PV cost of leasing at the firm's 8 percent after-tax cost of debt is $707,189.

3.   a.   The Net Advantage to Leasing (NAL) is $817,197 – $707,189 = $110,008, and hence the trucks should be leased.

4. d. Place the lessor's cash flows on a time line:

	0 5.4%	1	2	3	4	5 Years
Outlay[a]	-1,000,000					
Dep. tax savings[b]		80,000	128,000	76,000	48,000	44,000
Lease pymt (AT)[c]	123,000	123,000	123,000	123,000	123,000	
Residual value (AT)[d]						84,000
Maintenance (AT)[e]	-6,000	-6,000	-6,000	-6,000	-6,000	
	-883,000	197,000	245,000	193,000	165,000	128,000

Notes:

[a]Cost of purchasing the trucks.

[b]This is each year's depreciation expense times the lessor's tax rate of 40 percent.

[c]After-tax lease payment = $205,000(1 − 0.40) = $123,000.

[d]After-tax residual value = $100,000 − ($100,000 − $60,000)(T) = $84,000.

[e]After-tax maintenance payment = $10,000(1 − T).

The lessor's NPV of the lease investment is the PV of the net cash flows when discounted at the after-tax opportunity cost of capital or 9%(1 − T) = 9%(0.6) = 5.4%. NPV = -$78,625.

5. c. Cost of owning: Net investment = $250,000.

	0 4.8%	1	2	3	4 Years
Loan Payments[a]		-75,480.20	-75,480.20	-75,480.20	-75,480.20
Interest tax savings[b]		8,000.00	6,224.63	4,307.24	2,236.45
Maintenance (AT)	-3,000	-3,000.00	-3,000.00	-3,000.00	
Dep. tax savings[c]		33,000.00	45,000.00	15,000.00	7,000.00
Residual value (AT)[d]					15,000.00
	-3,000	-37,480.20	-27,255.57	-59,172.96	-51,243.75

Notes:

[a]Loan amortization schedule:

Year	Beg. Bal.	PMT	Int.	Prin. Repymt.	End. Bal.
1	$250,000.00	$ 75,480.20	$20,000.00	$ 55,480.20	$194,519.80
2	194,519.80	75,480.20	15,561.58	59,918.62	134,601.18
3	134,601.18	75,480.20	10,768.09	64,712.11	69,889.07
4	69,889.07	75,480.20	5,591.13	69,889.07	0.00
		$301,920.80	$51,920.80	$250,000.00	

[b]Interest tax savings = Interest$(1 - T)$.

[c]Depreciation schedule:

Year	Factor	Depreciation Expense	Tax Savings
1	0.33	$ 82,500	$ 33,000
2	0.45	112,500	45,000
3	0.15	37,500	15,000
4	0.07	17,500	7,000
	1.00	$250,000	$100,000

[d]Residual value (AT) = $25,000$(1 - T)$ = $15,000.

PV cost of owning at 4.8% = $157,470.

Cost of leasing:

	0 4.8% 1	2	3	4 Years
Lease payments (AT)[a]	-42,600	-42,600 -42,600	-42,600	

Notes:

[a]$71,000$(1 - T)$ = $42,600.

PV cost of leasing at 4.8% = $159,046.

Thus, owning is $157,470 – $159,046 = $1,576 less costly than leasing, so the firm should purchase the printing press.

6. **a.** Lessor's analysis:

	0 4.8%	1	2	3	4 Years
Net cost	-250,000				
Maintenance	-3,000	-3,000	-3,000	-3,000	
Dep. tax savings		33,000	45,000	15,000	7,000
Net residual value					15,000
Lease payment	42,600	42,600	42,600	42,600	
	-210,400	72,600	84,600	54,600	22,000

The lessor's NPV at 4.8 percent = $1,577.

7. **e.** The lessee would be indifferent if the cost of leasing were equal to $157,470, the PV of owning. Thus,

$157,470 = PMT(PVIFA_{4.8\%,4})(1.048)$
$157,470 = PMT[(1-(1/1.048)^4)/0.048](1.048)$
$157,470 = PMT(3.56249)(1.048)$
$\quad\quad PMT = \$42,177.70.$

Note that this payment is after taxes, so it must be "grossed up" to calculate the lease payment before taxes. Lease payment (BT) = $42,177.70/0.6 = $70,296.17, or approximately $70,296.

CHAPTER 21
HYBRID FINANCING: PREFERRED STOCK, WARRANTS, AND CONVERTIBLES

OVERVIEW

In earlier chapters, we have examined common stock, various types of long-term debt, and leasing. In this chapter, we examine three other sources of long-term capital: preferred stock, which is a hybrid security that represents a cross between debt and common equity; warrants, which are derivative securities; and convertibles, which are hybrids between debt (or preferred stock) and warrants.

OUTLINE

Preferred stock is a hybrid—it is similar to bonds in some respects and to common stock in others. Preferred stock resembles bonds in that it has a par value, and like a bond's coupon payments, preferred dividends are fixed in amount and must be paid before common stock dividends. On the other hand, if earnings are not sufficient to cover the preferred dividend, the directors can omit the dividend without subjecting the company to potential bankruptcy.

- ■ Accountants generally view preferred stock as equity, and hence show it on the balance sheet as an equity account. However, from a finance perspective preferred stock lies somewhere between debt and common equity—it imposes a fixed charge and thus increases the firm's financial leverage, yet omitting the preferred dividend does not force a company into bankruptcy.

- ■ Some of the basic features of preferred stock are listed below.
    - ❑ The dividend is either stated as a percentage of par, as so many dollars per share, or both ways. If the preferred dividend is not earned, the company does not have to pay it.
    - ❑ Most preferred issues are *cumulative*, meaning that the cumulative total of all unpaid preferred dividends must be paid before dividends can be paid on the common stock.

- ❑ Unpaid dividends are called *arrearages*. Dividends in arrears do not earn interest; they only grow from additional nonpayments of the preferred dividend.
- ❑ Preferred stock normally has no voting rights. However, most preferred issues stipulate that the preferred stockholders can elect a minority of the directors if the preferred dividend is omitted.

■ Preferred stock is less risky than bonds from the viewpoint of the issuing corporation.

■ Preferred stock is riskier than bonds to investors for the following reasons:
- ❑ Preferred stockholders' claims are subordinated to those of bondholders in the event of liquidation.
- ❑ Bondholders are more likely to continue receiving income during hard times than are preferred stockholders.

■ Investors require a higher after-tax rate of return on a given firm's preferred stock than on its bonds.

■ Since 70 percent of preferred dividends is exempt from corporate taxes, preferred stock is attractive to corporate investors.

■ About half of all preferred stock issued in recent years has been convertible into common stock.

■ Some preferred stocks are similar to perpetual bonds in that they have no maturity date, but most new issues now have specified maturities.

■ Many preferred issues are callable by the issuing corporation, which can also limit the life of the preferred.

■ Nonconvertible preferred stock is virtually all owned by corporations, which can take advantage of the 70 percent dividend exclusion to obtain a higher after-tax yield on preferred stock than on bonds.

■ The volume of preferred stock financing is geared to the supply of money in the hands of corporate investors.

■ For issuers, preferred stock has a tax disadvantage relative to debt—interest expense is deductible while preferred dividends are not.

■ Two important innovations in preferred stock financing have occurred in recent years.

- ❏ *Adjustable rate preferred stocks (ARPs)* tie their dividends to the rate on Treasury securities instead of paying fixed dividends.
- ❏ *Money market,* or *market auction, preferred stocks* are, from the investor's point of view, a low risk 7-week maturity security which can be sold between auction dates at close to par value.

- ■ Preferred stock has the following advantages from the issuer's standpoint:
  - ❏ The obligation to pay preferred dividends is not contractual; passing a preferred dividend cannot force a firm into bankruptcy.
  - ❏ The firm avoids the dilution of common equity that occurs when common stock is sold.
  - ❏ Since preferred sometimes has no maturity, and since preferred sinking fund payments, if present, are typically spread over a long period, preferred issues reduce the cash flow drain from repayment of principal that occurs with debt issues.

- ■ Preferred also has the following disadvantages from the issuer's standpoint:
  - ❏ Since preferred dividends are not tax deductible, preferred stock usually has a higher after-tax cost than debt financing. However, the tax advantage of preferred stocks to corporate purchasers lowers their pre-tax cost and thus their effective cost.
  - ❏ Preferred dividends are considered to be a fixed cost. Therefore, their use, like that of debt, increases financial risk and thus the cost of common equity.

A warrant is a certificate issued by a company which gives the holder the right to buy a stated number of shares of the company's stock at a specified price for some specified length of time.

- ■ Generally, warrants are distributed with debt as an incentive for investors to buy long-term debt with a lower coupon rate than would otherwise be required.
  - ❏ Warrants are long-term call options that have value because holders can buy the firm's common stock at the exercise price regardless of how high the market price climbs.
  - ❏ The option offsets the low interest rate.

- ■ The key issue in setting the terms of a bond with warrants is valuing the warrants.
  - ❏ The straight-debt value can be estimated quite accurately.
  - ❏ The Black-Scholes Model cannot be used to value a warrant. Instead, more sophisticated and accurate models are used.
  - ❏ Price paid for bond with warrants = Straight-debt value of bond + Value of warrants.
    - There is a major difference between call options and warrants. When call options are exercised, the stock provided to the optionholder comes from the secondary

market, but when warrants are exercised, the stock provided to the warrantholders are newly issued shares.

- The exercise of warrants dilutes the value of the original equity, which could cause the value of the original warrant to differ from the value of a similar call option.

■ Warrants generally are used by small, rapidly growing firms as "sweeteners" to make their bonds or preferred stocks more attractive. However, after AT&T became the first large and financially strong corporation to use warrants, their use by such firms became commonplace.

■ A bond with warrants has some characteristics of debt and some characteristics of equity. It is a *hybrid security* that provides the financial manager with an opportunity to expand the firm's mix of securities and thus to appeal to a broader group of investors.

■ Most warrants are *detachable* and can be traded separately from the bond or preferred stock with which they were issued.

■ Warrants generate additional equity capital when they are exercised.
- The *exercise price* on warrants is generally set 20 to 30 percent above the market price of the stock on the date the bond is issued.

■ There are three conditions which encourage holders to exercise their warrants:
- If the market price is above the exercise price, and the warrants are about to expire, holders will exercise their options and purchase stock.
- Since warrants pay no dividends, holders will be inclined to exercise them and obtain common stock as the common dividend is increased.
- A *stepped-up exercise price* will also induce holders to exercise their warrants.

■ Warrants generally bring in funds only if funds are needed. Warrants generally produce needed funds as the company grows and as the stock price increases over the exercise price.

■ When warrants are exercised a transfer of wealth is evident, but that transfer is both expected and gradual and is also in the best interest of the firm.

■ The component cost of an issue with warrants can be estimated by placing the expected cash flows associated with the issue on a time line and then calculating the IRR of the stream.
- The expected rate of return to investors is the before-tax cost to the company.

■ Although the interest rate on the bond will be less than the rate on a similar straight debt issue, the total cost rate of the issue, including the opportunity cost of the warrants, will usually be somewhere between the firm's costs of straight debt and equity because the riskiness of a bond with warrants falls between that of debt and equity.

Convertible securities are bonds or preferred stocks which, under specified terms and conditions, can be exchanged for common stock at the option of the holder.

■ Conversion of a bond or preferred stock, unlike the exercise of a warrant, does not provide capital: debt (or preferred stock) is simply replaced on the balance sheet by common stock. However, conversion does lower the debt ratio improving the firm's financial strength.

■ The *conversion ratio (CR)* specifies the number of common shares that will be received for each bond or share of preferred stock that is converted.

■ The *conversion price, P_c,* is the effective price paid for the common stock when conversion occurs. For example, if a bond is issued at its par value of $1,000 and can be converted into 40 shares of common stock, the conversion price would be

$$P_c = \$1,000/CR = \$1,000/40 = \$25 \text{ per share.}$$

Someone buying the bond and then converting it would, in effect, be paying $25 per share for the stock.

■ The conversion price of a bond is typically set at about 20 to 30 percent above the prevailing market price of the common stock at the time the convertible issue is sold. Thus, if the common stock is selling for $20.83 at the time the convertible is issued, the conversion price might be set at 1.2($20.83) = $25. This would produce a conversion ratio of CR = 40:

$$CR = \$1,000/P_c = \$1,000/\$25 = 40.$$

■ The actual market price of a convertible bond can never fall below the higher of its straight-debt value or its conversion value. The higher of those two values is called the *floor price.*

■ The bond's market value will typically exceed its floor value.
 ❑ It will exceed the straight-bond value because the option to convert is worth something.
 ❑ The convertible's price will also exceed its conversion value because holding the convertible is equivalent to holding a call option, and, prior to expiration, the option's true value is higher than its expiration value.

■ Like a bond with warrants, the expected cost rate on convertible debt can be estimated by placing the issue's expected cash flows on a time line. Also, like debt with warrants, the costs should lie between the issuing firm's cost of straight debt and its cost of common stock, because, from the investors' viewpoint, a convertible is riskier than straight debt but less risky than common stock.

■ Convertible issues have two important advantages from the issuer's standpoint:
  ❑ By giving investors an opportunity to realize capital gains, a firm can sell debt with a lower interest rate or preferred stock with a lower dividend yield.
  ❑ Convertibles provide a way of selling common stock in the future at prices higher than those currently prevailing.

■ From the standpoint of the issuer, convertibles have three important disadvantages:
  ❑ If the stock price does not increase, investors will not convert and the company will be stuck with debt (or preferred) rather than equity in its capital structure.
  ❑ Convertibles typically have a low coupon interest rate, and the advantage of this low-cost debt will be lost when conversion occurs.
  ❑ If the firm's stock price rises sharply, it would have been better off if it had used straight debt in spite of its higher cost and then sold the common shares at the higher price and refunded the debt.

■ Typically, convertibles contain a call provision that enables the issuing firm to force holders to convert.

■ When convertible debt is issued, actions to increase the company's riskiness may increase the convertible debt's value as well as the common stock's value. Thus, some of the gains to shareholders from taking on high-risk projects may be transferred to convertible bondholders. This reduction in benefits to shareholders decreases the incentive for managers to substitute assets, and hence lowers agency costs. This same general logic applies to convertible preferred and warrants.

Convertible debt can be thought of as straight debt with nondetachable warrants. Thus, it might appear that debt with warrants and convertible debt are more or less interchangeable. However, a closer examination reveals differences.

■ The exercise of warrants brings in new equity capital, while the conversion of convertibles results only in an accounting transfer.

■ A second difference involves flexibility. Most convertible issues contain a call provision that allows the issuer either to refund the debt or to force conversion, depending on the relationship between the conversion value and call price. However, most warrants are not callable, so firms generally must wait until maturity for the warrants to generate new equity capital.

■ Generally, maturities also differ between warrants and convertibles. Warrants typically have much shorter maturities than convertibles, and warrants typically expire before their accompanying debt matures.

■ Warrants usually provide for fewer future common shares than do convertibles because with convertibles all of the debt is converted to common whereas debt remains outstanding when warrants are exercised.

■ In general, firms that issue debt with warrants are smaller and riskier than those that issue convertibles.

■ Bonds with warrants typically require issuance costs that are about 1.2 percentage points more than the flotation costs for convertibles.

Firms must take into account outstanding warrants or convertible securities when reporting earnings per share.

■ Firms with warrants or convertible securities outstanding must reflect these securities when they report earnings per share to stockholders. A firm could report earnings per share in one of three ways:
- ❑ *Basic EPS*, where earnings available to common stockholders are divided by the average number of shares actually outstanding during the period.
- ❑ *Primary EPS*, where earnings available are divided by the average number of shares that would be outstanding if those warrants and convertibles "likely to be exercised or converted in the near future" had actually been exercised or converted.
- ❑ *Diluted EPS*, which is similar to primary EPS except that *all* warrants and convertibles are assumed to be exercised or converted regardless of the likelihood of this occurring.
- ❑ Under SEC rules, firms are required to report both basic and diluted EPS.

SELF-TEST QUESTIONS

Definitional

1.   Preferred stock has characteristics similar to both _____ and _____ _____.

2.   The _____ _____ feature means that preferred stockholders must receive all dividends in arrears before common dividends may be paid.

3.   Warrants and convertibles may make a company's securities more attractive to a broader range of _____ and hence lower its _____ ____ _____.

4.   A(n) _____ is a long-term call option to buy a stated number of shares of _____ _____ at a specified _____.

5.   Warrants are often attached to a(n) _____ issue in order to induce investors to purchase the issue at a relatively low _____ rate.

6.   The _____ price of a warrant is generally set at about ____ to ____ percent above the stock's market price.

7.   When they are exercised, warrants add additional _____ _____ to a firm's capital structure.

8.   Warrants will certainly be exercised if the stock's market price is above the _____ price and the warrant is about to _____.

9.   Holders of warrants will have an extra incentive to convert to _____ _____ as the company increases the _____ on its common shares.

10. Almost all warrants are _____ and can be traded separately from the debt or preferred stock with which they were issued.

11. Convertible bonds or preferred stocks may be exchanged for _____ _____ at the option of the holder.

12. The _____ _____ specifies the number of shares of common stock that will be received for each bond that is converted.

13. The _____ _____ is the effective price paid for one share of common stock upon conversion.

14. When a convertible bond is issued, the conversion price is determined by dividing the _____ _____ of the bond by the number of shares received on conversion.

15. Selling a convertible issue may have the effect of selling _____ _____ at a price higher than the market price prevailing at the time the convertible is issued.

16. If a firm's stock price does increase, the company can force _____ of convertible bonds by including a(n) _____ _____ in the bond indenture.

17. It may be unwise for a firm to sell a convertible issue if it anticipates that its _____ _____ will increase rapidly in the near future.

18. In reporting its earnings, a firm with warrants and convertible securities must report both _____ EPS and _____ EPS.

19. The higher of a convertible bond's straight-debt value or its conversion value is called the _____ _____.

20. _____ _____ _____ _____ tie their dividends to the rate on Treasury securities instead of paying fixed dividends.

Conceptual

21. Preferred stock is generally viewed as equity by bondholders and as debt by common stockholders.

    a. True   b. False

22. The coupon interest rate on convertible bonds is generally set higher than the rate on similar nonconvertible issues.

    a. True   b. False

23. Primary EPS shows what EPS would have been if all warrant and convertibles had been converted prior to the reporting date.

    a. True   b. False

24. Investors are willing to accept lower interest (or dividend) yields on convertible securities in the hopes of later realizing capital gains.

    a. True   b. False

25. The conversion of a convertible bond replaces debt with common equity on a firm's balance sheet, but it does not bring in any additional capital.

    a. True   **b.** False

26. The market price of a warrant may be substantially above its expiration value.

    a. True   **b.** False

27. The advantage to the corporation of using preferred stock financing is:

    a. Preferred dividends are tax deductible.
    b. Preferred stockholders bear no risk of ownership.
    c. The returns on preferred stock are always higher than on bonds.
    d. The firm can retain control and limit the profit sharing of new investors.
    e. Preferred stockholders always have voting rights.

SELF-TEST PROBLEMS

1. The Clayton Corporation has warrants outstanding that permit the holder to purchase one share of common stock per warrant at $30. What is the expiration value of Clayton's warrants if the common stock is currently selling at $20 per share?

    a. -$20   **b.** -$10   **c.** $5   **d.** $10   **e.** $20

2. Refer to Self-Test Problem 1. Calculate the expiration value if the common stock is now selling at $40 per share.

    a. -$20   **b.** -$10   **c.** $0   **d.** $10   **e.** $20

3. White Corporation has just sold a bond issue with 10 warrants attached to each bond. The bonds have a 20-year maturity, an annual coupon rate of 12 percent, and they sold at the $1,000 initial offering price. The current yield to maturity on bonds of equal risk, but without warrants, is 15 percent. What is the value of each warrant?

    a. $22.56   **b.** $21.20   **c.** $20.21   **d.** $19.24   **e.** $18.78

(The following data apply to the next four Self-Test Problems.)

Central Food Brokers is considering issuing a 20-year convertible bond that will be priced at its par value of $1,000 per bond. The bonds have a 12 percent annual coupon interest rate, and each bond could be converted into 40 shares of common stock. The stock currently sells at $20 per share, has an expected annual dividend of $3.00, and is growing at a constant 5 percent per year. The bonds are callable after 10 years at a price of $1,050, with the price declining by $5 per year thereafter. If, after 10 years, the conversion value exceeds the call price by at least 20 percent, management will call the bonds.

4. What is the conversion price?

   a. $20   **b.** $25   **c.** $33   **d.** $40   **e.** $50

5. If the yield to maturity on similar nonconvertible bonds is 16 percent, what is the straight-debt value?

   a. $1,000.00   **b.** $907.83   **c.** $812.22   **d.** $762.85   **e.** $692.37

6. What is the conversion value in Year 10?

   a. $800.73   **b.** $1,000.50   **c.** $1,148.01   **d.** $1,222.18   **e.** $1,303.12

7. If an investor expects the bond issue to be called in Year 10, and he plans on converting it at that time, what is the investor's expected rate of return upon conversion?

   a. 12.0%   **b.** 12.2%   **c.** 13.6%   **d.** 14.4%   **e.** 15.3%

ANSWERS TO SELF-TEST QUESTIONS

1.	bonds (debt); common stock (equity)	10.	detachable
2.	cumulative dividends	11.	common stock
3.	investors; cost of capital	12.	conversion ratio
4.	warrant; common stock; price	13.	conversion price
5.	debt; interest	14.	par value
6.	exercise (striking); 20; 30	15.	common stock
7.	common equity	16.	conversion; call provision
8.	exercise (striking); expire	17.	stock price
9.	common stock; dividend	18.	basic; diluted

19. floor price   **20.**   Adjustable rate preferred stock

21.   a. Preferred stock is treated as debt by common stockholders since preferred dividends must be paid before common dividends. Bondholders have a priority claim on cash flows over preferred stockholders and also priority in the event of liquidation and therefore view preferred stock as equity.

22.   b. The coupon interest rate is lower because investors expect some capital gains return upon conversion. Note, however, that the overall required rate of return is higher for the convertible issue.

23.   b. Primary EPS includes only those shares from warrants and convertibles likely to be converted in the near future. Diluted EPS includes all shares.

24.   a. However, the investor is including the expected capital gain as part of his required return, so the total required return on convertibles is higher than on a straight security with similar other features.

25.   a. The bond is turned in to the company and replaced with common stock. No cash is exchanged.

26.   a. A warrant is a call option, and hence its value depends not only on its expiration value, but also on its time to maturity, the price volatility of the underlying stock, and the risk-free rate.

27.   d. By setting a fixed dividend, management can limit the degree of profit sharing by preferred stockholders and also retain control since preferred stockholders normally do not have voting rights.

SOLUTIONS TO SELF-TEST PROBLEMS

1.   b. Expiration value = Market price − Exercise price. When P_0 = $20, the Expiration value = $20 − $30 = -$10.

2.   d. When P_0 = $40, the Expiration value = $40 − $30 = $10.

3. e. First, find the straight-debt value:

$$V = INT(PVIFA_{k,n}) + M(PVIF_{k,n}) = \$120(PVIFA_{15\%,20}) + \$1,000(PVIF_{15\%,20})$$
$$= \$812.22.$$

Thus the value of the attached warrants is $\$1,000 - \$812.22 = \$187.78$. Since each bond has 10 warrants, each warrant must have a value of $\$18.78$.

4. b. P_c = Par value/Shares received = $\$1,000/40 = \$25.00$.

5. d. $V = INT(PVIFA_{k,n}) + M(PVIF_{k,n})$
$$= \$120(PVIFA_{16\%,20}) + \$1,000(PVIF_{16\%,20}) = \$762.85.$$

6. e. $C_t = P_t CR;\ C_{10} = P_{10}CR = \$20(1.05)^{10}(40) = \$1,303.12$.

7. c. This is solved by finding the value of k_c in the equation:

$$\text{Price paid} = INT\left(PVIFA_{k_c,n}\right) + \text{Expected conversion value}\left(PVIF_{k_c,n}\right)$$
$$\$1,000 = \$120\left(PVIFA_{k_c,10}\right) + \$1,303.12\left(PVIF_{k_c,10}\right)$$
$$k_c = 13.6\%.$$

CHAPTER 22
CURRENT ASSET MANAGEMENT

OVERVIEW

About 60 percent of a typical financial manager's time is devoted to working capital management, and many students' first jobs will involve working capital. This is particularly true of smaller businesses, where new job creation is especially rapid. Therefore, working capital is an essential topic.

Working capital policy involves two basic questions: (1) What is the appropriate amount of current assets for the firm to carry, both in total and for each specific account, and (2) how should current assets be financed? This chapter addresses the first question, while Chapter 22 addresses the second question.

OUTLINE

It is useful to begin by reviewing some basic definitions and concepts.

■   *Working capital*, sometimes called *gross working capital*, is defined as current assets, while *net working capital* is defined as current assets minus current liabilities.

■   *Net operating working capital (NOWC)* is defined as operating, or non-interest bearing, current assets minus operating, or non-interest charging, current liabilities. Generally, NOWC is equal to cash, accounts receivable and inventories less accounts payable and accruals.

■   The *current ratio*, which is calculated as current assets divided by current liabilities, is intended to measure liquidity.

■   The *quick ratio*, which also attempts to measure liquidity, is calculated as current assets less inventories, divided by current liabilities. The quick ratio is an "acid test" of a company's ability to meet its current obligations.

■   The most comprehensive picture of a firm's liquidity is obtained by examining its *cash budget*, which forecasts a firm's cash inflows and outflows, and thus focuses on what really counts, the firm's ability to generate sufficient cash inflows to meet its required cash outflows.

■   *Working capital policy* refers to the firm's policies regarding target levels for each category of current assets and how current assets will be financed.

■   *Working capital management* involves both setting working capital policy and carrying out that policy in day-to-day operations.

A firm's current asset levels rise and fall with business cycles and seasonal trends. At the peak of such cycles, businesses carry their maximum amounts of current assets.

■   There are three alternative policies regarding the total amount of current assets carried. Each policy differs with regard to the amount of current assets carried to support any given level of sales, hence in the turnover of those assets.

  ❑   A *relaxed current asset investment policy* is one where relatively large amounts of cash, marketable securities, and inventories are carried, and where sales are stimulated by the use of a credit policy that provides liberal financing to customers and a corresponding high level of receivables.

  ❑   A *restricted current asset investment policy* is one where holdings of cash, securities, inventories, and receivables are minimized. Current assets are turned over more frequently, so each dollar of current assets is forced to "work harder."

  ❑   A *moderate current asset investment policy* is between the two extremes.

  ❑   Generally, the decision on the current assets level involves a risk/return tradeoff. The relaxed policy minimizes risk, but it also has the lowest expected return. On the other hand, the restricted policy offers the highest expected return coupled with the highest risk. The moderate policy falls in between the two extremes in terms of expected risk and return.

  ❑   Changing technology can lead to dramatic changes in the optimal current asset investment policy.

■   Working capital consists of four main components: cash, marketable securities, inventory, and accounts receivable.

■   For each type of asset, firms face a fundamental tradeoff: current assets are necessary to conduct business, and the greater the holdings of current assets, the smaller the danger of running out, hence the lower the firm's operating risk. However, holding working capital is costly; so, there is pressure to hold the amount of working capital carried to the minimum consistent with running the business without interruption.

The concept of working capital management originated with the old Yankee peddler, who would borrow to buy inventory, sell the inventory to pay off the bank loan, and then repeat the cycle. That general concept has been applied to more complex businesses, and the cash flow cycle concept is used for analyzing the effectiveness of a firm's working capital management.

■ The cash conversion cycle model focuses on the length of time between when the company makes payments and when it receives cash inflows.

■ The *inventory conversion period* is the average length of time required to convert materials into finished goods and then to sell those goods.

■ The *receivables collection period* is the average length of time required to convert the firm's receivables into cash, that is, to collect cash following a sale.

■ The *payables deferral period* is the average length of time between the purchase of materials and labor and the payment of cash for them.

■ The *cash conversion cycle* nets out the inventory conversion period, the receivables collection period, and the payables deferral period.
  ❑ It equals the length of time between the firm's actual cash expenditures to pay for productive resources and its own cash receipts from the sale of products—the average length of time a dollar is tied up in current assets.
  ❑ Cash conversion cycle = Inventory conversion period + Receivables collection period – Payables deferral period.

In today's world of intense global competition, working capital management is receiving increasing attention from managers striving for peak efficiency. In fact, the goal of many leading companies today is zero working capital.

■ Proponents of *zero working capital* claim that a movement toward this goal not only generates cash but also speeds up production and helps businesses make more timely deliveries and operate more efficiently.

■ The concept has its own definition of working capital: Inventories + Receivables – Payables.
  ❑ The rationale here is (1) inventories and receivables are the keys to making sales, but (2) inventories can be financed by suppliers through accounts payable.

■ Reducing working capital and thus increasing turnover has two major financial benefits.
  ❑ Every dollar freed up by reducing inventories or receivables, or by increasing payables, results in a one-time contribution to cash flow.
  ❑ A movement toward zero working capital permanently raises a company's earnings.

■   The most important factor in moving toward zero working capital is increased speed. The best companies are able to start production after an order is received yet still meet customer delivery requirements. This system is known as *demand flow* or *demand-based management*, and it builds on the just-in-time method of inventory control.

❑   Demand flow management is broader than just-in-time because it requires that all elements of a production system operate quickly and efficiently.

■   A focus on minimizing receivables and inventories while maximizing payables will help a firm lower its investment in working capital and achieve financial and production economies.

Cash is a nonearning asset. Excessive cash balances reduce the rate of return on equity and hence the value of a firm's stock. Thus, the goal of cash management is to minimize the amount of cash the firm must hold in order to conduct its normal business activities, yet at the same time, to have sufficient cash (1) to take trade discounts, (2) to maintain its credit rating, and (3) to meet unexpected cash needs.

■   Firms hold cash for two primary reasons:

❑   Transactions balances are held to provide the cash needed to conduct normal business operations.

❑   Compensating balances are often required by banks for providing loans and services.

■   Two secondary reasons are also cited:

❑   Precautionary balances are held in reserve for random, unforeseen fluctuations in cash inflows and outflows.

❑   Speculative balances are held to enable the firm to take advantage of bargain purchases.

■   Firms do not segregate funds for each of these motives, because the same money often serves more than one purpose, but firms do consider all four factors in setting their overall cash positions.

■   An ample cash balance should be maintained to take advantage of *trade discounts* and favorable business opportunities, to help the firm maintain its credit rating, and to meet emergency needs.

A cash budget projects cash inflows and outflows over some specified period of time.

■   The basis for a cash budget is the sales forecast, the level of fixed assets and inventory that will be required to meet the forecasted sales level, and the times when payment must be made.

- Cash budgets can be created for any interval, but firms typically use a daily cash budget forecasted over the next month, plus less detailed monthly cash budgets for the coming year.
  - The monthly cash budgets are used for planning purposes, and the daily or weekly budgets for actual cash control.

- A typical cash budget consists of three sections.
  - The *collections and purchases worksheet* summarizes the firm's cash collections from sales and cash purchases for materials.
  - The *cash gain or loss section* lays out the cash inflows and outflows, and the "bottom line" of this section is the net cash gain or loss.
  - The *loan requirement or cash surplus section* summarizes the firm's cumulative need for loans and cumulative surplus cash.

- If the firm's cash inflows and outflows are not uniform over the budget interval, say monthly, the cash budget could seriously understate the firm's cash needs.

- The cash budget can be used to help set the firm's *target cash balance*, the desired cash balance that a firm plans to maintain in order to conduct business. This is accomplished by incorporating uncertainty into the budget, and then setting a target balance which provides a cushion against adverse conditions.

- Note that the cash budget focuses on the physical movement of cash, and hence depreciation cash flow does not appear directly in the budget. It does, however, affect the amount of taxes shown.

- Since the cash budget represents a forecast, all the values in the table are *expected* values.

- Spreadsheet programs such as *Lotus 1-2-3* and *Microsoft Excel*, are particularly well suited for preparing and analyzing the cash budget.

- The target cash balance probably will be adjusted over time, rising and falling with seasonal patterns and with long-term changes in the scale of the firm's operations.

Cash management has changed significantly over the last two decades as a result of an upward trend in interest rates and technological developments.

- From the early 1970s to the mid-1980s, there was an upward trend in interest rates that increased the opportunity cost of holding cash. This encouraged financial managers to search for more efficient ways of managing the firm's cash.

- Technological developments, particularly computerized electronic funds transfer mechanisms, changed the way cash is managed.

- Effective cash management encompasses proper management of cash inflows and outflows, which entails (1) improving forecasts of cash flows, (2) synchronizing cash inflows and outflows, (3) using float, (4) accelerating collections, (5) getting available funds to where they are needed, and (6) controlling disbursements.

- Synchronizing cash inflows and outflows provides cash when it is needed and thus enables firms to reduce cash balances, decrease bank loans, lower interest expense, and boost profits.

- *Check clearing* is the process of converting a check that has been written and mailed into cash in the payee's account.

- *Float* is defined as the difference between the balance shown in a firm's (or individual's) checkbook and the balance on the bank's records. A firm's *net float* is a function of its ability to speed up collections on checks received (*collections float*) and to slow down collections on checks written (*disbursement float*).

Several techniques are now used to speed collections and to get funds where they are needed.

- A *lockbox plan* is a procedure which speeds up collections and reduces float through the use of post office boxes in payers' local areas.
  - Customers mail checks to a post office box in a specified city. A local bank then collects the checks, deposits them, starts the clearing process, and notifies the selling firm that payment has been received.
  - Processing time is further reduced because it takes less time for banks to collect local checks.

- Firms are increasingly demanding payments of larger bills by wire, or even by automatic electronic debits, whereby funds are automatically deducted from one account and added to another.

Marketable securities typically provide much lower yields than a firm's operating assets, yet they are often held in sizable amounts.

- In many cases companies hold marketable securities for the same reasons they hold cash.

- While these securities are not as liquid as cash, in most cases they can be converted to cash on very short notice.

- Marketable securities provide at least a modest return, while cash yields nothing.

■ William Baumol first recognized that the tradeoff between cash and marketable securities is similar to the one firms face when setting the optimal inventory level.

  ❑ He applied the EOQ inventory model to determine the optimal level of cash balances.

  ❑ He suggested that cash holdings should be higher if costs are high and the time to liquidate marketable securities is long.

Inventory, which may be classified as supplies, raw materials, work-in-process, and finished goods, is an essential part of virtually all business operations.

■ Inventory levels depend heavily upon sales. Since inventory is acquired before sales can take place, an accurate sales forecast is critical to effective inventory management.

■ Errors in the establishment of inventory levels quickly lead either to lost sales or to excessive carrying costs.

■ Proper inventory management requires close coordination among the sales, purchasing, production, and finance departments. The sales/marketing department is generally the first to spot changes in demand. These changes must be worked into the company's purchasing and manufacturing schedules, and the financial manager must arrange any financing needed to support the inventory buildup. Lack of coordination among departments, poor sales forecasts, or both, can lead to disaster.

The twin goals of inventory management are (1) to insure that the inventories needed to sustain operations are available, but (2) to hold the costs of ordering and carrying inventories to the lowest possible level.

■ Inventory costs are divided into three categories: carrying costs, ordering and receiving costs, and the costs that are incurred if the firm runs short of inventory.

  ❑ *Carrying costs* generally rise in direct proportion to the average amount of inventory held. Carrying costs associated with inventory include cost of the capital tied up, storage and handling costs, insurance, property taxes, and depreciation and obsolescence.

  ❑ *Ordering costs*, which are considered to be fixed costs, decline as average inventory increase, that is, as the number of orders decrease. Ordering costs include the costs of placing and receiving orders.

  ❑ The *costs of running short* include loss of sales, loss of customer goodwill, and disruption of production schedules.

Inventory management also involves the establishment of an inventory control system. These systems vary from the extremely simple to the very complex.

■ One simple control procedure is the *red-line method*. A red line is drawn inside the bin where the inventory is stocked. When the red line shows, an order is placed.

■ The *two-bin method* has inventory items stocked in two bins. When the working bin is empty, an order is placed and inventory is drawn from the second bin.

■ Large companies employ much more sophisticated *computerized inventory control systems*. The computer starts with an inventory count in memory. As withdrawals are made, they are recorded by the computer, and the inventory balance is revised. Orders are automatically placed once the reorder point is reached.

■ The *just-in-time (JIT) system* coordinates a manufacturer's production with suppliers' so that raw materials arrive from suppliers just as they are needed in the production process. It also requires that component parts be perfect; therefore, JIT inventory management has been developed in conjunction with total quality management (TQM).

■ Another important development related to inventory is *out-sourcing*, which is the practice of purchasing components rather than making them in-house. Out-sourcing is often combined with just-in-time systems to reduce inventory levels.

■ A final point relating to inventory levels is the *relationship between production scheduling and inventory levels*. Inventory policy must be coordinated with the firm's manufacturing and procurement policies, because the ultimate goal is to *minimize total production and distribution costs*, and inventory costs are just one part of the picture.

Carrying receivables has both direct and indirect costs, but it also has an important benefit—granting credit will increase sales.

■ *Accounts receivable* are created when a firm sells goods or performs services on credit rather than on a cash basis. When cash is received, accounts receivable are reduced by the same amount.

■ The total amount of accounts receivable outstanding is determined by (1) the volume of credit sales and (2) the average length of time between sales and collections.

■ The investment in receivables, like any asset, must be financed in some manner.

Receivables must be actively managed to insure that the firm's receivables policy is effective. There are two commonly used methods to monitor a firm's receivables.

■ The *days sales outstanding (DSO)*, also sometimes called the average collection period (ACP), measures the average length of time it takes a firm's customers to pay off their credit purchases.
  ❑ The DSO is calculated by dividing the receivables balance by average daily credit sales.

- ❑ The DSO can be compared with the industry average and the firm's own credit terms to get an indication of how well customers are adhering to the terms prescribed and how customers' payments, on average, compare with the industry average.

- ■ An *aging schedule* breaks down a firm's receivables by the ages of the accounts, and it points out the percentage of receivables due that are attributable to late paying customers.

- ■ Management should constantly monitor both the DSO and the aging schedule to detect trends, to see how the firm's collection experience compares with its credit terms, and to see how effectively the credit department is operating in comparison with other firms in the industry.

- ■ Both the DSO and aging schedule can be distorted if sales are seasonal or if a firm is growing rapidly. A deterioration in either the DSO or the aging schedule should be taken as a signal to investigate further, but not necessarily as a sign that the firm's credit policy has weakened.

The major controllable determinants of demand are sales prices, product quality, advertising, and the firm's credit policy. The credit policy consists of (1) the credit period, (2) credit standards, (3) collection policy, and (4) discounts.

- ■ The *credit period* is the length of time for which credit is granted. Increasing the credit period often stimulates sales, but there is a cost involved in carrying the increased receivables.
  - ❑ A firm's regular *credit terms* include the credit period and discount.

- ■ *Credit standards* refer to the financial strength and creditworthiness a customer must exhibit in order to qualify for credit.
  - ❑ Setting credit standards requires a measurement of *credit quality*, which is defined in terms of the probability of a customer's default.
  - ❑ Credit evaluation is a well-established practice, and a good credit manager can make reasonably accurate judgments of the probability of default by different classes of customers.
  - ❑ Computerized information systems can assist in making better credit decisions, but in the final analysis, most credit decisions are really exercises in informed judgment.

- ■ *Collection policy* refers to the procedures the firm follows to collect past-due accounts. The collection process can be expensive in terms of both out-of-pocket expenditures and lost goodwill, but at least some firmness is needed to prevent an undue lengthening of the collection period and to minimize outright losses. A balance must be struck between the costs and benefits of different collection policies.

- The last variable in the credit policy decision is the firm's *cash discount policy*. Cash discounts attract customers and encourage early payment but reduce the dollar amount received on each discount sale.
  - Offering discounts should cause a reduction in the days sales outstanding, because some existing customers will pay more promptly in order to get the discount.
  - If sales are seasonal, a firm may use *seasonal dating* on discounts. Seasonal dating is the offering of terms to induce customers to buy early by not requiring payment until the purchaser's selling season, regardless of when the goods are shipped.

- Other conditions may also influence a firm's overall credit policy.
  - It is sometimes possible to sell on credit and assess a carrying charge on the receivables that are outstanding, making credit sales more profitable than cash sales.
  - It is illegal for a firm to charge prices or to set credit terms that discriminate between customers unless these differential prices are cost-justified.
    - The same holds true for credit—it is illegal to offer more favorable credit terms to one customer or class of customers than to another, unless the differences are cost justified.

SELF-TEST QUESTIONS

Definitional

1. Current assets are also referred to as _____ _____.

2. _____ working capital is defined as _____ assets minus current _____.

3. The goal of cash management is to _____ the amount of _____ the firm must hold in order to conduct its normal business activities.

4. Precautionary balances are maintained in order to allow for random, unforeseen fluctuations in cash _____ and _____.

5. _____ balances are maintained to pay banks for services they perform.

6. Efficient cash management is often concerned with speeding up the _____ of checks received and slowing down the _____ of checks issued.

7. One method for speeding the collection process (through the use of post office boxes in payers' local areas) is the use of a(n) _____ system.

8. The difference between a firm's balance on its own books and its balance as carried on the bank's books is known as _____.

9. Inventory is usually classified as _____, _____ _____, _____-____- _____, and _____ _____.

10. The twin goals of inventory management are to provide the inventory needed for operations at the _____ _____.

11. Storage costs, obsolescence, and other costs that _____ with larger inventory are known as _____ costs.

12. Ordering and receiving costs are _____ related to average inventory size.

13. Inventory control systems that require suppliers to deliver items as they are needed are called _____-____-_____ systems.

14. _____ _____ are created when goods are sold or services are performed on credit.

15. A firm's outstanding accounts receivable will be determined by the _____ of credit sales and the length of time between _____ and _____.

16. Sales volume and the collection period will be affected by a firm's _____ _____.

17. Extremely strict credit standards will result in lost _____.

18. Credit terms generally specify the _____ for which credit is granted and any _____ _____ that is offered for early payment.

19. The optimal credit terms involve a tradeoff between increased _____ and the cost of carrying additional _____ _____.

20. _____ policy refers to the manner in which a firm tries to obtain payment from past-due accounts.

21. Two popular methods for monitoring receivables are _____ _____ and the _____ _____ _____.

22. Credit sales may be especially profitable if a(n) _____ charge is assessed on accounts receivable.

23. The most comprehensive picture of a firm's liquidity is obtained by examining its _____ _____, which forecasts a firm's cash inflows and outflows.

24. _____ _____ _____ refers to the firm's policies regarding target levels for each category of current assets and how current assets will be financed.

25. A(n) _____ current asset investment policy is one where relatively large amounts of cash, marketable securities, and inventories are carried, and where sales are stimulated by the use of a credit policy that provides liberal financing to customers and a corresponding high level of receivables.

26. A(n) _____ current asset investment policy is one where holdings of cash, securities, inventories, and receivables are minimized.

27. Firms hold cash for two primary reasons: _____ and _____ balances.

28. _____ _____ _____ defines working capital as inventories plus receivables less payables.

29. _____ _____ management is a system where firms are able to start production after an order is received, yet still meet customer delivery requirements, and it builds on the just-in-time method of inventory control.

30. A typical cash budget consists of three sections: the _____ and _____ worksheet, the cash _____ or _____ section, and the cash surplus or loan requirement section.

31. The _____ cash balance is the desired cash balance that a firm plans to maintain in order to conduct business.

32. _____ _____ typically provide much lower yields than a firm's operating assets, yet they are often held in sizable amounts and are held for the same reasons firms hold cash.

33. _____-_____ is the practice of purchasing components rather than making them in-house.

34. _____ _____ is defined in terms of the probability of a customer's default.

35. The _____ _____ period is the average length of time required to convert materials into finished goods and then to sell those goods.

36.   The _____ _____ period is the average length of time required to convert the firm's receivables into cash, that is, to collect cash following a sale.

37.   The _____ _____ period is the average length of time between the purchase of materials and labor and the cash payment for them.

38.   The _____ _____ _____ is the average length of time a dollar is tied up in current assets.

Conceptual

39.   A firm changes its credit policy from 2/10, net 30, to 3/10, net 30. The change is to meet competition, so no increase in sales is expected. The firm's average investment in accounts receivable will probably increase as a result of the change.

   a. True   **b.** False

40.   An aging schedule is constructed by a firm to keep track of when its accounts payable are due.

   a. True   **b.** False

41.   If a credit policy change increases the firm's accounts receivable, the entire increase must be financed by some source of funds.

   a. True   **b.** False

42.   Which of the following actions would *not* be consistent with good cash management?

   a. Increasing the synchronization of cash flows.
   b. Using lockboxes in funds collection.
   c. Maintaining an average cash balance equal to that required as a compensating balance or that which minimizes total cost.
   d. Minimizing the use of float.
   e. None of the above; all are consistent with good cash management.

43. The costs of a stock-out do *not* include

    a. Disruption of production schedules.
    b. Loss of customer goodwill.
    c. Depreciation and obsolescence.
    d. Loss of sales.
    e. Answers c and d above.

44. The goal of credit policy is to

    a. Minimize bad debt losses.
    b. Minimize DSO.
    c. Maximize sales.
    d. Minimize collection expenses.
    e. Extend credit to the point where marginal profits equal marginal costs.

SELF-TEST PROBLEMS

1. The Mill Company has a daily average collection of checks of $250,000. It takes the company 4 days to convert the checks to cash. Assume a lockbox system could be employed which would reduce the cash conversion period to 3 days. The lockbox system would have a net cost of $25,000 per year, but any additional funds made available could be invested to net 8 percent per year. Should Mill adopt the lockbox system?

    a. Yes; the system would free $250,000 in funds.
    b. Yes; the benefits of the lockbox system exceed the costs.
    c. No; the benefit is only $10,000.
    d. No; the firm would lose $5,000 per year if the system were used.
    e. The benefits and costs are equal; hence the firm is indifferent toward the system.

(The following data apply to the next three Self-Test Problems.)

Simmons Brick Company sells on terms of 3/10, net 30. Gross sales for the year are $1,200,000 and the collections department estimates that 30 percent of the customers pay on the tenth day and take discounts; 40 percent pay on the thirtieth day; and the remaining 30 percent pay, on average, 40 days after the purchase. Assume 360 days per year.

2. What is the days sales outstanding?

    a. 10 days   **b.** 13 days   **c.** 20 days   **d.** 27 days   **e.** 40 days

3. What is the current receivables balance?

    a. $60,000   **b.** $70,000   **c.** $75,000   **d.** $80,000   **e.** $90,000

4. What would be the new receivables balance if Simmons toughened up on its collection policy, with the result that all nondiscount customers paid on the thirtieth day?

    a. $60,000   **b.** $70,000   **c.** $75,000   **d.** $80,000   **e.** $90,000

5. Haberdash Inc. last year reported sales of $12 million and an inventory turnover ratio of 3. The company is now adopting a just-in-time inventory system. If the new system is able to reduce the firm's inventory level and increase the firm's inventory turnover ratio to 7.5, while maintaining the same level of sales, how much cash will be freed up?

    a. $2,400,000   **b.** $1,600,000   **c.** $4,000,000   **d.** $3,000,000   **e.** $5,250,000

ANSWERS TO SELF-TEST QUESTIONS

1.	working capital	20.	Collection
2.	Net; current; liabilities	21.	aging schedules; days sales outstanding
3.	minimize; cash	22.	carrying
4.	inflows; outflows	23.	cash budget
5.	Compensating	24.	Working capital policy
6.	collection; payment	25.	relaxed
7.	lockbox	26.	restricted
8.	float	27.	transactions; compensating
9.	supplies; raw materials; work-in-process; finished goods	28.	Zero working capital
		29.	Demand flow (based)
10.	lowest cost	30.	collections; purchases; gain; loss
11.	increase; carrying	31.	target
12.	inversely	32.	Marketable securities
13.	just-in-time	33.	Out-sourcing
14.	Accounts receivable	34.	Credit quality
15.	volume; sales; collections	35.	inventory conversion
16.	credit policy	36.	receivables collection
17.	sales	37.	payables deferral
18.	period; cash discount	38.	cash conversion cycle
19.	sales; accounts receivable		

39. b. No new customers are being generated. The current customers pay either on Day 10 or Day 30. The increase in trade discount will induce some customers who are now paying on Day 30 to pay on Day 10. Thus, the days sales outstanding is shortened which, in turn, will cause a decline in accounts receivable.

40. b. The aging schedule breaks down accounts receivable according to how long they have been outstanding.

41. b. Receivables are based on sales price which presumably includes some profit. Only the actual cash outlays associated with receivables must be financed. The remainder, or profit, appears on the balance sheet as an increase in retained earnings.

42. d. Management should try to maximize float.

43. c. Depreciation and obsolescence are inventory carrying costs.

44. e. The goal of credit policy is to maximize overall profits. This is achieved when the marginal profits equal the marginal costs.

SOLUTIONS TO SELF-TEST PROBLEMS

1. d. Currently, Mill has 4($250,000) = $1,000,000 in unavailable collections. If lockboxes were used, this could be reduced to $750,000. Thus, $250,000 would be available to invest at 8 percent, resulting in an annual return of 0.08($250,000) = $20,000. If the system costs $25,000, Mill would lose $5,000 per year by adopting the system.

2. d. 0.3(10 days) + 0.4(30 days) + 0.3(40 days) = 27 days.

3. e. Receivables = (DSO)(Sales/360) = 27($1,200,000/360) = $90,000.

4. d. New days sales outstanding = 0.3(10) + 0.7(30) = 24 days.
Sales per day = $1,200,000/360 = $3,333.33.
Receivables = $3,333.33(24 days) = $80,000.00.

Thus, the average receivables would drop from $90,000 to $80,000. Furthermore, sales may decline as a result of the tighter credit and reduce receivables even more.

Also, some additional customers may now take discounts, which would further reduce receivables.

5. a. Inventory turnover ratio$_{Old}$ = Sales/Inventory
    $$3 = \$12,000,000/I$$
    $$3I = \$12,000,000$$
    $$I = \$4,000,000.$$

    Inventory turnover ratio$_{New}$ = Sales/Inventory
    $$7.5 = \$12,000,000/I$$
    $$I = \$12,000,000/7.5$$
    $$I = \$1,600,000.$$

    Cash freed up = $\$4,000,000 - \$1,600,000 = \$2,400,000$.

CHAPTER 23
SHORT-TERM FINANCING

OVERVIEW

Working capital policy involves decisions relating to current assets, including decisions about financing them. Since about half of the typical firm's capital is invested in current assets, working capital policy and management are important to the firm and its shareholders. In fact, about 60 percent of a financial manager's time is devoted to working capital policy and management, and many finance students' first assignments on the job will involve working capital. For these reasons, working capital policy is a vitally important topic.

This chapter first explains alternative current asset financing policies and the advantages and disadvantages of short-term financing. Then the nature of accruals and trade credit and their respective costs are covered. Finally, the cost of bank loans, how to choose a bank, the use of commercial paper, and the use of security in short-term financing are considered.

OUTLINE

A firm's current asset levels and financing requirements rise and fall with business cycles and seasonal trends. At the peak of such cycles, businesses carry their maximum amounts of current assets. Similar fluctuations in financing needs can occur over these cycles, typically, financing needs contract during recessions, and they expand during booms.

- Current assets rarely drop to zero, and this fact has led to the development of the idea of *permanent current assets*. These are the current assets on hand at the low point of the cycle.

- Seasonal current assets are defined as *temporary current assets*.

- The manner in which the permanent and temporary current assets are financed is called the firm's *current asset financing policy*.

- ❑ The *maturity matching, or "self-liquidating," approach* matches asset and liability maturities. Defined as a moderate current asset financing policy, this would use permanent financing for permanent assets (permanent current assets and fixed assets), and use short-term financing to cover seasonal and/or cyclical temporary assets (fluctuating current assets).
- ❑ The *aggressive approach* is used by a firm which finances all of its fixed assets with long-term capital but part of its permanent current assets with short-term, nonspontaneous credit.
- ❑ A *conservative approach* would be to use permanent capital to meet some of the cyclical demand, and then hold the temporary surpluses as marketable securities at the trough of the cycle (storing liquidity). Here, the amount of permanent financing exceeds permanent assets.

There are advantages and disadvantages to the use of short-term financing.

- ■ A short-term loan can be obtained much faster than long-term credit.

- ■ Short-term debt is more flexible since it may be repaid if the firm's financing requirements decline. Long-term debt can be retired, but this will probably involve a prepayment penalty. In addition, flotation costs are higher for long-term debt than for short-term credit and long-term loan agreements always contain provisions that constrain the firm's future actions.

- ■ Short-term interest rates are normally lower than long-term rates. Therefore, financing with short-term credit usually results in lower interest costs.

- ■ Short-term debt is generally more risky than long-term debt for two reasons.
  - ❑ Short-term interest rates fluctuate widely while long-term rates tend to be more stable and predictable, and hence the interest rate on short-term debt could increase dramatically over a short period.
  - ❑ Short-term debt comes due every few months. If a firm does not have the cash to repay debt when it comes due, and if it cannot refinance the loan, it may be forced into bankruptcy.

Different types of short-term funds have different characteristics. One source of short-term funds is accrued wages and taxes, which increase and decrease spontaneously as a firm's operations expand and contract. This type of debt is "free" in the sense that no interest is paid on funds raised through accruals. However, a firm cannot ordinarily control its accruals.

Accounts payable, or trade credit, is the largest single category of short-term debt. Trade credit is a "spontaneous" source of funds because it arises from ordinary business transactions. Most firms make purchases on credit, recording the debt as an account payable.

■ An increase in sales will be accompanied by an increase in inventory purchases, which will automatically generate additional financing.

■ The cost of trade credit is made up of discounts lost by not paying invoices within the discount period.
   ❑ For example, if credit terms are 2/10, net 30, the cost of 20 additional days' credit is 2 percent of the dollar value of the purchases made.
   ❑ The following equation may be used to calculate the nominal percentage cost, on an annual basis, of not taking discounts:

$$\frac{\text{Nominal annual}}{\text{cost}} = \frac{\text{Discount \%}}{100 - \text{Discount \%}} \times \frac{360}{\frac{\text{Days credit is}}{\text{outstanding}} - \frac{\text{Discount}}{\text{period}}}.$$

   ❑ For example, the nominal cost of not taking the discount when the credit terms are 2/10, net 30, is

$$\frac{\text{Nominal annual cost}} = \frac{2}{98} \times \frac{360}{30 - 10} = 0.0204(18) = 0.367 = 36.7\%.$$

   ❑ In effective annual interest terms, the rate is even higher. Note that the first term on the right-hand side of the nominal cost equation is the periodic cost, and the second term is the number of periods per year. Thus, the effective annual rate is:

$$(1.0204)^{18} - 1.0 = 1.439 - 1.0 = 43.9\%.$$

■ Trade credit can be divided into two components: *Free trade credit* is that credit received during the discount period. *Costly trade credit* is obtained by foregoing discounts. This costly component should be used only when it is less expensive than funds obtained from other sources.
   ❑ Financial managers should always use the free component, but they should use the costly component only after analyzing the cost of this capital to make sure that it is less than the cost of funds which could be obtained from other sources.
   ❑ Competitive conditions may permit firms to do better than the stated credit terms by taking discounts beyond the discount period or by simply paying late. Such

practices, called *stretching accounts payable*, reduce the cost of trade credit, but they also result in poor relationships with suppliers.

Bank loans appear on a firm's balance sheet as notes payable and represent another important source of short-term financing. Bank loans are not generated spontaneously but must be negotiated and renewed on a regular basis.

■ About two-thirds of all bank loans mature in a year or less, although banks do make longer-term loans.

■ When a firm obtains a bank loan, a *promissory note* specifying the following items is signed: the amount borrowed, the interest rate, the repayment schedule, any collateral offered as security, and other terms and conditions to which the bank and the borrower have agreed.

■ Banks normally require regular borrowers to maintain *compensating balances* equal to 10 to 20 percent of the face value of the loan. Such required balances increase the effective interest rate on the loan.

■ A *line of credit* is an informal agreement between a bank and a borrower indicating the maximum credit the bank will extend to the borrower.
  ❑ Many lines of credit have a "clean-up" clause requiring the borrower to have a zero balance on the loan for some period during the year.
  ❑ The clean-up clause prevents the line of credit from becoming a permanent source of financing.

■ A *revolving credit agreement* is a formal line of credit often used by large firms. Normally, the borrower will pay the bank a commitment fee to compensate the bank for guaranteeing that the funds will be available. This fee is paid in addition to the regular interest charge on funds actually borrowed.
  ❑ Note that a revolving credit agreement is very similar to an informal line of credit, but with an important difference: The bank has a *legal obligation* to honor a revolving credit agreement, and for this it receives a commitment fee. Neither the legal obligation nor the fee exists under the informal line of credit.

The interest cost of loans will vary for different types of borrowers and for all borrowers over time. Rates charged will vary depending on economic conditions, the risk of the borrower, and the size of the loan. Interest charges on bank loans can be calculated in one of several ways listed below.

- *Regular, or simple, interest.* The nominal interest rate is divided by the number of days in the year to get the rate per day. This rate is then multiplied by the actual number of days during the specific payment period, and then times the amount of the loan.

$$\text{Interest rate per day} = \frac{\text{Nominal rate}}{\text{Days in year}}.$$

Interest charge for period = (Days in period)(Rate per day)(Amount of loan).

  ❑ The effective rate on the loan depends on how frequently interest must be paid—the more frequently, the higher the effective rate. The best procedure to use is to lay out all the cash flows on a time line and solve for the interest rate.

- *Discount interest.* Under this method, the bank deducts interest in advance. The effective annual rate of interest on a discount loan is always higher than the rate on an otherwise simple interest loan.

  ❑ To find the effective interest rate on a discount loan, lay out all the cash flows on a time line (remembering to subtract out the interest paid in advance) and solve for the interest rate.
  ❑ The firm actually receives less than the face amount of the loan.

    Funds received = Face amount of loan (1.0 − Nominal interest rate).

  ❑ The face amount of the loan can be calculated as follows:

$$\text{Face amount of loan} = \frac{\text{Funds received}}{1.0 \; - \; \text{Nominal rate (decimal)}}.$$

  ❑ Shortening the period of a discount loan lowers the effective rate of interest.

  ❑ *Installment loans: add-on interest.* Interest charges are calculated and then added on to the amount received to determine the loan's face value, which is paid off in equal installments. The borrower has use of the full amount of the funds received only until the first installment is paid.
  ❑ To determine the effective rate of an add-on loan, lay out all the cash flows on a time line and solve for the interest rate.
  ❑ The payments are calculated as the amount to be repaid, which consists of principal plus the total interest divided by 12.
  ❑ *Annual percentage rate (APR)* is a rate reported by banks and other lenders on loans when the effective rate exceeds the nominal rate of interest.

$$\text{APR} = \text{(Periods per year)(Rate per period)}.$$

Choosing a bank involves an analysis of the following variables:

■ *Willingness to assume risks.* Some banks are quite conservative, while others are more willing to make risky loans.

■ *Advice and counsel.* A bank's ability to provide counsel is particularly important to firms in their formative years.

■ *Loyalty to customers.* This variable deals with a bank's willingness to support customers during difficult economic times.

■ *Specialization.* A bank may specialize in making loans to a particular type of business. Firms should seek out a bank which is familiar with their particular type of business.

■ *Maximum loan size.* This is an important consideration for large companies when establishing a borrowing relationship because most banks cannot lend to a single customer more than 15 percent of the bank's capital accounts.

■ *Merchant banking.* Originally the term applied to banks which not only loaned depositors' money but also provided its customers with equity capital and financial advice. In recent years, commercial banks have been attempting to get back into merchant banking, in part because their foreign competitors offer such services, and U. S. banks compete with foreign banks for multinational corporations' business.

■ *Other services.* The availability of services such as providing cash management services, assisting with electronic funds transfers, and helping firms obtain foreign exchange should also be taken into account when selecting a bank.

Commercial paper, another source of short-term credit, is an unsecured promissory note. It is generally sold to other business firms, to insurance companies, to banks, and to money market mutual funds. Only large, financially strong firms are able to tap the commercial paper market.

■ Maturities of commercial paper range from a few days to nine months, with an average of about five months.
   ❑ Interest rates on prime commercial paper generally range from 1 1/2 to 3 percentage points below the stated prime rate, and about 1/8 to 1/2 of a percentage point above the T-bill rate. However, rates fluctuate daily with supply and demand conditions in the marketplace.

❑ A disadvantage of the commercial paper market vis-a-vis bank loans is that the impersonal nature of the market makes it difficult for firms to use commercial paper at times when they are in temporary financial distress.

For a strong firm, borrowing on an unsecured basis is generally cheaper and simpler than on a secured loan basis because of the administrative costs associated with the use of security. However, lenders will refuse credit without some form of collateral if a borrower's credit standing is questionable.

SELF-TEST QUESTIONS

Definitional

1. In the maturity matching approach to working capital financing, permanent assets should be financed with _____ capital, while _____ assets should be financed with short-term credit.

2. Some firms use short-term financing to finance permanent assets. This approach maximizes _____ _____, but also has the _____ _____.

3. Short-term borrowing provides more _____ for firms that are uncertain about their _____ borrowing needs.

4. Short-term borrowing will be less expensive than borrowing long-term if the yield curve is _____ sloping.

5. Short-term interest rates fluctuate _____ than long-term rates.

6. _____ wages and taxes are a common source of short-term credit. However, most firms have little control over the _____ of these accounts.

7. Accounts payable, or _____ _____, is the largest single source of short-term credit for most businesses.

8. Trade credit is a(n) _____ source of funds in the sense that it automatically increases when sales increase.

9. Trade credit can be divided into two components: _____ trade credit and _____ trade credit.

10. Free trade credit is that credit received during the _____ period.

11. _____ trade credit should only be used when the cost of the trade credit is less than the cost of _____ sources.

12. The instrument signed when bank credit is obtained is called a(n) _____ _____.

13. Many banks require borrowers to keep _____ _____ on deposit with the bank equal to 10 or 20 percent of the loan's face value.

14. Maturities on commercial paper generally range from _____ to _____ months, with interest rates set about 1 1/2 to 3 percentage points _____ the _____ rate.

15. A(n) _____ loan is one where collateral such as _____ or _____ have been pledged in support of the loan.

16. A(n) _____ ____ _____ is an informal agreement between a bank and a borrower as to the maximum loan that will be permitted.

17. The fee paid to a bank to secure a revolving credit agreement is known as a(n) _____ fee.

18. If interest charges are deducted in advance, this is known as _____ interest, and the effective rate is higher than the _____ interest rate.

19. With a(n) _____ loan, interest charges are calculated and then added on to the amount received to determine the loan's face value, and then it is paid off in equal amounts per period.

20. Commercial paper can only be issued by _____, _____ _____ firms.

21. _____ current assets are those current assets on hand at the low point of a business cycle.

22. Seasonal current assets are defined as _____ current assets.

23. Competitive conditions may permit firms to do better than the stated credit terms by taking discounts beyond the discount period or by simply paying late; such practices are called _____ _____ _____.

24. A(n) _____ _____ _____ is a formal line of credit often used by large firms.

25. _____ the period of a discount loan lowers the effective rate of interest.

26. _____ _____ _____ is a rate reported by banks and other lenders on loans when the effective rate exceeds the nominal rate of interest, and its is calculated as the number of periods per year times the rate per period.

27. The _____ of accounts receivable is characterized by the fact that the lender not only has a claim against receivables but also has recourse to the borrower.

28. _____, or selling accounts receivable, involves the purchase of accounts receivable by the lender, generally without recourse to the borrower.

29. The _____ _____ is an instrument acknowledging that the goods are held in trust for the lender.

30. _____ _____ financing uses inventory as a security and requires public notification.

Conceptual

31. The matching of asset and liability maturities is considered desirable because this strategy minimizes interest rate risk.

   a. True   **b.** False

32. Accruals are "free" in the sense that no interest must be paid on these funds.

   a. True   **b.** False

33. The effect of compensating balances is to decrease the effective interest rate of a loan.

   a. True   **b.** False

34. Which of the following statements concerning commercial paper is most correct?

    a. Commercial paper is secured debt of large, financially strong firms.

    b. Commercial paper is sold primarily to individual investors.

    c. Maturities of commercial paper generally exceed nine months.

    d. Commercial paper interest rates are typically 1 1/2 to 3 percentage points above the stated prime rate.

    e. None of the above statements is correct.

35. Which of the following statements is most correct?

    a. If you had just been hired as Working Capital Manager for a firm with but one stockholder, and that stockholder told you that she had all the money she could possibly use, hence that her primary operating goal was to avoid even the remotest possibility of bankruptcy, then you should set the firm's working capital financing policy on the basis of the "Maturity Matching, or Self-Liquidating, Approach."

    b. Due to the existence of positive maturity risk premiums, at most times short-term debt carries lower interest rates than long-term debt. Therefore, if a company finances primarily with short-term as opposed to long-term debt, its expected TIE ratio, hence its overall riskiness, will be lower than if it finances with long-term debt. Therefore, the more conservative the firm, the greater its reliance on short-term debt.

    c. If a firm buys on terms of 2/10, net 30, and pays on the 30th day, then its accounts payable may be thought of as consisting of some "free" and some "costly" trade credit. Since the percentage cost of the costly trade credit is lowered if the payment period is reduced, the firm should try to pay earlier than on Day 30, say on Day 25.

    d. Suppose a firm buys on terms of 2/10, net 30, but it normally pays on Day 60. Disregarding any "image" effects, it should, if it can borrow from the bank at an effective rate of 14 percent, take out a bank loan and start taking discounts.

    e. Each of the above statements is false.

SELF-TEST PROBLEMS

(The following data apply to the next three Self-Test Problems.)

A firm buys on terms of 2/10, net 30, but generally does not pay until 40 days after the invoice date. Its purchases total $1,080,000 per year.

1.   How much "non-free" trade credit does the firm use on average each year?

    a. $120,000   **b.** $90,000   **c.** $60,000   **d.** $30,000   **e.** $20,000

2.   What is the nominal cost of the "non-free" trade credit?

    a. 16.2%   **b.** 19.4%   **c.** 21.9%   **d.** 24.5%   **e.** 27.4%

3.   What is the effective cost rate of the costly credit?

    a. 16.2%   **b.** 19.4%   **c.** 21.9%   **d.** 24.5%   **e.** 27.4%

4.   Lawton Pipelines Inc. has developed plans for a new pump that will allow more economical operation of the company's oil pipelines. Management estimates that $2,400,000 will be required to put this new pump into operation. Funds can be obtained from a bank at 10 percent discount interest, or the company can finance the expansion by delaying payment to its suppliers. Presently, Lawton purchases under terms of 2/10, net 40, but management believes payment could be delayed 30 additional days without penalty; that is, payment could be made in 70 days. Which means of financing should Lawton use? (Use the nominal cost of trade credit.)

    a. Trade credit, since the cost is about 12.24 percent.
    b. Trade credit, since the cost is about 3.13 percentage points less than the bank loan.
    c. Bank loan, since the cost is about 1.13 percentage points less than trade credit.
    d. Bank loan, since the cost is about 3.13 percentage points less than trade credit.
    e. The firm could use either since the costs are the same.

(The following data apply to the next four Self-Test Problems.)

You plan to borrow $10,000 from your bank, which offers to lend you the money at a 10 percent nominal, or stated, rate on a 1-year loan.

5.   What is the effective interest rate if the loan is a discount loan?

    a. 11.1%   **b.** 13.3%   **c.** 15.0%   **d.** 17.5%   **e.** 20.0%

6. What is the effective interest rate if the loan is an add-on interest loan with 12 monthly payments?

    a. 11.5%   **b.** 13.3%   **c.** 15.0%   **d.** 17.5%   **e.** 19.5%

7. What is the effective interest rate if the loan is a discount loan with a 15 percent compensating balance?

    a. 11.1%   **b.** 13.3%   **c.** 15.0%   **d.** 17.5%   **e.** 20.0%

8. Under the terms of the previous problem, how much would you have to borrow to have the use of $10,000?

    a. $10,000   **b.** $11,111   **c.** $12,000   **d.** $13,333   **e.** $15,000

9. Gibbs Corporation needs to raise $1,000,000 for one year to supply working capital to a new store. Gibbs buys from its suppliers on terms of 4/10, net 90, and it currently pays on the 10th day and takes discounts, but it could forego discounts, pay on the 90th day, and get the needed $1,000,000 in the form of costly trade credit. Alternatively, Gibbs could borrow from its bank on a 15 percent discount interest rate basis. What is the effective annual cost rate of the lower cost source?

    a. 20.17%   **b.** 18.75%   **c.** 17.65%   **d.** 18.25%   **e.** 19.50%

ANSWERS TO SELF-TEST QUESTIONS

1.	permanent (long-term); temporary	13.	compensating balances
2.	expected return; greatest risk	14.	one; nine; below; prime
3.	flexibility; future	15.	secured; receivables; inventory
4.	upward	16.	line of credit
5.	more		
6.	Accrued; size (amount)	17.	commitment
7.	trade credit	18.	discount; simple (or nominal or stated)
8.	spontaneous		
9.	free; costly	19.	installment
10.	discount	20.	large; financially strong
11.	Costly; alternative	21.	Permanent
12.	promissory note	22.	temporary

23.	stretching accounts payable		**27.**	pledging
24.	revolving credit agreement		**28.**	Factoring
25.	Shortening		**29.**	trust receipt
26.	Annual percentage rate		**30.**	Warehouse receipt

31.   b.   The matching of maturities minimizes default risk, or the risk that the firm will be unable to pay off its maturing obligations, and reinvestment rate risk, or the risk that the firm will have to roll over the debt at a higher rate.

32.   a.   Neither workers nor the IRS require interest payments on wages and taxes that are not paid as soon as they are earned.

33.   b.   Compensating balances increase the effective rate because the firm is required to maintain excess non-interest-bearing balances.

34.   e.   Commercial paper is the unsecured debt of strong firms. It generally has a maturity from one to nine months and is sold primarily to other corporations and financial institutions. Rates on commercial paper are typically below the prime rate.

35.   d.   Statement a is false; the conservative approach would be the safest current asset financing policy. Statement b is false; short-term debt fluctuates more than long-term debt, thus, the greater the firm's reliance on short-term debt, the riskier the firm. Statement c is false; it makes no difference in the cost if the firm pays on Day 25 versus Day 30 in this instance. Statement d is true; if the firm can "stretch" its payables the nominal cost is 14.69% (the effective cost is 15.66%). Thus, the firm should obtain the 14% bank loan to take discounts as this is the lowest cost to the firm.

SOLUTIONS TO SELF-TEST PROBLEMS

1.   b. $1,080,000/360 = $3,000 in purchases per day. Typically, there will be $3,000(40) = $120,000 of accounts payable on the books at any given time. Of this, $3,000(10) = $30,000 is "free" credit, while $3,000(30) = $90,000 is "non-free" credit.

2.   d.   Nominal cost $= \dfrac{\text{Discount \%}}{100 - \text{Discount \%}} \times \dfrac{360}{\text{Days credit is} \; \underset{}{-} \; \text{Discount}}$
$\text{outstanding} \text{period}$

$$= \frac{2}{100 - 2} \times \frac{360}{40 - 10} = \frac{2}{98} \times \frac{360}{30} = 24.5\%.$$

3.   e.   The periodic rate is 2/98 = 2.04%, and there are 360/30 = 12 periods per year. Thus, the effective annual rate is 27.4 percent:

$$\left(1 + \frac{k_{\text{Nom}}}{m}\right)^{12} - 1.0 = (1.0204)^{12} - 1.0$$

$$= 1.2742 - 1.0 = 0.2742 = 27.4\%.$$

4.   c.   Face amount $= \dfrac{\$2,400,000}{1 - 0.10}$
$= \$2,666,667.$

Interest to be deducted in advance = 0.10 × \$2,666,667 = \$266,667.

```
0   I = ?                                          1  Year
├─────────────────────────────────────────────────┤
2,666,667                                      -2,666,667
-266,667
2,400,000
```

Using a financial calculator, enter N = 1, PV = 2400000, PMT = 0, and FV = -2666667; and then solve for I to get the effective cost of the loan, 11.11%.

Credit terms are 2/10, net 40, but delaying payments 30 additional days is the equivalent of 2/10, net 70. Assuming no penalty, the nominal cost is as follows:

$$\text{Nominal cost} = \frac{\text{Discount \%}}{100 - \text{Discount \%}} \times \frac{360}{\text{Days credit is} \; \underset{}{-} \; \text{Discount}}$$
$$\text{outstanding} \text{period}$$

$$= \frac{2}{100 - 2} \times \frac{360}{70 - 10} = \frac{2}{98} \times \frac{360}{60} = 0.0204(6) = 12.24\%.$$

Therefore, the loan cost is 1.13 percentage points less than trade credit.

5.   a.   Face amount $= \dfrac{\$10,000}{1 - 0.10}$

$= \$11,111.$

Interest to be deducted in advance $= 0.1 \times \$11,111 = \$1,111.$

Using a financial calculator, enter N = 1, PV = 10000, PMT = 0, and FV = -11111; and then solve for I to get the effective cost of the loan, 11.11%.

6.   e.   The amount to be repaid is $10,000 plus $1,000 of interest, or $11,000. The monthly payment is $11,000/12 = $916.67.

The time line for the loan is:

```
     0    I = ?   1                              12 Months
     ├───────────┼──────────────────────────────────┤


  10,000  -916.67                              -916.67
```

With a financial calculator, enter N = 12, PV = 10000, PMT = -916.67, FV = 0, and solve for I = 1.49767%. However, this is a monthly rate. The effective rate is found as $(1 + 0.0149767)^{12} - 1 = 19.529\% \approx 19.5\%.$

7.   b.   Face amount of loan $= \dfrac{\$10{,}000}{1-0.10-0.15}$

$$= \$13{,}333.$$

Interest to be deducted in advance $= 0.1 \times \$13{,}333 = \$1{,}333.$
Compensating balance $= 0.15 \times \$13{,}333 = \$2{,}000.$

```
    0   I = ?                                    1  Year
    ├──────────────────────────────────────────────┤
 13,333                                         -13,333
 - 1,333                                        +  2,000
 - 2,000                                        -11,333
 10,000
```

Using a financial calculator, enter N = 1, PV = 10000, PMT = 0, and FV = -11333; and then solve for I to get the effective cost of the loan, 13.3%.

8.   d. $\dfrac{\$10{,}000}{1-0.15-0.10} = \$13{,}333.$

0.15($13,333) = $2,000 is required for the compensating balance, and 0.10($13,333) = $1,333 is required for the immediate interest payment.

9.   c.   Accounts payable:
Nominal cost = (4/96)(360/80) = 0.04167(4.5) = 18.75%.
EAR cost= $(1.04167)^{4.5} - 1.0 = 20.17\%.$

Cost of notes payable:
Face amount of loan $= \dfrac{\$1{,}000{,}000}{1-0.15}$

$$= \$1{,}176{,}471.$$

Interest to be deducted in advance $= 0.15 \times \$1{,}176{,}471 = \$176{,}471.$

```
    0   I = ?                              1  Year
    |────────────────────────────────────|
  1,176,471                            -1,176,471
  -  176,471
  1,000,000
```

Using a financial calculator, enter N = 1, PV = 1000000, PMT = 0, and FV = -1176471; and then solve for I to get the effective cost of the loan, 17.65%.

CHAPTER 24
DERIVATIVES AND RISK MANAGEMENT

OVERVIEW

Risk management can mean many things, but in business it involves identifying events that could have adverse financial consequences for the firm and then undertaking actions to prevent and/or minimize the damage caused by these events. Years ago, corporate risk managers dealt primarily with insurance—they made sure the firm was adequately insured against fire, theft, and other casualties and that it had adequate liability coverage. More recently, however, the scope of risk management has been broadened to include such things as controlling the costs of key inputs or protecting against changes in interest rates or exchange rates. In addition, risk managers try to insure that actions designed to hedge against risks are not actually increasing risks.

Since perhaps the most important aspect of risk management involves derivative securities, we begin the chapter with a discussion of derivatives. *Derivatives* are securities whose values are determined, in whole or in part, by the market price (or interest rate) of some other asset. Derivatives include options, whose values depend on the price of some underlying stock; interest rate and exchange rate futures and swaps, whose values depend on interest rate and exchange rate levels; and commodity futures, whose values depend on commodity prices.

OUTLINE

Investors dislike risk. Most investors hold well-diversified portfolios, so at least in theory the only "relevant risk" is systematic risk.

- You might expect a corporate executive to say that beta is the type of risk they were concerned about. However, the executive would probably define risk as: "The possibility that our future earnings and free cash flows will be significantly lower than we expect."

- A company's value depends on its profits and free cash flow.

- The long-run value of a stock depends on the present value of its expected future free cash flows, discounted at the weighted average cost of capital (WACC).

- ❑ WACC will change only if a particular action causes a change in the cost of debt or equity, or the target capital structure.

- ■ If investors use *"homemade" hedging*, then the stock of a company that hedges its own operations should be the same as it would be if the company did not hedge its operations.

- ■ A 1998 survey reported that 83 percent of firms with market values greater than $1.2 billion engage in *risk management*, and that percentage is surely even higher today.

- ■ Here are several plausible reasons companies might try to manage risk:
  - ❑ *Debt capacity.* Risk management can reduce the volatility of cash flows, which decreases the probability of bankruptcy.
  - ❑ *Maintaining the optimal capital budget over time.* Smoothing out the cash flows can alleviate the problem of not meeting capital needs in the most efficient manner.
  - ❑ *Financial distress.* Risk management can reduce the likelihood of low cash flows, hence of financial distress.
  - ❑ *Comparative advantages in hedging.* Firms generally have lower transactions cost due to a larger volume of hedging activities. Also, managers know more about the firm's risk exposure than outside investors, hence managers can create more effective hedges. Effective risk management requires specialized skills and knowledge that firms are more likely to have.
  - ❑ *Borrowing costs.* Firms can sometimes reduce input costs, especially the interest rate on debt, through the use of derivative instruments called "swaps".
  - ❑ *Tax effects.* Companies with volatile earnings pay more taxes than more stable companies due to the treatment of tax credits and the rules governing corporate loss carry forwards and carry backs.
  - ❑ *Compensation systems.* Many compensation systems establish "floors" and "ceilings" on bonuses or else reward managers for meeting targets. So, even if hedging does not add much value for stockholders, it may still be beneficial to managers.

An historical perspective is useful when studying derivatives. One of, if not, the first formal markets for derivatives was the futures market for wheat.

- ■ *Hedging* with futures lowered aggregate risk in the economy.

- ■ The earliest futures dealings were between two parties who arranged transactions between themselves. Soon, though, middlemen came into the picture, and trading in futures was established.
  - ❑ The Chicago Board of Trade was an early market place for this dealing, and *futures dealers* helped make a market in futures contracts. This improved the efficiency and lowered the cost of hedging operations.

■ *Speculators* then entered the scene. Speculators add capital and players to the derivatives market, and this stabilizes the market. Risk to the speculators themselves is high, but their bearing that risk makes the derivatives markets more stable for the hedgers.

■ *Natural hedges* are situations where aggregate risk can be reduced by derivatives transactions between two parties (called *counterparties*). These exist for many commodities, for foreign currencies, for interest rates on securities with different maturities, and even for common stocks where portfolio managers want to "hedge their bets."

■ Hedging can also be done in situations where no natural hedge exists. Here one party wants to reduce some type of risk, and another party agrees to sell a contract which protects the first party from a specific event or situation.

■ The derivatives markets have grown more rapidly than any other major market in recent years for a number of reasons.
  ❑ Analytical techniques have been developed to help establish "fair" prices, and having a better basis for pricing hedges makes the counterparties more comfortable with deals.
  ❑ Computers and electronic communications make it much easier for counterparties to deal with one another.
  ❑ Globalization has greatly increased the importance of currency markets, and the need for reducing the exchange rate risks brought on by global trade.

■ Derivatives do have a potential downside. These instruments are highly leveraged, so small miscalculations can lead to huge losses. Also, they are complicated, hence not well understood by most people. This makes mistakes more likely with less complex instruments, and it makes it harder for a firm's top management to exercise proper control over derivatives transactions.

There are many types of derivatives, including forward contracts, futures, swaps, structured notes, inverse floaters, and a host of other "exotic" contracts.

■ *Forward contracts* are agreements where one party agrees to buy a commodity at a specific price at a special future date and the other party agrees to make the sale.

■ A *futures contract* is similar to a forward contract, but with three key differences.
  ❑ Futures contracts are "marked to market" on a daily basis, meaning that gains and losses are noted and money must be put up to cover losses.
  ❑ With futures, physical delivery of the underlying asset is virtually never taken—the two parties simply settle up with cash for the difference between the contracted price and the actual price on the expiration date.

- ❑ Futures contacts are generally standardized instruments that are traded on exchanges, whereas forward contracts are generally tailor-made, are negotiated between two parties, and are not traded after they have been signed.

- ■ In a *swap* two parties agree to swap something, generally obligations to make specified payment streams. Most swaps today involve either interest payments or currencies.
  - ❑ Note that swaps can involve *side payments*, additional payments needed to get the other party to agree to the swap.
  - ❑ Originally, swaps were arranged between companies by money center banks, which would match up counterparties. Such matching still occurs, but today most swaps are between companies and banks, with the banks then taking steps to ensure that their own risks are hedged.

- ■ A *structured note* often means a debt obligation which is derived from some other debt obligation.
  - ❑ Zeroes formed by stripping T-bonds were one of the first types of structured notes.
  - ❑ Another important type of structured note is backed by the interest and principal payments on mortgages, *collateralized mortgage obligations*.
  - ❑ Investment bankers can create notes called IOs, for Interest Only, which provide cash flows from the interest component of the mortgage amortization payments, and POs, for Principal Only, which are paid from the principal repayment stream.

- ■ A floating rate note has an interest rate that rises and falls with some interest rate index. With an *inverse floater*, the rate paid on the note moves counter to market rates.
  - ❑ Thus, if interest rates in the economy rose, the interest rate paid on an inverse floater would fall, lowering its cash interest payments. At the same time, the discount rate used to value the inverse floater's cash flows would rise along with other rates. The combined effect of lower cash flows and a higher discount rate would lead to a very large decline in the value of the inverse floater. Thus, inverse floaters are exceptionally vulnerable to increases in interest rates.

Risk can be classified in many ways and different classifications are commonly used in different industries.

- ■ Here's one list that provides an idea of the wide variety of risks to which a firm can be exposed: pure risks, speculative risks, demand risks, input risks, financial risks, property risks, personnel risks, environmental risks, liability risks, and insurable risks.

Firms often use the following three-step approach to risk management: (1) identify the risks faced by the firm, (2) measure the potential impact of the risks identified, and (3) decide how each relevant risk should be handled.

- ■ There are several techniques to help minimize risk exposure:

- ❏ *Transfer the risk to an insurance company.* Often, it is advantageous to insure against, and hence transfer, a risk. However, insurability does not necessarily mean that a risk should be covered by insurance. Thus, it might be better for the company to *self-insure*, which means bearing the risk directly rather than paying to have another party bear the risk.
- ❏ *Transfer the function that produces the risk to a third party.* In some situations, risks can be reduced most easily by passing them on to some other company that is not an insurance company.
- ❏ *Purchase derivative contracts to reduce risk.* Firms use derivatives to hedge risk.
- ❏ *Reduce the probability of occurrence of an adverse event.* In some instances, it is possible to take action to reduce the probability that an adverse event will occur.
- ❏ *Reduce the magnitude of the loss associated with an adverse event.*
- ❏ *Totally avoid the activity that gives rise to the risk.*

- ■ Risk management decisions, like all corporate decisions, should be based on a cost/benefit analysis for each feasible alternative. The same financial management techniques applied to other corporate decisions can also be applied to risk management decisions.

Firms are subject to numerous risks related to interest rate, stock price, and exchange rate fluctuations in the financial markets. For an investor, one of the most obvious ways to reduce financial risks is to hold a broadly diversified portfolio of stocks and debt securities; however, derivatives can also be used to reduce the risks associated with financial and commodity markets.

- ■ One of the most useful tools for reducing both *security and commodity price exposure* is to *hedge* in the futures markets.
    - ❏ Futures contracts are divided into two classes, *commodity futures* and *financial futures*.
        - • Commodity futures are contracts that are used to hedge against price changes for input materials.
        - • Financial futures are contracts that are used to hedge against fluctuating interest rates, stock prices, and exchange rates.
    - ❏ When futures contracts are purchased, the purchaser does not have to put up the full amount of the purchase price; rather, the purchaser is required to post an initial *margin*. However, investors are required to maintain a certain value in the margin account, called a *maintenance margin*.
    - ❏ An *option* is similar to a futures contract, but it merely gives someone the right to buy (call) or sell (put) an asset, but the holder of the option does not have to complete the transaction. A futures agreement, on the other hand, is a definite agreement on the part of one party to buy something on a specific date and a specific price, and the other party agrees to sell on the same terms.

■ Firms are exposed to losses due to changes in security prices when securities are held in investment portfolios, and they are also exposed during times when securities are being issued. In addition, firms are exposed to risk when floating rate debt is used to finance an investment that produces a fixed income stream. These types of risk can be reduced by using *derivatives*. *Futures and swaps* are two types of derivatives used to manage security price exposure.

❑ *Futures markets* are used for both speculation and hedging: *Speculation* involves betting on future price movements; *hedging* is done by a firm or individual to protect against a price change that would otherwise negatively affect profits.

• There are two basic types of hedges: (1) *long hedges*, in which futures contracts are bought in anticipation of (or to guard against) price increases, and (2) *short hedges*, where a firm or individual sells futures contracts to guard against price declines.

❑ A *perfect hedge* occurs when the gain or loss on the hedged transaction exactly offsets the loss or gain on the unhedged position.

❑ The futures and options markets permit flexibility in the timing of financial transactions, because the firm can be protected, at least partially, against changes that occur between the time a decision is reached and the time when the transaction will be completed.

• A *swap* is another method for reducing financial risks. It is an exchange of cash payment obligations, in which each party to the swap prefers the payment type or pattern of the other party.

■ Although the corporate use of derivatives to hedge risk is a relatively new phenomenon, it has caught on like wild fire. In fact, more than 90 percent of large U. S. companies use derivatives on a regular basis.

❑ There is, however, a downside to derivatives. Hedging is invariably cited by authorities as a "good" use of derivatives, whereas speculating with derivatives is often cited as a "bad" use.

❑ Hedging allows managers to concentrate on running their core business without having to worry about interest rate, currency, and commodity price variability. However, if derivatives are improperly constructed or used for speculation purposes, they have the potential to create very large losses in very short periods.

■ CFOs, CEOs, and board members should be reasonably knowledgeable about the derivatives their firms use, should establish policies regarding when they can and cannot be used, and should establish audit procedures to ensure that the policies are actually carried out. Moreover, a firm's derivatives position should be reported to stockholders.

SELF-TEST QUESTIONS

Definitional

1. _____ _____ generally involves the management of unpredictable events that have adverse financial consequences for the firm.

2. There are six reasons risk management might increase the value of a firm. Risk management allows corporations (1) to increase their _____ ____ _____, (2) to maintain their capital budget over time, (3) to avoid costs associated with _____ _____, (4) to utilize their comparative advantages in hedging relative to the hedging ability of individual investors, (5) to reduce both the risks and costs of borrowing by using _____, and (6) to reduce the higher _____ that result from fluctuating earnings.

3. Firms often use a three-step approach to risk management: (1) _____ the risks faced by the firm, (2) _____ the potential impact of the risks identified, and (3) decide how each relevant risk should be handled.

4. To _____-_____ means bearing the risk directly rather than paying to have another party bear the risk.

5. Risk management decisions, like all corporate decisions, should be based on a(n) _____/_____ analysis for each feasible alternative.

6. _____ are generally standardized instruments that are traded on exchanges and that are "marked to market" daily, but where physical delivery of the underlying asset is virtually never taken.

7. Futures markets are used for both hedging and speculation: _____ involves betting on future price movements, while _____ is done by a firm or individual to protect against price changes that could otherwise negatively affect profits.

8. _____ are securities whose values are determined by the market price (or interest rate) of some other asset.

9. A(n) _____ is an exchange of cash payment obligations, in which each party to the transaction prefers the payment type or pattern of the other party.

10. A(n) _____ _____ often means a debt obligation which is derived from some other debt obligation, for example, collateralized mortgage obligations.

11. The two parties involved in derivatives transactions are called _____.

12. _____ _____ are situations where aggregate risk can be reduced by derivatives transactions between two parties.

13. _____ _____ are agreements where one party agrees to buy a commodity at a specific price at a specific future date and the other party agrees to make the sale.

14. A floating rate note has an interest rate that rises and falls with some interest rate index. With a(n) _____ _____, the rate paid on the note moves counter to market rates.

15. _____ futures are contracts that are used to hedge against price changes for input materials.

16. _____ futures are contracts that are used to hedge against fluctuating interest rates, stock prices, and exchange rates.

17. There are two basic types of hedges: (1) _____ hedges, in which futures contracts are bought in anticipation of (or to guard against) price increases, and (2) _____ hedges, where a firm or individual sells futures contracts to guard against price declines.

Conceptual

18. The two basic types of hedges involving the futures market are long hedges and short hedges, where the words "long" and "short" refer to the maturity of the hedging instrument. For example, a long hedge might use stocks, while a short hedge might use 3-month T-bills.

   a. True   b. False

19. Speculators add capital and players to the derivatives market; thus, this tends to make the market unstable.

   a. True   b. False

20. A perfect hedge occurs when the gain or loss on the hedge transaction exactly offsets the loss or gain on the unhedged position.

   a. True   b. False

21. A swap is a method for reducing financial risk. Which of the following statements about swaps, if any, is *incorrect*?

    a. A swap involves the exchange of cash payment obligations.

    b. The earliest swaps were currency swaps, in which companies traded debt denominated in different currencies, say dollars and pounds.

    c. Swaps are generally arranged by a financial intermediary, who may or may not take the position of one of the counterparties.

    d. A problem with swaps is the lack of standardized contracts, which limits the development of a secondary market.

    e. None of the statements are incorrect; all of the above statements are correct.

22. Which of the following statements regarding futures and forward contracts is most correct?

    a. Futures contracts are similar to forward contracts except for the length of time the contract is outstanding.

    b. Forward contracts are "marked to market" on a daily basis, while futures contracts are not "marked to market."

    c. With forward contracts, physical delivery of the underlying asset is virtually never taken.

    d. Forward contracts are generally standardized instruments that are traded on exchanges, whereas futures contracts are generally tailor-made, are negotiated between two parties, and are not traded after they have been signed.

    e. All of the above statements are false.

23. Which of the following statements is most correct?

    a. Recently, the scope of risk management has been broadened to include things like controlling the costs of key inputs or protecting against changes in interest rates on exchange rates.

    b. Hedging with futures raises the aggregate risk in the economy.

    c. Corporations on whose stocks options are written have nothing to do with the option market.

    d. The actual market price of an option lies below the exercise value at each price of the common stock, although the premium rises as the stock price increases.

    e. Statements a and c are correct.

SELF-TEST PROBLEMS

1. What is the implied interest rate on a Treasury bond ($100,000) futures contract that settled at 101-2?

    a. 5.91%   **b.** 7.55%   **c.** 8.25%   **d.** 8.05%   **e.** 7.73%

2. Refer to Self-Test Problem 4. If the interest rate was 8.50 percent, what would be the contract's new value?

    a. $101,062.50   **b.** $100,235.33   **c.** $97,875.42   **d.** $76,153.41   **e.** $99.189.44

ANSWERS TO SELF-TEST QUESTIONS

1.	Risk management	**9.**	swap
2.	use of debt; financial distress; swaps, taxes	**10.**	structured note
		11.	counterparties
3.	identify; measure	**12.**	Natural hedges
4.	self-insure	**13.**	Forward contracts
5.	cost/benefit	**14.**	inverse floater
6.	Futures	**15.**	Commodity
7.	speculation; hedging	**16.**	Financial
8.	Derivatives	**17.**	long; short

18.   b.   Long hedges are futures contracts bought to guard against price increases, while short hedges are futures contracts sold to guard against price declines.

19.   b.   These very things tend to stabilize the market.

20.   a.   This statement is correct.

21.   d.   This is not a problem with swaps.

22.   e.   Futures contracts are similar to forward contracts except for three key differences: (1) Futures contracts are "marked to market," (2) With futures contracts, physical delivery of the underlying asset is virtually never taken, and (3) futures contracts are standardized instruments that are traded on the exchange.

23. e. Statement b is false because hedging lowers the aggregate risk in the economy. Statement d is false because an option's market value lies above its exercise value at each price of the common stock, although the premium declines as the stock price increases. Since statement a and c are correct, the proper choice is statement e.

SOLUTIONS TO SELF-TEST PROBLEMS

1. a. Futures contract settled at 101 2/32% of $100,000 contract value, so PV = 1.010625 × $1,000 = 1,010.625 × 100 bonds = $101,062.50. Using a financial calculator, we can solve for k_d as follows:
N = 40; PV = -1010.625; PMT = 30; FV = 1000; solve for I = k_d = 2.9544% × 2 = 5.9088% ≈ 5.91%.

2. d. If the interest rate was 8.50%, then we would solve for PV as follows:
N = 40; I = 8.50/2 = 4.25; PMT = -30; FV = 1000; solve for PV = $761.5341 × 100 = $76,153.418.

CHAPTER 25
BANKRUPTCY, REORGANIZATION, AND LIQUIDATION

OVERVIEW

The financial manager of a failing firm must know how to ward off his or her firm's total collapse and thereby reduce its losses. The ability to hang on during rough times often means the difference between the firm's forced liquidation versus its rehabilitation and eventual success. At the same time, an understanding of business failures and bankruptcies, their causes, and their possible remedies is also important to financial managers of successful firms, because they must know their firms' rights when their customers or suppliers go bankrupt.

OUTLINE

A number of factors combine to cause business failures. Case studies show that financial difficulties are usually the result of a series of errors, misjudgments, and interrelated weaknesses that can be attributed directly or indirectly to management, and signs of potential financial distress are generally evident before the firm actually fails.

■ Although bankruptcies are more common among smaller firms, it is clear that large firms are not immune. It is interesting to note that whereas the failure rate per 10,000 businesses fluctuates with the state of the economy, the average liability per failure has tended to increase over time. This is due primarily to inflation, but it also reflects the fact that some very large firms have failed in recent years.

■ Government and industry seek to avoid failure among larger firms. For financial institutions the reason for this is to prevent an erosion of confidence and a consequent run on the banks. The fact that bankruptcy is a very expensive process gives private industry strong incentives to avoid outright bankruptcy.

Financial distress begins when a firm is unable to meet scheduled payments or when cash flow projections indicate that it will soon be unable to do so.

■   Several questions arise as to how a firm should proceed:
- ❑ Is the situation temporary or a permanent problem?
- ❑ If temporary, can an agreement with creditors be worked out; if permanent, who should bear the losses?
- ❑ Is the company "worth more dead than alive"?
- ❑ Should the firm file for bankruptcy or use informal procedures?
- ❑ Who should control the firm while it is being liquidated or rehabilitated?

Because of costs associated with formal bankruptcy, it is desirable to reorganize or liquidate a firm outside formal bankruptcy through use of informal settlement procedures.

■   *Informal reorganization* can be used in the case of an economically sound company in temporary distress. Voluntary plans, called *workouts,* usually require some type of *restructuring* of the firm's debt.
- ❑ A debt restructuring begins with a meeting between the failing firm's managers and creditors. An *adjustment bureau* run by the creditor managers' association often arranges the meeting. A great deal of negotiation is involved to reach a final debt restructuring agreement.
- ❑ Management draws up a list of creditors with the amounts of debt owed.
- ❑ The company develops information showing the value of the firm under different scenarios.
- ❑ The information is then shared with the firm's bankers and other creditors. This information, when presented in a credible manner, will often convince creditors that they would be better off accepting something less than the full amount of their claims rather than holding out for the full face amount.
- ❑ Creditors often prefer an *extension* because it promises eventual payment in full. In an extension, creditors postpone the dates of required interest or principal payments, or both.
- ❑ In a *composition*, creditors voluntarily reduce their fixed claims on the debtor by accepting a lower principal amount, by reducing the interest rate on the debt, by accepting equity in place of debt, or by accepting some combination of these changes.
- ❑ Such voluntary settlements are not only informal and simple but also relatively inexpensive because legal and administrative expenses are held to a minimum. Creditors often recover more money, and sooner, than if the firm were to file for bankruptcy.
- ❑ Perhaps the biggest problem in informal reorganizations is in getting all the parties to agree to the voluntary plan. This problem is called the *holdout problem.*

■ *Informal liquidation* is the result of determining that a firm is more valuable dead than alive. *Assignment* is an informal procedure for liquidating a firm, and it usually yields creditors a larger amount than they would receive in a formal bankruptcy liquidation. In an assignment, the title to the debtor's assets is transferred to a third party, known as an assignee or trustee, who is instructed to liquidate the assets through a private sale or public auction and then to distribute the proceeds among the creditors on a pro rata basis. Assignments are feasible only if the firm is small and its affairs are not too complex.

A firm is officially bankrupt when it files for bankruptcy with a federal court. Formal bankruptcy proceedings are designed to protect both the firm and its creditors. Chapter 11 of the 1978 Bankruptcy Reform Act deals with business reorganization.

■ If the problem is temporary insolvency, then the firm may use bankruptcy proceedings to gain time to solve its cash flow problems without asset seizure by its creditors.

■ If the firm is bankrupt in the sense that liabilities exceed assets, the creditors can use bankruptcy procedures to attempt to ensure that the firm's owners do not siphon off assets which should go to creditors.

Two problems often arise to stymie informal reorganizations and thus force debtors into formal Chapter 11 bankruptcy.

■ The *common pool problem* occurs because individual creditors have an incentive to foreclose on the firm even though it is worth more collectively as an ongoing concern. A solution to the common pool problem is the Chapter 11 *automatic stay provision*, which limits the ability of creditors to foreclose unilaterally on the debtor to collect their individual claims.

■ *Fraudulent conveyance* statutes, which are part of debtor-creditor law, protect creditors from unjustified transfers of property by a firm in financial distress.

■ The *holdout problem* can also make it difficult to reorganize a firm's debts. If all creditors agreed to a reorganization plan, it would benefit the creditors and the firm simultaneously. However, there is an advantage for a creditor to "hold out" since his or her claim would be higher than that of those who would agree to a lower settlement. Thus, it is likely that none of the creditors would accept the offer. Because of this problem, it is easier for a firm with few creditors to informally reorganize than it is for a firm with many creditors.

In bankruptcy, it is much easier to gain acceptance of a reorganization plan, because the bankruptcy court will lump the creditors into classes.

- A *cramdown* is a procedure in which the court mandates a reorganization plan in spite of dissent.

Filing for bankruptcy under Chapter 11 has several benefits besides automatic stay and cramdown that are not inherent in informal restructurings.

- Interest and principal payments may be delayed without penalty until a reorganization plan is approved.

- The firm is permitted to issue *debtor in possession (DIP) financing* which enhances the ability of the firm to borrow funds for short-term liquidity purposes, because such loans are senior to all previous unsecured debt.

- The debtor firm's managers are given the exclusive right for 120 days after filing to submit a reorganization plan, plus another 60 days to obtain agreement on the plan from the parties affected.

- Under the early bankruptcy laws, most formal reorganization plans were guided by the *absolute priority doctrine*. This doctrine holds that creditors should be compensated for their claims in a rigid hierarchical order, and that senior claims must be paid in full before junior claims can receive even a dime. An alternative position, the *relative priority doctrine*, holds that more flexibility should be allowed in a reorganization, and that balanced consideration should be given to all claimants. Current law represents a movement away from absolute priority and toward relative priority.

The primary role of the bankruptcy court in a reorganization is to determine the fairness and the feasibility of proposed plans of reorganization.

- The *fairness* doctrine states that claims must be recognized in the order of their legal and contractual priority.

- The primary test of *feasibility* in a reorganization is whether the fixed charges after reorganization will be adequately covered by earnings.

- Recently a new type of reorganization called *prepackaged bankruptcy* combines the advantages of both the informal workout and formal Chapter 11 reorganization. Here the debtor firm gets all, or most of, the creditors to agree to the reorganization plan prior to filing for bankruptcy. Then, a reorganization plan is filed along with the bankruptcy petition. If enough creditors have signed on before the filing, a cramdown can be used to bring reluctant creditors along.

- ❑ The three primary advantages of a prepackaged bankruptcy are (1) reduction of the holdout problem, (2) preserving creditors' claims, and (3) taxes.

If a company is "too far gone" to be reorganized, then it must be liquidated.

- ■ Liquidation should occur when the business is worth more dead than alive, or when the possibility of restoring it to financial health is so remote that the creditors run a higher risk of greater loss if operations are continued.

- ■ Chapter 7 of the Federal Bankruptcy Reform Act addresses three important problems during a liquidation:
  - ❑ It provides safeguards against fraud by the debtor.
  - ❑ It provides for an equitable distribution of the debtor's assets among the creditors.
  - ❑ It allows insolvent debtors to discharge all their obligations and thus be able to start new businesses unhampered by the burden of prior debt.

- ■ The distribution of assets in a liquidation under Chapter 7 is governed by the following priority of claims: (1) Past due property taxes, (2) secured creditors, (3) trustee's costs, (4) expenses incurred after an involuntary case has begun but before a trustee is appointed, (5) wages due workers if earned within 3 months prior to filing the bankruptcy petition, (6) claims for unpaid contributions to employee benefit plans, (7) unsecured claims for customer deposits, (8) taxes due, (9) unfunded pension plan liabilities, (10) general (unsecured) creditors, (11) preferred stockholders, and (12) common stockholders.

Normally, bankruptcy proceedings originate after a company cannot meet its current obligations. However, bankruptcy law also permits a company to file for bankruptcy if its financial forecasts indicate that a continuation of current conditions would lead to insolvency.

Many critics today claim that current bankruptcy laws are not doing what they were intended to do.

- ■ Before 1978, most bankruptcies ended quickly in liquidation. Then, Congress rewrote the laws giving companies more opportunity to stay alive, believing that this was best for managers, employees, creditors, and stockholders.

- Critics believe that bankruptcy is good business for consultants, lawyers, and investment bankers, who reap hefty fees during bankruptcy proceedings, and for managers, who continue to collect their salaries and bonuses as long as the business is kept alive.

- Bankruptcy cases can drag on in court for many years, depleting assets that could be sold to pay off creditors and shareholders. In effect, critics say, maintaining companies on life support does not serve the interests of the parties that bankruptcy laws were meant to protect.

SELF-TEST QUESTIONS

Definitional

1. _____ _____ can be used in the case of an economically sound company in temporary distress. Voluntary plans, called _____, usually require some type of restructuring of the firm's debt.

2. Creditors often prefer a(n) _____ because it promises eventual payment in full.

3. In a(n) _____, creditors agree to reduce their fixed claims on the debtor.

4. _____ is an informal procedure for liquidating a firm, and it usually yields creditors a larger amount than they would receive in a formal bankruptcy liquidation.

5. Two problems often arise to stymie informal reorganizations and thus force debtors into formal Chapter 11 bankruptcy: the _____ _____ _____ and the _____ _____.

6. A(n) _____ is a procedure in which the court mandates a reorganization plan in spite of dissent.

7. _____-____-_____ financing enhances the ability of the firm to borrow funds for short-term liquidity purposes, because such loans are senior to all other unsecured debt.

8. The _____ doctrine states that claims must be recognized in the order of their legal and contractual priority, while the primary test of _____ in a reorganization is whether the fixed charges after reorganization will be adequately covered by earnings.

Conceptual

9. Financial distress begins when a firm is unable to meet scheduled payments to creditors, not when the firm's cash flow projections indicate that it will soon be unable to do so.

   a. True   **b.** False

10. Bankruptcies are more common among larger firms than smaller firms.

    a. True   **b.** False

11. Informal reorganization can be used in the case of an economically sound company in temporary distress. One type of voluntary plan is called a workout.

    a. True   **b.** False

12. Which of the following statements is most correct?

    a. In an extension, creditors voluntarily reduce their fixed claims on the debtor by accepting a lower principal amount, by reducing the interest rate on the debt, by accepting equity in place of debt, or by accepting some combination of these changes.
    b. Technical insolvency occurs when a firm's book value of total liabilities exceeds the true market value of its assets.
    c. Although many people use the term bankruptcy to refer to any firm that has "failed," a firm is not legally bankrupt unless it has filed for bankruptcy under federal law.
    d. Both statements a and c are true.
    e. All of the statements are false.

13. Which of the following statements is most correct?

    a. The automatic stay provision provided for in Chapter 11 is only granted to certain debtors in bankruptcy. It limits the ability of creditors to foreclose unilaterally on the debtor to collect their individual claims and, as a result, it provides a solution to the holdout problem.
    b. Fraudulent conveyance statutes, which are a part of debtor-creditor law, protect creditors from unjustified transfers of property by a firm in financial distress.
    c. In a cramdown, creditors postpone the dates of required interest or principal payments, or both.
    d. The common pool problem occurs because individual creditors have an incentive to foreclose on the firm even though the firm is worth more collectively as an ongoing concern.
    e. Both statements b and d are true.

SELF-TEST PROBLEMS

1. The Stanton Marble Company has the following balance sheet:

Current assets	$15,120	Accounts payable	$ 3,240
		Notes payable (to bank)	1,620
		Accrued taxes	540
		Accrued wages	540
		Total current liabilities	$ 5,940
Fixed assets	8,100	First mortgage bonds	2,700
		Second mortgage bonds	2,700
		Total mortgage bonds	$ 5,400
		Subordinated debentures	3,240
		Total long-term debt	$ 8,640
		Preferred stock	1,080
		Common stock	7,560
Total assets	$23,220	Total liabilities and equity	$23,220

The debentures are subordinated only to the notes payable. Suppose Stanton Marble goes bankrupt and is liquidated with $5,400 being received from the sale of the fixed assets, which were pledged as security for the first and second mortgage bonds, and $8,640 received from the sale of current assets. The trustee's costs total $1,440. How much will the holders of subordinated debentures receive?

a. $2,052   **b.** $2,448   **c.** $3,240   **d.** $2,709   **e.** $3,056

(The following data apply to the next three Self-Test Problems.)

The Lockwood Corporation's balance sheet and income statement are as follows (in millions of dollars). Lockwood and its creditors have agreed upon a voluntary reorganization plan. In this plan, each share of the $6 preferred will be exchanged for one share of $2.40 preferred with a par value of $37.50 plus one 8 percent subordinated income debenture with a par value of $75. The $10.50 preferred issue will be retired with cash.

Balance Sheet:

Current assets	$336	Current liabilities	$ 84
Net fixed assets	306	Advance payments	156
Goodwill	30	Reserves	12
		$6 preferred stock, $112.50 par value	
		(2,400,000 shares)	270
		$10.50 preferred stock, no par, callable	
		at $150 (120,000 shares)	18
		Common stock, $1.50 par value	
		(12,000,000 shares)	18
		Retained earnings	114
Total assets	$672	Total claims	$672

Income Statement:

Net sales	$1,080.0
Operating expense	1,032.0
Net operating income	$ 48.0
Other income	6.0
EBT	$ 54.0
Taxes (50%)	27.0
Net income	$ 27.0
Dividends on $6 preferred	14.4
Dividends on $10.50 preferred	1.3
Income available to common stockholders	$ 11.3

2. What is the value (in millions of dollars) of total assets on the balance sheet?

   a. $680   **b.** $620   **c.** $636   **d.** $654   **e.** $645

3. What is the value (in millions of dollars) of the new preferred stock?

   a. $105   **b.** $90   **c.** $110   **d.** $80   **e.** $95

4. What is the net income available to common stockholders (in millions of dollars) after the proposed recapitalization takes place?

   a. $17   **b.** $11   **c.** $14   **d.** $13   **e.** $16

(The following data apply to the next six Self-Test Problems.)

At the time it defaulted on its interest payments and filed for bankruptcy, the Southeastern Manufacturing Company (SMC) had the following balance sheet (in thousands of dollars). The court, after trying unsuccessfully to reorganize the firm, decided that the only recourse was liquidation under Chapter 7. Sale of the fixed assets, which were pledged as collateral to the mortgage bondholders, brought in $1,600,000, while the current assets were sold for another $800,000. Thus, the total proceeds from the liquidation sale were $2,400,000. Trustee's costs amounted to $200,000; no single worker was due more than $2,000 in wages; and there were no unfunded pension plan liabilities.

Current assets	$1,600	Accounts payable	$ 200
		Accrued taxes	160
		Accrued wages	120
		Notes payable	720
		Total current liabilities	$1,200
Net fixed assets	2,400	First mortgage bonds[a]	1,200
		Second mortgage bonds[a]	800
		Debentures	800
		Subordinated debentures[b]	400
		Common stock	200
		Retained earnings	(600)
Total assets	$4,000	Total claims	$4,000

Notes:

[a]All fixed assets are pledged as collateral to the mortgage bonds.
[b]Subordinated to notes payable.

5. How much of the proceeds (in thousands of dollars) from the sale of assets remain to be distributed to general creditors after distribution to priority claimants?

    a. $432   **b.** $500   **c.** $375   **d.** $300   **e.** $320

6. How much of the proceeds (in thousands of dollars) do the second mortgage holders receive after distribution to general creditors and subordination adjustments are made?

    a. $400   **b.** $451   **c.** $51   **d.** $375   **e.** $500

7. How much of the proceeds (in thousands of dollars) do the holders of the subordinated debentures receive after distribution to general creditors and subordination adjustments are made?

   a. $51   **b.** $102   **c.** $142   **d.** $0   **e.** $25

8. How much of the proceeds (in thousands of dollars) from the liquidation do the common stockholders receive?

   a. $0   **b.** $51   **c.** $25   **d.** $102   **e.** $142

ANSWERS TO SELF-TEST QUESTIONS

1. Informal reorganization; workouts
2. extension
3. composition
4. Assignment
5. common pool problem; holdout problem

6. cramdown
7. Debtor-in-possession
8. fairness; feasibility

9. b. Financial distress also begins when the firm's cash flow projections indicate that it will soon be unable to meet scheduled payments to creditors.

10. b. Just the reverse is true; however, large firms are not immune to bankruptcy.

11. a. This statement is correct.

12. c. Statement a is false; it describes a composition, not an extension. Statement b is false; a firm is considered technically insolvent if it cannot meet its current obligations as they fall due. Statement c is true. Thus, statements d and e are both incorrect.

13. e. Statement a is false; automatic stay is granted to all debtors in bankruptcy and it is a solution for the common pool problem. Statement b is true. Statement c describes an extension, not a cramdown. Statement d is true; thus, statement e is correct.

SOLUTIONS TO SELF-TEST PROBLEMS

1. a.

Claimant	Claim Amount (1)	Priority Distribution and General Creditor (2)	Subordinate Adjustment (3)	Percent of Claim (4)
Accounts payable	$ 3,240	$ 2,448	$ 2,448	75.56%
Notes payable	1,620	1,224	1,620	100.00
Accrued taxes	540	540	540	100.00
Accrued wages	540	540	540	100.00
1st mortgage bonds	2,700	2,700	2,700	100.00
2nd mortgage bonds	2,700	2,700	2,700	100.00
Subord. debentures	3,240	2,448	2,052	63.33
Preferred stock	1,080	0	0	0.00
Common stock	7,560	0	0	0.00
Trustee	1,440	1,440	1,440	100.00
Total	$ 24,660	$ 14,040	$ 14,040	56.93%

Explanation of the columns:

(1)   Values are taken from the balance sheet.

(2)   Since the firm's total debt obligations (including trustee costs) equals $16,020 and only $14,040 is received from the sale of assets, the preferred and common stockholders are wiped out. These stockholders receive nothing.

   The $5,400 from the sale of fixed assets is immediately allocated to the mortgage bonds. The holders of the first mortgage bonds are paid off first, so they receive $2,700. The remaining $2,700 from the sale of fixed assets is allocated to the second mortgage bonds, so these bondholders are also paid off.

   By law, trustee expenses have first claim on the remaining available funds, wages have second priority, and taxes have third priority. Thus, these claims are paid in full.

   We now have $6,120 remaining and claims of $8,100, so the general creditors will receive 75.56 cents on the dollar:

$$\frac{\text{Funds available}}{\text{Unsatisfied debt}} = \frac{\$14,040 - \$5,400 - \$1,080 - \$1,440}{\$3,240 + \$1,620 + \$3,240} = 0.7556.$$

General creditors are now initially allocated 75.56 percent of their original claims.

(3)   This column reflects a transfer of funds from the subordinated debentures to the notes payable to the bank. Since subordinated debentures are subordinate to bank debt, notes payable to the bank must be paid in full before the debentures receive anything. The notes are paid in full by transferring the difference between their book value and initial allocation ($1,620) $1,224 = $396) from

subordinated debentures to notes payable. This reduces the allocation to subordinated debentures and increases the allocation to notes payable by $396.

(4)   Column 3 ÷ Column 1.

2.   d.   The pro forma balance sheet follows (in millions of dollars):

Current assets[a]	$318	Current liabilities	$ 84
Net fixed assets	30	Advance payments	156
Goodwill	30	Reserves	12
		Subordinated debentures[b]	180
		$2.40 preferred stock, $37.50 par value	
		(2,400,000 shares)[c]	90
		Common stock, $1.50 par value	
		(12,000,000 shares)	18
		Retained earnings	114
Total assets	$654	Total claims	$654

Notes:
[a]$336 million - $18 million = $318 million used to retire the $10.50 preferred stock.
[b]2,400,000 shares H $75 par value = $180 million.
[c]2,400,000 shares H $37.50 par value = $90 million.

3.   b.   See the balance sheet shown in response to Self-Test Problem 2.

4.   c.   The pro forma income statement (in millions of dollars) follows:

Net sales	$1,080.0
Operating expense	1,032.0
Net operating income	$ 48.0
Other income	6.0
EBIT	$ 54.0
Interest expense[a]	14.4
EBT	$ 39.6
Taxes (50%)	19.8
Net income	$ 19.8
Dividends on $2.40 preferred[b]	5.8
Income available to common stockholders	$ 14.0

Notes:
[a]0.08($180 million par value) = $14.4 million.
[b]$2.40(2,400,000 shares) = $5.76 million . $5.8 million.

5.   e.   Distribution to priority claimants (in thousands of dollars):

Proceeds from the sale of assets	$2,400
Less:	
1. First mortgage (paid from sale of fixed assets)	1,200
2. Second mortgage (paid from sale of fixed assets)	400
3. Fees and expenses of bankruptcy	200
4. Wages due to workers	120
5. Taxes due	160
Funds available for distribution to general creditors	$ 320

Distribution to general creditors (in thousands of dollars):

General Creditor Claims	Amount of Claim	Pro Rata Distribution[a]	Distrib. After Subord. Adj.[b]	% of Orig. Claim Received
Unsat. 2nd mortgage	$ 400	$ 51	$ 51	56%[c]
Accounts payable	200	25	25	13
Notes payable	720	91	142	20
Debentures	800	102	102	13
Subord. debentures	400	51	0	0
Total	$2,520	$320	$320	

Notes:

[a]Pro rata distribution: $320/$2,520 = 0.127 = 12.7%.

[b]Subordinated debentures are subordinated to notes payable. Unsatisfied portion of notes payable is greater than subordinated debenture distribution so subordinated debentures receive $0.

[c]Includes $400 from sale of fixed assets received in priority distribution.

6.   b.   See the distribution worksheet shown in response to Self-Test Problem 5.

7.   d.   See the distribution worksheet shown in response to Self-Test Problem 5.

8.   a.   Because the amount of funds available for distribution to general creditors is $320,000 and the total claims of these general creditors is $2,520,000, the common stockholders will receive nothing.

CHAPTER 26
MERGERS, LBOs, DIVESTITURES, AND
HOLDING COMPANIES

OVERVIEW

Most corporate growth occurs by internal expansion, which takes place when a firm's existing divisions grow through normal capital budgeting activities. However, the most dramatic examples of growth, and often the largest increases in stock prices, result from *mergers*, the first topic covered in this chapter. *Leveraged buyouts*, or *LBOs*, occur when a firm's stock is acquired by a small group of investors rather than by another operating company.

Since LBOs are similar to mergers in many respects, they are also covered in this chapter. Conditions change over time, and, as a result, firms often find it desirable to sell off, or *divest* major divisions to other firms that can better utilize the divested assets. *Divestitures* are also discussed in the chapter. Finally, we discuss the *holding company* form of organization, wherein one corporation owns the stock of one or more other companies.

OUTLINE

Several reasons have been proposed to justify corporate mergers.

■ One major reason for mergers is *synergy*.
   ❑ If Companies A and B merge to form Company C, and if C's value exceeds that of A and B taken separately, then synergy is said to exist.
   ❑ Synergism can arise from four sources:
      • Operating economies
      • Financial economies
      • Differential management efficiency
      • Increased market power

- □ Operating and financial economies, as well as increases in managerial efficiency, are socially desirable. However, mergers that reduce competition are both undesirable and illegal.

- ■ *Tax considerations* can provide an incentive for mergers.
  - □ A highly profitable firm might merge with a firm which has accumulated tax losses so as to put these losses to immediate use.
  - □ A firm with excess cash and a shortage of internal investment opportunities might seek a merger rather than pay the cash out as dividends, which would result in the shareholders paying immediate taxes on the distribution.

- ■ Occasionally, a firm will merge with another because it thinks it has found a "bargain," that is, *assets can be purchased below their replacement cost.*
  - □ However, if the capital markets are efficient, stock prices represent the fair market value of the underlying assets.
  - □ The fact that a firm's market value is far below its replacement or book value does not, in itself, make the firm an attractive acquisition candidate.

- ■ *Diversification* is often cited by managers as a rationale for mergers.
  - □ Diversification may bring some real benefits to the firm, especially by reducing the variability of the firm's earnings stream, which benefits the firm's managers, creditors, and other stakeholders.
  - □ However, by simply holding portfolios of stocks, stockholders can generally diversify more easily and efficiently than can firms.

- ■ Financial economists like to think that business decisions are based only on economic considerations. However, some business decisions are based more on managers' personal motivations than on economic factors.
  - □ Some mergers occur because managers want to increase the size of their firms, and hence gain more power, prestige, and monetary compensation.
  - □ Other mergers occur because managers want to keep their jobs, so they merge with other firms to make the firm less attractive to hostile suitors. This type of merger is called a *defensive merger*.

- ■ Firms are generally valued in the markets as ongoing firms. However, some firms are worth more if they are broken up and then sold off in pieces. Thus, some acquisitions are motivated by the fact that a firm's *breakup value* is greater than its current market value.

There are four primary types of mergers.

- A *horizontal merger* occurs when one firm combines with another in the same line of business.

- A *vertical merger* exists when firms combine in a producer-supplier relationship.

- A *congeneric merger* occurs when the merging companies are somewhat related, but not to the extent required for a horizontal or vertical merger.

- A *conglomerate merger* occurs when completely unrelated enterprises combine.

Five major "merger waves" have occurred in the United States. The high level of merger activity that is still going on has been sparked by several factors.

- Five major "merger waves" have occurred in the U. S.
  - In the late 1800s consolidations occurred in the oil, steel, tobacco, and other basic industries.
  - In the 1920s the stock market boom helped financial promoters consolidate firms in a number of industries.
  - In the 1960s conglomerate mergers were the rage.
  - In the 1980s LOB firms and others began using junk bonds to finance all manner of acquisitions.
  - Currently, strategic alliances are being formed to enable firms to compete better in the global economy.

- In general, the mergers in the 1990s have been significantly different from those of the 1980s.
  - In the 1980s mergers were financial transactions in which buyers sought companies that were selling at less than their true values as a result of incompetent or sluggish management.
  - In the 1990s most of the mergers have been strategic in nature. Companies are merging to gain economies of scale or scope and thus be better able to compete in the world economy.
  - Other differences between the 1980s and the 1990s are the way the mergers were financed and how the target firms' stockholders were compensated.
  - In the 1990s there has been an increase in cross-border mergers. Many of these mergers have been motivated by large shifts in the value of the world's leading currencies.

In most mergers, one company, the target company, is acquired by another, the acquiring company.

■   In a *friendly merger*, the management of the target company approves the merger and recommends it to their stockholders.

    ❑   Under these circumstances a suitable price is determined, and the acquiring company will simply buy the target company's shares through a friendly *tender offer.*

    ❑   Payment will be made either in cash, or in the stock or debt of the acquiring firm.

■   A *hostile merger* is one in which the target firm's management resists the takeover. The target firm's management either believes the price offered is too low, or it may simply want to remain independent.

    ❑   Under these circumstances, the acquiring company may make a hostile tender offer for the target company's shares. This is a direct appeal to the target firm's stockholders asking them to exchange their shares for cash, bonds, or stock in the acquiring firm.

    ❑   The number of hostile tender offers has increased greatly during the past several years.

Mergers are regulated by both the state and federal governments.

■   Federal laws place three major restrictions on acquiring firms.

    ❑   Acquirers must disclose their current holdings and future intentions within 10 days of amassing at least 5 percent of a company's stock, and they must disclose the source of the funds to be used in the acquisition.

    ❑   Target shareholders must be given at least 20 days to tender their shares.

    ❑   If the tender price is increased during the 20-day open period, all shareholders who tendered prior to the new offer must receive the higher price.

■   Many states now have merger laws which restrict the actions that can be taken by raiders.

    ❑   One such law restricts the ability of a raider to vote the shares they have acquired; that is, the merger must be approved by disinterested shareholders.

    ❑   Other state laws limit the use of *golden parachutes,* onerous debt-financing plans, and some types of *poison pills* to protect target stockholders from their own managers.

While merger analysis may appear simple, there are a number of complex issues involved.

■ The acquiring firm must perform a capital budgeting-type analysis. If it appears that the target firm can be purchased for less than its intrinsic value, then the offer should be made.

■ However, the target firm's shareholders must believe that a "fair" price is being offered. Otherwise, they will not tender their shares.

■ Several methodologies are used to value firms. Two commonly-used methods are the *discounted cash flow analysis* and the *market multiple method*. Regardless of the valuation methodology, two factors must be recognized.
  ❑ Any changes in operations occurring as a result of the proposed merger that will impact the value of the business must be considered in the analysis.
  ❑ The goal of merger valuation is to set the value of the target business's equity, or ownership position.

■ The *discounted cash flow approach* to valuing a business involves the application of capital budgeting procedures to an entire firm rather than to a single project.
  ❑ To apply this method, two key items are needed: (1) a set of pro forma statements that develop the incremental cash flows expected to result from the merger, and (2) a discount rate, or cost of capital, to apply these projected cash flows.
  ❑ In a pure *financial merger*, in which no synergies are expected, the incremental postmerger cash flows are simply the expected cash flows of the target firm if it were to continue to operate independently.
  ❑ In an *operating merger*, in which the two firms' operations are to be integrated, or if the acquiring firm plans to change the target firm's operations to get better results, then forecasting future cash flows is even more complex.

■ Merger cash flows, unlike capital budgeting cash flows, *must include* interest expense.
  ❑ The target firm usually has embedded debt that will be assumed by the acquiring company.
  ❑ The acquisition is often financed partially by debt.
  ❑ If the subsidiary is expected to grow in the future, new debt will have to be issued over time to support its expansion. Thus, debt costs must be explicitly included in the cash flow analysis.

■ With debt costs included in the cash flow analysis, the resulting net cash flows accrue solely to the equity holders of the acquiring firm; thus, we are using the *equity residual method*.
  ❑ This is in contrast to the corporate value model where the free cash flows, which belong to all investors not just shareholders, are discounted at the WACC.

- ❑ Both methods lead to the same estimate of equity value.

- ■ The *appropriate discount rate is a cost of equity* rather than an overall cost of capital. The cost of equity used must reflect the underlying riskiness of the target company's assets and the riskiness of the financing mix used for the acquisition.

- ■ A risk analysis could be performed on the cash flows.
  - ❑ Sensitivity analysis, scenario analysis, and/or Monte Carlo simulation could be used to get a feel for the risks involved with the acquisition.

- ■ The Security Market Line can then be used to determine the target firm's postmerger cost of equity.

- ■ The present value of the incremental merger cash flows is the maximum price that the acquiring firm should pay for the target company.

- ■ Another method of valuing a target company is *market multiple analysis*, which applies a market-determined multiple to some measure of earnings such as net income or earnings per share. The basic premise is that the value of any business depends on the earnings that the business produces.
  - ❑ Note that earnings (or cash flow) measures other than net income can be used in the market multiple approach. Another commonly used measure is *earnings before interest, taxes, depreciation, and amortization (EBITDA)*.

- ■ Although the DCF method has strong theoretical support, one has to be very concerned over the validity of the estimated cash flows and the discount rate applied to those flows.

- ■ The market multiple method is more ad hoc, but its proponents argue that earnings estimates for a single year, or for a few years, are much more likely to be accurate than the many years of cash flows that must be estimated in the DCF approach and it avoids the problem of having to estimate a discount rate.
  - ❑ The market multiple method has problems of its own. One concern is the comparability between the firm being analyzed and the firm (or firms) that set the market multiple. Another concern is how well does one year of earnings capture the value of a firm that will be operated for many years into the future, and whose earnings could soar due to merger-related synergies.

- ■ The terms of a merger include three important elements:
  - ❑ *The price to be paid* determines whether the shareholders of the acquiring company or the shareholders of the target company reap the greater benefits from the merger.

- If there were no synergistic benefits, the maximum bid would be equal to the current value of the target company. The greater the synergistic gains, the greater the gap between the target's current price and the maximum the acquiring company could pay.
- The greater the synergistic gains, the more likely a merger is to be consummated.
- The issue of how to divide the synergistic benefits is critically important in any merger analysis.
- Where in the range the actual price will be set depends on the negotiating skills of the two management teams and on the bargaining positions of the two parties as determined by fundamental economic conditions.
- The acquiring firm keeps its maximum bid secret, and it plans its bidding strategy carefully and consistently with the situation.

□ *Postmerger control of the firm*, which is of great interest to managers due to their concern for their jobs.
□ *The structure of the offer* is how to pay for the merger—in cash, in securities of the acquiring firm, or in some combination of the two.

■ An acquiring firm may wish to change the capital structure of the target once it is acquired. This can change the analysis in several ways:
□ The cash flows to the shareholders may be higher or lower.
- Interest expense is higher.
- The retentions needed for growth are lower because of the higher debt level.
□ Beta will increase, so the discount rate will be higher.
□ The bid price is affected through the value of the firm and the per share price.
- The value of the firm may be higher or lower based on the new cash flows and the new discount rate.
- The maximum bid price is the total value of the target after the capital structure change, minus the target's debt before the acquisition.

Once the value of the target is estimated, the acquiring firm must decide on the structure of the takeover bid.

■ The acquiring firm can either buy the target's assets or buy shares of stock directly from the target's shareholders.

■ The structure of the bid is extremely important since it affects:
□ The capital structure of the postmerger firm.
□ The tax treatment of both the acquiring firm and the target firm's stockholders.

- ❑ The ability of the target firm's stockholders to reap the rewards of future merger-related gains.
- ❑ The types of federal and state regulations that apply to the merger.

- Target shareholders do not have to pay taxes on the their takeover proceeds if their shares are paid for by stock in the acquiring firm (at least 50 percent of the payment must be in stock). If the offer is predominantly cash or debt securities, taxes will have to be paid.

- If the acquiring firm elects to write up the target company's assets for tax purposes, the target company must pay a capital gains tax on the write-up. However, it can then depreciate the assets from their new, higher value.

Mergers are handled in either of two basic ways: (1) as a pooling of interests or (2) as a purchase.

- In theory, a *pooling of interests* is a merger among equals, hence the consolidated balance sheet is simply the sum of the two merging company's balance sheets.

- Under the *purchase* method, one firm is assumed to have bought another in much the same way it would buy any capital asset, paying for it with cash, debt, or stock of the acquiring company.
  - ❑ If the price paid is exactly equal to the acquired firm's *net asset value*, which is defined as its total assets minus its liabilities, then the consolidated balance sheet will be identical to that under pooling.
  - ❑ If the price paid exceeds the net asset value, then asset values will be increased to reflect the price actually paid, whereas if the price paid is less than the net asset value, then assets must be written down when preparing the consolidated balance sheet.

- Significant differences can also arise in reported profits under the two accounting methods.
  - ❑ If asset values are increased, this must be reflected in a higher depreciation charge and also in a higher cost of goods sold if inventories are written up.
  - ❑ Also, *goodwill* represents the excess paid for a firm over its adjusted net asset value. Goodwill is written off, or amortized, over a period corresponding to not more than 40 years.

- Several conditions must be met to use the pooling method, the most important of which is that the acquisition must be paid for with common stock of the acquiring firm.

- Nevertheless, about 90 percent of all recent acquisitions over $100 million have used pooling, which does not lower the combined firm's reported earnings.

In many situations it is hard to identify an acquirer and a target firm. Thus, the merger appears to be a true "merger of equals." There are several steps to go through in this type of analysis.

- Develop pro forma financial statements for the consolidated corporation.
  - ❑ The key set of figures is the projected consolidated free cash flows available to stockholders.

- Estimate the new company's cost of equity, and use that rate to discount the equity flows of the consolidated company.
  - ❑ This is the value of the equity of the consolidated company.

- Decide how to allocate the new company's stock between the two sets of old stockholders.
  - ❑ A key issue is how to divide the synergistic-induced value between the two sets of stockholders.
    - One basis for the allocation is the relative pre-announcement values of the two companies.
  - ❑ Control of the consolidated company is also a key issue.

Investment bankers play an important role in merger activities.

- The major investment banking firms have merger and acquisition (M&A) departments which help to match merger partners.

- These same investment bankers can also help a firm fend off an unwanted suitor.
  - ❑ Sometimes a *white knight* will be lined up to acquire a firm that is trying to avoid being taken over by an unfriendly suitor.
  - ❑ In other situations, a *white squire* may be sought to buy shares in the target firm, hold them, and then vote in favor of current management.
  - ❑ Investment bankers can also recommend *poison pills*, which are actions that effectively destroy the value of the firm in the event of merger, and hence drive off unwanted suitors.

- Investment bankers are often used to help establish the offering price. Generally, both the acquiring and target firms will use investment bankers to help establish a price and also to participate in the negotiations.

- Investment banking firms also engage in *risk arbitrage*, which means speculating in the stocks of companies that are likely takeover targets.

- They help finance mergers too.

Recent merger activity has raised two questions: (1) Do corporate acquisitions really create value, and , (2) if so, how is this value shared between the parties?

- Researchers attempt to answer questions such as this by examining the relative stock price performance of merging firms around the merger announcement date.

- On average, the stock prices of target companies have increased by 20-30 percent upon the merger announcement.

- However, the stock prices of acquiring firms have tended to remain unchanged.

- Thus, the evidence strongly indicates that acquisitions do create value, but that shareholders of target firms reap virtually all of the benefits.

Mergers are one way for two companies to completely join assets and management, but many firms are striking cooperative deals which fall short of merging. Such cooperative amalgamations are called corporate alliances, and they occur in many forms.

- *Joint ventures* are an important type of alliance.
  - Joint ventures are controlled by a combined management team formed by the parent companies.
  - Joint ventures are operated independently from the parent companies.

- Other types of alliances include cross-licensing, consortia, joint bidding, and franchising.

In a leveraged buyout (LBO), a small group of equity investors, usually including current management, acquires a firm in a transaction financed largely by debt.

- The debt is serviced by the cash flows generated by the acquired company's operations and by the sale of some of its assets.
  - Often, some of the assets must be sold to service the debt.
  - In other instances, the LBO firm plans to sell off divisions to other firms that can gain synergies.
  - The heavy debt burden forces management to operate very efficiently.

■ Usually, after several years of being privately held, the firm has been streamlined and made more efficient. Then, the owners recover their equity investment by going public again.

Although corporations do more buying than selling of productive assets, selling, or divestiture, does take place.

■ There are three primary types of *divestitures*:
   ❏ A division may be *sold to another firm*. This is the most common form of divestiture.
   ❏ In a *spin-off*, a division may be set up as a corporation, with the parent firm's stockholders then being given stock in the new corporation on a pro rata basis.
   ❏ In a *carve-out*, a minority interest in a corporate subsidiary is sold to new shareholders, so the parent gains new equity financing yet retains control.
   ❏ In a *liquidation*, the assets of a division are sold off piecemeal, rather than as a single entity.

■ There are a variety of reasons cited for divestitures:
   ❏ It appears that, on occasion, investors do not properly value some assets when they are part of a large conglomerate. Thus, divestiture can occur to enhance firm value.
   ❏ Often, firms will need to raise large amounts of cash to finance expansion in their core business, or to reduce an onerous debt burden, and divestitures can raise the needed cash.
   ❏ Sometimes, assets are just no longer profitable and must be liquidated.
   ❏ Firms that are struggling against bankruptcy often have to divest profitable divisions just to stay alive.
   ❏ The government sometimes mandates divestiture on antitrust grounds.

A holding company is a firm that holds large blocks of stock in other companies and exercises control over those firms. The holding company is often called the parent company and the controlled companies are known as subsidiaries or operating companies. Holding companies may be used to obtain some of the same benefits that could be achieved through mergers and acquisitions. However, the holding company device has some unique disadvantages as well as unique advantages.

■ Advantages of holding companies include the following:
   ❏ *Control with fractional ownership*. Effective control of a company may be achieved with far less than 50 percent ownership of the common stock.

❏ *Isolation of risks.* Claims on one unit of the holding company may not be liabilities to the other units. Each element of the holding company organization is a separate legal entity.

■ Disadvantages of holding companies include the following:
❏ *Partial multiple taxation.* Consolidated tax returns may be filed only if the holding company owns 80 percent or more of the voting stock of the subsidiary. Otherwise, intercorporate dividends will be taxed. Note, though, that firms that own over 20 percent but less than 80 percent of another corporation can deduct 80 percent of the dividends received from taxable income, while firms that own less than 20 percent may deduct only 70 percent of the dividends received.
❏ *Ease of enforced dissolution.* It is much easier for the Justice Department to require disposal of a stock position than to demand the separation of an integrated business operation.

■ The holding company device can be used to control large amounts of assets with a relatively small equity investment. The substantial leverage involved in such an operation may result in high returns, but it also involves a high degree of risk.

SELF-TEST QUESTIONS

Definitional

1. If the value of two firms, in combination, is greater than the sum of their separate values, then _____ is said to exist.

2. Synergistic effects may result from either _____ economies or _____ economies.

3. The Justice Department may be concerned about the _____ implications of a proposed merger.

4. A(n) _____ merger takes place when two firms in the same line of business combine, while the combination of a steel company with a coal company would be an example of a(n) _____ merger.

5. The merger of two completely unrelated enterprises is referred to as a(n) _____ merger.

6. A firm which seeks to take over another company is commonly called the _____ company, while the firm it seeks to acquire is referred to as the _____ company.

7. A merger may be described as "friendly" or "hostile," depending upon the attitude of the _____ of the target company.

8. A(n) _____ _____ is a request by the acquiring company to the target company's _____ to submit their shares in exchange for a specified price or specified number of shares of stock.

9. A(n) _____ merger combines the business activity of the two firms with the expectation of _____ benefits.

10. _____ mergers do not combine the business operations of two firms, and no operating economies are expected.

11. Merger analysis is very similar to _____ _____ analysis.

12. In valuing the target firm, the analysis focuses on the cash flows that accrue to the stockholders of the _____ firm.

13. A(n) _____ _____ occurs when two firms combine parts of their companies to accomplish specific, limited objectives.

14. A pro rata distribution of stock in a new firm which was formerly a subsidiary is called a(n) _____.

15. Unless a holding company owns at least ____ percent of the shares of a subsidiary company, it may be subject to multiple _____ on a portion of any intercorporate _____.

16. A(n) _____ merger is a merger that occurs to make the firm less attractive to hostile suitors.

17. A(n) _____ merger occurs when the merging companies are somewhat related, but not to the extent required for a horizontal or vertical merger.

18. A(n) _____ merger is one in which the target firm's management resists the takeover.

19.   Two commonly-used methods to value firms are _____ _____ _____ and _____ _____ analyses.

20.   Merger cash flows, unlike capital budgeting cash flows, must include _____ expenses.

21.   A(n) _____ _____ is sometimes lined up to acquire a firm that is trying to avoid being taken over by an unfriendly suitor.

22.   A(n) _____ _____ may be sought to buy enough of the target firm's shares to block a merger.

23.   _____ _____ are actions that effectively destroy the value of the firm in the event of a merger, and hence drive off unwanted suitors.

24.   Investment banking firms engage in _____ _____, which means speculating in the stock of companies that are likely takeover targets.

25.   In a(n) _____ _____ a small group of investors, usually including top management, acquires a firm in a transaction financed largely by debt.

26.   _____ occurs when the assets of a division are sold off piecemeal, rather than as an operating entity.

27.   Mergers are handled in either of two basic ways: (1) as a(n) _____ ____ _____ or as a(n) _____.

28.   _____ represents the excess paid for a firm over its adjusted net asset value.

29.   In a(n) _____-_____, a minority interest in a corporate subsidiary is sold to new shareholders, so the parent gains new equity financing yet retains control.

Conceptual

30.   In a financial merger, the expected postmerger cash flows are generally the sum of the cash flows of the separate companies.

   a. True   b. False

31. Interest expense must be explicitly included in the incremental cash flow analysis for a merger.

    a. True   **b.** False

32. The holding company device can be used to take advantage of the principle of financial leverage. Thus, the holding company can control a great deal of assets with a limited amount of top-tier equity.

    a. True   **b.** False

SELF-TEST PROBLEMS

(The following data apply to the next four Self-Test Problems.)

TransCorp, a large conglomerate, is evaluating the possible acquisition of the Chip Company, a transistor manufacturer. TransCorp's analyst projects the following postmerger incremental cash flows (in millions of dollars):

	2002	2003	2004	2005
Net sales	$200	$230	$250	$270
Cost of goods sold	130	140	145	150
Selling/administrative expense	20	25	30	32
EBIT	$ 50	$ 65	$ 75	$ 88
Interest	10	12	13	14
EBT	$ 40	$ 53	$ 62	$ 74
Taxes (40%)	16	21	25	30
Net income	$ 24	$ 32	$ 37	$ 44
Retained earnings	12	13	14	15
Cash available to stockholders	$ 12	$ 19	$ 23	$ 29
Terminal value				400
Net CF	$ 12	$ 19	$ 23	$429

The acquisition, if made, would occur on January 4, 2002. All cash flows above are assumed to occur at the end of the year. Chip currently has a market value capital structure of 10 percent debt, but TransCorp would increase the debt to 50 percent if the acquisition were made. Chip, if independent, pays taxes at 30 percent, but its income would be taxed at 40 percent if consolidated. Chip's current market-determined beta is 1.80. Its estimated postmerger beta is 2.67.

The cash flows above include the additional interest payments due to increased leverage and asset expansion, and the full taxes paid by TransCorp on the Chip income stream. Depreciation-generated funds would be used to replace worn-out equipment, so they would not be available to TransCorp's shareholders. Retained earnings would be used, in addition to new debt, to finance required asset expansion. Thus, the net cash flows are the flows that would accrue to TransCorp's stockholders. The risk-free rate is 10 percent and the market risk premium is 5 percent.

1. What is the appropriate discount rate for valuing the acquisition?

   a. 10.00%   **b.** 15.00%   **c.** 19.00%   **d.** 21.75%   **e.** 23.35%

2. What is the value (in millions of dollars) of the Chip Company to TransCorp?

   a. $197.73   **b.** $206.42   **c.** $219.78   **d.** $322.85   **e.** $429.00

3. Chip has 5 million shares outstanding. Chip's current market price is $32.50. What is the maximum price per share that TransCorp should offer?

   a. $32.50   **b.** $37.50   **c.** $41.37   **d.** $43.96   **e.** $46.93

4. TransCorp should offer Chip's stockholders $32.625 per share.

   a. True   **b.** False

ANSWERS TO SELF-TEST QUESTIONS

1.	synergy	13.	joint venture
2.	operating; financial	14.	spinoff
3.	antitrust	15.	80; taxation; dividends
4.	horizontal; vertical	16.	defensive
5.	conglomerate	17.	congeneric
6.	acquiring; target	18.	hostile
7.	management	19.	discounted cash flow; market multiple
8.	tender offer; stockholders	20.	interest
9.	operating; synergistic	21.	white knight
10.	Financial	22.	white squire
11.	capital budgeting	23.	Poison pills
12.	acquiring	24.	risk arbitrage

25. leveraged buyout	**28.** Goodwill
26. Liquidation	**29.** carve-out
27. pooling of interests; purchase	

30. a. In a financial merger, no synergistic effects are anticipated.

31. a. The target firm generally has embedded debt that is being assumed by the acquiring firm. Since these costs are not marginal, they must be specifically included in the analysis.

32. a. This statement is true, but the leveraging which occurs in a holding company organization significantly increases the riskiness of the firm.

SOLUTIONS TO SELF-TEST PROBLEMS

1. e. $k_s = 10\% + (5\%)2.67 = 23.35\%$.

2. c. $V = \dfrac{\$12\,\text{million}}{(1.2335)^1} + \dfrac{\$19\,\text{million}}{(1.2335)^2} + \dfrac{\$23\,\text{million}}{(1.2335)^3} + \dfrac{\$429\,\text{million}}{(1.2335)^4}$

$\quad = \$219.78\,\text{million}$.

3. d. $\$219.78\,\text{million}/5\,\text{million} = \$43.96$.

4. b. It does not make sense to offer Chip's shareholders just a little above the current market price. Not enough shares would be tendered to gain control, the expenses would be for naught, and other firms could be induced to make competing bids.

OVERVIEW

As the world economy becomes more integrated, the role of multinational firms is increasing. Although the same basic principles of financial management apply to multinational corporations as well as to domestic ones, financial managers of multinational firms face a much more complex task. The primary problem, from a financial standpoint, is the fact that the cash flows must cross national boundaries.

These flows may be constrained in various ways, and, equally important, their values in dollars may rise or fall depending on exchange rate fluctuations. This means that the multinational financial manager must be constantly aware of the many complex interactions among national economies and their effects on international operations.

OUTLINE

A multinational, or global, corporation is one that operates in an integrated fashion in a number of countries. The growth of multinationals has greatly increased the degree of worldwide economic and political interdependence.

■ Companies, both U. S. and foreign, go "international" for six primary reasons:
  After a company has saturated its home market, growth opportunities are often better in foreign markets.
  Many of the present multinational firms began their international operations because raw materials were located abroad.
  Because no single nation holds a commanding advantage in all technologies, companies are scouring the globe for leading scientific and design ideas.
  Still other firms have moved their manufacturing facilities overseas to take advantage of cheaper production costs in low-cost countries.
  Firms can avoid political and regulatory hurdles by moving production to other countries.

Finally, firms go international so that they can diversify, and consequently, cushion the impact of adverse economic trends in any single country.

■ Over the past 10 to 15 years, there has been an increasing amount of investment in the U. S. by foreign corporations, and in foreign nations by U. S. corporations. These developments suggest an increasing degree of mutual influence and interdependence among business enterprises and nations, to which the United States is not immune.

In theory, financial concepts and procedures are valid for both domestic and multinational operations. However, there are six major factors which distinguish financial management as practiced by firms operating entirely within a single country from management by firms that operate globally.

■ Cash flows will be denominated in different currencies, making exchange rate analysis necessary for all types of financial decisions.

■ Economic and legal differences among countries can cause significant problems when the corporation tries to coordinate and control worldwide operations of its subsidiaries.

■ The ability to communicate is critical in all business transactions. U. S. citizens are often at a disadvantage because we are generally fluent only in English.

■ Values and the role of business in society reflect the cultural differences that may vary dramatically from one country to the next.

■ Financial models based on the traditional assumption of a competitive marketplace must often be modified to include political (governmental) and other noneconomic facets of the decision.

■ *Political risk,* which is seldom negotiable and may be as extreme as *expropriation,* must be explicitly addressed in financial analysis. Political risk varies from country to country.

An exchange rate specifies the number of units of a given currency that can be purchased for one unit of another currency.

■ An *exchange rate* listed as the number of U. S. dollars required to purchase one unit of foreign currency is called a *direct quotation.* The number of units of foreign currency that can be purchased for one U. S. dollar is called an *indirect quotation.* Normal practice in the U. S. is to use indirect quotations for all currencies *other than British pounds, for which direct quotations are given.*

■ Converting from one foreign currency to another foreign currency may require the use of *cross rates*. For example, if the direct quotation between pounds and dollars is $1.7875 and the indirect quotation between francs and dollars is FF5.6344, the cross rate between pounds and francs can be calculated as follows:

$$\text{Cross rate} = \frac{\text{Dollars}}{\text{Pound}} \times \frac{\text{Francs}}{\text{Dollar}} = \frac{\text{Francs}}{\text{Pound}}$$

$$= 1.7875 \text{ dollars per pound} \times 5.6344 \text{ francs per dollar}$$

$$= 10.0715 \text{ francs per pound}.$$

■ The tie-in with the dollar ensures that all currencies are related to one another in a consistent manner. If this consistency did not exist, currency traders could gain profits by buying undervalued currencies and selling overvalued currencies. This process, known as arbitrage, works to bring about an equilibrium.

The International Monetary Fund (IMF) was the center of a fixed exchange rate system that operated for 25 years after World War II.

■ Under this system, the U. S. dollar, which was linked to gold by a fixed price of $35 per ounce, was the base currency, and the relative values of all other currencies to the dollar were controlled within narrow limits, but then adjusted periodically.
Currency fluctuations depend on supply and demand and capital movements. However, these fluctuations were kept within limits by the actions of the various central banks, which bought or sold currency to maintain specific prices.
If a country *devalued* its currency, then fewer units of another currency would be required to buy one unit of the devalued currency. Its "price" would be reduced, making the country's goods cheaper and thus stimulating exports and discouraging imports. A country could devalue its currency only with the approval of the IMF.

■ In 1971, the *fixed exchange rate system* was replaced by a system under which the U. S. dollar was permitted to "float."
A *floating exchange rate system* is one under which currency prices are allowed to reach their own levels without much governmental intervention.
The present managed floating system permits currency rates to move without any specific limits, but central banks do buy and sell currencies to smooth out exchange rate fluctuations.

■ The inherent volatility of exchange rates under a floating system increases the uncertainty of the cash flows for a multinational corporation. This uncertainty is known as *exchange rate risk*, and it is a major factor differentiating a global corporation from a purely domestic one.

■ Concerns about exchange rate risk have spurred attempts to stabilize currency movements. In 1979, the European Monetary System (EMS) was formed.
Participants agreed to limit fluctuations in their exchange rates so that rates stayed within a prespecified range.
It was felt that this arrangement would preclude the frequent disruptions to international trade and economic health that were caused by the vagaries of a floating foreign exchange market.

■ European nations are now moving toward an alternative to the EMS. Under the Treaty of Maastricht, participants in the European Monetary Union (EMU) agreed to move to a common currency called the "Euro."

■ In today's floating exchange rate environment, many countries have chosen to peg their currencies to one or more major currencies.
Countries with *pegged exchange rates* establish a fixed exchange rate with another major currency, and then the values of the pegged currencies move together over time.

■ Not all currencies are *convertible*. A currency is convertible when the issuing nation allows it to be traded in the currency markets and is willing to redeem the currency at market rates.

Importers, exporters, and tourists, as well as governments, buy and sell currencies in the foreign exchange market, which consists of a network of brokers and banks based in New York, London, Tokyo, and other financial centers.

■ The rate paid for delivery of currency no more than two days after the day of trade is called the *spot rate*.

■ When currency is bought or sold and is to be delivered at some agreed-upon future date, usually 30, 90, or 180 days into the future, a *forward exchange rate* is used.
If one can obtain more of the foreign currency for a dollar in the forward market than in the spot market, then the forward currency is less valuable than the spot currency, and the forward currency is said to be selling at a *discount*.
If a dollar will buy fewer units of a currency in the forward market than in the spot market, then the forward currency is worth more dollars than the spot currency, and the forward currency is said to be selling at a *premium*.

Market forces determine whether a currency sells at a forward premium or discount, and the relationship between spot and forward exchange rates is summarized in a concept called interest rate parity.

■   *Interest rate parity* holds that investors should expect to earn the same return in all countries after adjusting for risk.

■   Interest rate parity is expressed as follows:

$$\frac{\text{Forward exchange rate}}{\text{Spot exchange rate}} = \frac{(1+k_h)}{(1+k_f)}.$$

Both the forward and spot exchange rates are expressed in terms of the amount of home currency received per unit of foreign currency.
k_h and k_f are the periodic interest rates in the home country and foreign country.

■   Interest rate parity shows why a particular currency might be at a forward premium or discount.
Notice that a currency is at a forward premium whenever domestic interest rates are higher than foreign interest rates.
Discounts prevail if domestic interest rates are lower than foreign interest rates.
Arbitrage forces interest rates back to parity.

Market forces work to ensure that similar goods sell for similar prices in different countries after taking exchange rates into account. This relationship is known as purchasing power parity.

■   *Purchasing power parity*, sometimes referred to as the law of one price, implies that the level of exchange rates adjusts so that identical goods cost the same amount in different countries.

■   The equation for purchasing power parity is

$$P_h = (P_f)(\text{Spot rate}) \text{ or Spot rate} = \frac{P_h}{P_f}.$$

P_h is the price of the good in the home country.
P_f is the price of the good in the foreign country.
The spot market exchange rate is expressed as the number of units of home currency that can be exchanged for one unit of foreign currency.

■   Notice that PPP assumes there are no transportation or transaction costs, or regulations, which limit the ability to ship goods between countries. In many cases, these assumptions are incorrect, which explains why PPP is often violated.
Products in different countries are rarely identical. Frequently, there are real or perceived differences in quality, which can lead to price differences in different countries.

■   Parity relationships are extremely useful in judging and anticipating future conditions.

Relative inflation rates have many implications for multinational financial decisions. Relative inflation rates will greatly influence future production costs at home and abroad. Equally important, they have a dominant influence on relative interest rates and exchange rates.

■   A foreign currency, on average, will depreciate at a percentage rate approximately equal to the amount by which its country's inflation rate exceeds the U. S. inflation rate. Conversely, foreign currencies in countries with less inflation than the U. S. will, on average, appreciate relative to the U. S. dollar.

■   Countries experiencing higher rates of inflation tend to have higher interest rates. The reverse is true for countries with lower inflation rates.

■   Gains from borrowing in countries with low interest rates can be offset by losses from currency appreciation in those countries.

There exists a well developed system of international capital markets.

■   Americans can invest in world markets by investing in the stock of U. S. multinational corporations or by buying the bonds and stocks of large corporations (or governments) headquartered outside the United States.
Investment by U. S. firms in foreign operating assets is called *direct investment*.
Investment in foreign stocks and bonds is called *portfolio investment*.

■   The *Eurodollar market* is essentially a short-term market for handling dollar-denominated loans and deposits made outside the United States.
A *Eurodollar* is a U. S. dollar deposited in a bank outside the United States.
The major difference between a dollar on deposit in Chicago and a dollar on deposit in London is the geographic location. The deposits do not involve different currencies, so exchange rate considerations do not apply. However, Eurodollars are outside the direct control of the U. S. monetary authorities, so U. S. banking regulations, including reserve requirements and FDIC insurance premiums, do not apply.

If interest rates in the United States are above Eurodollar rates, these funds will be sent back and invested in the United States, while if Eurodollar deposit rates are significantly above U. S. interest rates, more dollars will be sent out of the United States.

Interest rates on Eurodollar deposits (and loans) are tied to a standard rate known as the *London Interbank Offer Rate (LIBOR)*, the rate of interest offered by the largest and strongest London banks on dollar deposits of significant size.

■　Two international bond markets have developed which trade in long-term funds.

Foreign bonds are bonds sold by a foreign borrower but denominated in the currency of the country in which the issue is sold.

Eurobonds are bonds sold in a country other than the one in whose currency the issue is denominated.

Eurobonds appeal to investors for several reasons.

- Generally, they are issued in bearer form rather than as registered bonds, so the names and nationalities of investors are not recorded.

- Most governments do not withhold taxes on interest payments associated with Eurobonds.

■　New issues of stock are sold in international markets for a variety of reasons.

Firms are able to tap a much larger source of capital than their home countries.

Firms want to create an equity market presence to accompany operations in foreign countries.

Large multinational companies also occasionally issue new stock simultaneously in multiple countries.

■　In addition to direct listing, U. S. investors can invest in foreign companies through *American Depository Receipts (ADRs)*, which are certificates representing ownership of foreign stock held in trust.

There are several important differences in the capital budgeting analysis of foreign versus domestic operations.

■　Cash flow analysis is much more complex for overseas investments.

Usually a firm will organize a separate subsidiary in each foreign country in which it operates.

Any dividends or royalties repatriated by the subsidiary must be converted to the currency of the parent company and thus are subject to exchange rate fluctuations.

Dividends and royalties received are normally taxed by both foreign and domestic governments.

Some governments place restrictions, or exchange controls, on the amount of cash that may be remitted to the parent company in order to encourage reinvestment of earnings in the foreign country.

The only relevant cash flows for analysis of an international investment are the financial cash flows that the subsidiary can legally send back to the parent.

- The cost of capital may be higher for foreign investments because they may be riskier than domestic investments.

    Exchange rate risk refers to the fact that exchange rates may fluctuate, increasing the uncertainty about cash flows to the parent company.

    Political risk refers to the possibility of *expropriation* and to restrictions on cash flows to the parent company.

- Companies can take steps to reduce the potential loss from expropriation in 3 major ways.

    Finance the subsidiary with local capital.

    Structure operations so that the subsidiary has value only as a part of the integrated corporate system.

    Obtain insurance against economic losses from expropriation.

Companies' capital structures vary among countries. Evidence suggests that companies in Germany and the United Kingdom tend to have less leverage, whereas firms in Canada appear to have more leverage, relative to firms in the United States, France, Italy, and Japan.

The objectives of working capital management in the multinational corporation are similar to those in the domestic firm but the task is more complex.

- The objectives of cash management in the multinational corporation are to speed up collections and to slow disbursements, to shift cash rapidly from those parts of the business that do not need it to those parts that do, and to obtain the highest possible risk-adjusted rate of return on temporary cash balances. The same general procedures are used by multinational firms as those used by domestic firms, but because of longer distances and more serious mail delays, lockbox systems and electronic funds transfers are especially important.

- Granting credit is more risky in an international context because, in addition to the normal risks of default, the multinational corporation must also worry about exchange rate changes between the time a sale is made and the time a receivable is collected. Credit policy is generally more important for a multinational firm than for a domestic firm.

Much of the U. S.'s trade is with poorer, less-developed countries; thus, granting credit is generally a necessary condition for doing business.
Nations whose economic health depends upon exports often help their manufacturing firms compete internationally by granting credit to foreign countries.

■ The physical location of inventories is a complex consideration for the multinational firm. The multinational firm must weigh a strategy of keeping inventory concentrated in a few areas from which they can be shipped, and thus minimize the total amount of inventory needed to operate the global business, with the possibility of delays in getting goods from central locations to user locations around the world. Exchange rates, import/export quotas or tariffs, the threat of expropriation, and taxes all influence inventory policy.

SELF-TEST QUESTIONS

Definitional

1. The _____ _____ determines the number of units of one currency that can be exchanged for another.

2. International financial transactions were carried out under a(n) _____ _____ _____ system from the end of World War II until 1971.

3. The organization which controlled the fixed exchange rate system was the _____ _____ _____, which served as a world central bank.

4. Under the fixed rate system, the relative values of various currencies were based on the ____ ____ _____, and were controlled within narrow limits, but then adjusted periodically.

5. Countries with export surpluses and a strong currency might have to _____ their currencies upward.

6. In 1971, the _____ rate system was replaced by one that permitted the U. S. dollar to _____ against other currencies.

7. Evaluation of foreign investments involves the analysis of dividend and royalty cash flows that are _____ to the parent company.

8. Some foreign governments restrict, or block, the amount of income that can be repatriated to encourage _____ in the foreign country.

9. _____ risk refers to the possibility of restrictions on cash flows or the outright _____ of property by a foreign government.

10. A dollar deposited in a non-U. S. bank is often called a(n) _____.

11. Investment by U. S. firms in foreign operations is called _____ investment, while the purchase of foreign bonds and stock by U. S. citizens or firms is called _____ investment.

12. _____ bonds are bonds sold by a foreign borrower but denominated in the currency of the country in which the issue is sold.

13. A(n) _____ corporation is one that operates in an integrated fashion in a number of countries.

14. An exchange rate listed as the number of U. S. dollars required to purchase one unit of foreign currency is called a(n) _____ quotation. The number of units of foreign currency that can be purchased for one U. S. dollar is called a(n) _____ quotation.

15. _____ is the process that works to bring about an equilibrium among exchange rates.

16. A currency is _____ when the issuing nation allows it to be traded in the currency markets and is willing to redeem the currency at market rates.

17. Countries with _____ exchange rates establish a fixed exchange rate with another major currency, and then the values of these currencies move together over time.

18. The rate paid for delivery of currency no more than two days after the day of trade is called the _____ rate.

19. When currency is bought or sold and is to be delivered at some agreed-upon future date a(n) _____ exchange rate is used.

20. _____ _____ parity holds that investors should expect to earn the same return in all countries after adjusting for risk.

21. _____ _____ parity, sometimes referred to as the law of one price, implies that the level of exchange rates adjusts so that identical goods cost the same amount in different countries.

22. The _____ _____ _____ rate is the rate of interest offered by the largest and strongest London banks on dollar deposits of significant size.

23. _____ are bonds sold in a country other than the one in whose currency the issue is denominated.

24. _____ _____ _____ are certificates representing ownership of foreign stock held in trust.

25. A currency is at a(n) _____ premium whenever domestic interest rates are higher than foreign interest rates.

Conceptual

26. Financial analysis is not able to take into account political risk.

    a. True   **b.** False

27. When a central bank of a country buys and sells its currency to smooth out fluctuations in the exchange rate, the system is referred to as a managed floating system.

    a. True   **b.** False

28. A foreign currency will, on average, appreciate at a percentage rate approximately equal to the amount by which its inflation rate exceeds the inflation rate in the United States.

    a. True   **b.** False

29. The cost of capital is generally lower for a foreign project than for an equivalent domestic project since the possibility of exchange gains exists.

    a. True   **b.** False

30. Which of the following statements concerning multinational cash flow analysis is *not* correct?

    a. The relevant cash flows are the dividends and royalties repatriated to the parent company.

    b. The cash flows must be converted to the currency of the parent company and, thus, are subject to future exchange rate changes.

    c. Dividends and royalties received are normally taxed only by the government of the country in which the subsidiary is located.

    d. Foreign governments may restrict the amount of the cash flows that may be repatriated.

SELF-TEST PROBLEMS

1. The "spot rate" for Greek drachmas is 0.0313 U. S. dollars per drachma. What would the exchange rate be expressed in drachmas per dollar?

    a. 0.0313 drachmas per dollar   **d.** 319.4890 drachmas per dollar
    b. 3.1300 drachmas per dollar   **e.** 400.0000 drachmas per dollar
    c. 31.9489 drachmas per dollar

2. The U. S. dollar can be exchanged for 942.1432 Italian lire today. The Italian currency is expected to appreciate by 10 percent tomorrow. What is the expected exchange rate tomorrow expressed in lire per dollar?

    a. 836.1935 lire per dollar   **d.** 958.2334 lire per dollar
    b. 841.3167 lire per dollar   **e.** 965.9813 lire per dollar
    c. 847.9289 lire per dollar

3. You are considering the purchase of a block of stock in Galic Steel, a French steel producer. Galic just paid a dividend of 10 francs per share; that is, $D_0 = 10$ francs. You expect the dividend to grow indefinitely at a rate of 15 percent per year, but because of a higher expected rate of inflation in France than in the United States, you expect the franc to depreciate against the dollar at a rate of 5 percent per year. The exchange rate is currently 5 francs per U. S. dollar, but this ratio will change as the franc depreciates. For a stock with this degree of risk, including exchange rate risk, you feel that a 20 percent rate of return is required. What is the most, in dollars, that you should pay for the stock?

    a. $20.90   **b.** $31.70   **c.** $46.00   **d.** $53.60   **e.** $60.34

4. Refer to Self-Test Problem 3. Now assume that the franc is expected to appreciate against the dollar at the rate of 1 percent per year. All other facts are unchanged. Under these conditions, what should you be willing to pay for the stock?

   a. $20.90   b. $31.70   c. $46.00   d. $53.60   e. $60.34

5. A currency trader observes that in the spot exchange market, one U. S. dollar can be exchanged for 130.99 Spanish pesetas or for 1.3395 Swiss francs. How many Swiss francs would you receive for every peseta exchanged?

   a. 0.005699   b. 0.010226   c. 63.468975   d. 97.790220   e. 175.461105

6. A deluxe refrigerator costs $1,300 in the United States. The same refrigerator costs 2,250 Dutch guilders. If purchasing power parity holds, what is the spot exchange rate between guilders and the dollar? In other words, according to the spot rate calculated, how many guilders would you receive for every dollar exchanged?

   a. 0.5778   b. 0.6375   c. 1.2349   d. 1.7308   e. 2.0345

7. 6-month U. S. T-bills have a nominal rate of 8 percent, while default-free German bonds that mature in 6 months have a nominal rate of 6 percent. In the spot exchange market, one German mark equals $0.70. If interest rate parity holds, what is the 6-month forward exchange rate? In other words, how many U. S. dollars would you receive for every German mark exchanged in 6 months?

   a. $0.7068   b. $0.7280   c. $0.7498   d. $0.6933   e. $0.6875

ANSWERS TO SELF-TEST QUESTIONS

1. exchange rate
2. fixed exchange rate
3. International Monetary Fund (IMF)
4. U. S. dollar
5. revalue
6. fixed; "float"
7. repatriated
8. reinvestment
9. Political; expropriation
10. Eurodollar
11. direct; portfolio
12. Foreign
13. multinational
14. direct; indirect
15. Arbitrage
16. convertible
17. pegged
18. spot
19. forward
20. Interest rate

21.	Purchasing power		**24.**	American depository receipts
22.	London Interbank Offer		**25.**	forward
23.	Eurobonds			

26. b. Political risk must be explicitly addressed by international financial managers.

27. a. This statement is correct.

28. b. The foreign currency will depreciate if its inflation rate is higher than that of the United States.

29. b. The cost of capital is generally higher because of exchange risk and political risk.

30. c. Dividends and royalties received will generally also be taxed by the U. S. government, but the total taxes paid to both governments will not exceed that which would be paid had the earnings occurred in the United States.

SOLUTIONS TO SELF-TEST PROBLEMS

1. c. The exchange rate for drachmas per dollar would be the reciprocal of the exchange rate of dollars per drachma: 1/(0.0313 dollars per drachma) = 31.9489 drachmas per dollar.

2. c. 942.1432(0.90)/$1.00 = 847.9289 lire per dollar.

3. a. First, the valuation equation must be modified to convert the expected dividend stream to dollars:

$$D_t = D_0(1 + g)(ER),$$

where ER = exchange ratio. ER = 1/5 today, but if francs depreciate at a rate of 5 percent, it will take more francs to buy a dollar in the future. The value of ER at some future time (t) will be

$$ER_t = \frac{\text{Dollars}}{\text{Francs}} = \frac{1}{5(1.05)^t}.$$

Therefore, D_t in dollars may be calculated as follows:

$$D_t \text{ (in dollars)} = (10 \text{ francs})(1 + g)^t (ER_t)$$

$$= \frac{\$10(1.15)^t}{5(1.05)^t}$$

$$= \frac{\$2(1.15)^t}{(1.05)^t}$$

$$= \$2\left(\frac{1.15}{1.05}\right)^t$$

$$= \$2(1.0952)^t.$$

Thus, if the dividend in francs is expected to grow at a rate of 15 percent per year, but the franc is expected to depreciate at a rate of 5 percent per year against the dollar, then the growth rate, in dollars, of dividends received will be 9.52 percent. We can now calculate the value of the stock in dollars:

$$\hat{P}_0 = \frac{D_1}{k_s - g} = \frac{\$2(1.0952)}{0.20 - 0.0952} = \frac{\$2.1904}{0.1048} = \$20.90.$$

4. e. Solve the problem as above: $ER_t = 1(1.01)^t/5$.

$$D_t \text{ (in dollars)} = (10 \text{ francs})(1 + g)^t \left(\frac{(1.01)^t}{5}\right)$$

$$= (\$10/5)(1.15)^t(1.01)^t$$

$$= \$2(1.1615)^t.$$

Thus, the franc dividend is expected to increase at a rate of 15 percent per year, and the value of these francs is expected to rise at the rate of 1 percent per year, so the expected annual growth rate of the dollar dividend is 16.15 percent. We can now calculate the stock price:

$$\hat{P}_0 = \frac{D_1}{k_s - g} = \frac{\$2(1.1615)}{0.20 - 0.1615} = \frac{\$2.3230}{0.0385} = \$60.34.$$

5. b. $1 = 130.99$ Spanish pesetas; $1 = 1.3395$ Swiss Francs; Swiss francs/peseta = ?

$$\text{Cross rate: } \frac{\text{Dollar}}{\text{Peseta}} \times \frac{\text{Swiss Franc}}{\text{Dollar}} = \frac{\text{Swiss Franc}}{\text{Peseta}}.$$

Note that an indirect quotation is given for the Spanish peseta; however, the cross rate formula requires a direct quotation. The indirect quotation is the reciprocal of the direct quotation. Since $1 = 130.99$ Spanish pesetas, then 1 peseta = 0.007634.

$$\frac{\text{Swiss Franc}}{\text{Peseta}} = 0.007634 \times 1.3395 = 0.010226 \text{ Swiss francs per peseta.}$$

6. d.
$$P_h = P_f \text{ (Spot rate)}$$
$$1{,}300 = 2{,}250 \text{(Spot rate)}$$
$$\frac{1{,}300}{2{,}250} = \text{Spot rate}$$
Spot rate $= \$0.5778$.

1 guilder = 0.5778. This is a direct quotation. However, the problem asks for how many guilders would you receive for every dollar exchanged, an indirect quote. To obtain the answer, take the reciprocal of $0.5778 = 1/0.5778 = 1.7308$ guilders per 1 U. S. dollar.

7. a.
$$\frac{\text{Forward exchange rate}}{\text{Spot exchange rate}} = \frac{(1 + k_h)}{(1 + k_f)}$$

$$k_h = \frac{8\%}{2} = 4\%.$$

$$k_f = \frac{6\%}{2} = 3\%.$$

Spot exchange rate $= \$0.70$.

$$\frac{\text{Forward exchange rate}}{\$0.70} = \frac{1.04}{1.03}$$
$$1.03 \text{(Forward exchange rate)} = \$0.7280$$
$$\text{Forward exchange rate} = \$0.7068.$$